MAN'S STRUGGLE FOR FOOD

Harvey Benham

Professor Emeritus
University of Wisconsin, Green Bay

UNIVERSITY
PRESS OF
AMERICA

D1421078

LANHAM • NEW YORK • LONDON

University Press of America,™ Inc.

4720 Boston Way
Lanham, MD 20706

3 Henrietta Street
London WC2E 8LU England

Library of Congress Cataloging in Publication Data

Benham, Harvey.
    Man's struggle for food.

    1. Food—History. I. Title.
TX353.B46   338.1'9   80-67188
ISBN 0-8191-1518-5   AACR2
ISBN 0-8191-1519-3 (pbk.)

THIS BOOK IS DEDICATED TO THE MEMORY OF
THE LATE SIR JACK DRUMMOND, WHO AS
PROFESSOR OF BIOCHEMISTRY AT UNIVERSITY
COLLEGE LONDON DURING MY Ph.D. PROGRAM,
PROVIDED THE INITIAL STIMULUS.

ACKNOWLEDGEMENTS

There is a great deal of useful material to which I have referred in the bibliography. I am, however, particuarly indebted to three sources: Food in History, by Reay Tannahill; Six thousand years of bread, by Heinrich Jacobs; and The Englishman's Food, by the late Sir Jack Drummond and Anne Wilbraham. A Short History of the English People, by John Richard Green, published in four volumes in 1894, has provided an endless source of worthwhile illustrations.

Some of this material formed the basis for a course entitled Nutrition and Culture, presented once a year from 1973 to 1978 at the University of Wisconsin-Green Bay. I am indebted to my many students, whom I hope to have stimulated.

In the preparation of the manuscript, I am especially grateful to our daughter Dr. Barbara Benham, who by her untiring interest and constructive criticisms helped the book's progress in its early stages. I also acknowledge the typing skills and expertise of Kathy Rodriguez in preparing the final copy.

Finally, I commend my wife Sylvia for her patience throughout.

Harvey Benham
2 Windy Oaks Court
Little Rock, Arkansas 72205
USA.

TABLE OF CONTENTS

1. EARLY MAN.   1- 16
      hunting for food--Neanderthal man--
      Cromagnon man--food gathering--fire--
      pottery

2. NEOLITHIC REVOLUTION.   17-36
      wild grain--early farming--domestication
      settlements--river civilisations--atti-
      tudes towards animals--food supplies

3. EGYPT AND SUMER.   37-49
      The Nile--cultural advances--risen bread--
      attitudes towards agriculture--defores-
      tation and desiccation

4. THE JEWS.   51-58
      early history--agriculture--unleavened
      bread--food customs and taboos

5. GREECE.   59-85
      Hesiod--agriculture--food of the early
      Greeks--Solon--the cult of Demeter--
      early medicine

6. ROME: REPUBLIC TO EMPIRE   87-101
      early days--the republic--eating habits--
      farming--the turning point

7. ROME: EMPIRE TO FALL.   103-114
      decline in public morality--annona--
      the welfare state--last years of empire

8. THE DARK PERIOD.   115-127
      After Rome's fall--the beginnings of
      feudalism--land--taxation--hunger--the
      Church

9. THE NORDIC PEOPLES.   129-144
      the mongols--settling down--culture of
      the nordic peoples--the horse--growth
      of the towns--problems of food quality--
      the guilds

10. LIVING IN THE MIDDLE AGES.   145-174
     the people's food--the manors--advances
     in agriculture--the horse--growth of the
     towns--problems of food quality--the
     guilds

11. CHANGE.   175-194
     the Black Death--its aftermath--wool--
     food of the wealthy--food quality--pun-
     ishment for wrongdoing--plight of the
     poor

12. FOOD ASPECTS OF THE NEW TOWNS.   195-208
     Venice and trade--spices--Vasco da Gama
     and Magellan--fish--salt

13. MAN'S GRAINS.   209-220
     oats and coarse grains--preference for
     wheat--attitude of the church--white bread

14. WORLD DISCOVERY.   221-232
     early times in India--Hinduism--Guatama--
     influence of Buddhism on eating habits--
     ritual pollution

15. ISLAM.   233-248
     foundations--Mohammed--the Koran--food
     habits--conflicts with Crhistianity--
     Islam and India

16. OPENING UP A NEW WORLD.   249-263
     Columbus--Mexico and Cortez--maize--
     trade and shipping--Peru and Pizarro

17. THE POTATO.   265-283
     from Peru to Ireland

18. SCURVY   285-295
     sea voyages--Vasco da Gama--Jacques
     Cartier--land scurvy--scurvy in recent
     times--functions of ascorbic acid

19. THE SEVENTEENTH CENTURY.   297-327
     diets after Elizabeth I--food for the
     towns--vegetables--food for the poor--

       middle and upper classes--travel--Italy--
       France--Spain--coffee--drinking--the
       green sickness

20. AVITAMINOSIS A.   329-342
       early deprivation of the milk supply--
       vegetables--eye conditions--later short-
       ages

21. THE EIGHTEENTH CENTURY.   343-381
       improvements in wages--increase in
       population--new industries--advances in
       agriculture--nutritional deterioration
       after 1750--from plenty to scarcity--
       transportation

22. FRANCE IN THE EIGHTEENTH CENTURY. 383-399
       starvation--seeds of revolution--
       Parmentier--1789--Napoleon--Peace of
       Paris

23. THE NINETEENTH CENTURY.   401-416
       exhaustion after Napoleon--industrial
       conditions--reformers--prison diets--
       deterioration of the diet

24. RICKETS.   417-433
       early history--diet--animal rickets--
       cod liver oil--modern findings

25. NINETEENTH CENTURY AMERICA. 435-447
       wheat versus rye--Europe's need for
       grain--wheat and maize--railroads--
       Chicago--revolution in milling

26. NINETEENTH CENTURY NUTRITION. 449-457
       white bread--life in the sɪums

27. STRIDES IN FOOD PRESERVATION. 459-467
       salt--canning--refrigeration--other
       advances in food--science of nutrition

28. BERI-BERI.   469-477
       asiatic background--rice--thiamin

29. RECENT TIMES.   479-489
      World War I--nutritional advances--
      World War II--food packaging--nutrition
      of infants--needs for the future

    LIST OF ILLUSTRATIONS   491-493

x

PREFACE

"The history of man from the beginning has been the history of his struggle for daily bread."

Josue de Castro: The Geography of Hunger (1955)

The purpose of this book is to approach man's struggle for food from the historical perspective. Food supplies are traced from the cave to the present. Connections are made between advances in lifestyle and the acquisition of new technologies on the one hand, and the availability of food for the people on the other. It will be seen how land has been slowly transformed from its natural state. At first it was used for food production and agriculture, and then, rather more rapidly, for non-food purposes which are not necessarily essential for human survival.

Relationships are traced between food scarcity and the gradual concentration of land into fewer and fewer hands. Throughout recorded history the pattern has repeated itself over and over. The vigor of a civilisation declines as its nutritional situation deteriorates, and both are tied to the way land is owned and utilised.

One of the purposes of this book is to call attention to the basic needs of men, rather than to their desires. Attitudes about food which stemmed from religious beliefs and practices are noted, since they frequently had a profound and pervasive effect upon both individual human behaviour, and upon social patterns associated with food production, preparation and consumption.

Efforts in the past to regulate food quality, and the punishments connected with failure to do so, are described as a further effort by man to protect himself through social organisation, against abuses, disease, and those individuals who, throughout the ages, have been ready to take advantage of others.

xi

Over the centuries, the gradual refinement of foods as well as their greater variety have contributed to the well-being of the people. It is too early as yet to judge whether these results are progressive or retrogressive, at least in terms of twentieth century nutrition. The mechanisation of food processing which began in the nineteenth century, has now reached such proportions in many parts of the world that its effects on future generations cannot as yet be guessed.

Chapters on the voyages of discovery in the sixteenth and seventeenth centuries deal with new foods and habits, and the impact that these had on various cultures.

Inflation and debasement of the coinage are old difficulties and have often been connected with food supply and demand. Solutions to these complex problems today will not be found without weighing the consequences of solutions attempted, with or without success, in days gone by.

The book is addressed to a wider audience than food and nutrition students. Those who would seek ways out of our present world food dilemmas may find much in it of interest. But it contains no panacea and gives no assured answers. It seeks to call attention to the recurring theme of hunger, and to the numerous occasions in the past when circumstances similar to those we confront today have existed in earlier civilisations.

We should not be either surprised or angry regarding our predicaments. They have happened before. Our task is to apply what we can learn from history to the thoughtful and intelligent solution of our present and future problems.

1.   EARLY MAN

HUNTING FOR FOOD

To begin at the beginning is not easy. For
when was the beginning? For three to five million
years, palaeolithic ape-man coexisted with the
larger mammals, and learned to adapt to his environment. Fossil remains related to human evolution
are to be found in the early Pleistocene deposits
in south and east Africa. This early ancestor,
Australopithecanus, was a small-brained, large-
jawed creature, capable of bipedalism. He first
of all stood on three feet and ultimately on two,
in order to free the fore-limbs for picking up a
rock to hurl at some other creature. He had the
inestimable advantage of the apposition of thumb
and fingers, allowing a strong grasp of objects.
In addition, by standing he was able to free his
hands for manipulation. This was surely a most
important attribute, for it enabled this man-type
to progress upward over his fellow creatures.

His wits became sharper, and he competed with
the lion, the hyena and the sabre-toothed tiger, who
shared his hunting grounds. He learned to climb
trees for safety, and developed his eyesight better, perhaps at the expense of his sense of smell.
But he could not live all of his time in the trees,
for a shortage of eggs, nestlings and fruit might
force him to come down to forage on the ground as
well. There he could better obtain lizards, tor-
toises, moles and other kinds of life, including
plump insects.

The women of the species began the earliest
types of food gathering. As wild plant species
appeared she gathered nuts and berries; she gathered insects such as ants, locusts and grasshoppers;
and when near oceans, shellfish. As time went on
these early man-types made increased use of tools.
Their wits became more refined so that they ceased
to use their teeth for fighting one another, and
instead learned to use tools as weapons also. The

1

teeth changed shape, and what would ultimately
become human speech began to develop.

The earth began to cool off a million years
ago, and there had to be adaptation to cold and
ice. About half a million years ago, there
appeared Pithecanthropus erectus, that is, man
standing up. He was apparently about five feet
in height, but he was evidently able to take on
the tiger, rhinoceros and buffalo, because their
bones are to be found littering his caves.

Anthropologists look at the earliest relics
for evidence of this life of long ago. Sometimes
a pattern of nutrition can be gleaned, if only
approximately. Some event of geological and
natural significance, a sealed cave, for example,
may afford a record of a particular time. In
such caves remains of early man have been found,
skulls with brain cavities of substantial volume,
and many teeth. There are also fragments of the
bones of many other animals, especially the long
bones. We can only surmise that after gorging
as much on the carcass of a fallen animal as he
and his friends could manage, they would have
dragged the leg back to the cave to be eaten at
leisure. But what is informative is that the long
bones found in these instances have frequently
been split lengthwise, undoubtedly to scoop out
and eat the marrow, for which they hungered.*

For at some stage there must have been a
transition from a largely vegetarian diet to a
hunting economy which provided a significant
amount of meat. But this did not apply to many
of the other ape-like creatures. Presumably
monkeys and apes which are predominantly vegetarian evolved from the tree-living hominids. Even
baboons, which differ from most other non-human
primates in that they live on the ground, are
also predominantly vegetarian, eating as they do
a great variety of plant species. And so man's
ancestors ate seeds and other vegetable foods,
and became scavengers in the plains and forests.
Gorillas, chimpanzees and orang-utans are all

* in modern parlance, they needed the iron, and
the phospholipids, as we need them today.

2

clearly vegetarian. How would one have believed
that Homo would rise up to dominate the other
species? All have much the same digestive system,
and all can handle meat.

But man adapts, can live anywhere, and explores
to find his food, wandering with the seasons if
need be. It is important to know what is the so-
called ideal diet. This means that we must know
what man ate before he invented agriculture. For
this diet served him well for millennia, during
which time he must have adapted himself to a particular choice of foods. We cannot escape the con-
clusion that this somehow must represent the ideal
diet. It was a precarious existence at best, but
those males and females who did survive to reproductive age are in fact our ancestors. "As I
understand it", writes John Yudkin, "man and his
immediate ancestors, emerging as a distinct species
two million years ago, were hunters as well as
gatherers of food; their diet contained a not
inconsiderable quantity of meat, being as they
were, omnivorous. Therefore he was not so likely
to suffer from food shortages, as were those
species living on a more restricted diet."

In the palaeolithic period crustaceans were
eaten by coastal-dwelling people when and where
available. Such a mode of life would have provided
a nourishing diet; for shellfish contain, in
addition to good protein, considerable quantities
of glycogen, and are satisfactory if eked out with
vegetable food; no animal flesh is necessary.

NEANDERTHAL MAN

During one of the cold spells, about 75,000
B.C., there appeared a larger-brained man than
Homo erectus, whom we have called Homo sapiens.
He left burial places so that we have certain
clues as to his life.

Neanderthal man spent much time in caves,
and some interesting findings have survived. The
size and shape of their thigh bones indicate
a lot of squatting, especially in the women. It

is allowable to deduce that osteomalacia and birth difficulties might have been common. Their calcium and vitamin D requirements may not have been satisfied, particularly if the weather were cloudy even when they were outside. However, early hunting man had very little damage to his teeth, and no caries.

Over the centuries, he came a skilled hunter; he learnt how to stalk animals, and the use of disguise for this purpose.* He learned the mating calls of animals, and even knew the practice of stampeding large herds of wild animals over cliffs in a communal enterprise. He used fire sometimes but not apparently universally; and he used many kinds of tools.

Neanderthal man disappeared in the later Paleolithic period for reasons that are not entirely clear. One is left with the speculation that bone deficiencies may have had something to do with their demise. Bone deficiencies are said to have eliminated the Greenland colony of Eric the Red in recent times. This colony was founded in 950 A.D., and not finally wiped out until 1,500 A.D. Their skeletons have been studied and found to be deficient. Perhaps this was how the Neanderthalers failed in what may have been similar conditions 50,000 years ago.

CROMAGNON MAN

About 30,000 years ago there appeared on the Eurasian continent men who were vastly more skilled than the Neanderthalers. These men, whom we call Cromagnon, were hunters as well as artisans. They used fish-hooks and sinew for sewing garments, to keep out the elements. They used bone and horn for hunting weapons, and thus had many more tools than earlier man had for attacking prey, and one another.

They lived in Europe for at least 10,000 years, and found food relatively easy to obtain. The climate was improving and the last of the glaciers were retreating. As the ice age receded and the

* the use of hunting cloths today in the mountains of central Asia may have evolved from very early beginnings.

4

STAMPEDING OVER A CLIFF: CAVE PAINTING

northern regions unfroze, there appeared vast
rivers, lakes and inland water systems. New forms
of life became plentiful; fish, waterfowl, and
birds. Numerous small mammals also made their
appearance, thus providing man with additional,
and less hazardous, sources of food.

In addition there were large animals, mammoths,
reindeer, rhinoceros, bison, reindeer, ibex and
bears. They all made use of the new land uncovered
as the glaciers retreated. The rigor of life still
kept the numbers of human beings down, so that
there was enough food for all.

There was differentiation now between the hunter and the hunted. When the wild animals migrated
to higher and cooler elevations in the summer,
and to lower places in the winter, so too the
dwellings of the clans of Cromagnon men would
adapt to fit such migrations. For where the animals found food and water, so too did man.

Cromagnon man made use of fire although he
may not have systematically generated it. It is
not known when the method of the whirl-stick came
into practice, but this was one of the earliest
uses of friction applied to man's needs. He
used animal bones as fuel and could split a warm
bone to get at the marrow.

Near Bruvin in Moravia there is a heap of
bones representing the remains of over 2,000 mammoths, driven to death by stampeding over a cliff.*
The immense accumulation of bones at the European
killing cliffs indicates that Cromagnon man had
little use for the fleshy parts of these larger
animals. Otherwise he would have dragged the
bones with the meat attached to his caves, for leisurely consumption. But the muscle meat, which
we have come to prize so highly, was for him merely the troublesome husk surrounding the valuable
portions.

When he and his companions had succeeded in
the hunt one day, the probably drank some of the

* Native Americans can still remember such an event
  in Montana; it was done to kill buffalo and to
  judge by the bone dust there, it had been happening long before horses were used for stampeding.

6

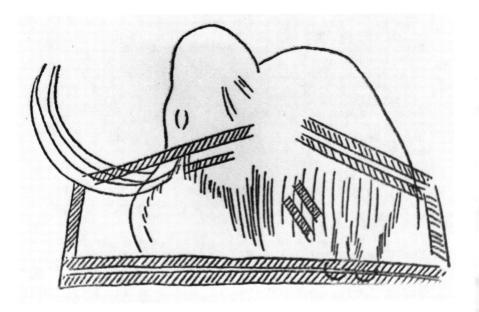

Trapped Mammoth: Cave Painting

blood while it flowed. Then they would have ripped
open the carcass to get at the liver, heart and
spleen; the pancreas and the brain would also be
prized parts. After they were satiated they
would chew the ends of the softer bones, and scoop
out the marrow from the split long bones. Thus
they were assured of their own nutrition, especially as regards bones, teeth and red blood cor-
puscles.

    Inspection of some of the sites where bones
are to be found has yielded some interesting information about the diets of these early peoples.

They would smash the brain cases to get at the
brain tissue, providing them with the phospholipids which are so necessary to good nutrition.
In the case of the skulls, it is interesting
to note that the number of mandibles found at a
site is very nearly the same as the total number
of animals found. This is not true for other
bones. A lot of the smaller bones are missing,
possibly because they were left for the dogs or
other small predatory animals hovering around
the caves and camps. The reason which the
Brothwells propose is fascinating. It so happens
that removal of the mandible is necessary in
order to get easily at the tongue, which was (and
is) rightly regarded as a choice morsel, and not
under any circumstances to be left behind.

If they were successful in killing a large
beast, a mammoth for example, it would be necessary
to carve it up then and there. But to remain on
hand for long, with other fierce, four-legged predators hovering nearby, would have been suicidal.
So they probably devised some kind of litter.
The entire community might have been enlisted to
cart the carcass back to camp. In this way attitudes towards food would have developed; sharing
the hunters' success; general rejoicing; feast and
feast times, frequently to coincide later with the
sun's changes. There would be enjoyment and
sociability. And the light and warmth of the cave
must have had a humanizing effect.

In a hundred centuries Cromagnon man did not
domesticate any animals, this was in the future.
They did not make any great advances in weapons or
tools. They did not even attain the bow and arrow,
but they did have crude harpoons. But food was
plentiful, and there were several ways to obtain
it. Driving off a hyena from an unfinished meal
might be an easy way to a food supply. A hyena's
dentition is such that it cannot pick the bones
very clean; a newly-born hyena might afford easy
prey now and then. This could have then led to
further stimulus to perfect hunting techniques.

Thus Cromagnon man had a great variety of
foodstuffs close at hand, and this assurance permitted him a certain amount of security. It reduced the anxieties inherent in the life of the
day-to-day hunting and collecting communities of
earlier times. It was thus that they were inclined
to turn their attention to decorating caves and
other forms of art.

FOOD GATHERING

While the men were out hunting, the women
were doing the gathering. This had been going on
for millennia. In the course of time the women
of the species would have learned which plants,
berries and nuts were edible; she possibly would
have tested these out on smaller animals; for baby
animals of various species would be picked up
after the kill and brought into the camp; this
was before real domestication took place. When she
erred she paid for it by sickness and even death
for herself and her children. So we must salute
early woman as the instrument by which all the
selection of everything that we have now growing
on this earth was made down through the centuries.

But she will have often chosen wisely, so that
she and her children could grow well and strong.
They had to see to it that they did not poison
themselves and their families. For those who did
not survive to adulthood are not our ancestors.

At some time while she was out gathering, she
may well have wondered why it might not be possible
to make things grow where and when she wanted them,
instead of randomly. She will have noticed, for
example, that when the camp left in the spring for
higher ground, and returned sometime later, luxur-
iant growth had occured in the refuse piles of the
earlier camp. An old seed, lodged in a hillock
and slow to sprout, would have first taught her
that new plants would grow from it. To these primitive peoples it must have seemed little short of
miraculous to find that plants that were needed
for food sprang up by his very huts and paths.

9

And as these plants established themselves, the
collecting range was diminished, in other words
they did not have to go far in order to gather them.
The richer nitrogenous soils in the vicinity of
the dwellings enabled the seeds to establish themselves firmly. Thus it was that gathering changed
almost imperceptibly into harvesting, although
as yet there was no conscious planting.

In this way a kind of symbiosis arose between
the logical demands of the plants on the one hand,
and the food needs of man on the other, with his
excreta forming the linkage. It is not too far-
fetched to suggest that it is this situation that
might have been the basis for so many folk-tales
and legends, which attributed the growing of useful plants to gods and other supernatural beings.

Thus, as Hawkes has suggested, agriculture
developed along three lines: gathering; then harvesting close at hand; and finally and much later;
sowing or planting. But in any event food was
becoming more available as these findings took root
in men's consciousness. However it was not always
possible to use all the food as it became available.
Even in the best of situtations it would have been
possible to take back to camp only selected portions of the kill. It would have been evident very
early on that food suffered rapid putrefaction unless the temperature were cold enough to afford
some degree of protection. Thus early ideas of
food preservation arose from this. Having observed that chilling would allow the meat to keep
longer, they would place it in various hiding-
places, or caches, situated strategically along
the way; they would return later to find the meat
preserved, an important milestone in our story.

In hotter and dryer circumstances, it is
probable that natural drying would have been appli-
cable. The strip of dried meat, of biltong, eaten
by some African tribes today is probably very similar to the dried meat with which their ancestors
must have been familiar millennia ago.

FIRE

Man first got hold of fire in some natural form, and learned eventually how to keep it alight. He did not know how to generate it for some time after he first used it; he was eventually to learn that too. The use of the whirl-stick has been mentioned, but at some point, probably about 56,000 years ago, he discovered ways of striking flints together, which enabled him to tame fire and to generate it at will. According to modern dating methods, one finds from soot residues and other manifestations of fire, that Pithecanthropus erectus did discover fire. It was to alter his eating habits enormously.

Neanderthal man discovered that alterations in food could be achieved by placing it on hot stones near fire, and in this way cooking was achieved for the first time. In addition to its use in cooking food, fire had a number of other advantages. In the first place it frightened away wild animals from the camps at night; secondly it introduced a humanizing effect as the clans would gather around it for warmth and reassurance. And it was later to be useful in signals and as a communicating device.

But our emphasis is on food, and here the effects may have been even more far-reaching than the mere cooking of it, important though this was. According to Leopold and Ardrey the cooking of the food removed certain toxic substances which might be present; such a change would certainly have enhanced the human life span and prospects for survival. For cooking may disarm toxic substances through accelerated oxidations at the elevated temperature, to form harmless products; protein toxins are certainly denatured by heat, and this applies especially to the common enzyme inhibitors, which are often protein or polypeptide in nature. Such enzyme inhibitors may be present in cereals and legumes, such as cyanogens and toxic alkaloids. Cooking would remove these.

11

Just as observations about the effects of cold temperatures on food preservation were carried forward as part of man's advancement, so too the effects of cooking were soon to be seen and valued. For if the fortunes of the hunt went well one day, early man ate. But if on the following day no prey fell to his club, he and his family went hungry.

However, he soon learnt that if he passed the meat over the fire, it did not spoil and could be eaten days later. The discovery of roasting solved food storage problems for that time. But as yet there was no cooking as such, for man had no vessels that could withstand a direct flame; pottery was thousands of years away.

Roasting as the first method may have got started when someone accidentally dropped a piece of meat into the fire, and could not retrieve it until the fire had died down. They would then have found that the meat had lost some of its weight, and a good deal of its flavor. They would then have found that this shrinkage would have been much less if they had placed the meat in the embers after the fire had died down. After this great observation it was but a small step to place a flat stone by the side of the fire, this could produce enought heat to bake turnips, onions and similar vegetables in their jackets.

At about this time, man also found that roasting grains enabled him to remove the outer husks more easily, that part which was tough and unyielding. Roasting would also have killed the germ, so that grain could be stored without sprouting. But this is ahead of our story.

A type of oven has recently been excavated in Moravia, Czechoslovakia. It dates from about 25,000 years ago, and consists of tiny pits in which hot pebbles were placed. For a roaring camp fire had nothing to recommend it to these early peoples; they rather used to dig a pit in order to control the fire. These pits, lined with stones and with clay if they happened to have it handy, were filled with water. Hot stones from the fire were man-handled into the pit, which heated the water. But boiling foods in water was not possible until much later when pottery was discovered.

POTTERY

Natural containers such as turtle shells may have preceded pottery. The people who lived in Central America, and lived in rock shelters, about 7,000 B.C., began to use stone cooking pots, made by chipping away at the stone, which was so plentiful. In Central Asia such cooking pots were also used; they were found by the author in Afghanistan in the 1960's. True pottery was not to evolve until about 6,000 B.C.

An earlier form of pottery may have occurred, as so often happens, inadvertently. The caked and dirty piglet which had been so carelessly laid down in the mud, when cooked, tasted so much better than its cleaner kin. The clay had hardened around it and given it a little encasement. Another possibility leading to the discovery of true pottery may have arisen as a result of the use of wicker baskets. By 6,000 B.C. man had, as we shall see, domesticated a number of plants, many of them with reed-like stems. Weaving these inedible parts of the plants was an old discovery, and baskets were used to store grain by lining them with mud clay. These may have been subjected to a fire one day, and all the wickerwork and reeds burnt away. But the clay became hard and strong, and watertight.

We cannot know the details of such advances; but we do know that man could conjecture and reason about his problems. He might have applied his thinking process as follows: what would happen if he were to make a pot without the wickerwork, dry this useless vessel in the sun, and then deliberately fire it? Over centuries it would seem that pottery was developed from such simple beginnings.

The first pottery was made by building up the pots with the fingers alone. Late stone-age Egyptians at least before 6,000 B.C. showed beautiful pottery made in this way. As the Neolithic revolution proceeded, the idea of a wheel to turn

13

the pot was introduced, at first on a stone slab
turned by a minion. The concept of the wheel
and axle developed from this, and so the present
potter's wheel got its start. Later on still,
the foot pedal made the services of the assistant
unnecessary.

Thus arose the pot. And with it came a revolution in cooking, and a revolution in nutrition.
For stews and mixtures could now be concocted.
The family could avail themselves of a variety
of mixtures of herbs, vegetables and meat. This
was a great cultural advance and the patterns of
living changed very markedly. The cauldron (pot-
au-feu) of the middle ages, and today's stewing
pot stem from these early beginnings.

And so man now became the eater of cooked
foods for the first time. And for the first time
he and his family could look forward to regular
meals, planned, cooked and served hot. This was
of course conditional upon food being available
in the first place. Our story will develop more
and more along the lines of the scarcity of food
for the majority of the world's people, which
pertains right up to the present time.

It is now time to retrace our steps in order
to see the changes in man's understanding and control over other living things. We must look into
the whole process of domestication.

REFERENCES

3   IDEAL DIET: Yudkin, John; Archaeology and the nutritionist; from Ucko and Dimbleby: a collection of original research papers; pp 547-552 (1969).

4   NEANDERTHALERS: Coon, Carleton; The Origin of Races; chap. 11, 520-534 (1962).

6   FOOD OF CROMAGNON MAN: Brothwell, Don and Patricia; Food in Antiquity; a survey of the diet of early peoples; London, 1969.

6   WHIRL-STICK: Breasted, J.H. Ancient Times: a history of the early world; chap. 1, p 8 (1916).

8   TONGUE AS AN ARTICLE OF EARLY DIETS: Brothwell, Don and Patricia; ibid.

11   TOXIC SUBSTANCES REMOVED BY COOKING: Leopold, A. Carl, and Ardrey, Robert; Science 176, 511 (1972).

11   HUMANISING EFFECT OF COOKING: Coon, Carleton: The Story of Man, p 63 (1954).

12   "IF HE PASSED MEAT OVER THE FIRE..2 Jacob, H.E. Six thousand years of bread. chap. 3 p 6 (1944).

13   EARLY POTTERY: Breasted, J.H. ibid p 33 fig 16.

15

THE NEOLITHIC REVOLUTION

The new stone age period indeed saw a revolution in human cultural development. In addition to the development of pottery and weaving, man learned to make better weapons for hunting. Most importantly he learned to domesticate both plants and animals.

And so the long path in time leads eventually to ourselves. It leads from a hominid group which abandoned four-limb brachiation in favor of hind-limb bipedalism. Man, once on that path was unique as no other animal had ever been. He developed greater skill in abstraction and in communication, with ever-increasing use of energy sources. He advanced tool invention, tool development, community sense and political sophistication. But the first of the energy sources which he needed was that provided by the sun.

WILD GRAIN

As the glaciers retreated and the climate mellowed, fields of wild grain spread across the land. It was stimulated in the late winter by the cool moist air; it could come to fruition early, before the dry parching winds of summer came to destroy it. These fields of wild grain could seed themselves, and did so. Soon rippling fields of wild barley and wild wheat appeared on suitable land. The evidence of the existence of these cereal types is found in a study of pollen grains found in caves, as has been elaborated by Flannery and by Wright.

Wheat at low altitudes could defeat the particular kinds of weeds which coexisted with it. But at higher altitudes and cooler climes the weeds flourished. And the farmers who gathered these crops at that time saw this change. They came to harvest the weeds rather than the wheat. One of these weeds was a grass, a member of what we now

call the Gramineae family; it was later to be known
as rye. Another of these weeds was oats.

But early man's crop of grass seeds was often
pilfered before he could harvest it; it was subject
to insect infestation, to the encroachments of
rodents, and to the predations of that thief of
old, the wind. Man had to break his favorite
grasses of their bad habit of yielding to the wind.
And so he came to cultivate those crops whose seed
clung to the ear longest. From this arose cultivated wheat and rye. These new varieties had
fruit that clung to the pedicle so firmly, that
it could be removed only by trampling, shaking or
beating. That is by the process which we call
threshing. Thus man was able to transform the wild
grain into a domesticated type. This means that
man is in charge. It is he who has to plant it,
for the wind can no longer sow it. Without man
the grain would disappear, for it can reproduce
itself only when man sows it.

Many of the principal crops that were developed were taken to areas further north, or else
to higher altitudes. Wheat, barley, rice, flax
and even soybeans were found to be less well
adapted to the harsher conditions of the soils up
there; weeds on the other hand were better adapted
to such conditions; hence the percentage of weeds
increased until at last the weed became the crop
and the crop the weed. Thus rye, for example, became the crop in northern Europe, in the Baltic
areas particularly. This thesis has been elaborated by Vavilov.

But the weeds have a real purpose; they represent rapidly evolving races of plants which are
able to exchange genes with the crop through occasional bursts of hybridisation. They act as reservoirs of variability, which are extremely important
in the evolution of the crop itself. We may well
be in danger at the present time, because we are
trying to decrease the variability instead of increasing it.

"Cultivated plants are from one point of view, nature's misfits". They cannot form part of climax vegetation, but have to take advantage of disturbed (i.e. ploughed), open soils, or of such poor soils that nothing without the quick tenacious power of plants which can store large quantities of food could survive. As Hawkes has said, this question of the development of cultivated plants has been one of the most important phenomena in the history of mankind.

EARLY FARMING

It seems that these early farmers made a living by diversifying their activities rather than by concentrating on one food source. Around 8,000 years ago the inhabitants of the hills around the fertile crescent came to know their habitat so well that they were beginning to domesticate both plants and animals, of which they had acquired certain kinds during the long course of their hunting and gathering activities.

Sickle blades dating from 9,000 B.C., and grinding stones dating from 10,500 B.C. have been found, denoting the earliest types of agricultural activities. Residues found in the excavation of a settlement at Ali Kosch, dating from about 7,500 B.C., reveal the various types of foods that were eaten at that time. There were ungulate meats, grasses, legumes, nut meat and mussels. They also had pistachios and almonds, good sources of energy. Combinations of twenty or so foods in this era made the farmers of that time better nourished than are their successors in present-day Iraq, as Helbaek has noted.

Of course there were setbacks. Sometimes a period of desiccation set in, affecting a wide area of the tropics, where before there had been ample rainfall, and what are called pluvial conditions. As a result, former hunting populations of the areas of India and Africa, which had previously supported them, were evidently forced to concentrate along sources of permanent water, at springs and

19

oases, or along waterways. A site at Anau in southern Turkmenistan yields this hypothesis. With the
gradual shrinkage of the dimensions of habitable
areas, and the disappearance of the herds of wild
animals, man concentrated on the oases. He was
forced to find new means. of support.

Consequently he began more and more to utilize
the native grasses, and from among these he learned
the different seeds which were found growing on the
dry land, and in the marshes around the water holes.
This enforced concentration of the people around
the oases, according to Childe, brought about the
first step in the selection and evolution of a
whole array of cereals; for the new conditions of
water shortage led to an intensified search for
means of nourishment.

Animals and men would be herded together
around pools and wadis, that were growing increasingly isolated and far apart. Such enforced jux-
taposition might of itself promote that sort of
symbiosis between man and beast which was to become
so important, and characterizes the herdsman: in a
word, the domestication of animals.

As Childe has stated, the resulting emanci-
pation from dependency on the whims of the environment gave the impetus for that economic revolution
heralded by the invention of food production as
such. Given enough food resources, intensified
food collecting provided the basis for large
settlements of size and importance. Through the
cultivation of plants, as Heiser has said, man
became able to produce more food with less effort.
More mouths of feed were no longer disastrous,
but rather advantageous, for with more bodies to
till and reap, food could be produced more effi-
ciently. Accordingly the clan which had been living
in a cave 100,000 years earlier, and long before
that, now settled down beside a river somewhere,
forming the first prehistoric river civilizations.

There were other advances at this time. The
women, our ancestral mothers, had to devise ways of

planting the seeds of these new crops. At first a grubbing stick was used, to help the earth receive the seed. They would plant in the holes the seeds of Father Millet, the oldest of the grains. The women tended these plants, for they nourished their children and made strong men out of them.

One day, we can conceive, when out digging holes with this stick, one of the women found it to be too burdensome; so she requested her man to bind a long stick to a shorter one at right angles, securing them with tough grass. This tool, which was to develop into the hoe enabled her to hack at the ground, putting her weight behind the blow. For many thousands of years she cultivated her gardens with this hoe, raising her grasses and her vegetables. This kind of culture is called horticulture.

Such labor is rather inefficient. It is shallow and merely scratches the surface. But it led to the great discovery that seeds dropped into the ground yielded a harvest a few months later. But then they had to stay around in order to guard the crop from predators and other marauders. Hence arose settlements and communities. But these early settlements did not last long because these rudimentary farmers did not understand the art of manuring. And they did not have a plough, not realizing that it is necessary to turn the earth over fairly deeply. Therefore, fertile land was turned into desert land rather quickly. And so the importance of water was further demonstrated, for plants as well as for animals. The first rudiments of irrigation were conceived at about this time.

And so whereas man had been a hunter and a gatherer, he is now becoming a herdsman and a grower, both together. He began deliberate cultivation and settlements; the next step was that the first villages were established. Irrevocably land and property values began to occupy men's thoughts.

During this neolithic period, the farmers grew emmer wheat, einkorn wheat, two-row barley, linseed, lentils, and peas, with rye grass and other weeds as well.

DOMESTICATION

The objective of domestication of both plants and animals was always to increase the available food. Farmers who concentrate mainly on the growing of plants have land holdings or territories which are extremely small compared with those of hunters and gatherers. An extended family of a dozen persons may farm no more than a few acres; a dozen such families grouped together in a village community may hold a total of a few square miles of land, much of which would be grazing land for herds and flocks. On the other hand, as pointed out by Watts and Watts, herdsmen who concentrate mainly on the nurture of their animals usually have much larger territorial claims than do farmers. The need for more grazing land not uncommonly would force the herdsman to migrate for hundreds of miles seasonally with their animals in order to find adequate supplies of grass. Even such nomads, however, would sow grain at one season in fields which they would sometimes own, returning to gather the crop at a later time. And so agriculture and husbandry were often combined to some degree.

But how did domestication of animals begin in the first place? We do not know exactly, but there are some guidelines. The reindeer, feeding on glacial water which lacks salt, is driven to search for natural salt. Where humans congregated, it must have been noted that reindeer would accept human urine as a source of salt. With this bait, man succeeded in enticing reindeer into his camps. Thus was built up an interdependence which has to play an integral role in all domestication of animals.

Man learned that animals could in some circumstances be approached, and the early hunters would have noticed that they could make pets of

baby wild animals, which in these cases would be
spared rather than killed and eaten. Man has
allowed the dog to frequent his camps to clean up
the offal of his prey and the refuse from his
feasts. Well before the Neolithic revolution, a
small Asiatic wolf was domesticated, about 11,000
years ago. Although the dog's ancestors had provided food for man for millions of years prior to
this time, it was soon to be realized that this
animal was more valuable alive than dead. His
speed, sense of hearing and of smell, were to prove
most useful, supplementing as they did those of
his master.

As Childe says:

> "under conditions of desiccation, the
> cultivator has the chance of a attach-
> ing to his menage, not only isolated young
> beasts, but also remnants of complete
> herds, comprising animals of all ages
> and both sexes."

Man was quick to realize the advantages of
having a group of half-tamed beasts hanging around
the periphery of his camps, to act as a reserve of
game easily caught. He was thus well on his way to
domestication.

Other conditions of the time assisted in
developing it even further. The fields of wild
grain referred to above attracted a number of
smaller animals who were multiplying in the open
shade around the periphery of the forests. In
addition, raids by wild goats and sheep were a
serious threat to the food supply. Consequently,
a method of bringing them under control was
essential. One way to do this was to adopt baby
wild animals and bring them into the camp; as they
matured in a semi-domesticated fashion, they would
be crossed with a wild sire, thus developing an
indigenous flock. Possibly this was done with
goats first, who then provided a useful service
as clearers of the ground, because they would kill
plants by defoliation. Sheep were likewise domes-

ticated, at least by 8,900 B.C. In due time, goats, sheep, and cattle were to form man's livestock, as they were slowly brought into a domestic state.

The sheeps' woollen skins, before spinning was known, were useful as clothing. However, flocks of sheep eat one hundred pounds of fodder per sheep per week. Consequently, the herdsman would have to travel constantly in search of new grazing lands. They would have to drive their herds up hill to pastures in the spring. But now a regular company of village inhabitants would have to accompany the herd, in order to ward off wild beasts and to milk the female animals. And they must take with them supplies of food and other kinds of equipment. In some cases, the number of people that had to accompany the herds might be quite small; but in some of the more arid parts of the world, such as Persia, Sumer, and what was later to be called Afghanistan, the bulk of the community would have to abandon its villages and make off into the hills with their herds. The nomadic way of life was born of this necessity.

Domestication of animals required certain hitherto undeveloped skills and attributes. It requires a full stomach, for the kill-and-eat instinct which had been the rule of life previously had to be overcome. It required observation and patience; there had to be time for cogitation and reflection. The connection between copulation and pregnancy had to be well understood. Man had to exercise restraint and discrimination in using his reserve of animals. He must refrain from frightening the beasts unnecessarily. He must be sure to refrain from killing the youngest, tamest and tenderest for meat; in fact he had to learn to kill and eat the more obstreperous and unmanageable animals, and to retain the more docile.

Thus man had begun to establish domestic breeds which were tamer than their forebears; in fact he had started the process of selective breeding. In learning at close range about the processes of reproduction, he was able to exercise con-

trol over the breeding of his stock. He would learn
to improve his animals by allowing only those with
desirable features to breed. He must learn about
his animals' needs for food and water, and he must
study the life of the beasts at close range. Instead of merely driving the herd away when the
time came for sowing his crops again, he had to
follow the beasts and guide them to where there
would be suitable pasture and water. He must be
prepared to ward off predators. In effect man made
the animals dependent upon him, and the responsi-
bilities which this involved had important implications, as we shall see.

An important feature in this whole process was
that man developed an understanding of procreation.
He concept of death accompanied this thinking. He
was also able to understand the characteristics
of animals were in fact passed on from one generation to the next.

Thus man finally had control over the sources
of food energy. By domesticating plants, man
acquired the primary food sources, and thus became
lord and master. By gaining control over animals,
man acquired the means to concentrate greatly the
food sources available to him, in the shape of
animals who do the converting for him. In a very
real sense, man, by the process of domestication,
gained control over some of the sun's energy.
Through this control he has increased his food
supply, with the result that he can live longer,
and reproduce his kind in greater numbers.

Now man had several features which were to
alter his life style and his culture permanently;
skins for clothing, and for water containers;
fat for cooking and for salves; tallow for lamps;
dung as fuel (though not yet as fertilizer) and
finally a draught animal for pulling a stick plow,
his first power tool. For perhaps when the hoe
got stuck deeply in the ground, they tied to it
one of their bulls. And he pulled, not upward
as man did with his hoe, but along. In some such

25

way as this the earth was "torn open". This in
turn was to lead to a series of myths and cults
concerning the earth and its fruitfulness, which
will be dealt with later.

As a result of these developments, the food
supply improved immeasurably. Milk began to be
a supplement to the diet, added to the diet of
fish, game, and such other fauna as might be
trapped or killed. Cattle especially represented
food which did not run away. It denoted an early
form of plenty. In later times wealth was to be
measured in cattle.* Other animals also had their
functions. Dogs were useful in hunting, for warning of an approaching enemy, for corralling sheep,
and last but not least, for companionship. Cats
were useful in the control of small rodents, which
were always a threat to food supplies. Swine
were useful as scavengers, as were poultry; the
latter in addition supplied food and eggs. Asses
were used as pack animals, camels for freight
and elephants for work. Man had suddenly acquired
a whole array of assistants to do his bidding.

Finally horses, developed in Asia but not
before about 3,000 B.C., were to become especially
important to man. They could transport a man fast;
they lessened fatigue; they were useful in battle,
giving additional speed as well as extra height,
from which to spear an enemy or an animal. The
horse could give a man speed in fleeing from a more
powerful enemy, or if attacking, extra height to
club him over the head. And the horse was to give
man a sense of freedom from his earth-bound state.

All of these advances affected nutrition,
directly or indirectly. Food became more plentiful,
always provided that the enemy did not invade.
And so man became a herdsman and a grower whereas
before he had been a hunter and a gatherer. But
one did not supersede the other in a clear-cut
fashion. At first the women were the ones engaged in the sedentary pursuits of agriculture,
while the men still went out hunting. For centuries the serious business of the chase occupied the

* flock of cattle: "pecus" (Latin); our word pecuniary
comes from this source.

men of the community, up until quite recent times.

SETTLEMENTS

As has already been mentioned, when our ancestors began deliberate cultivation, settlements
came into being. Villages were established, and
property values began to occupy men's thoughts.
Territoriality came into play as a human force;
there was social differentiation; there were haves
and have nots. Men began to gain power over other
men. This was the beginning of the process which
we call history.

Whereas nomadic peoples lead a precarious life
of movement, the early pastoral peoples tended to
live in tents instead of excavated shelters. They
used vessels of leather, and basketry, instead
of heavy ceramic pots and metal tools. Consequently there is very little evidence of a durable
nature left behind for the archaeologist to discover. Tents do not even leave postholes where
they once stood.

It appears from the evidence available that
from about 15,000 to 9,000 B.C. there was overall
occupation of a region around what is now Turkey
and Syria. The peoples of this region produced
flint tools which what we now call the blade-tool
culture; there were rock shelters and even open
air sites. Round stone-founded structures have
been found, about six metres in diameter, with
hearths, storage-pits and bins. The supposition
is made that sickle-blades were to be used at this
time for wild wheat and barley. Apparently there
were village farming communities at Jarmo, dated
7,000 B.C. This site has yielded evidence of two
kinds of wheat, barley, certain legumes; a goat
a sheep and a dog. By 5,000 B.C. this type of
living was probably transferred to Egypt as well.

According to Sauer, agriculture did not originate from a growing or chronic shortage of food;
people living in the shadow of famine do not have
the means or the time to take the slow and leisurely

27

experimental steps that are necessary if food
supply is to develop in a better and more varied
way. The improvement of plants by selection and
better cultivation was accomplished by a people
living at a comfortable margin above the mere
subsistence level. Sauer's argument is that the
needy and miserable societies are not inventive,
for they lack the leisure for introspection, reflection and discussion. The hearts of domestication are to be found in those areas where there is
a marked diversity of plants and animals, and where
there is a goodly variety of raw materials to experiment with. This implies well diversified terrain,
and perhaps also a variety of climate.

Sauer reasons that primitive cultivators
could not at first have established themselves in
large river valleys, if these were subject to floods.
It is probable that agriculture began in the wooded
lands, higher up. Here biological activity tends
to be high, and offers the maximum probability of
a wide variety of species, and thus assures a better
and more reliable food supply. Likewise habitats
at forest and woodland margins are likely to have
been preferentially selected. At the boundaries
between forest and steppe, between forest and sav-
annah, and between forest and coast, it could have
been easier than elsewhere to combine vegetable
and animal protein supplies, for the people could
hunt herbivores and catch fish, at the same time
gathering wild plants.

The more assured and better balanced diet which
this variety affords would also have reinforced
tendencies to establish sedentary settlements in
these very areas. In the uplands the people would
have opened up new land by deadening trees. For
this purpose goats were useful, because the damage
trees at the base so severely that in a relatively
short period the trees would die and could be
removed. In this way, goats were an additional
useful resource for man. This is probably what
happened in the highlands of Abyssinia, and the
resulting erosion has produced the silt for the
Egyptian civilization to rely upon as a source of

soil nourishment from that day to this.

Even though, with the help of goats they might deaden the ultimately remove trees, they were unable to eradicate the vigorous and tenacious grasses, so that early farming became woodland farming. But a planted clearing anywhere is a feast set out for all manner of wild creatures, whether they walk, fly or crawl. They come in to raid fruits, leaves and roots. What is food for man is also food for beast. Therefore by day and night someone must be alert to drive off the unbidden wild guests. This is where the animals of the farmyard were often useful. For man soon learned that to plant a field and leave it until the harvest meant loss of the harvest.

RIVER CIVILIZATIONS

It is now clear that the early settlements on higher ground had within them the seeds of their own destruction. For over time erosion of the slopes took hold, and these areas often turned into deserts. This was because of the type of agriculture practiced. In turn men were to learn about the importance of water, and so they tended to settle down near water. The clustering of groups in permanent settlements and villages was possible along waterways and river systems; they would select stream junctions, lake outlets and rapids. They also learned about canalization and irrigation in a primitive sort of way.

Thus it came about that richer crops could be grown in such areas, this in turn led to the growth of towns along these waterways. These served as lines of communication with other villages. Man learned new skills; fibres were used for nets and wood for boats and paddles. In such ways exchange of ideas was fostered. The new communities sometimes grew into towns which later became famous: Cairo, Baghdad, Benares, (Varanasi), Khartoum.

Important among the early civilizations are those situated along the Indus River, Moenjodaro and Harappa. Excellent evidence has been uncovered to denote the developed life style of the period. There to be seen are the remains of irrigation systems, places for bathing, drainage schemes and housing. Of particular interest to us is the extensive brickwork, including storage buildings for what must have been bountiful harvests. Rooms are differentiated for various tasks, showing a specialization in the lives of the people which is quite remarkable for that time, which was between 3,500 and 3,000 B.C.

Transportation along the rivers on long rafts, canoes and logs made cultural exchange and trade possible. This led to warfare and territoriality. But it also led to peace and collaboration, followed by intermarriage, and thereby the establishment of larger units and tribes. These might learn eventually to act together in a common cause and a nation came into being.

Eventually trade had its beginnings, assisted by two developments; some early genius took the potter's wheel and turned it upright, and with a like companion wheel set an axle between them. From such a beginning arose a cart, to be the forerunner of our present-day transportation system.* The second important advance at this time was the concept of a sailboat, which was later to be fully developed by the Phoenicians. Travel could now be overland and on the sea, as well as up and down rivers. The interplay between groups which resulted from these advances was an incalculable force.

ATTITUDES TOWARDS ANIMALS

The idea that animals were property was soon well established. The nomad groups particularly valued those animals that traveled well. They were used as pack animals; camels, asses and donkeys.

Other ideas born of agriculture were soon to pervade men's consciousness. When the earth was being torn open by the hoe as it was pulled by the

* We still use the term "axle" in assessing the tolls on certain roads.

bull, they began to fear both the bull and the hoe.
Trembling that they had outraged the Great Spirit,
they were inclined to fill in the furrow that they
had made. But there were those who said, "let
us put the male seed of the grasses into the womb
of the earth mother". And they did so, but did
not feel safe in so doing. They begged the earth
to forgive them for cutting her open; they gave
presents as propitiation. For they feared that
the earth might open up and swallow them all.

But nothing of the kind happened. The earth
on the contrary blessed those who had aided her
reproductive powers. Everything grew taller and
greener. And so they sanctified the hoe. It
was discovered much later, probably by the early
Chinese, that a dragged spade works better than
a dragged hoe. It turned the earth better. From
these early beginnings arose the properly-curved
moldboard plow of later times. Sauer has noted
a religious motive for the domestication of animals,
although at first there was little realization of
what was happening. For at first there had been
merely a gradual association of two species; man
and dog; man and goat, etc. This was a new concept. But the interesting part of it is that
these animals were pre-adapted by their respective
evolutions to be of service to one another in a
mutually beneficial manner. But man had no idea
of this; he had at first no conception of the future
value of their milk or their wool. But he soon
learned how to benefit from these new associations.
New uses of animals included their value as decoys
in hunting. Even their value as pets in the community, for the children particularly, predisposed
man in his attitude towards them.

When the development of infantile-appearing
strains of cattle suggested to early man that
these were somehow special, and they were certainly
more tractable, then it was conceived that they
could be put to various ritual uses. Represen-
tations indicate that the first-known harnessing
of cattle was to sleighs or wagons in religious
processions. Mesopotamian frescoes show priests

31

plowing and performing other tasks of husbandry.
They are also shown performing rites in the sac-
rificing of an animal, or in processions within
the temple precincts. The use of cattle for secular purposes in performing labor seems to have
derived from their prior use in sacred tasks.

The castration of a bull which was to lead
to the tractable ox was a significant advance,
and it had a religious connotation. Neither the
taming effect nor the development of more tender
meat could have been foreseen.

Representational art sometimes gives us clues
as to the habits of man at the time. The famous
frescoes at Ur not only show priests milking cattle,
but also a drawing of a bull with a ring through
its nose, presumably therefore tame. Other art
works of the time show the sacrificial uses of
animals, which by the time of early Jewry were of
great importance. The sacrificial use of animals
brings up the question of blood. It may be noted
that blood was not only used as a food when beasts
were slaughtered, but in all probability the drawing of blood from large animals was practiced by
some cultures. In a tomb of Rameses III is a
kitchen scene with blood being caught in a bowl.

FOOD SUPPLIES

Before proceeding to a consideration of the
great periods of Egypt and Sumer, it may be well
to note the situation as regards food supplies.
The milk of tamed animals was an enormous addition
to the better nutrition of the people. Its use
had an interesting history. Reindeer milk was
used by northern communities who as we have seen
brought this animal under domestication quite early.
The milk of yaks and asses has been used in restricted areas. If camels' milk is regarded as the
sweetest, mares' milk has long been regarded as
superior. Some Asian tribes have commonly mixed
mares' milk with millet meal, and have even mixed
blood with it. The use of sourmilk, butter and
cheese must have quickly followed the milking of

32

animals. It was important in Sumer, and milking scenes from Ur show the method used by the shepherds. A man in seated rocking a narrow-necked jar. Two men are close by seen straining the resulting liquid, no doubt removing the butter.

And so now man has at his disposal a wider variety of foods. Not only has he sources of meat on a reliable basis, but also a large variety of plant crops as well. His diet would become richer in carbohydrates, especially when animal meat was scarce. In the first place he would rely on molluscs for additional sources of food when he lived near the oceans. Oysters, cockles, mussles and whelks are more abundant per unit area than any other animal food; however, they do involve wasted labor in collecting, because they produce the greatest bulk of refuse for a given quantity of edible substance of any food. "One suspects", says J. G. Evans, "that shellfish as a main article of food were eaten for lack of something better, rather than from choice; or in bad seasons, or when unfamiliar surroundings presented challenges which could not at first be overcome."

In order to see the transition involved to the advent of walled towns, about 3,000 B.C., it is useful to trace three time-frames in communities in western Iran. The first pre-history time-frame was a period of semi-nomadic hunting and gathering, lasting until about 8,000 B.C.; the second era, called early dry-farming, plus the domestication of goats and sheep, involved the production primarily of emmer wheat and two-row barley. This period, lasting until about 5,500 B.C., illustrates the first permanent villages, early hornless sheep, and cereal grain supplies showing a mixture of wild and domesticated characteristics. The third period involved the bread wheats, triticum; six-row barley, lentils, grass peas, domestic cattle and dogs. This era brings us down to about 3,000 B.C.

It is around these permanent living sites that we can see the creation of the open habitats necessary for the cultivation of the weedy ancestors

33

of our later cultigens. We can begin to distin-
guish between root crops and seed crops. The common denominator of root crops is that through
their ability to store starch, they are well adapted to withstand long dry spells. They mature
quickly once the rainy season is over and the ground
warms up. Thus they derive from areas with markedly seasonal climates. This root culture, as
we call it, conuco, makes small demands upon the
soil and plant nutrients. However, the production
of seed crops, such as maize and beans, removes
much of the soil fertility at harvest. Milpar,
as we call it, is therefore much more damaging to
the ecosystem than is conuco. Provided that the
ground is deep enough, conuco can be succesfully
grown, even on steep slopes without causing erosion.
The milpar system however much more easily gets
out of equilibrium.

According to Hawkes, we can establish that
cultivated plants arose from a rather restricted
number of plant families and in a rather restricted
area of the globe; they seem to have come mainly
from the group Gramineae, the grasses, and the
Leguminosae. The others are almost nil, except a
certain number of herbs. This merely means that
the majority of plants known to mankind have remained firmly wild, and have never been domesticated.

The processes of domestication enabled the
people of those days to feed themselves better.
This, in turn, produced larger, viable groups of
people, who gathered together under a common plan
of living. Thus were young nations born, and
society evolved into the very important civilizations of those times. Of importance to us are the
peoples of Egypt and of Sumer.

REFERENCES

17   WILD GRAIN: Flannery, Kent V: Pre-histor-
      ic Agriculture; from Ucko and Dimbleby
      pp 75-100 (1970).

17   Wright, H. E. The environmental setting for
      plant domestication in the near east:
      Science 194, 385-389 (1976).

18   WEEDS: Vavilov, Nicholas I; Geographical
      regularities in the distribution of cul-
      tivated plants Leningrad 1927.

19   CULTIVATED PLANTS: Hawkes, J. G. from Ucko
      and Dimbleby; ibid, p 21-25.

19   SICKLE BLADES: Garrodd,Proc. Brit. Acad. 43,
      211-217 (1958).

19   FOOD IN IRAQ: Helbaek, Hans; Domestication
      of food plants in the old world; Science
      130, 365-372 (1959).

20   FOOD PRODUCTION: Childe, V. Gordon; Man
      makes himself, chap. 5, p 63 (1936).

20   PLANT CULTIVATION: Heiser, Charles B.
      Seed to Civilisation, pp 191-207 (1973).

21   EARLY PLANT DOMESTICATION: Heiser, Charles
      B., Bioscience 19, 228-231 (1969).

21   HOE CULTURE: Clark, Grahame and Piggott,
      Stuart, Prehistoric societies: chap. 8;
      Origins of farming (1970).

21   FIRST RUDIMENTS OF IRRIGATION: Flannery,
      Kent V. The ecology of early food produc-
      tion in Mesopotamia, Science 147, 1247-
      1256 (1969).

22   EARLY NEOLITHIC PLANTS: Sauer, Carl O. The
      domestication of animals and food stuffs.
      MIT Press, Cambridge, Mass. (1952).

22   TERRITORIAL CLAIMS OF HERDSMEN: Watts,
       Richard J. and Patti Jo; The domestication
       of plants and animsals (1969).

23   "UNDER CONDITIONS OF DESICCATION.." Childe,
       V. Gordon, Pre-historic man; chap. 5
       p 67 (1967).

24   SHEEPS' WOOLLEN SKINS USEFUL AS CLOTHING..
       Flannery, Kent V. Pre-historic agriculture,
       from Streuver's collection of papers;
       chap. IV, p 51 (1970).

25   INCREASED FOOD SUPPLY: Ucko, P. J. and
       Dimbleby, G. W. The domestication and
       exploitation of plants and animals; Aldine
       1969.

27   VILLAGE FARMING COMMUNITIES AT JARMO: Butz,
       Karl W. from Streuver; chap. XII, pp 200-
       235 (1970).

28   "NEEDY SOCIETIES NOT INVENTIVE.." Sauer, C. O.
       from Streuver, chap. XX.

29   LOSS OF HARVEST TO PREDATORS. Sauer, C. O.
       ibid.

31   RELIGIOUS MOTIVE FOR DOMESTICATION OF ANI-
       MALS.. Sauer, C. O. ibid.

32   TOMB OF RAMESES III. Breasted, James H.;
       The development of religion and thought
       in ancient Egypt (1916).

33   EXPLOITATION OF SHELLFISH. Evans, J.G. in
       Ucko; Hawkes, J. G. from Ucko and Dimbleby.
       ibid.

One important consequence of the neolithic
revolution, involving as it did the domestication
of animals and plants, was that man became a "pre-
dator of the soil." For the first time, he began
to upset the natural balance, with the result that
deserts were created, for example, in parts of the
formerly fertile Sumerian empire. In a very real
sense, man had begun to step outside nature rather
than remain a part of it.

It did not happen this way in Egypt and, for
that reason, Egypt's history was far different
from that of Sumer (Babylon). The Nile River made
the difference -- it did his farming for him. The
Nile, one branch of which rises in Abyssinia, car-
ries the overflow water after the torrential spring
rains in the uplands. It takes some time for a
river to flow from source to mouth, especially when
it is nearly two thousand miles long. The Nile
overflowed its banks very gently in September and
then retreated, leaving the rich black soil, or
alluvium.

This rich soil was carried all the way from
the mountains of Abyssinia and deposited for the
Egyptian farmer. The Nile god worked all year
for the Egyptians with a precision unknown in other
cultures up to that time. A nation that experienced this kindness, this bounty for thousands
of years on a regular basis had to believe that
the Nile acted with conscious intent. (Later on,
the Greeks were to assume a materialistic conception of these events which would have left the
Egyptians aghast. The Greeks, for example, would
wonder whether the Nile had a source, and if so,
where it was. The Egyptians would have considered
it blasphemous to ask the question, let alone to
search out the very delivery-chamber of their god).

Not only did the Nile god bear irrigating
waters, but the alluvial soil also carried precious
grains of gneiss, slate, and iron oxide washed out

from the upland hills. The forests in the highlands had begun to be cut so that animals could
graze on the grasses which could then grow in place
of trees. Man was thus starting the erosion of his
upland soil, by planting grain on it where trees
once had stood.

An occurrence as regular as the river's phases
prompted the development of a calendar. There were
three seasons in a year, each one hundred and
twenty days long. The new year for the Egyptians
started with the flooding of the river over its
banks, and this period later came to be called
July. It corresponded also with Sirius, the dog
star, which was in ascendance at that time. The
receding of the waters in September enabled planting to be done in October, and the sprouting of the
grain occurred in early November. That was the
beginning of the second season, when the grain grew
and came to fruition. The harvest in March denoted
the beginning of the third season and this was the
time of year when the Egyptians waited patiently
for the flooding to begin again in July.

The Egyptians called themselves chemet, or
"sons of chemi," the black earth, and they traced
their origin and their name to the divine act
which brought them the rich soil in which they sowed
their wheat. They could plant their crops without
plowing, for the sun baked the topsoil as the river
retreated, and the Egyptian farmer would sow his
wheat in the resulting cracks and fissures. The
sun's drying action also aerated the soil, which
helped to produce a better yield. The Egyptians
soon learned, however, that they were going to do
better if they were to plow. The stick plow was
invented, and it is not too different from the ones
in use in the hinterland of Afghanistan today.
Egyptian farmers also resorted to vigorous hoeing
to break up the clods for further soil improvement.
It is startling, but important for us to realize
that in 1,000 B.C. Egypt was producing as rich a
crop of grain as it does in the twentieth century.

Egypt under the Pharoahs was run like one great manorial estate. The entire farming population filled the granaries with grain and, in turn, those same granaries were emptied to feed the entire population. The serfs of the community received "less, but sufficient," and "the great ones, more." Every Egyptian lived in dependence upon the Pharoah; personal freedom had not been accorded to them but the lack of personal freedom, on the other hand, freed each individual from having to worry about his food. Since all cropland belonged to the Pharoah, they were all renters. They had to relinquish one-fifth of the crop, and the rest they could keep for food, feed, and seed. This arrangement is not a bad one, given later history of farming communities. In a few centuries Egypt's population increased a hundredfold. It has been estimated that by the third millenium B.C., the Egyptian peasant could produce three times as much food as he and his family of six needed to sustain them. Consequently, a surplus was available to feed workers on the massive tomb and flood-control projects.

A lot of work was needed annually in order to
keep the irrigation ditches in repair. The annual
flooding would wipe out signs of the borders of
men's property and, although the farmers were
renters, they did have their piece of land to attend
to. Thus the Nile forced the Egyptians, of necessity, to become surveyors and arithmeticians. The
Nile governed the science of Egypt and the Egyptians
developed mathematical precision in these matters.
They also developed astronomy, because they were
very conscious of the sun and seasons, and the
stars in their appointed courses. Today we can
see evidence of all this mathematical activity
in the hieroglyphs found in the surviving tomb
monuments.

At some point, the ancient Egyptians also
developed the art of making risen bread, and this
knowledge at once elevated them above all the rest
of the then-known world: Sumer, Syria, and the
other peoples around the Mediterranean, who were
still living on flat breads, porridges, meal, and
toasted grains for centuries after. In fact, up
to and including Roman times, this uninteresting
fare was staple in most cultures. The Germans,
when they were to meet the Romans much later,
knew only oat groats. The Assyrians, who were
contemporaries of the Egyptians, used hot slices
of barley flat cakes which they enlivened with
honey.

But the advances to come arose because the
Egyptians saw around a corner before anybody else
did. Instead of fearing, as all other peoples did
at the time, that their food might decay, the
Egyptians set aside their dough until it did
decay, and then observed with pleasure the results--
a process of fermentation. When the cells of
yeast fell upon a mixture of Nile water and meal,
fermentation occurred. The bubbles of gas could
not escape from the tenacious material and the
gas puffed up the dough, loosening it and light-
ening it. In the course of baking the acid and
alcohol did, of course, escape, but the open tex-

40

ture remained.* The Egyptians were especially concerned with results, and this procedure yielded a product entirely different from what had been known before. However, this kind of dough could not be baked outdoors, on coals of fire or on hot stones, nor in the way they had toasted their groats for centuries.

For risen dough, an enclosed oven is needed and the Egyptians invented this hitherto-unknown device by building hollow earthen mounds to house the cooking fire. In so doing, they entrusted their food to supernatural forces, for you cannot see inside an oven. The black earth used for building the ovens was called, as we have seen, chemia, and unknown substances in this chemia were the gift of the Nile god. The known substances in the dough were coupled within the confines of the oven according to some unknown law. Thus, to the Egyptians the oven was the first magic cauldron, the "womb of chemistry."

The image of fertility has survived in the vernacular--the early ovens, with their resenblance to a pregnant woman's abdomen, left their mark in sayings that are still used. For example, the Germans were wont to say when a girl was coming to term with her baby: "There is a loaf in the oven." It is still a way of announcing a pregnancy.

The Egyptians were to develop bread-making to a high art and eventually recorded fifty varieties. They learned to keep a piece of sourdough for inoculation of the next batch. Bread was included in their diet and it became important enough to figure in inscriptions and hieroglyphics, and to be left in a dead man's tomb in order that he should be able to eat on his way across the river. The tombs of Kings show the royal bakery to be an important feature of those times.

Now in modern times we know that both wheat and rye contain gluten. Gluten is the elastic part of the dough that allows it to stretch so well and

* The scientific details of this process were not truly known until Vanleeuwenhoek saw yeast cells under his microscope in the eighteenth century.

Food in the tomb

yet hold the texture. Barley had been used by the
Egyptians and other cultures for bread, but now
with this new bread-making process barley fell out
of favor. This was because barley contains very
little gluten, and many of the other grains contain none at all. Thus arose the emphasis on wheat
for bread which has remained a part of Western
culture ever since. Wheat, developed and grown in
Egypt, affected the civilizations of both Greece
and Rome. Their rise and their fall were inextricably bound up with wheat, as we shall see in later
chapters.

The wages of workers in the time of the Pharoahs were paid in produce: bread, beer, beans, onions, dried meat, fat, and salt.* The leisured elite, by contrast wanted for nothing and partook of luxurious banquets complete with entertainment: dancing girls, dwarfs, fools, wrestlers, and storytellers.

The Nile delta region was prolific in growing melons, grapes, onions, garlic, and olives. From earliest times, fish were preserved by both salting and drying. Grapes were dried for raisins. Beans, parsley, radishes, and leeks were also common. Figs, too, became important in ancient times, and baskets of figs have been found among Egyptian tomb offerings. The Egyptians were quite concerned about their health and believed that most illnesses had their source in the digestive system. As a result they often fasted. The mild laxative effect of figs may have commended itself to them.

What did the Egyptians believe that affected their way of living? Their chief ethic was represented by a goddess called Maat, who personified the concepts of order, truth, justice, and rightousness. These denoted the fitness of things, which the Egyptians believed was built into the world at the time of creation.

For the Egyptian official, Maat meant dealing justly in his daily activities. For the peasant or fellahin it meant working hard and honestly. Maat was the handiwork of the god rather than of mens' consciences. A god-given changelessness was the paramount idea and everything was exactly as it should be, fixed and proper. There was no Garden of Eden, no Golden Age, no Armageddon in Egyptian mythology.

The Egyptians thought of the afterlife as a duplication of the best moments of earthly existence.

* Even today, bread is central to the fellahin's diet. He will break open his round breads and stuff inside whatever additional food Allah has blessed him with -- vegetables, chopped meat, fish, and so forth.

There was nothing morbid about it, and it was honestly and confidently prepared for. Every Egyptian
of means was busy collecting earthly things to
take along with him in his tomb. Artsts were comm-
issioned to decorate the walls of the tomb with the
things the deceased would be using in the hereafter.
There would be scenes of sailing, hunting, fishing,
banqueting. The tasks to be undertaken by his
servants would also be portrayed on the walls of
the tomb.

SUMER

Egypt's food supply was assured by the regenerating waters of the Nile, and the country could
have survived without external trade, at least as
far as food is concerned. But for the people
of Sumer, further East, life was hard. They could
not survive as the Egyptians were able to do, working as they did with the almost exhausted soils
of Mesopotamia. The Tigris and Euphrates rivers
did not provide the same regenerating force which
the Nile did, and the people had to leave the rivers
for higher ground when the lowland soil became too
poor to farm. They used irrigation canals whenever they could, but it became too difficult to
make a living off soils which had been impoverished
by repeated herding and cropping. Consequently
Sumer--also called Babylon--was unable to continue
as a power, whereas Egypt has been able to survive
until the present day.

When the replacement of stone age tools with
bronze tools was taking place, copper and tin
were required. Bronze was being made in Sumer long
before the Egyptians knew about it. Bronze is
rather soft, but it did take an edge for a weapon
such as the neolithic people never had. It was
also possible to make other items from bronze --
plates and cups, for instance. Egypt had neither
copper nor tin, and so had to go on expeditions
to find them. Possessiveness and territoriality
as regards resources led eventually to skirmish and
warfare.

There were other advances. The Sumerian
farmer had developed a curved sickle, resembling
a sheep's jaw. This flint-toothed instrument was
very efficient for grass cutting and was not improved
upon until metal blades came into use many centuries
later.

The very first agricultural records of which
we are aware appeared in a document dating from
2,500 B.C., which was similar to our present Farmers'
Almanac. The document advised: "When you are about
to plant your fields keep your eye on the man who
plants barley. Let him drop the grain uniformly
two fingers deep. Use up one shekel of barley for
each garush of land (6-7 yards). If the barley
seed does not sink in properly change your coulter,
the tongue of the plow."

These advances heralded an improvement in crop
yields and in quality, especially of wheat and
barley. Provided that sufficient water was available, this was an era of comparative plenty in
Sumer. Populations grew, and mere subsistence was
replaced by the development of specialized skills
and occupations other than food production. Eventually the Sumerians learned that a given area of
land put down to wheat or barley filled more stomachs than the same land given over to livestock.
"Civilized" man replaced meat with grain as his
staff of life, and it has remained so ever since.

The change from a meat to a predominantly grain
diet was a far-reaching one, for it immobilized
large numbers of people by keeping them tied to the
land they farmed. It increased their consciousness
of boundaries and frontiers. Thus it was an early
step towards national consciousness, and it led to
friction between nomadic herdsmen and settled grain
eaters. As we shall see later the meat eaters, full
of protein energy, frequently came off best.

The average person in those days had a largely vegetarian diet consisting of barley, wheat,
and millet. The people also ate chick peas, lentils,
and beans, turnips, onions, leeks and garlic, cucum-

45

bers, mustard, cress, and fresh lettuce. Everyday meals in the days of the Sumerian empire were probably made up of barley bread, plus onions and a handful of beans washed down with beer. For variety, there was sometimes fish. Beef and veal were popular for those who could afford them, but a slaughtered animal had to be consumed quickly if it was not to turn putrid. Mutton was common, because the Sumerians emphasized herding. Goats' meat was acceptable, as was pork.

Centuries later, both the Jews and the Moslems rejected pork. The pig was disliked at first because it resisted herding, because it was not herbivorous, and because it had little stamina. Later it was feared, loathed, and finally rejected altogether.

As new cities arose in the Babylonian empire, there had to be also agreements in economic structure and in the underlying measurements of the buildings. As has been so well pointed out by Childe, the surplus wealth of Mesopotamia was providing for miners, smelters and other artisans who made no contribution to communal food supplies. Metal became common, pots are manufactured by men on the wheel instead of by women building them up as of old. The cylinder seal is adopted for labelling property and for signing documents. Babylonic cuneiform script is widely adopted for recording transactions; slavery was adopted for ensuring that the mines of Sinai were kept running for the benefit of the metal trade. All of these special activities were to require more food to be produced by fewer people, so that the large non-food-producing groups could be fed adequately.

The changes brought by the new Greek conquerors, such as Alexander, were to bring a shadow over the great Sumerian empire. It was to be a thousand years before a revivification process set in. This was to arise in ways entirely unforseen.

Although copper sometimes occurs in the native state, tin does not. Tin must be smelted, a process which requires the use of carbon in the form of wood charcoal for reducing the oxide ores. The demand for trees to use for wood charcoal contributed to the deforestation of the Sumerian hillsides and, in later times, to those of Greece as well.

During the neolithic era, man had farmed with just a few basic tools: the hoe, harrow, rake and mallet. These just scratched the surface of the light soils of those regions, and their use led rapidly to erosion. About 3,000 B.C., oxen were tamed and thus deep plowing became possible. Improved soil preparation and aeration due to this deep plowing enabled more soil nutrients to become available, and true agriculture began.

Babylonian Plowing Scene, fourteenth century B.C., from seal impression.

REFERENCES

37 REGULARITY OF THE NILE: Jacob, Heinrich; Six thousand years of bread, p 19 (1944).

38 "SONS OF CHEMET": Breasted, James H. Development of Religion and thought in ancient Egypt (1912).

39 THE PHAROAHS: Erman, Adolph; Life in ancient Egypt; (1885); trans. Blackman (1925).

39 POPULATION OF EGYPT: Breasted, James H. Ancient Times; a history of the early world; chap. III: Egypt (1916).

40 "LOOSENING THE DOUGH". Pliny the Elder; Natural History, Book XVIII, 26-27; Ist century A.D.

41 BAKING IN EGYPT DURING THE MIDDLE KINGDOM: Larsen, Hjalner. (1936).

42 EVERYDAY LIFE IN ANCIENT EGYPT: Shorter, A.W. (1932).

43 BREAD AS PAYMENT AND AS MONEY: Jacob, H. ibid p 31-32.

43 USE OF FIGS: Columella; VII, 10 (200 A.D.).

43 MAAT, GODDESS OF TRUTH AND RIGHTNESS: Steindorff, Georg; Religion of the ancient Egyptians, (1905), chap. IX, p 83.

44 ARTISTRY OF THE TOMBS: Emery, Walter B.: Archaic Egypt (1961).

45 "CHANGE YOUR COULTER, THE TONGUE OF YOUR PLOW." Kramer, Samuel Noah; The Sumerians, their history, culture and character; Appendix I; Farmers' Almanac, p 341, (1963).

45   GROWTH OF SUMER'S POPULATION: Childe, Gordon;
        "Man makes himself"; chap. VII p 137-8.

46   USE OF PORK: Kees, Herman; Ancient Egypt
        and cultural topography. (1961).

46   EARLY FOOD PRODUCTION IN SUMER: Flannery,
        Kent V.: Ecology of early food production
        in Mesopotamia; Science 147, 1247-1256,
        (1965).

47   EARLY SEEDS IN SUMER: Heiser, Charles B.:
        Seed to Civilisation; seedsaat Sarmo
        dated about 6,750 B.C. p 6 (1973).

The early history of the Jews is inextricably connected to that of Egypt. The figure who stands out in this period is Joseph, one of the many sons of Jacob. His large family of brothers were hostile to him, and as a result Joseph was sold as a slave. He grew up in Egypt, and eventually became known as possessing the gift of interpretation of dreams. With this gift, he was able to bargain for payment, and ultimately gained his freedom.

The Pharoah adopted the ex-slave, and used his gift of vision for his own purposes. In time, Joseph was made Grand Vizier of Egypt. As such, he was responsible for the gathering of one-fifth of the grain as taxes, and also for the public storage of grain. For this important position he needed authority from the Pharoah, whose signet ring was copied for Joseph's use in the execution of his duties.

Joseph was anxious to re-unite with his family, in particular his brothers, Reuben, Benjamin, and Simeon. They did not at first recognize him, but when they did, he invited his entire family to move to Egypt and to settle in the land of Goshen, which was good pastoral land.

The Pharoah apparently was delighted with this arrangement. Joseph told his brothers, however, to stress to the Egyptians that they were shepherds rather than farmers; otherwise he knew that there might be some risks in settling in this border area. In this way, Joseph saw to it that his family would not come into close contact with the bread-eating Egyptians. This was because the Egyptians considered pastoral peoples inferior -- people who lived in the company of their animals were regarded as unclean by a society that specialized in bread. The Egyptians continually looked down upon the Bedouin. "I caused the Bedouin to go as dogs", says the Instruction of King Amenemhet, who ruled from 1965 to 1955 B.C. For the Egyptians were agriculturalists par excellence, and their bread was risen bread, nice and white.

And so the early Hebrews lived their own life as nomadic herders, and only occasionally became tillers of the soil. They must have been astonished to encounter a people like the Egyptians, who spent their lives making bread. The Hebrews did learn the art of risen breadmaking from the Egyptians, but they could not use it consistently until they settled down. They could not transport ovens, which have to be a part of a permanent dwelling. So the Jews baked no bread until they were on their own land.

They did, however, eat their bread much like the Bedouin tribes have done ever since those times -- either they parched the grain on hot stone floors, as described in the Book of Ruth; or they set flat cakes to bake slowly between layers of slow-burning dung. If they did have a hearth, they were able to roast the dough in the ashes. But it was still a flat cake, and not bread.

In the early history of the Jews as a settled people, each family tried to have its own oven, and the baking was done by the women. As cities arose, men took over the baking and more people tended to buy their bread from these bakers than to make it at home. The early breads were fairly flat, small and round. At least three were needed for a meal. That is why the Jews broke their bread rather than cutting it; thence arose the phrase, "the breaking of bread," and, ultimately, "breakfast."

And when the Isrealites, led by Moses, later departed from Egypt in such haste, they took the dough "before it was leavened, their kneading-cloths being bound up in their clothes upon their shoulders." Having finally escaped from Egypt, they baked "unleavened cakes of the dough which they had brought forth out of the land of Egypt," and Moses enjoined them: "There shall be no leavened bread eaten."

This became part of the sanctification of the Jewish faith, commemorated each year at the Passover. And it was thus that the Jews had both a sacred bread and a profane bread: profane bread, such as the Egyptians had taught them to make, could be eaten at ordinary times. But in the presence of God and his emissaries, only unleavened bread could be eaten.*

Their God, Jehovah, was worshipped in a tent, or tabernacle, which had no resting-place. The God of a pastoral people disdained bread that took a whole day to bake. And a very powerful taboo arose from these beliefs. For why did the Jews not bring leavening into the presence of God? It was the same leavening that they ate at other times of the year. One possibility is that bread was a sacrificial food, and as such it could not be in the slightest degree tainted. Risen bread involves a process of fermentation (decay) which might well have been considered to be unclean.

All foods offerered to God must be free of taint. Meat was held to be palatable for two days only; after that it could not be sacrificed to God. LIkewise, vegetables could not be brought to the altar after two days. In the Middle-Eastern climate this was entirely logical. Sourness and rottenness were one and the same thing, namely fermentation. How could one offer to God something which was in a state of decay? Milk, too, so quick to sour in that hot climate, was not considered an acceptable offering to God, and was never brought to the altar. This is interesting, because other Semitic peoples like the Carthaginians and the Arabians did not hesitate to do this.

Much later Mohammed was to teach that yeast was not a destroyer, but a giver of life. Islam has used various forms of fermented milk for over a thousand years, as kefir, mast and yoghurt. All of these ways of preserving milk were regarded as good and constructive uses of the fermentation process.

* This idea of unleavened bread was carried right through into the Christian celebration of the Mass.

LAND

After the Jews had left Egypt and settled to
the East, the question of land ownership soon arose.
Moses, brought up in the Egyptian court, had seen
that in Egypt all the land belonged to the Pharoah.
Eternal servitude was the result for the common
people. Moses rejected that notion, because his
people wanted, above all else, to be free. Not
just free of the Pharoah, but intrinsically free
to live as they felt they must. And so Moses drew

Moses giving his Constitution
to the sons of Israel

up a constitution which limited the freedom of the
land in a novel way: Moses reasoned that if the
land did not belong to a single Pharoah or King,
then it should not belong to some lesser persons

54

either. And he also recognized that if every Jew
in Canaan were to be granted an equal portion of
land, with freedom to dispose of it exactly as he
wanted to, in a very short time the rich cattle owners
would displace the poorer landowners, and the situation would turn out to be worse than in the
beginning. So Moses decreed that nobody could sell
the land, because its owner was the Lord God.
"The land shall not be sold, forever. For the
land is mine", saith the Lord.

And so, in the Jewish culture, there was no
private property in land. Boundary marks were sacred, agrarian usary was a sin, and land speculation
was eliminated altogether. Of course, the laws
were flouted and circumvented, but they did exist,
and no other people had such laws. (The modern
ideas about the Israeli kibbutzim really date back
to the communal ideas of Moses). The Romans never
had such laws, and we shall see the consequences.
In fact, the strife between those who own land and
the vast numbers of ordinary people who own no
land goes on throughout history and right up to the
present day.

Many peoples have struggled with this problem.
Feelings about land run very deep. For example,
the native Americans had a special regard for land;
they said that it belonged to the Great Spririt,
and that they were only renters of it. This became
an acute problem when they were deprived of their
land by the oncoming pioneers.

FOOD

What did the Jewish people eat in those early
days? They ate meat chiefly after animal sacrifices, for they soon learned to burn only the
entrails. They used wheat or barley cooked with
lamb or mutton, very much the same sort of diet
that the Moslems were later to use. Game was
hunted, and nuts were a favorite food of those
who could afford them. Locusts and wild honey are
mentioned as well. The common people ate bread

and fish, beans, lentils, cucumbers and onions. They enjoyed a fine red wine from Palestine "for the afflicted heart."

How do food habits arise? Some of them are lost in the mists of antiquity. Among the old Semitic peoples, there was a rule that men and women should not see each other eat. So the custom arose that the man would eat alone, and his wife and children would eat at another time, and possibly at another place. Covering the mouth while eating and drinking were sometimes said to prevent the evil eye -- it is thought that this belief originated from the watching of others eat by hungry people, who might then be envious. Others believed that a homeless evil spirit might wander into their open mouths and cause trouble.

Some foods were considered clean: for example animals that chewed their cud, and whose hooves are cloven. Cattle, sheep and goats fulfill both these requirements, but swine are unclean because they do not chew their cud, although their hooves are cloven. Camels are unclean because although they chew the cud, their hooves are not cloven. Fish with both scales and fins are clean; thus eels and shellfish are not allowed. Birds of prey and most insects are unclean, and so is the internal fat of any animal.

Meat and dairy foods are eaten separately, on separate dishes and at separate times. During Passover, flour and other grains cannot be used, neither can leavening agents or malt. This is in commemoration of the flight from Egypt.

REFERENCES

51 JOSEPH SOLD AS A SLAVE: Genesis, 37.

51 JOSEPH GRAND VIZIER OF EGYPT: Genesis, 39.

51 PHAROAH'S SIGNET RING: Genesis, 41, v 42.

51 "AND TO SETTLE IN THE LAND OF GOSHEN.."
    Genesis, 45, v 10.

51 "I CAUSED THE BEDOUIN TO GO AS DOGS." Erman,
    Adolph L. Literature of the Ancient Egypt-
    ians, (1894), tr. Blackman, II, 4 p 74.

52 "THE JEWS BAKED NO BREAD UNTIL THEY WERE ON
    THEIR OWN LAND"..Jacob, H. H. Six thousand
    Years of Bread. (1944), chap 13, p 34-6.

52 GRAIN PARCHED ON STONE FLOORS. Book of Ruth,
    2, 14.

52 "THEIR KNEADING-CLOTHS UPON THEIR SHOULDERS.."
    Exodus 12, v 34.

55 "THE LAND SHALL NOT BE SOLD, FOREVER."
    Leviticus, 25, v 23.

56 WINE FOR THE AFFLICTED HEART: Proverbs,
    31, v 5,6.

56 CAMELS ARE UNCLEAN..Deuteronomy, 14, v 7.

EARLY DAYS

Our main source for descriptions of life in
the early Greek days is Hesiod, whose father, having failed in business, bought a farm in the hill
country of Boeotia, at a place called Helikon.
There Hesiod kept his father's sheep, and learned
the stars, the seasons, and a considerable body of
lore about farming in general. Hesiod set down his
advice to the world in a remarkable poem, called
Works and Days. It became famous in his day, and
his lines were quoted, echoed, and paraphrased in
all parts of the Greek world, and later in the
Roman world as well. It is an important work for
our topic, because it deals with all aspects of the
raising of food.

> "First get a house and a woman, and an ox
> for the plow, and have your tools ready in
> the house...get two nine-year-old oxen;
> they are in their prime then, and they
> will not get to fighting and break the
> plow...and get a man of forty for your
> plowman; a younger man gets bored and
> wants companionship...and don't stint his
> food..."

The poetry of his writing, even in an English
translation, is unsurpassed:

> "...when the might of the fierce sun is
> ceasing from its sultry heat and mortals
> move more lightly--for then Sirius goes
> but little over the heads of mortal men
> by day, and takes a greater share of the
> night--at that season the wood that you
> cut is most proof against worms, when it
> is letting fall its leaves and ceasing to
> grow. So then cut wood, remembering to
> do all work in due season..."

"...and mark when you hear the cry of the
crane crying high on the clouds year by
year; it gives the signal for plowing
and warns us of the season of rainy winter,
and it grieves the heart of a man that
has no oxen. Then it is time to feed up
your curly-haired oxen in the byre...."

"... pray then to Zeus of the earth and
holy Demeter in full weight, when first you
begin your plowing. You take the end of
the plow-tail in your hand and come down
on the backs of your oxen with your goad
as they tug on the peg that holds the yoke-
straps. And let a little slave follow
behind with a mattock to give trouble to
the birds by hiding the seed...."

And in mid-September, the vintage:

"...but when Sirius and Orion are come
into the mid-heaven, and rosy-fingered
Dawn looks upon Arcturus, then, Perses,
cut and bring home all your clustering
grapes; and show them to the sun ten days
and nights, and keep them five days in the
shade, and on the sixth pour off into
jars the gifts of Dionysus, the joy of
many...."

Hesiod's chief message was to work incessantly.
Addressing his brother Perses he says, "...but
do you ever remember my bidding: work, noble Perses, so that hunger may hate you and fair-crowned
Demeter may love you and fill your barns."

This canny old Greek farmer had comments about
his times, and he was largely pessimistic. "We
live in an iron age, even harder than the age of
bronze, and the days of gold are far away...." And,
he continued with an air of resignation: "...the
nobles who govern are predatory and corrupt, but
it is no use complaining."

60

Hesiod comsidered the farmer's life in Greece to be a hard life, and warned against subdivision of the land into too many plots too small to support a family:

"One son is the best number to leave behind you, for so will wealth increase. Or, if you have a second son, you should die old, at least not until you have built up an estate large enough to stand division."

He also advised his readers to eat less in the winter, and "...if you are hungry, go to bed, for the long winter nights are a great help."

Thus we learn from Hesiod what Greek life was like about the ninth century B.C.* As long as the human population of Greece was small at that time, a farmer could subsist with his family in some sort of comfort. They grew wheat and barley, they tended a few olive trees, fig trees, and grapevines; perhaps they might keep a pig or two, and possibly a goat for milk and cheese.

The average diet of early Greek towns and villages was inferior to that of the farmer. The town dweller and his family had to be content with a diet of beans, lentils, leeks, onions, and turnips. They ate maza, a barley porridge or paste; barley flat bread, and a handful of olives. Very occasionally the town-dweller would have salt fish, but meat was a rarity and wine a luxury. The average Greek who was slightly better-off would eat various kinds of bread, as well as wine, cakes, and honey.

By 650 B.C., population pressure began to build up and the land itself became worked over more thoroughly, so that most of the population was forced to live on poorer land than before. The rest of this chapter will show how this came to pass.

* Hesiod's close observations of the stars and other phenomena, especially eclipses, have enabled modern scholars to date his writings with some accuracy, at or soon after 850 B.C.

AGRICULTURE

In Sumer it took thousands of years to strip the land; how could it happen so rapidly in Greece? For the Greeks were using marginal land by 600 B.C.

According to the records, the Greeks were not very good agriculturalists. The people did not practice rotation of crops, but left their fields fallow half the time, thus losing production every other year. And when they did plant the following year, they planted the same crops as previously. Homer mentioned manuring in his writings, but the Greek landowners as a whole did not practice it.

The main problem was how to get enough food to eat, and that food had to be grain. Meat had almost disappeared from the average diet. The need for grain forced the Greek city-states to develop an import-export economy based on imperialistic arrangements. For this they needed ships, which required precious wood. Wood could only be obtained from those same forests that were needed to knit the soil together, and to provide acorns for the pigs. Nevertheless, timber was taken in order to build the fleet to carry imported grain and exported wine and olive oil.

Secondly, as the city-states grew, houses were built largely of wood, since not every house could be made of stone or marble. The third factor which contributed to denuding the forests was the advance in metallurgy, for that technology required larger and larger amounts of wood charcoal.

The soil, no longer fed by dead leaves and held together by tree roots, was washed down the steep hillsides by the torrential rains that occasionally occur in Greece, the result was that the hills lost their soil and the valleys lost their fertility.

At the same time, the power of Greece relative to other nations grew, and slaves were introduced

from Egypt and Asia Minor. This increased the
number of people living on the same amount of land.
The lot of the peasant grew harder, and he got
into debt. Many farmers abandoned the soil, and
settled for a nomadic life. Sometimes they could
eke out a meager living from the sea. Some of
them learned piracy, and from that, trade.

MEALS IN GREECE

Apart from the many public banquets, the average meals were not lavish. At first both the
peasants and the well-to-do had similar diets. But
as time passed, Athens became the center of magnificence in the then-known world. At that point,
the diets of the rich and the poor became sharply
differentiated.

A large variety of commodities were available
in Athens. The meat most often used was oxen,
sheep, goats, or swine. Swine meat (pork) was used
extensively, either roasted, salted, or smoked,
or made into sausages. (There are records showing
that sausages were sometimes adulterated with the
flesh of dogs or asses). Several kinds of poultry
were used, as well as game such as hare. Fish were
eaten in great quantities, even by the poor, especially sardines, which have been important in the
Greek diet ever since.

Grain was used for bread and for porridges,
and these were chiefly made of wheat and barley,
since rye was despised as being food fit only for
barbarians. Only the well-to-do ate risen bread,
either white or brown. The average Greek peasant
or city-dweller could not afford an oven, and
bread had to be obtained from a bakery. The poor
ate maza instead, which must have resembled polenta,
still used in southern Greece today.

Green vegetables were used for salads. As-
paragus, radishes, mushrooms, lentils, and peas
were common. Onions and garlic were relished, and
eaten raw with bread. Nuts were a very important

part of the diet of the Mediterranean world, as well as that of the Middle East. Certain kinds of black walnuts are the best source of iron, and were available to many people; almonds also are a good source of both iron and protein. Salt, pepper, and various spices such as sesame, coriander, caraway and mustard were also known.

For the better-off, fruit, cheese, and cakes were available, and honey was used as a sweetener. Butter was not used. Wine was drunk, but not usually very much, unless the meal was to be followed by a symposium. During a symposium, wine and other dainties would be served, and dancing girls were featured. The wine was usually mixed with water, either one to one, or even two to three. This is still the custom in many parts of Greece.

As Athens became more and more conscious of its intellectual prowess and eminence, and therefore more self-assured, it also paid the penalty for excesses. As time passed, foods became more and more exotic, and sometimes even ridiculous.

Athenians entertained a great deal, when they could afford it. People would frequently stop by for a short time before going on to a second place. For those brief visits, they would be served hors d'oeuvres; literally, "instead of the works," rather than a full meal. Eventually this custom grew to be considered miserly, and today, hors d'oeuvres are served in addition to, rather than instead of, the main meal.

OLIVES

At first, Athens had not be interested in trade, but as the years went by and Greek soil was depleted as a result of deforestation and poor farming techniques, the Greeks became more and more dependent on other nations for essential foods, especially grain. Of necessity, therefore, Athens had become a booming trade center by 600 B.C. and carried on a brisk trade, exporting olive oil in exchange for the badly-needed grain.

Harvesting olives.

Laws prohibited the export of all agricultural commodities except olive oil, because if other foods were exported, there would have been insufficient food for the Greeks themselves. Because of these laws, the Greek farmer often sold everything he had, and planted olive trees so that he could export the oil. This was disastrous environmentally, even if it made sense economically. The olive tree has a long tap root that goes deep down into the subsoil, enabling it to reach the nutrients in the limestone. Because of this, it does not knit the topsoil. It can grow on those bare hills, although it was not in fact the proper crop. Any rains which wash away the topsoil around an olive tree, nevertheless do not damage the tree. But there is no topsoil for other crops. Such plantings really damaged the soil. Two hundred years later, Plato was to describe the white limestone outcroppings and the bare hills -- the Greek landscape is still famous for its brilliance, but it was bought dearly, at the expense of the people. It took thousands of years of improper soil husbandry to deplete the soils of Sumer, but only hundreds to destroy the once-fertile soils of Greece.

SOLON

Greek imperialism, which nurtured a new class of "nouveaux riches", produced a number of new problems, including class conflict and the denial of citizenship rights; by 594 B.C., there was utter turmoil.

Out of this turmoil arose the gigantic figure of Solon, an Athenian aristocrat from an old and respected family. He had been a merchant, and rose to influence in Athens as a mediator. He stood on the side of the poor against the aristocrats, but he was not really a radical. We should call him, rather, an enlightened moderate.

The problems which Solon faced were enormous. Civil war or tyranny were imminent. All elements of society were at odds. Because of many debts, small farmers were likely to have fallen into a

serf-like situation called "hectemorrage".
The "hectemoros" was required to give one-sixth of
his produce to his creditor, usually a rich landowner. If he failed, he and his family might
have to pay for it in enslavement.

Coinage also contributed to the small farmer's
indebtedness. By means of coinage, the middle-sized
landowner could accumulate wealth, but the poor
suffered because products increased in price, especially those intended for export. Poor farmers
could not easily switch to the cultivation of those
goods which fetched the best prices, because it
required time and investment, of which the poor had
neither. It takes well over twelve years for an
olive tree to bear its first fruit, and from three
to four years for a vine to bear grapes. A farmer
near the subsistence level could not survive in the
meantime; thus Greek society became stratified into
the very rich, the very poor, and a new commercial
or entrepreneurial class.

Solon, realizing the situation, attached the
rich for their greed, which, he said, was "...rous-
ing up civil strife and sleeping war." He instituted a number of reforms, the first of which was
an effort to deal with the problems of the "hectemoros". A law called "Seisachtheia", which meant
"shaking off the burdens," was enacted; its effect
was to cancel all debts and to forbid all further
loans on the security of the person. He also
purchased Athenians who had been sold as slaves
abroad, and returned them to Athens. He freed the
land, and spoke of removing the "horoi", the
markers placed on land to show that it was not
mortgaged.

Solon divided the citizenry formally into four
classes: the "pentakosoi medimnoi", the "five-
hundred bushel men," the large landowners; the
"hippoi", or knights; the "zuigitoi", or yoke-men;
and the "thetes", or common folk. The top class
had all the rights to become chief officials, the
hippoi could accede to all posts except those at
the very top, and zuigitoi could hold lesser offices,

67

and the thetes were only allowed to vote and not to
hold office at all.

Solon's skillful administrations and just laws
were only successful temporarily. He never did
break the power of the old aristocrats, especially
in religious offices and in the power structure.

GREEK CITY-STATES

A city-state organization was described by
Aristotle, who defined a "polis" as a partnership
of clans and families, "...living well; its object
a full and independent life." The concept of citizenship arose from this set of social relationships.

Both Aristotle and Plato astutely observed
that the key to the polis was "autarkia": self-
sufficiency. They pointed out that ideally this
self-sufficiency should exist in all facets of life.
Aristotle specified six necessary components of
"autarkia": food supply, handicrafts, arms, money
supply, religion, and the legal system; and the
occupations common to each.

"Autarkia" worked well in early Greece, during
the ninth, eighth and seventh centuries B.C. But
after the polis got to be a certain size, its very
complexity militated against self-sufficiency,
and thus against independence. When communities
were separated from one another by the geography
of land and sea, they were forced to be self-
sufficient. But in time, excess population demanded the establishment of colonies, and this encouraged trade. In addition, outside contacts
introduced new cultures and prevented stagnation.
All this created a new world order, for which the
polis was not suited.

Athens and Sparta represented the extremes in
self-sufficiency, and both extremes led to the
failure of the polis and of its conceptual foundation,
"autarkia". Sparta, almost totally isolated and
independent, decayed; whereas Athens became incredibly vital as a result of increasing dependency on
other nations.

Because Sparta had ample land to feed her sparse population she never became involved in colonization but instead developed isolationist attitudes. Due to limited contacts with the outside world, her arts and crafts became stagnant and deteriorated. Although Sparta was militarily strong because her citizens were professional soldiers, the fabric of her society was weakened from within. Though victorious in the Peloponnesian War against Athens (431-404 B.C.), Sparta never benefitted by this victory because she was on the verge of collapse anyway: for Sparta lacked administrative skills and acumen, and became static at the very time that Athens was ready to surge forward.

These same Peloponnesian Wars played havoc with the countryside and with the crops. As a result the Greek peasant, wherever he lived, was so burdened with debt that he had to sell out to the speculators, and he left the familiar countryside for the doubtful haven of the city. An impoverished family of three would be reduced to eating only greens and turnips, iris rhizones and a few lupin seeds. They would gather wild pears if they could, and perhaps find a dried fig or an occasional grasshopper. A family of five would be reduced to eating barley paste, and little else.

The soil would grow perhaps seven or eight bushels of wheat per acre in good years. In bad years, the people would go hungry and famines were frequent. As in all cases before and since, historical movements of great significance were accompanied by substantial dietary changes. The decline of Athens from 450 B.C. onwards was to produce a loss of variation in the diet -- what we call a balanced diet became almost impossible to achieve, and nutritional deficiencies and diseases appeared in the culture.

In addition to a nutritional decline and food scarcity, there were occasional outbreaks of unfamiliar infections. Thucydides left a vivid impres-

sion of one such disaster, which occured in 429
B.C. and left Athens quite demoralized. The
disease killed off as many as one-quarter of the
army, and particularly affected the cities, through
the ports of Piraeus and other places. The disease
created so many antibodies in the bloodstreams
of the surviving Athenians that the chain of infection could not be maintained, and it burnt
itself out in a single season, leaving as quietly
as it had come. According to William McNeil in
his fascinating book, Plagues and People, this
epidemic was probably measles.

As the third century B.C. progressed, the power
of Greece declined and that of Rome grew. The
Punic Wars between Rome and Carthage dominated the
Mediterranean scene until 201 B.C. Rome was
determined to neutralize the Greek power of Philip
of Macedon, and in this Rome was successful. By
196 B.C., Roman troops were withdrawn from Greece,
which was henceforth to be free. Peace broke
down, however, and another war in 146 B.C. ended
with the total destruction of Corinth.

FOOD IN GREECE

The Greeks made a number of contributions to
progress in food cultivation. That of figs, particularly, reached a high state of perfection.
The Greeks had learned from Eastern peoples that
a more sturdy fig tree could be achieved by hanging the branches of the wild-goat fig, "Caprificus",
into the boughs of the female cultivated tree.
This caprification process assisted pollination
and increased the yield. It was a very early type
of genetic cross, possibly the first of its kind.

The fig became very important nutritionally,
and its export was forbidden at one time. The
staple foods were cereals of various kinds, combined with olive oil, grapes and figs. Vegetables
grown locally had to be harvested by May, before
the torrid Greek summer put an end to agricultural
productivity altogether. There was little or no

irrigation, as there were no rivers (such as the
Tigris and Euphrates in Sumer and the Nile in
Egypt) to help things along.

Only the rich had fresh fish, even though one
is never far from the sea in Greece. Bees were
kept in large numbers, for other sources of sugar
were not known. Also unknown were potatoes, lemons,
oranges, and tomatoes. Salt was reclaimed from
the sea in salt pans, much as it is today on the
coast of India; it was carried into the interior
towns and traded for slaves. Hence the phrase,
"a man is worth his salt".

Wine was kept cold in summer by bringing snow
and ice down from the mountains into cool caves.
Beer was known, since the Egyptians and Sumerians
had produced it for centuries; but the Greeks despised beer, as most wine-drinking people still do.

Even today the food of the poor Greeks is
much the same as it was then, except for the addition of citrus, coffee, tea, sugar, and tomatoes.
The Greeks did not seem to adopt potatoes as readily as did many of the northern European cultures.

THE CULT OF DEMETER

A country or an empire can last only so long
as the people are fed. In Greece, the events which
led to the harvest became part of a whole mythology, around which the people wove a fabric of
religious observances. Thunder, rain, and the
growing of plants were all significant events,
and were related to the seasons of the year. The
Greeks, observing this connection, wove a cult
around it.

Demeter was the daughter of Cronon and Rhea,
and was thus one of the great Olympians. These
gods and goddesses lived on Mount Olympus, and
occasionally came down to earth. Demeter was first
coveted by Poseidon, god of the sea, but she did
not care for him and so refused him. In order to

71

escape from him, she fled from Mount Olympus and, disguising herself, lived on earth in a cave. In order to bring her back to Olympus, Zeus himself intervened, and because of this intervention she returned to Olympus and resumed her place among the immortals.

Then Zeus himself coveted her, but she rejected him also. In order to deceive her, Zeus took on the form of a bull. The daughter who was born to Demeter as a result of this encounter was named Kore'. At heart, Demeter loved Jasion the plowman, a mortal. According to legend, she lay with him in a thrice-plowed field, and by him she had a son, named Plutus. Zeus was jealous of Jasion, and struck him down with thunderbolts, but Jasion's descendants have survived, as generations of plowmen.

The legend of Demeter is concerned with her daugher Kore', whose father was Zeus himself. One day Kore' was out picking flowers in a field and saw a beautiful narcissus. She ran to pick it, and the earth opened up and Hades appeared. Hades was the god of the underworld, and the brother of Zeus. Hades seized Kore' and carried her with him down into the bowels of the earth.

Demeter was overcome with grief, and resolved to seek for her daughter. She ranged up and down the earth on foot, trying to find out where Kore' had gone. Hecate informed Demeter that Kore' had gone off with Hades. Demeter was overwhelmed with this news, and decided to withdraw from Olympus, and to take on the guise of an old woman. She hired herself out as a nurse to the family of the king of Eleusis, and stayed there for some time. While there, she used her power to impart certain gifts to the king and his family. She showed them the first ear of corn, and how to hitch oxen to a plow. She showed them how to till the soil to yield harvests, and she gave them the olive tree.

Still, Demeter was grieving for her daughter, and retired to a temple that she had made at Eleusis. Remaining there for awhile, she prepared for mankind a cruel and terrible year, during which the earth would refuse to give forth any crop. The whole of mankind would have perished, had not Zeus himself intervened. He sent his messenger to Demeter to plead with her not to carry out her plan, but she was implacable, and stated flatly that she would not allow the earth to bear fruit unless she saw her daughter again. Finally Zeus sent word down to his brother Hades, to return young Kore' (who since her sojourn in the underworld had changed her name to Persephone). Hades complied with this wish, but before sending his young wife up to the earth again he tempted her with pomegranate seeds. This fruit was the symbol of marriage, and the effect of eating it was to render the union of a man and a woman indissoluble.

When Kore', now Persephone, returned to her mother, Demeter was overjoyed. But she said, "Surely thou hast not eaten of anything whilst in the regions below the earth? For if thou hast not eaten, thou shalt live with me on Olympus; but if thou hast, then thou must return to the depths of the earth." When Persephone admitted to having eaten the fatal pomegranate, it seemed that Demeter must again lose her daughter.

Appealing to Zeus, Demeter agreed to a compromise: that Persephone would live for one-third of the year with her husband underground, and for two-thirds of the year with her mother. Being satisfied with this arrangement, Demeter set aside her anger and bade the soil be fertile again. The vast earth was soon covered with leaves and flowers. And before she returned to Olympus, Demeter taught the kings of the earth her divine science, and initiated them into the mysteries of growing things.

Thus the Greeks explained why each year when the cold weather arrived, the earth took on an

aspect of mourning and sadness -- that was the time
when Persephone went to join her husband in the
deep shadows. But when the spring came, the earth
put on its mantle of a thousand flowers to greet
the return of Persephone.

A whole cult developed around the legends of
Demeter and Persephone, and the disappearance
and later return of Persephone were the occasions
of great festivals in Greece. Demeter was considered to be the goddess in charge of all agriculture and related persuits; and the return of Persephone brought back the growing-season each year.

In the sequence of making bread, the sowing
and the reaping were men's work, and the threshing
was done by the trampling of the oxen. In the
making of flour one entered the women's sphere,
but in order to make the flour the grain had to be
crushed. The Greeks felt that, in order to obtain
bread man should appease the soul of the tortured
wheat, and that its living soul as it became bread
should be honored. Because the earth, in which
the apparently dead wheat seed is sown, is the
same earth in which the bodies of the dead are
laid, Demeter was also thought to have power over
the destruction or the resurrection of human souls;
so those who did not attend the rites of the cult
of Demeter were thought to be damned.

All Athens, all Greece, and parts of Italy
participated in the great "celebration of the
bread." It was the proudest feast of the ancient
world. A procession in honor of Demeter represented the four months when Persephone would rest
in the arms of the god of the underworld, now
equated with death. Because Demeter had searched
for her daughter on foot, all went on foot, rich
and poor alike. Various rituals were performed
as the rather sombre procession went on its way.
On the third day the priests of Bacchus, the god
of wine, were introduced, and the remainder of
the procession took on a spirit of revelry. This
custom was carried on for over 1100 years, from
700 B.C. to at least 400 A.D. People would come

from all over the known world to participate in it.

The cult of Demeter was a rival to Christianity, because it gave its initiates a life of the soul after death, or could punish by withholding this eternal life. In this regard, it was a significant competitor to Christianity.

It is interesting to note that when Alaric the Goth came down towards Rome in 394 A.D., he came into contact with this cult, and felt that it had merit even though it was entirely different from the northern cults. He tried to prevail upon the Christian monks not to destroy the temple at Eleusis, but by then the Christians were determined to eradicate the cult. They destroyed the statues, and rushed into the temple shouting "Christus panis!" A mightier bread god than Demeter had come into the world.

EARLY MEDICINE

The Greek thinkers of the fifth and fourth centuries B.C. were seekers after the original principle of all things. They strove to put into comprehensible form all the essential elements that go to make up man and his environment. It was the Sicilian Empedocles (circa 500-430 B.C.), who held that the four elements -- earth, air, fire, and water -- were fundamental. From them, according to the proportion in which they were combined, all other substances originate.

Hippocrates (circa 460-377 B.C.) was about thirty years old when Empedocles died. That his thinking was influenced by the teachings of the older man is evident in his writings. The essential life process for human beings, according to Hippocrates, is the interplay between the individual and his environment. He reasoned that each of the four elements had its characteristic quality. Earth was dry, water moist, fire hot and air cold. There are four possible combinations of these without the contradiction of opposites; hot and moist; cold and moist; hot and dry; cold and dry. Combinations of these possibilities producing a blending or complexion in an individual, and this determined his behavior. For example, one in whom heat and moisture were dominant would be of sanguine temperament; if cold and moist, a phlegmatic temperament would result; hot and dry and cold and dry corresponded, respectively, to choleric and melancholic dispositions.

For each complexion there was a corresponding appropriate humour. These humours were the discernible bodily fluids: blood, phlegm, yellow bile, and black bile. According to Hippocrates and the classical theory of Greek medicine, health existed in an individual when the humours were present in the body in proper proportion to each other. When one or another happened to be in excess a dyscrasia or abnormal mixture, resulted. The Greeks considered disease to arise this way. For if one of the four elements were greatly in excess in the environment, this would tend to produce a corresponding excess of that humour in the patient's body. (The "environment", in this case, included not merely the "airs, waters, and places" described by Hippocrates, but also all the food ingested by the patient).

All foodstuffs were also thought to be composed of the same four elements, and their digestibility as well as their nutritive value were determined accordingly. Thus arose a sort of classification of foods, and diets were prescribed along these lines. By means of diet, the Greeks thought that they could alter the disposition of a growing person to conform with the accepted norms of the time. Children were to be nourished with meats and drinks which were moderately hot and moist, and thereby, they thought, the growing adolescent would take on more of the sanguine temperament, in place of the phlegmatic one of childhood. Later on, as manhood approached, an element of the choleric disposition would be engendered by feeding salads, "meats of grosser substance, and wine allayed with water." And in old age, when the natural heat and strength of the body was declining, hot and moist meats and drinks were once again encouraged.

These traditions were set forth in the Hippocratic school, and became invested with the aura of dogma for many centuries. Six hundred years after Hippocrates, Galen was to pull the Hippocratic ideas and theses together into a monumental compilation, which was to guide the Latin world and beyond for many centuries. Although these writings were not known in Europe during the Dark Ages, they were treasured at that time as a part of the Arabic libraries of Alexandria and other cultural centers of the Mediterranean world.

It is significant to note that the classification of disease also had a long tradition in China. Before the sixth century B.C., Ho the Physician had divided diseases into six classes. These six classes derived from excesses of one or another of the six aspects of "chi", the breath of life, or "subtle wind." (This concept was similar to the Greek concept of pneuma). As time passed, the six elements were reduced to five -- the same four Hippocrates had specified, plus a fifth, metal.. Some of these were classified as "yin", (cool, moist) and others as "yang" (hot). These elements influenced the Chinese diet also.

India, too, settled on five basic elements, and introduced another thought concerning the human condition. It was generally agreed that children imbibed not only nourishment, but also temperament and morale through their mother's milk. In fact, this was a pervasive believe in many parts of the world. Long before Greece, as far back as the early Indian Upanishads, it was written that a newborn child was dependent upon its mother for both its health and its temperament.

GALEN

By the time Galen was born, classical Greece was several hundred years in the past and the Roman Empire ruled the Mediterranean world. The two civilizations had blended, and the use of Greek was diffused throughout the eastern part of the Roman empire. Even in the western part, it was still used as the language of culture.

It is difficult to overestimate the debt we owe to Galen. Born about 130 A.D., Galen was a prominent Roman citizen who wrote a large number of authenticated works which we still possess. (These are in Greek, but parallel Latin translations also exist). Galen's work digests and assimilates the earlier works, from Hippocrates until his own time. Galen takes the position that the organism takes on, or assimilates, what is natural to it -- and rejects the rest. In dealing with disease, Galen stressed hygiene. He noted constitutional differences in people, and emphasized that advice on health matters should be given only by qualified doctors. He made derogatory remarks about people who wrote treatises on health and yet were not able to keep themselves healthy: "...healer of others, himself a mass of sores...."

REGIMEN SANITATIS

At the risk of getting ahead chronologically, it is now appropriate to deal with the developments of health and diet as propounded in the early middle ages. Early in the centuries after Christ, a school had been founded at Salerno, and it was already famous by 1,000 A.D. This school was to revive the Galen-Hippocrates theories and philosophy. For one day late in the eleventh century a man known as Constantine the African came to Salerno. He set about translating many works of learning from Arabic into Latin. These works had been lost, mislaid or neglected by the western world during the Dark Ages. Fortunately, the Arabs had translated them into their language and kept them safely in their libraries.

Among the works which he translated were those of Galen. This body of knowledge came to be known as the "Regimen Sanitatis", and has been called that ever since. The attitudes which arose from these teachings were to dominate medical and health

thinking for many centuries afterwards. The returning Crusaders also heard of these works and
helped to spread the doctrine in Europe. It is
said that Robert Duke of Normandy, eldest son of
William the Conqueror, visited Salerno on the way
back from the First Crusade, to get healing help
for his wounds, but this has not been corroborated.

Among the many claims set forth in the Salerno
doctrine was the statement that it is possible
to live longer on a balanced diet. Thus the
balancing of the four elements referred to by
Hippocrates was returned to Europe after 1600
years.

One of the detrimental parts of the Salerno
dietary regime was that which prescribed fruit as
being cold and moist. It was therefore considered
unsuitable for children and infants, as well as
for nursing mothers. In the sixteenth century
voyages of discovery we shall note the prevalence
and the severity of scurvy. It is probably that
mothers for centuries before were denying themselves and their children the requisite vitamin
C. In passing, it is to be noted that Galen's
father lived to be 100 and never ate fruit.

All mediaeval writers on the subject said
that one must eat fruit sparingly. Much later
in Tudor times the following passage occurs in
"The Castel of Health" by Sir Thomas Elyot (1539):

"the nature which was in men at the
begynnyng, that nowe all fruits generally
are noyfulle (harmful) to man, and do
engender yil humour, and be oftentymes
the cause of putrified fevers, if they
be moche and continually eaten."

It should be remembered that fruit ripens in
summer and early autumn. This was also the time
when dysentery was prevalent. Thus an unjust
connection was made, and the true laxative effect
of fruit did nothing to allay the suspicion, which
has persisted up until quite recent times.

Nevertheless a certain amount of good sound nutrition did arise from the Regimen Sanitatis. Chapters on infant feeding precribed mother's milk, although animal milk must have been tried many times. If it were necessary to take a wet nurse, and it was commonly done, great care would be taken in choosing one, for they thought that if the nurse were a dolt or a drunkard the child would certainly take after her. If her milk contained traces of blood the child might grow up to be a murderer. After her moral qualities had been carefully examined they then looked at her milk. Wet nurses were enjoined not to eat strong herbs which flavor the milk, and, "thee shall refrain from all kinds of raw fruits..."

However Guillemeau, an authority writing in 1612 recommends that wet nurses be given plenty of herb soups from fresh herbs, but not strong ones.

In sixteenth century Florence, careful mothers would not have dreamt of allowing a wild Saracen woman to wet-nurse their children. Lest we get smug, note the following passage from recent times. It is quoted from "The Complete Indian Housekeeper and Cook" by Steele and Gardiner, published in London in 1888. The book is dedicated to:

"the english girls to whom fate may assign the task of being housemothers in our eastern empire."

In it this statement appears:

"One is felt impelled to ask, why the milk of a native woman should contaminate an English child's character, when that of the beasts is held to have no such power, were it not a clear case of racial prejudice..."

The question of when the child should be weaned has always been one of uncertainty, although

80

Guillermeau's book, entiteld "Child birth, or the Happy Deliverie of Women" is definite on the subject:

> "The childe must be nourished with milk only, till his foreteeth come forth both above and beneath."

After weaning the children were given bread crusts and milk. Their temperament at this point was thought to be hot and moist, "like unto ye seed of which they bee procreated." So the coldness and moistness of milk, plus the bread would engender a certain amoung of choler and melancholy. In other words it was an attempt, albeit a very early one, to balance a diet. Interestingly enough such a diet, using the bread which they had at that time is almost perfectly balanced by our standards. When the teeth appeared the child was given chicken bones to chew and at fifteen months the flesh of capon or partidge in small quantities.

Milk was regarded as a special fluid, derived from blood:

> "milke is made of blood twice concocted; for until it comes to the paps or udder, it is plaine bloude; but afterwards, by the proper nature of the paps, it is turned into milk."

The nutritive value of milk was well known:

> "a man may live with milke only, and it will serve him instead of meat and drinks and medicine."

All of these later statements derive from Greek medicine, but were hidden from Europe during the mediaeval period when no Greek writings were available.

The different character and value of milk from various species was recognised. Woman's milk was

held to be the best, followed by that of asses
and goats, and lastly, cow's milk. A quote
from the Salerno doctrine in 1603 reads as follows:

> "in great consumptions learned physicians
>   thinke,
> 'tis good a goat or camel's milk to drinke,
> Cowes' milk and sheepes' doe well, but yet
>   an asses'
> is best of all, and all the other passes."

It is very significant that the Mongols knew
this,* and gave their children mares' milk to
drink, and made their cheese and yoghurt only
from goats', sheeps' or cows' milk. Again we
are left to wonder at the knowledge which the
early peoples had, and which is now vindicated.
For modern analysis has discovered that mares'
milk is four times as high in vitamin C as is
cows' milk. Such vitamin C as there was would
have disppeared in the making of cheese, so that
this tallied with Mongol practice. It will be
remembered that the Mongols living a peripatetic
life on their steppes, were short of sources of
vitamin C, and nomads and wanderers do not tarry
for the harvest of fresh produce. In time they
had understood that mares' milk was sufficiently
good for their children to be saved for this
purpose. In addition it turns out that goats',
sheeps' and camels' milk are very high in fat and
protein, and therefore is easily assimilated by
the small child's stomach and intestinal tract.
These views and practices are very old, and derive
from Greek teachings, and even antedate the Greeks
very possibly. Yet they had substance today in
the light of modern analysis.

In addition milk was rightly thought to be
nutritious in spring and summer than in winter.
This ties in with the need for carotene and vitamin A, a deficiency which is today disastrously
widespread in many parts of Asia and Africa. Thus
the knowledge of foods was tied up very closely

* See Chapter 9

with the belief system of the people, a topic
which we shall follow rather closely as we proceed
forward towards the present time.

The Hippocratic School of Medicine was to
influence diet and health for well over a thousand
years. After this digression it is now necessary
to retrace our steps in time, in order to consider
the next giant on the world stage, Rome.

REFERENCES

59 HESIOD: Works and Days: trans. Mair, A.W.
    Oxford Univeristy Press (1908).

59 GREECE IN THE EIGHTH CENTURY, B.C. Burn. A.R.
    The World of Hesiod (1966).

60 "BUT IT IS NO USE COMPLAINING.." Hesiod; Works
    and Days p 39.

61 DIET OF THE EARLY GREEKS: Vickery, Kenon F;
    Food in early Greece; University of Illinois
    Bull. 34, 97, (1936). Loewenberg, Miriam
    E. et al; Food and Man, chap I p 29 (1968).

61 POPULATION PRESSURE: Burn. A.R. A traveller's
    history of Greece, chap 3, p 65 (1965).

62 BACKWARD AGRICULTURE: Jacob, Heinrich E. Six
    thousand years of bread. p 48 (1944).

62 GROWTH OF CITY-STATES: Kitto, H.D.F. The
    Greeks; chap V, The Polis, p 64 et seq.
    (1951).

63 MEALS IN GREECE: Zimmern, Sir Alfred. The
    Greek Commonwealth, (1911).

63 MAZA FOR THE POOR: Moritz, L.A. Grain mills
    and flour in classical antiquity, p 150
    (1958).

64 DEPLETION OF THE SOIL: Tannahill, Reay; Food
    in History, chap 4 p 76 (1973).

66   SOLON: Kitto, H.D.F. The Greeks; ibid chap 6
     p 100 (1951).

67   SEISACHTHEIA: Jacob, ibid p 49 (1944).

67   USE OF COINAGE: `Burn A.R. ibid p 110 (1965).

68   GREEK CITY-STATES: Andrews, W. The Greek
     World, chap 2 (1961).

69   SPARTA: Kitto, H.F.D. Classical Greece;
     the fifth century; Peloponnesian Wars.
     p 113 (1951).

69   "BARLEY PASTE AND LITTLE ELSE.." Athenaeus;
     The Deipnosophists a chaotic miscellany
     of food in the classical world; trans. Gulik,
     II, 55 (1927).

70   DISASTER IN GREECE: PROBABLY MEASLES: McNeill,
     Wm. M. Plagues and People, p 53 (1976).

71   CULT OF DEMETER: Burn. A.R. chap 6 #3 pp 134-6.

72   ELEUSIS: Jacob, Heinrich E. Ibix #24 pp 60-73:
     "Hymn to Demeter at her sanctuary at Eleusis.

75   GREEK MEDICINE: Brock. A.J. chap 9; the
     Humoral theory; chap 10: Diet. (1977).

76   HIPPOCRATES: Kitto. H.D.F. The Greek Mind
     pp 188-89.

76   COMPLEXIONS OR HUMORS: Kirk. G.S. The Greek
     World p 124-28 Singer, Dr. Charles; A
     short history of medicine (1928).

78   SCHOOL OF SALERNUM: History; Packard F.R.
     and Garrison F.H. (1922).

80   "THEE SHALL REFRAIN FROM ALL KINDS OF RAW
     FRUITS.." Elyot, Sir Thomas; The Castel of
     Helth (1539).

80   DIET OF WET NURSES: Guillemeau, Jacques;
     Child-birth, or the Happy Deliverie of
     Women; (1612).

80   INFLUENCE OF WET NURSE ON THE CHARACTER OF
           INFANT: Steele and Gardiner; The Complete
           Indian Housekeeper and Cook; (1888).

81   NATURE OF MILK: Cogan, Thomas; The Haven of
           Helth (1584).

81   VALUE OF MILK IN THE DIET: Platt, Sir Hugh,
           Esq., Sundrie new and artificial remedies
           against famine (1596).

82   THE SCHOOL OF SALERNUM: Harington, Sir John;
           (1608).

ROME: REPUBLIC TO EMPIRE

THE EARLY DAYS

The earliest Italic peoples were shepherds rather than farmers, as were the Greeks. Meat, wild fruit and nuts comprised the diet of the traditional founders of Roman civilization. Their tribal and pastoral life was reflected in the way they worshipped: for a long time milk, instead of wine, was used for sacrifices. The tribal units jointed with other settlements in their common needs for defense, worship, and trade. As the need for feeding larger groups of people became apparent, they turned to growing their own food as necessary. For this purpose, they descended from their familiar hills, and reached the fertile plains of the Po River, setting up a town at Alba Longa. On this site, with its seven hills, Romulus and Remus according to legend, started the city of Rome.

Early Roman agriculture was placed under the protection of the gods. By the time that Rome was officially founded (753 B.C.), the first citizens had already modified their earlier pastoral life and had settled on lands having definite boundaries. Termini, or posts marking the boundaries of land were ranged on long untilled strips, and were respected as sacred. The cattle, too, shared this sacred protection, and anyone who killed an ox was liable to the death penalty.

The implements of husbandry were rather crude: plows fashioned from tree trunks with forked branches; sickles, and axes. Early Romans cultivated spelt,* barley, and millet. Wheat was not known until about 450 B.C., according to Varro. Land was dispersed among the people; the largest fields did not exceed 20 jugera, or about 13 acres. The exceptions to this were the lands belonging to the King. The primitive measure of land was the yoke, which represented the area that a pair of

* spelt, an early form of hulled wheat.

oxen could till without resting. For some time, the average holding of the ordinary man was one yoke. This amount tended to increase later, when land was taken from conquered peoples.

The early citizens devoted all their time to agriculture, with the exception of the years they gave to army service. But rotation of crops was not practiced, crop succession was unsatisfactory; insufficient manure and other causes kept yields poor. Nevertheless, the people were self-sufficient and independent, and produced everything they needed for a rough but adequate life.

These country folk were much respected in the later years of the republic. As Vegetius said, "...farming, to be successful, implies certain qualities of moral character, and in turn produces them." Cato the Elder was later to say, "When our forefathers wished to speak of a good citizen, they called him a good colonist and a good farmer."

Thus arose the Roman republic. At first, there was no educated or leisure class, but only poor, hardworking peasants. What did these early Romans eat? In assessing the nutritional status of the average people, which is never easy, one must look to the staples. The fare was simple in the early days of the republic, with not much difference between the food of the poor and that of the more well-to-do. Basically, the Roman food was much like that of the Greeks, but at first they had more latitude and variety because of the greater fertility of the Italian peninsula. For centuries, the average Roman ate porridge and roasted fish, pickled and dried vegetables, ham and salt pork. They ate olives, raw beans, figs, and cheese. The most common vegetables were broad beans, lentils, chickpeas, lettuces, cabbages, and leeks. Fruits available were apples, pears, cherries, plums, and grapes. The favorite nuts were almonds, but chestnuts and walnuts were also available. The Roman poor used grain pastes, coarse bread bristling with chaff, millet porridges, and water.

The use of bread became general only at the beginning of the second century B.C. Prior to that time, grain was used in the preparation of puls, a gruel made of any grain, though usually wheat or barley. Rye was not cultivated, and oats were reserved for cattle feed.

The variety noted here gave the average early Roman a balanced diet which many might envy today. Meals were served at tables set up in the atrium, or hallway. Father, mother, and children all sat around it on stools or benches. Dishes were of common crockery or even wood. Table knives and forks were unknown, but the early Romans had spoons like ours. According to Johnston, the Samnite envoys found Manius Curius, conqueror of Pyrrhus in 275 B.C., eating his simple dinner of vegetables from an earthen bowl. A century later, the historian Plautus reports that even the wealthiest Romans at that time had no specially trained cooks. When a more elaborate dinner was given, a professional cook was hired, who brought with him not only his own helpers but his own utensils, just as some caterers do today.

THE REPUBLIC: (509-71 B.C.)

In the early days of the Republic, the Romans had good laws which protected the farmer. All land that was conquered belonged to the State, and there was virtually no private property. When meritorious soldiers returned from the wars, they were rewarded with land. The State settled them as farmers, and by tilling the soil these soldiers could, and did, become attached to it.

As new lands were conquered during the fifth and fourth centuries B.C., however, property did tend to become more concentrated in the hands of fewer people. The nobles who eventually gained control of the Senate arranged to acquire the lands of the conquered Samnites, Etruscans, and other peoples of Latium. They also ceased to pay into the State treasury the tithe tax which they owed

on their grain, and the double tithe which they
owed on their oil and wine. From being the stew-
ards of the State, they became large landowners
and oppressors of the common folk. They took
advantage of the wars to remove the boundaries
(termini) which earlier had been so sacred, and in
this way they laid hands on yet more property.
The Romans had customarily set aside for the benefit of the city one-third, or even sometimes two-
thirds, of the arable and pasture land of their
conquered enemies. All citizens, upon payment of
a fee called scriptura, had the right to pasture
their cattle on this public land. Gradually this
practice was done away with, and the prolonged
wars deprived the poor of any equitable partici-
pation in the public lands.

The farmer-exsoldier had nothing but his own
two hands, his wife, his oxen, and maybe a half-
grown son. He had scarcely enough manure to improve his land. It is easy to imagine how dis-
couraged these people must have become. The rich
would approach the poor farmer with blandishments,
and offer to purchase his land at a ridiculously
low price. The farmer often had no other choice
but to sell. Then he moved to the city where, without employment, he loitered in taverns and on the
public square, looking with hatred upon the State
which had cheated him.

And thus pasture land owned by large land-
holders gained on farmland owned by small-scale
farmers. The small holders who had been bought out
sometimes resumed a lease on fields which they
had previously owned. The situation got worse
and worse. In order to counter this trend, the
authorities developed a small-holding class to act
as an intervening group between the poor and the
wealthy. In 366 B.C., the laws of Licinus stated
that no one might possess more than 500 jugera,
(about 325 acres), or more than 500 sheep or
100 cattle. From 334 B.C. to 264 B.C., sixty-five
communities were founded by the Senate, and more
than 100,000 persons of all ages were settled in
colonial areas. But these measures, as we shall

see, did not really counteract the flow of land and wealth into the hands of the few.

Two great reformers appeared, who were determined to champion the cause of the farmers. They were two brothers. One day, the older of the two spoke at an assembly of the Senate words that had not been heard before:

"The men who fought for Italy, ready to die for her as soldiers, had at most a share in her air and light, but neither house nor roof to shelter them. These warriors are called masters of the world, but not a square foot of earth in this world belongs to them...:

Thus spoke Tiberius Gracchus in 150 B.C. He succeeded in putting through the assembly and the Senate the 500-jugera limit on land ownership. The Roman establishment, however, would have none of this, and hired an assassin who killed Tiberius as he was about to speak at another public meeting. The murdered Gracchus was mourned by the People's party and, because he had tried to help the farmer, he was subsequently elevated almost to the status of a martyr. This put considerable pressure on the Senate, which then passed a law to settle 80,000 new farmers in an attempt to calm public opinion.

Tiberius' younger brother, Caius Gracchus, wanted to carry on the work of his dead brother, but finally he too was either assassinated by the establishment or else driven to take his own life; historians are not sure which.

EATING HABITS

During all this time, the eating habits of the Romans were changing. Contact with Egypt introduced raised breads into the Roman diet for the first time, and soon a variety of breads were available. Interestingly enough, the different types of bread began to reflect the social class structure. There were three main grades of bread: black bread, made of coarsely-ground whole flour with the branny particles included. It was called by various names, but all of them indicated much the same thing -- that this was the bread for the common folk: panis plebeius, panis sordidus; and panis rusticus. It was also sometimes referred to as panis castrensis, that is, the bread for the soldiers in camp. Next there was a whiter grade of bread which, however, still had a coarse texture; it was known as panis secundarius. Thirdly, there was panis candidus, the best and the whitest.

In the last two centuries of the Republic, the simple lifestyle of earlier days changed. Although the lower classes continued to live frugally on dark breads, vegetables, and occasionally, a little meat, and better-off started to acquire more elaborate habits. Some of the very rich, aping Greek luxury without Greek refinement, became gluttons instead of gourmets. They ransacked the known world for rare and expensive foods, rather than content themselves with really palatable and delicate dishes.

The style of meals changed and became more elaborate. A separate dining room was introduced into the architecture, and the great houses had two or more. In place of stools and benches were couches and cushions. Special dinner clothes were worn. Every rich man's household had a high-priced chef with a staff of trained assistants. Between the two extremes of rich and poor there was a small middle class who sought a middle way.

Eating patterns were different in the city than they were in the country. In the country, the first meal of the day was short, light, and informal. No coffee or hot drinks were served. Bread was hard and coarse enough to keep the teeth bright and the jaws strong. The grit from the grindstones was sometimes found in it, but the bread was softened and made more palatable by

dipping it in wine or oil. It was often sprinkled
with salt, or accompanied by raisins, cheese, or
olives. Sometimes the better-off would add honey
and wine mixed together, or even milk. Workers
pressed for time seem to have eaten breakfast on
the way to work, and schoolboys would often stop
at a bakery on the way to buy a pancake for a hasty
meal.

In the country, the midday meal was the
largest of the day. It was called cena. Farmers
also adopted the habit of taking a rest after the
large cena. This siesta was a sensible arrangement when the climate was very hot. On the farm,
the day closed with an early light supper (vesper-
na). While farmers took their main meal at
midday, in the city the midday meal was light. It
was called prandium, and generally consisted of
bread, olives, cheese, fruit, nuts and cold meats
left over from the day before. Salads also might
figure in this very nutritious meal.

The busy life of the city tended to crowd
the largest meal to a later hour, and for the
wealthy, these city dinners were long -- sometimes
lasting for three to five hours -- and elaborate.
They consisted of a succession of long, slowly
eaten courses, interspersed by dancing, games,
stories, and drinking. The meal itself was divided
into three parts: gustus (what we would call the
appetizer), cena (the meal itself), and the
dessert, called secunda mensa.

For gustus there would be oysters or other
shellfish, salted or pickled fish, and uncooked
vegetables, especially onions and lettuce, Almost invariably there were piquant sauces with the
appetizers, in fact the Roman cuisine was noted for
its various elaborate sauces, called liquamen,
sylphium, and garum. Two eggs and a dash of
garum, for example, formed a simple and delicious
dish. Apples and other fruits were eaten as
secunda mensa. From these eating patterns arose
the saying, "ab ovo ad mala," (from eggs to apples).

93

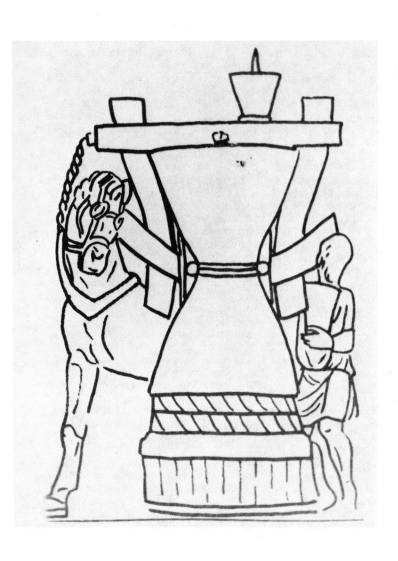

Roman rotary mill.

Today, we say "from soup to nuts," but the idea is precisely the same.

The average Roman family aspired to possess a silver salt cellar, as it was an important status symbol. It was placed in the center of the rectangular table, and important people were seated above the salt, lesser people below it. The lesson in humility in the Bible deals with this:

> "...rather, when thou art invited,
> go and take the lowest place (i.e.
> below the salt), that when he who
> invited thee sees this, he will say,
> Friend, go up higher; that thou begin
> to have honor."

Grain was converted into flour by the use of the saddle quern, which had been in use in Egypt long before the founding of Rome. The worker knelt at one end of a slanted rectangular base stone, and pushed the rubbing-stone (which was later shaped like a rolling-pin), back and forth over the angled base. This was hard work. Eventually, the rubbing stone became squarer and had a central slit through which the whole grain could be trickled. This at least saved the drudgery of lifting the rubbing-stone every time another handful of grain was added.

For thousands of years, the grinding motion had been back and forth. In early Greek times, it was discovered that a side-to-side motion eased the task considerably. The use of a lever enabled the momentum of the stone itself to reduce the physical effort demanded of the operator. This, in turn, led to the next logical development -- a rotary motion.

It had never been possible to drive animals back and forth to match the jerky motion of the old rubbing-stones, but it was possible to drive them around and around in a circle. With a large rotary mill and a couple of donkeys, the professional miller found himself in business.

In the days of the Republic, no specialized class of bakers existed. All baking was done by the housewife. She who had long been the wife of the farmer-warrior had been proud of her household work. However, as years went by and the society changed and became more stratified, women of the middle classes began to aspire to higher status and a life of greater ease. Mirror and rouge preserved youth, whereas leavening and baking brought on age. The ladies of the orient had known this for centuries, and now that the husbands of the Roman ladies began conquering the orient, the Roman ladies learnt it too.

Accordingly, professional bakers began to appear, and they relieved the women of home baking. For the possession of ovens was too costly for the average home, and before long ovens became the bakers' monopoly. Bakers became powerful, and the Roman government created a guild of bakers and gave them many favors and privileges. This guild had considerable influence in the religious life of Rome. The festival of Fornax, the oven goddess, celebreated on July 8, was an occasion for revelry.

FARMING

Farming practices in the days of the Republic have been well described by Cato, and later by Columella in his De Re Rustica (65 A.D.). Good plowing and fertilizing were considered essential. The plows were small and light, made of metal or wood. A field was turned over twice, the first time with the plow held straight in the furrow, and the second time at an angle. The plowing was done in close furrows, and the soil was sometimes worked over until it was almost as fine as dust. (Pliny gives an account of land that needed to be turned over nine times). Harrowing to cover the seed was considered by Roman farmers to be evidence of poor plowing. Good plowing, on the other hand, left no mark of the implement.

Farmyard manure was stored in piles, old and new separately. Ancient writers of the time advised a farmer who did not keep animals to have a compost heap using leaves, weeds, straw, ashes, and clippings. The Romans knew about enriching the soil with green manure, and also about planting legumes and then plowing them under. They practiced rotation of crops, first planting wheat, then barley, rye, or oats, and finally beans or peas on the same field. These remarkable advances demonstrate as well as anything the enormous strides taken by the Romans, from the early beginnings in agriculture which were so rudimentary.

The earlier farms were quite small, perhaps no more than 2 jugera (1.3 acres) or as much as 7 jugera (4.5 acres). When allotments from public lands were made in 393 B.C., farms of 7 jugera were allocated. Such a farm could be worked by the owner and one or two paid laborers, if such could be had. With hard labor and a few simple tools, the earlier Romans did intensive farming, rather like gardening.

But all this was to change. Following the Gracchus brothers' attempt at more equitable land distribution in 150 B.C., it seems that the State deserted its farmers and bowed in submission to the rich. The first consequence was that the large landowner left off raising grain, as it was more lucrative to use the land for pasture. The rich man, to be sure, sold grain; but it did not grow in Italy. It was brought in ships at extremely low freight rates from Rome's overseas possessions. For example, Roman legions razed Carthage to the ground, but were careful not to disturb the wheatfields. Thus Rome fed herself from her overseas possessions: Asia Minor, Egypt, and her North African colonies.

It is interesting to note that at this time, Italian soil was not used for supplying bread for Italian people. Cato, listing the various different uses of the land in order of their importance at the time, mentions vineyards, gardens, osier beds, olive plantations, grazing meadows and, only

sixthly, cornfields. Towards the end of the
Republic, meat was much more commonly eaten, birds
were raised, cheese was used, and garden products
of many kinds were grown. However, the fundamental task of raising grain was minimized.

The rich had it all their own way. After
the efforts of the Gracchus brothers, reaction set
in with the enactment of the Lex Thoria in 111 B.C.
This law abolished all contributions previously
paid by landowners; it suppressed the scriptura, the
fee paid by owners on each head of cattle pastured
in the Ager (public fields, or common-land); and
it converted into ownership the de facto occupation
which was their status until then.

THE TURNING POINT

History rarely provides a turning point between rise and fall of a civilization because
changes take place over a period of time, but if
there is such a date in Roman history it is 146
B.C. At that time, all conquests had been made,
all opposition to Rome's leadership had been removed, and all Grecian authority had been swept
away. Wealth and slaves poured into Rome from all
the conquered lands. With the removal of danger,
Roman citizens relaxed and looked around for ways
to enjoy themselves. Booty in the form of costly
furniture was brought back from Asia; new ideas
of table luxury came to be practiced, and various
imported foodstuffs of an exotic nature began to
differentiate the tables of the rich from those of
the poor.

The first thing that the rich did was to
despise a diet of vegetables. This view was to
prevail for centuries after. They expected not
one, but several meat courses. Later on, this
was to become absurdly ostentatious, just as it had
been in Greece centuries before. Romans would
favor such exotica as a wild sow with its belly
full of live thrushes, quinces stuck with thorns
to look like sea-urchins, roast pork carved into
models of fish or of songbirds, "lordly eggs warm

in their wisps of hay, together with the hens
that laid them," or a "plump kid with more milk in
him than blood".

Spain now sent abundant silver and gold, so
that luxurious drinking vessels appeared at the
tables of the rich to accompany the exotic foods.
In addition, brocaded carpets, perfumes, and cos-
metics made their appearance. Such was this wealth
that Roman citizens in Italy were not taxed for
over a century. It became unnecessary.

Eventually, however, such extravagance sparked
a reaction. There was the question of morality,
or controlling excesses and excessive expenditures.
Laws were passed against games of chance in an
attempt to curb gambling. Historians seem to agree
that it was the influx of wealth, mainly from the
East, which corrupted the traditional Roman way of
life. As noted by Barrow in The Romans, this wealth
brought about the rapid decay of old standards in
public and private conduct. The Mos Maiorum, the
general attitude of the majority of the people,
was corrupted. Ultimately, the various consuls in
the colonies saw to it that they enriched themselves
with each war. They even volunteered to fight in
order to enrich themselves personally.

At this time, also, a group of newly-rich
contractors and financiers, whose methods were
frequently fraudulent, arose to prominence in the
society. These were the publicani. The Senate
was not always able to control them. (This group
had become suspect by the time of Christ; thus
his reference to "publicans and sinners.")

Laws were passed in an effort to curb these
excesses. One law forbade the importation of wild
animals for shows, which had become a big business.
Another law sought to limit the size and expense
of parties. As late as 125 B.C. there is a record
of the censors fining a man for having too
expensive a house (However, soon after this, Lucius
Crassus -- a friend and supporter of Cicero -- was

99

to own one valued at three million sesterces.
Justice, it seems, has never been even-handed).

Towards the end of the Republic, Senators
evaded the rules forbidding them to have interests
in trade and industry. They transacted business
of all kinds through intermediaries. They were on
close terms with the publicani, as well as with
financiers and bankers. They readily sold their
estates and country houses and bought others,
speculating in the land and house property markets.

Credit was the great weapon of the aristo-
cracy against the lower classes. Mortgaged property
was appropriated by the rich. Usury, in the form
of absurdly high interest rates, was practiced
despite the "Laws of the Twelve Tables" which had
been enacted as early as 450 B.C. and which had
fixed interest rates at one percent per month.
In the face of these corrupt practices, secessions
and revolts among the lower classes occurred from
time to time, but they were at best only temporarily
successful.

After the Punic Wars (264-201 B.C.), Romans
were treated to a new kind of experience. There
were incessant military victories to be celebrated,
and the spoils taken from conquered Asiatic rulers
was brought to Rome and displayed to the public.
Romans were thus exposed to examples of luxurious
living, and demanded more and more for themselves,
including in particular the cruder types of
pleasure. Thus arose the circenses -- diversionary
spectacles to titillate, amuse, outrage, and hor-
rify the people. Amphitheatres to accomodate these
events were built in every province.

Thus the Roman world of this time offered a
spectacle of unheard-of prosperity. This prosperity, however, was not accompanied by unity. The
need for spectacles seemd to increase in proportion as incessant civil strife abolished security.

REFERENCES

87 "TERMINI, BOUNDARIES OF LAND.." Louis, Paul;
    Ancient Rome at Work; chap VII, (1927).

88 "A GOOD COLONIST AND A GOOD FARMER.." Cato
    the Elder: De Agri Cultura (168 B.C.).

89 MEALS IN THE EARLY DAYS: Barrow, R.H.: The
    Romans; (1949).

90 FARMING IN THE EARLY ROMAN TIMES: White,
    Kenneth, Roman Farming (1970).

90 LAND OF THE CONQUERED PEOPLES: Hamilton,
    Edith: The Roman Way (1963).

91 THE ANCIENT WORLD AT WORK: Mosse, Claude,
    (1969).

91 GRACCHUS BROTHERS: Cowell, F.R. The Revolu-
    tions of Ancient Rome, p 62 (1962).

92 MEALS IN ANCIENT ROME: Loewenberg et al. Food
    and Man, p 37 (1968).

92 VARIETIES OF BREAD: Parmelee, Prentice:
    Hunger and History (1951).

93 COURSES AT DINNER: Balsdon, J.P.V. Life and
    Leisure in ancient Rome. (1969).

95 "FRIEND, GO UP HIGHER..." Luke, 14, 7-12.

96 MIDDLE CLASS ROMAN WOMEN. Jacob, H.H. ibid
    p 78. (1944).

96 GOOD PLOUGHING. Pliny the Elder; Natural
    History, (23-79 A.D.).

96 "BOWED IN SUBMISSION TO THE RICH". Ferrero,
    Gugliemo; The Greatness and Decline of
    Rome; (1907).

97   LAND USES: Cato the Elder, ibid (186 B.C.).

98   LUXURIOUS LIVING. Wason, B: "Cooks, gluttons and gourmets;. (1962).

99   "A PLUMP KID WITH MORE MILK IN HIM THAN BLOOD.." Juvenal; 100 A.D. The Sixteen Satires; II, 66-74; tr. Green (1968).

100   LAWS OF THE TWELVE TABLES: Louis, Paul. ibid ch XV.

Things went from bad to worse; corruption of
the generals was followed by that of the armies
themselves. By 62 B.C., bribery was common, and
Julius Caesar was able to grasp at monarchy and
dictatorship. As a matter of fact, he got things
done, amongst which were the reform of the calendar
and the annexation of Britain. But the price of
order was the loss of liberty. The great contemporary historian Livy stated at the time that "we
have got to such a pitch that we can tolerate
neither our evils nor their remedies." Other historians of the period, also, were quick to note the
downward trends.

According to Plutarch, when the wealthy began
again to drive the poor off their land, the earlier
laws were partly effective, but only for a time.
The rich contrived to get these lands once more into
their own hands, often by assuming false names.
The poor were no longer ready, as they had formerly been, to serve in war; nor could they be careful
in the education of their children. In a short
time there were comparatively few freemen remaining
in the whole of Italy. The countryside now swarmed
with foreign-born slaves, confined in workhouses
and used by the rich to cultivate that same ground
from which they had displaced and dispossessed the
citizens.

Slavery had indeed become institutionalized
by the second century B.C., for foreign conquests
had brought countless prisoners of war to Rome.
Slaves were of many kinds: slaves by birth, that
is to say the children of slave women; free men
who were enslaved for various reasons; children
kidnapped by pirates or brigands and sold; children sold by their own fathers; and those guilty of
crimes which entailed loss of liberty. An endless
supply of slaves of both sexes and all ages
streamed from the slave markets. They were of the
most varied abilities: skilled cooks, musicians,

waiters, dancers, cupbearers -- as well as those without particular skills, used purely for manual labor.

Many professions, such as medicine and surgery, were in the hands of slaves or ex-slaves, for slaves could earn their freedom in a variety of ways, called manumissio. The freedom could be enacted by will, by enfranchisement; and by simple assertion by the master that the slave was free.

The nouveau riche class of Roman society had had very little formal schooling, but parents of this class wanted education for their children. They would hire learned Greeks as tutors. This was a matter of price and importance, for all scholarly works were written in Greek, and it was a long time before they were translated into Latin. The parents thus hired educated Greek slaves, called grammatici, to teach their children. These tutors were often very expensive: Pliny reports that one grammaticus is reported to cost 700,000 sesterces, a small fortune. Sometimes another slave would accompany the children to school, and as they went on foot, this slave came to be known as a pedagogus.

This slave-oriented society meant social debasement for a free man of birth and education. How could he compete in such a society without the wealth needed for ostentatious living? Therefore we witness the diminution and finally the disappearance of the middle class. Men of what had been the middle class went instead into the army, where they were not productive but destructive. Others, forced off their land, became idle city dwellers, the very people who were loudest in their demands for "panem et circenses" -- "bread and circuses."

The old farmers thought of the soil not as money but as life. A subsistence farming community doesn't generally make the mistake of thinking of the soil in financial terms alone. Rather, soil is held sacred, and must be preserved. These basic

tenets are as true today as they were then. But
they were neglected by the new Roman society. The
few rich got richer and the middle classes who had
formerly been powerful were impoverished and de-
graded. The poor lived in absolute misery. Where
in earlier times the land had been divided up into
small farms, under the Roman emperors it had
become consolidated into just a few huge ranches,
called latifundia, worked by slaves and tenant
farmers. For example, by the year 70 B.C., all
of Sicily belonged to just 84 owners. Moreover,
the tax collector appeared persistently to extort
money and goods from the tenant farmers who worked
the land for the absentee landlords.

There was no life in the country, and city
life looked more attractive. Farmland became
neglected. The soil was not cared for properly,
nor drained, so that malaria became common. Things
became progressively worse, and many of the common
folk lost all hope, "muffled their hands and threw
themselves into the Tiber."

Thus the great landholdings finally began to
destroy Rome and her empire.

ANNONA -- THE WELFARE STATE

Since the people had to be fed, Rome used
the wheat from Egypt to keep things going for
awhile. Because of the poverty of the general
population, aggravated by unemployment, the authorities organized the distribution of free Egyptian
grain to the poor, in an attempt to relieve the
crisis.

From the early days of the Republic, even as
far back as the sixth century, B.C., Rome had been
troubled by occasional famine. But by 123 B.C.
the problem had become chronic, and Caius Gracchus
had set a precedent by allowing all citizens to
buy grain from the public granaries at prices below those prevailing in the open market. This
practice, known as the annona, was established on

a regular basis and by 71 B.C., free grain was being distributed to 40,000 adult male citizens daily (panem quotidianum = daily bread). These recipients of free grain were called the plebs frumentaria.

Both Julius Caesar and his successor Augustus were faced with the same problem. Later still, Severus Augustus decreed that ready-made bread should be distributed instead of grain. The emperor Aurelian increased the allowance from one to 1½ pound, and added pork fat to the list of foodstuffs. In order to use up the wine paid in taxes by the winegrowers, the government decreed that it too should be given to the plebs frumentaria. The authorities had no choice but to do this, for unemployment was the terror of the Roman treasury. In certain cases the receipt of annona became hereditary, and the poor were thus encouraged to "multiply forever."

Not everybody at the time agreed with this policy. Sallust, the famous historian and a contemporary of Julius Caesar, spoke about it as follows: "...largitiones, qui rem publicam lacerunt." ("the handing out of largesse, which tears at the very fabric of public life"). Augustus Caesar tried to reduce the number of recipients of the dole, by refusing the annona to those "whose need is pretended." Grain speculation was rife in times of scarcity and the Caesars had to be prepared to dump grain onto the market to prevent undue speculation and the resulting instability in the price of bread.

This mass hunger was an unbelievable social nightmare. In former times hunger had only been local and temporary, but by 210 A.D. it was massive and pervasive. Roman writers of the time did not deal with it at all fully, largely because the ruling class had not as yet perceived it. The problems associated with this mass hunger were new: worked-out soil, the political control of wheat and bread, empire, conscription, and slavery. The bread-producing provinces, such as Egypt, were

stripped to feed other provinces. Since most of
the areas of the Empire had up to that time fed
themselves, there had been no transportation problems, no hoarding, and little speculation. Now all
these things arose at once. Hunger stalked the
Roman world.

Control of the grain fleet had become vital.
In 69 A.D., it was seized by the emperor Vespasian,
and the whole country was held up for ransom by
the Flavian family. As a result, they were given
power to rule, a clear case of blackmail.

In that same first century A.D., the mills
of Rome literally ground to a halt, because the
emperor Caligula requisitioned all of the animals
that had powered the millers' wheels. Later on,
the mills were to depend on water power and not
on animals. The Goths, infiltrating from the north
in the later days of the Empire, cut off the water
supply. In this way they could quickly win control
of a city. In order to ward off this complete
dependency, many households kept a saddle quern --
the ancient hand-millstone -- ready just in case
of emergency.

It was into such a world that Jesus Christ
was born. A carpenter's son, he nevertheless
time and time again used concepts and analogies
taken from agriculture and food. These were introduced into many parables: the sower; the harvest;
the wheat and the tares; wine; threshing and the
chaff; plowing; and herding and shepherding. When
Christ was asked, "What can you do to feed us in
this world?" he taught the people to ask for their
"panem quotidianum," their daily bread. This was
a reference to the bread that Caesar gave out daily
as the annona. The separation of church and state
was supported when Christ said, "Render unto Caesar
the things that are Caesar's; and unto God the
things that are God's." This meant paying taxes
and obeying the civil laws.

Christ was on earth a mere 33 years. During
that time and afterwards, the social and political

situation in the Empire went from bad to worse.
At long last it appeared that the Romans were in
no mood to cope with the hardships and problems of
conquest, nor with the administration of far-off
lands. More and more, control of the colonies
was given to those who lived there, particularly
to those who had seen service in the Roman army.

QVI BVS PVG NANTIBVS SIMMA GNIVS FERRV
MA TERNVS HA BILIS MISIT

The Roman army was composed of regiments from
all over the Empire. When a soldier's service was
finished, he received a copy of the record, kept
at Rome, authorizing his rights to Roman citizenship. His own copy on a double tablet or diploma,
might read as follows: "...the emperor Domitian
granted citizenship to the undermentioned soldiers,
cavalry and infantry..." and there followed a list
of the regiments and their countries of origin.
It continued: "...to them, their children, and
their posterity, he granted citizenship and the
rights of legal marriage with the wives to whom
they were married at the time of the grant; or
if unmarried, to the wives they married hereafter,
be it understood in respect of one wife to each
soldier..." Having received this proof of citizenship, the soldier would return to his homeland.
(Such a diploma, belonging to a legionnary of
that time, has been found in what is now Bulgaria).
The recipients were proud of their diploma.

The second right given was the right to vote
in elections. (Preserved under the walls of Pompeii are election posters dated 79 A.D.).

But the possession of a diploma, Roman citizenship, and the right to vote still did not provide the one really necessary thing -- food. Where
was the land on which to grow it? Grain was imported, but other parts of the Empire began to
produce the oil and the wine that previously only
Italy had produced. Consequently, there was now
nothing to export in return for the imported grain.
The Empire was experiencing rural depopulation and
agricultural decay, and the food supply of the
cities was in jeopardy.

In addition, enormous sums had to be found
to pay for soldiers needed to guard the frontiers
against the growing incursions of barbarians, and
to run stifling and extravagant bureaucracies,
which took root and flourished in all the provinces.
The once-flourishing cities of the provinces found
it harder to meet their expenses. Imperial taxes
increased. The value of money declined and debasement of the coinage was resorted to as inflation
skyrocketed. Lands went out of cultivation for
lack of labor; yet the army had to have supplies.
Ships were impressed to carry them, and the needs
of the civilian population took second place.

The people were asking, "shall I marry" "...
am I to be sold into slavery?" "Will I get my
salary?" "Should I quit?" "Shall I have to be a
member of the local council? " These were actual
questions put to an oracle in Egypt and preserved
for us on papyri. They were the thoughts and
worries of ordinary men and women of that chaotic
time.

A petition to the Emperor sent from Asia
Minor reads as follows:

"We are most atrociously oppressed
and squeezed by those whose duty it is
to protect the people...officers, sol-

109

diers, city magistrates and imperial
agents come to our village and take
us away from our work, and requisition
our oxen; they exact what is not due and
we suffer outragious injustices and
extortion."

The people of the provinces looked to Rome
in vain for guidance and material assistance, but
it was not forthcoming. Instead, Rome demanded
that each province should henceforth provide its
own defenses as well as its own grain.

LAST YEARS OF EMPIRE: DIOCLETIAN AND CONSTANTINE

The efforts of these two emperors, from 284
to 337 A.D., to restore some semblance of orderly
rule are almost certainly one reason why Rome could
last as long as it did. They effected certain wise
changes, and for awhile there was some hope of improvement. But under Constantine, the Empire was
divided into a western half, based on Roman civilization; and an eastern half, based on Byzantine culture. That the latter was to prove far more viable
than the former shows that Rome was unequal to the
task of creating a world state.

The third century A.D. was a time of social
and economic crisis. Institutions crumbled, and
the privileged position of Roman citizens faded
away. Ordinary people who used to be able to vote,
and to choose those who would represent them in the
Senate, now had to walk around with petitions in
their pockets to hand to the emperor should they
chance to meet him. He might then intercede.

Following the reigns of Diocletian and Constantine, the Roman world went into a steep decline.
The emperors were more often than not despotic;
the Senate lost its power; and municipal self-
government faded. The army deteriorated as well.

In the proud days of the Republic, the army
had been composed of volunteers from the most civilized provinces, and consisted for the most part of

110

the most enlightened inhabitants of the realm.
Now, the urban population shirked military service,
and the wealthy bought themselves off by means of
substitutes. The army wás forced to conscript
displaced agricultural laborers, those same dis-
gruntled and dispossessed people who hated the
State. The civilized upper classes grew less and
less accustomed to military service and sent inferior men into the ranks.

Finally the provinces became virtually
bankrupt. Development stopped, and parts of the
Empire went begging. The army, once the servant
of the Empire, became its master, and acted through
rulers whom it raised up and pulled down, according to its own caprice. The senatorial class was
ousted from provincial governorships and from military commands and replaced by officers of the army.

From 235 to 285 A.D. there were no fewer than
26 emperors, only one of whom died a natural death.
According to historian Paul Louis, "...the Roman
world gave way before a barbarian attack...because
the crumbling Empire no longer contained anything
worth saving, and life had become so cruel a
thing that no disorder, no violence and no subver-
sion could add to its difficulties..."

Perhaps this is too harsh a view. As Barrow
concludes, "The barbarian invasions were neither
catastrophic nor sudden, nor destructive and dis-
ruptive. Rome never fell; she turned into something else. Rome, superseded aṣ the source of
political power, passed into even greater supre-
macy as an idea. Rome, with the Latin language,
had become immortal..."

One might conclude with a statement taken
from Hyams' Soil and Civilization:

"...personal freedom to abuse soil
other commodities, in order to get a
fortune, a state of affairs which is
typical of the moral and social anarchy

111

of declining civilizations, is not
compatible with service to the community, or to any other social idea."

REFERENCES

103   "WE CAN TOLERATE NEITHER OUR EVILS NOR THEIR
      REMEDIES." Livy, History of Rome.

104   EXCESSES IN ROME: Barrow, R. H. ibid (1949);
      p 96.

104   Carcopino, Jerome: "Daily life in ancient
      Rome: people and city at the height of
      the empire. (1941).

105   SUPPLY OF SLAVES: Pierre: The Civilisation
      of Rome; pp 228-231 (1963).

105   LATIFUNDIA: Louis, Paul; ibid chap. VIII.

105   ANNONA: THE WELFARE STATE: Tenney, Frank;
      An economic survey of ancient Rome (1933);
      Fronto, Marcus Cornelius quoted in Tanna-
      hill, ibid p 85.

106   "LARGITIONES, QUI REM PUBLICAM LACERUNT."
      Sallust, (86-34 B.C.).

106   "PANEM ET CIRCENSES" Juvenal, The Sixteen
      Satires, X, 77-81.

107   BLACKMAIL OF THE FLEET. Tacitus; The Histor-
      ies, trans. K. Wellesley (1964); Prentice
      Parmelee, ibid (1951).

108   DIPLOMA: Barrow, R.H. The Romans; chap. IV
      p 93 (1949).

110   PETITIONS TO THE EMPEROR, Barrow, ibid p 172.

111   "THE ROMAN WORLD GAVE WAY BEFORE A BARBARIAN
      ATTACK." Louis, Paul. Ancient Rome at
      work, p 214 (1927).

111   ROME SURVIVED AS AN IDEA: Millar, Fergus;
      The Roman Empire and its neighbours.
      p 239 (1966).

AFTER ROME'S FALL

During the turbulent period after the break-up
of the Roman imperial system in the west, there was
confusion and difficulty all over Europe. Much
of the knowledge that the mediterranean world had
accumulated was either abandoned, neglected or even
lost during this time. "It would be idle to write
of states and rulers" says H. G. Wells.

Adventurers would seize a castle or a country-
side and rule uncertainly for a while. In Rome
itself the great arena of the colosseum had been
made into a privately owned castle, as had Hadrian's
tomb. The adventurers who had possession of these
strongholds waylaid each other, fighting and bickering in the ruinous streets of the once-famous city.
For ruinous it was: to illustrate, water had always been an abiding problem in Rome. There had
been either too much of it or too little. During
the years of the Roman Republic an increasingly
elaborate drainage system had been developed to
keep the marshes drained and the city dry. These
pipes cracked and burst in the neglected Rome of
the sixth century. Plague and pestilence devastated
the city. Popes prayed for deliverance, but there
was none.

One of the most important documents of this
period when the Roman empire was crumbling was
written by Salvian, whose father was a Gallic noble.
In 418 when Salvian was a young man the prefect
of the Gauls moved his capital from Trier to Arles.
Salvian's father decided to move there also with
his family, and the young man became a preacher and
a teacher in the cause of justice on earth. His
enlightening work, "De gubernatione Dei", survives,
and in it there are harsh words for the rich people
of Trier:

"Do you then seek public shows, O citizens
of Trier? Where, pray, are they to be

115

given? Over the pyres and the ashes, the body and the blood of the dead? The remains of a most unhappy people lie on the graves of their dead, yet you ask for circuses; the city is blackened with fire, yet you put on a festive countenance; all things mourn, yet you rejoice..."

"Now that the Roman commonwealth, already extinct, or at least drawing its last breath in that one corner where it seems to retain some life...is dying, strangled by the cords of taxation as if by the hands of brigands; still a great number of wealthy men are found, the burden of whose taxation is borne by the poor..."

This complaint was to be heard for a further thousand years. And other parts of the empire had also taken their habits and customs from the decadent examples described by Salvian. Spain, once Rome's most prized possession, became divided, and in 711 an Islamic army defeated the west Goths in a great battle. They occupied Spain and by 720 had reached the Pyrenees. They were not, however, to penetrate into France.

Salvian was emphatic in his condemnation of the life style of the remaining wealthy people:

"Even in my own country in the Gallic states, almost all men of high degree have been made worse by their misfortunes; I myself have seen men of lofty birth and honor, though already despoiled and plundered, less ruined nevertheless in fortune, than in morality. For ravaged and stripped though they were, something still remained to them of their property, but nothing of their character. The chief men of the civitas were reclining at feasts, forgetful of their honor, age, faith and rank, gorged with food, dissolute from wine-bibbing, wild with

116

shouting, giddy with revelry..."

Circenses at such a time? Evidently, yes; but
no panem; and certainly no annona. The common
people were left to fend for themselves.

THE BEGINNINGS OF FEUDALISM

Western Europe was a shattered civilisation,
without law, without administration, with roads destroyed and education disorganised. Because of
crime and brigandage, which went unpunished, men
turned to strong individual leaders rather than to in-
effectual committees.

Yet great numbers of people retained civilised
habits, ideas and traditions, in spite of the de-
gradation. A vigorous bishop or an ex-Roman of
ancient family might become powerful and attract
followers. The solitary man chose as his protector
the most active and powerful such leader, and became
his man. A process of political crystallisation
spread rapidly, and these associations formed what
was to develop into the feudal system. This social
structure became general over the Nordic areas of
Europe as well.

As soon as the Nordic peoples developed a
settled mode of living around and within the old
empire, there appeared levels in society. Starting out more or less equal, after three generations
one man would be working for another, selling his
strength to him. He would give up his freedom in
this way but in return bought the right to be fed
and protected against insecurities.

LAND

These inequalities of men with one another soon
began to be realised in the ownership of land. Celtic Britain was a grazing culture; every household
was supposed to possess cows. The tariffs of
composition, that is the lists of property of the
time, were all fixed in cows. Pigs, sheep and
goats are constantly mentioned. The use of milk,

and making of cheese and the salting of bacon are subjects that were frequently referred to in the chronicles of those times; hunting, fishing and the keeping of bees were carried on. This resulted in a high level of nutrition, as compared with later periods.

There was no land ownership, and wealth consisted of animals and other "mobilia". It is not clear exactly when soil cultivation arose in early Britain, but at any rate in Caesar's time it was still secondary in importance. Soil when it was owned belonged originally to groups, not to individuals. The Roman influence was a military one, and they did not attempt to deal with questions of ownership.

For reasons of organisation they set up villages, (vici) for the people of the land, who were known as pagani.

Following the Roman decline an individualistic approach to land and land ownership came to be developed. The significance of this change in the structure of society soon became apparent. Active agriculture began to be practised, and the mode of estimating land was based upon it. By the eighth century, over a thousand years after the Celtic times mentioned above, the land was assessed by the work of a plough-team with the requisite number of oxen for tillage. Standards were based on the work of a team of eight oxen, and natural subdivisions of the land were related to this method. The words bovate and virgate as land measurements date from this time. A virgate was about 40 acres and went with two cows: it was twice the area of a bovate.

The economic side of feudalism was characterised by groupings of men and estates based on principles inherited from the decaying Roman empire. When larger holdings were granted by the King, it was only on condition of its holder's service to the King's call. When these larger holdings were divided by their owners into smaller units, the sub-tenants were bound by the same conditions, in service to their lord.

"Hear, my Lord," swore the dependent, "I become liege man of yours for life and limb and earthly regard, and I will keep faith and loyalty to you for life and death, God help me." And he placed his hands between the lord's hands, as he knelt bareheaded on the ground before him. The kiss of the lord invested him with his fief, either land, or perhaps an office, the right to collect a toll, or the right to operate a mill. This fief was to descend upon him and his heirs forever. In reality this was private law in place of the vanished public law. In any event, it placed an army of adherents ready to do the lord's bidding; the King would ultimately have at his disposal the sum of all the feifdoms of the other lords of his realm. The notion of knightly association, devotion and personal service heralded the so-called age of chivalry.

Sometimes, particularly in France, invasions came from the north and the east. Loyal warriors would cluster around the kings, counts, bishops and abbotts. Thus the manors became political, legal and economic units. Whole villages became bound to the lord of the manor.

Ninth Century
Soldier

TAXATION

The people were required to give of their services and their goods. The taxes, rent or tribute due was elaborated over the years into a system. The tax due, or gafol, might be paid in money, ten

119

gafol-pence at Michaelmas. Or it might be in kind: at Easter a man might give a young lamb or two pence; on Martinmas Day 23 sesters' worth of barley and two hens.

In return, the peasant might be allotted more grass for his animals "if he ploughs for it." These arrangements are set forth in a document called Rectitudines singularum personarum (the rights of individual persons). By the tenth century one can see that series of encroachments on the people's property which has led over the centuries to other forms of unearned increment, such as our systems of ground rent, mining royalties and property taxes.

The requirements for the peasant's services were severe:

"for the cultivation of the arable, the peasant holdings will send their plough three or more days a week from sunrise until noon, with a full complement of beasts and laborers...later in the season the peasants will send their harrows to break up the sods and prepare the ground for the seed. When the harvest season comes all the population will have to turn out to help the lord's laborers."

A sense of the value of such work is expressed by the term used for it, precariae; that is, it is not supposed to be due, but has to be asked for, pre-arranged.

"And if this boon work has to be repeated several times the laborers get food and even ale from the manorial economy to keep them in good humour."

Thus wrote Aelfric in 1003, in his "Lex talionis".

HUNGER

During the Dark period, there were frequent times when hunger stalked the world. This was not new. Hunger had always existed; just as men died from old age, and from diseases, so they had died from hunger. This was especially true when grain became mouldy, or when cultivation was interrupted by war, which often happened.

At these times there was a breakdown of order, and killer bands used to roam through the country-side to waylay the travellers.

The forebears of the formerly nomadic peoples who were now settling down in Europe had been people of the east European and central Asian steppes. They had used horses for fast transportation and sudden war. They had been able to travel long distances, and were accustomed to killing their prisoners. They could not very well take them along with them, for there were no roads and no carts.

When their descendents settled down, they no longer used to kill their prisoners, because they found that they were of more value alive, as workers, than dead. As a result they adopted the institution of slavery which had been used in Egypt, Greece and Rome for thousands of years. There will be more to say about this later on.

In spite of these customs, great numbers of people managed to retain civilised habits, and to take a certain pride and responsibility for their people. The old ideas and traditions of the finer aspects of life were personified in the person of Charlemagne, King of the Franks and Lombards. He was the first ever to introduce measures to control food in the interests of the people, and as such he was far ahead of his time. In 774 he first forbad the export of grain from his kingdom. Following that he set maximum prices: one bushel of oats for one dinar; one bushel of barley for two dinars; for rye and what, three and four dinars respectively. He commanded the holders of royal offices to see to

it that the people did not die of hunger. He instituted welfare stations and a poor tax. The poor
were to be supplied with the "poor bread". It was
shaped like the Roman breads in the form of small
spheres; in French boules. The bread was known at
the time as pain de boule; from this arose the
French word for baker: "boulanger".

Such solicitude for the people's well-being
was rare indeed at that time. For hunger was becoming more than ever widespread. When various acts
of nature took away their harvests, it was usually
a famine of limited duration, and perhaps in one
area. The people might starve in one area, but in
the next province there would be food. One year
differed from another.

But in the period which we are now entering,
the purely local nature of famines changed. Hunger
became a permanent phenomenon, and appeared any and
everywhere. It attacked the poor people first. A
monk of Canterbury describes how the lowest in the
scale had to manage:

"...poor folk in cottages, charged with
children and the chief lord's rent;
that they with spinning may spare,
spend they it in househire, both in
milk and in meal, to make therewith
pap, to glut therewith their children that cry after food. Also themselves suffer much from hunger...there
is bread and penny ale for a pittance
(luxury); cold flesh and cold fish is
to them as baked venison; on Fridays
and fastingdays a farthing's worth of
mussles were a feast for such folk,
or so many cockles..."

And the lowest in the scale had to work the
hardest, in spite of food shortages. A part of
Aelfric's colloquoy had this to say:

"What sayest thou, plowman? How dost
thou do thy work?"

122

"Oh, my lord, hard do I work. I go
out at daybreak driving the oxen to
the field and I yoke them to the plow.
Nor is it ever so hard winter that I
dare loiter at home for fear of my
Lord; but the oxen yoked and the plowshare and coulter fastened to the plow,
every day must I plow a full acre or
more."

"Hast thou any comrade?"

"I have a boy driving the oxen with an
iron goad who is also hoarse with cold
and shouting."

"What more dost thou in the day?"

"Verily then I do more. I must fill
the bin of the oxen with hay; and
water them and carry out the dung.
Ha! Hard work it is, because I am
not free."

So it was a very hard time for the peasant.
Even lower than he was the slave or theow. In
wartime the slave class increased; but there were
also other reasons for this increase. The numbers
of the "unfree" were swollen by debt and by crime.
Famine also drove men to "bend their heads in the
evil days for meat." The debtor unable to dis-
charge his debt flung down his freeman's sword and
spear, and took up the laborer's mattock, and placed
his head as a slave within the master's hands. The
criminal whose kinsfolk would not make up the fine
became a crime-serf to the plaintiff.

Sometimes a father pressed for need sold
children and wife into bondage. The slave became
part of the live stock of the estate to be willed
away at death with horse or ox whose pedigree was
kept as carefully as his own. The cabins of the
unfree clustered around the home of the rich landowner as they had clustered around the villa of the
Roman gentleman. Plowman, shepherd, oxherd,

goatherd, dairymaid, hayward and woodward, were
often slaves in the early days.

The slave had no place in the justice court;
no kinsman to claim vengeance for his wrong. If
a stronger slew him, his lord claimed the damages;
if guilty of wrong-doing, "his skin paid for him"
under the lash. If he fled he might be chased like
a strayed beast, and flogged to death for his crime,
or burned to death if the slave were a woman.

THE CHURCH

What was the attitude of the Church towards
slavery? Christianity had become the state religion in at least part of the Roman empire in Constantine's time, 313 A.D. By the fifth and sixth
centuries Christianity had become firmly entrenched
throughout western Europe. The Church at this time
officially accepted slavery as a part of "Adam's
curse."

It was essential that man keep the rules, and
live a life free from sin. When those that had
lived a life of sin died, hell was awaiting them.
The Church sometimes painted hell as eternal fire;
at other times as a place of icy darkness of desolation. It was filled with oval white shapes,
heads hanging crookedly on bodies; with dark,
ravenous earthworms that stripped the ribs and drank
the blood.

> "...the head is cleft, hands disjointed,
> jaws gaping, mouth rent open; sinews are
> slackened, the neck gnawed through,
> fingers decayed, feet broken."

For now there was no home, no hope.

> "the soul, a small white disc was buffet-
> ed eternally from side to side in a
> terrible valley...and from the whole
> there exuded a foul stench; there howled
> lamentations and harsh laughter..."

124

Everything, the Church claimed, all small insects and fierce animals were in league, to remind man of his fall. Flies, for this purpose, invaded his food and drink. They disturbed his sleep, and lice molested him.

Anything new was considered dangerous, a crime against God, the Church, and the King. It was a treason to be punished in the proper manner: racking, then burning alive, to remind people of the hellish flames in which the miscreant would shortly be roasting.

One sees the Middle Ages set out like an expensive, Church-controlled boarding school; the pupils (people) are considered to be a rowdy, ill-disciplined crowd; never alone, never allowed to work out the rules for themselves. They play together at children's games: particularly soldiers and war. And after dinner, blind man's buff, ball and hot cockles. The authorities, behind their magnificence, their silks and velours, their chants and their incense, their mystery, bully and frighten the people into keeping the rules, condemning any originality as heresy, and threatening expulsion and hell.

But there was corruption in the Church itself, and in the authorities also. Funds were directed towards the very sins against which the Church thundered most vigorously. By 1321 this corruption, coupled with ignorance, were to bring about a change in the course of history, which was to affect among other things, food. As a result the Middle Ages would be ready for disintegration when the opportune moment arose.

REFERENCES

115 "IT WOULD BE IDLE TO WRITE OF STATES AND RULERS.." Wells, H.G. Outline of History; chap. xxxi, p 635 (1920).

116 "O CITIZENS OF TRIER?" Salvian; De Gubernatione Dei; Book IV, 89; quoted from the Mind of Latin Christendom, E. M. Pickman (1937).

116 GIDDY WITH REVELRY..Salvian, ibid.

117 AT FIRST NO LAND OWNERSHIP: de Coulanges, Fustel N; Origin of Property in land, (1927).

118 VIRGATE AND BOVATE: Peake, Harold J.E.: The English Village. chap. IX. (1922).

119 "I BECOME A LIEGE MAN OF YOURS.." Green, John Richard, A short history of the English people; Vol I, chap. II. 56 (1892).

120 "IF HE PLOWS FOR IT.." Liegermann: Rectitudines singularum personarum; Gesetze der angelsachsen; quoted from Vinogradoff: Growth of the English Manor, p 72 (1905).

120 REQUIREMENTS FOR PEASANTS" SERVICES: Aelfric: Lex talionis (1003); quoted in Peake, ibid (1922).

122 BOULANGER: Breasted, J.H. Ancient Times: a history of the early world, p 789 (1916).

122 POOR FOLK IN COTTAGES..Coulton, George G: The Mediaeval Village. (1925).

123 "WHAT SAYEST THOU, PLOWMAN?". Peake, ibid chap. IX.

123   "BEND THEIR HEADS IN THE EVIL DAYS FOR MEAT."
Green, J.R. ibid chap. I p 27;

124   "HIS SKIN PAID FOR HIM"..Green ibid p 28.

124   ADAM'S CURSE" Moffett, James; The first five
centuries of the Church (1938).

124   FOOD BEFORE THE NORMAN CONQUEST: Pullar, Phillippa; Consuming Passions: an historic
enquiry into certain English appetites.

It is appropriate at this time to retrace our
steps in order to take a look at the Nordic peoples
and their story; for they were to influence, and
even to dominate, the food of those times in
Europe, and for centuries to come.

When the "barbarians" overran Europe in the
fifth century it was considered the "funeral of the
world", according to one late Latin writer of the
time. He need not have been so pessimistic for
several good reasons.

It is true that the entire mediterranean world
underwent a profound change at this time. Once-
vigorous Roman-controlled cities became ghost towns
from which the population had fled. The northern
peoples, Goths, Visigoths, Vandals, Alemanni and
Franks, had lived close to the Roman empire without
having been able to reach the Mediterranean Sea.
They were different in a number of ways from the
southern Europeans. They possessed an immense new
vitality, living as they did on the excellent nutritive qualities of milk, cheese and meat.

They conquered not by numbers; it is claimed
that not more than 200,000 Visigoths took over
Spain with its population of an estimated six million. They achieved this by means of mobility,
guerilla strikes and sheer dynamism. They were
well prepared for this kind of movement.

The forebears of these tribes had subsisted
on their cattle and other animals; they were mobile
and nomadic; they could load their few belongings
onto wagons and go where they would. This kind of
life had been engendered by a long history of
travel with their flocks and herds, as far across
the steppes as the Gobi desert.

The ancestors of these people ranged the Eurasian heartland, from Mongolia and China to the

Northern Warrior

Ural Mountains, and were to influence all subsequent
history and diet as well.

THE MONGOLS

The enormous stretch of Eurasian land mass was
not forest but steppe. It was covered by natural
grasses which prevented soil erosion, and which
also demanded that the inhabitants were hunters
as well as nomads. They took their own animals with
them, and hunted wild animals. These circumstances
led to their interest in stock-breeding. Sometimes
they would settle for a while, until that land
became eroded, worn out and could not revive. Whole
clans would then be crowded out of the settled areas
and become nomadic once more.

A highly complex organizational system developed around this mobile society. Pasture land became
too important to be settled by the ancient law of
survival of the fittest. Some kind of fair allo-
cation of grazing land had to be assured. Ultimately, the economy of the steppes came to be ritualized.

It was from such a culture as this that the
Mongols came later. Their descendents today are to
be seen as the "kuchis" of Afghanistan. These
people still use the same black tents, called "yurts",
plastered with beef tallow to make them waterproof.
They move upland in the summer, and down towards
Pakistan in the winter. For they are always on the
move in search of water for their animals and themselves. The water holes dried up, especially after
the climatic changes brought about by shifts in the
wind currents, about 300 A.D. Recently it has been
theorized by Huntingdon and others that from about
2,000 B.C. to about 300 A.D., the depression track
followed a path through the Mediterranean region,
from Gibraltar, to the Black and Caspian seas. Clim-
atologists now claim that the main depression track
reverted to a more northerly course after 300 A.D.,
with catastrophic effects in the climate of those
regions. This has affected the whole subsequent
history, inasmuch as the aridity of the whole regions forced migrations into new paths. The central
Asian steppes were badly affected by this, so that
nomadic people had to strike out afresh in order to
find water.

This incessant movement of peoples sent a
number of Chinese border tribes westward to join
with Iranian herdsmen and with Mongols from the
forests of Siberia. These groupings were later to
form in Europe a people known as the Huns, about
100 A.D. One of their leaders was to be Attila the
Hun, known in Roman history. Even in World War I,
the British were apt to refer to the Germans as
the "Huns".

When the nomads encroached upon their settled
neighbors, they were not always welcome. But under
duress, the communities would allow the nomadic
groups to stay on their land; for even if there
was little forage to be had, yet the exhausted
field would benefit by the dung of the animals.
They would encamp there and then move on. Such a
symbiotic relationship between herders and the
settled communities exists to this day in parts of
Asia. The later English laws of jus faldae, men-

tioned in a subsequent chapter, are an offshoot of
this idea. The main difference is that in the case
of the nomads, they could enforce their will on
the communities. In the case of the later landowners in England, the peasants' animals were
commandeered by the lord to lend the benefit of
the dung to his fields.

Thus we have a situation in which the fiery,
black-browed horsemen from the steppes, well nourished upon animal protein foods, were usually able
to overcome their more stolid carbohydrate-fed
neighbors. These rugged men, bow-legged from constant riding, had large heads and massive chests,
to withstand the parching days and freezing nights
of the deserts and steppes. Their flocks and herds
provided for almost all of their needs: housing,
clothing, transportation, food and milk.

They developed the sheepskin coats which they
turned with the wool in and the skin out, for
warmth. They did not do any weaving, as the settled Chinese of those times did. They had no time
to weave; they tanned the skins with urea from the
urine of their animals, and even made tanned leather
shields.

FOOD OF THE MONGOLS

Centuries later we are able to learn something
about the descendents of these people. Marco Polo
in his remarkable thirteenth century writings gives
a detailed description of the Mongol armies. He
describes how, on the long trail, they would drink
the blood of their own horses. Half an imperial
pint could be drawn each tenth day without doing
any harm to the horses. This was enough to sustain
a rider, if he were to change mounts each day, without in any way impairing their efficiency. He would
thereby have a string of horses and would be able
to travel without provisions. They knew how to
puncture a vein in the neck and to stanch it again.
It was especially important to them that they
should be able to proceed without fires of any kind;
otherwise detection would be easy. The element of
surprise was all-important. "The Assyrian came

down like a wolf on the fold."

Even before Marco Polo, in the ninth century, a Chinese traveller into the Berber country recorded that "people often stick a needle into the veins of cattle and draw blood, which they drink raw, mixed with milk." This persisted until recent times, preserved in certain recipes. In seventeenth century Ireland, a French traveller noted that"

> "the peasants bleed their cows, and boil the blood with some of the milk and butter that came from the same beast; with a mixture of savoury herbs, this makes one of their most delicious dishes."

In Tyrone and Derry counties, the blood was even preserved; it was allowed to coagulate in layers, salted and cut up for later use. These types of blood recipes are the forerunners of the "drisheen" or blood pudding.

In Africa such customs also prevail. The Masai warriors of Kenya shoot a special arrow with a little barb in it into the neck of their cattle, bleed the animal and then close up the wound with a plug.

There are cultural offshoots to these food customs. Tales of werewolves and vampires, which suck innocent blood, have crept into our stories. And indeed very severe injunctions have been placed upon the use of blood as a food, nutritionally excellent though it is. This is particularly true of the regulations set forth in the Koran:

> "Carrion, blood and the flesh of swine; these are forbidden unto you."

Because the nomad horsemen of old had many horses, it is nor surprising that mares' milk was fully used by them, another cause of their exuberant good health.

According to our present knowledge about food values, the Mongols of old received ample protein, fat, vitamins A and D and most of the B vitamins. Their protein was complete. But with fresh fruits and vegetables either impossible to get out in the steppes, or out of favor, why did they not get scurvy?

This is one of those inexplicable things wherein primitive logic gets to work, possibly over long periods of time. We now realize that milk is not a good source of vitamin C, especially cows' milk. Human milk has at least twice as much, and as we now know, mares' milk has four times as much as cows' milk. We have to admire these people. They drank their mares' milk, but the milk of other species was allowed to curdle, and the forerunners of cheese and yogurt appeared. How did they know that mares' milk was superior? How did they know that what little vitamin C exists in cows' milk would be decreased in the curdling process?

Since neolithic times, milk had been known to "sour" rapidly on standing, and later, man discovered how to curdle it purposefully. It is even possible that, before the advent of pottery, man knew to place milk into an animal's stomach, where the rennin still present would curdle it into soft curds.

Dried milk so familiar to us today was known to the Mongols centuries back. Marco Polo wrote"

"for they first bring their milk to the boil; at the appropriate moment they skim off the cream that floats to the surface, and put it in another vessel to be made into butter; because so long as it (the cream) remained, the milk could not be dried..."

"then they left the milk (skimmed) in the sun to dry; when they are going on an expedition they take about ten pounds of

this concentrated milk. Each morning
they take out about half a pound of it,
put it into a gourd, with as much water
as they please; then while they ride, the
milk in their flask dissolved into a
fluid, which they drink. And this is
their breakfast..."

The nomadic peoples did not go short of milk,
but other societies did, and substitutes were developed. In particular, coconuts in India and
many parts of Africa; hickory nuts and pecans in
North America; walnuts and almonds in Europe and
many parts of the Middle East. Soybeans were used
in China before Christ's time. They were all
looking for the necessary fat. They did not at the
time know the other virtues of milk.

In hindsight it is easy to see that nutritional excellence was a feature of the new conquerors
of Europe. This was to be seen later in the time
of Genghis Khan. Fighting hand to hand, rather
than by surprise, necessitates that you outlast
your opponent. It is not hard to see that protein
quality, as well as quantity, is an important feature in the diets, and indeed, of the success, of
these peoples.

It is well to remember that these were the
ancestors of the same people who were to sit astride
Europe for centuries and from whom many of us are
descended. It is now time to return to the Europe
of the middle ages, in order to follow the fortunes
of these same people.

SETTLING DOWN

Those Nordic peoples who had been living next
door to the Roman empire for some time had already
learned the advantages of a modest agriculture.
When they shifted to a new place, the usually
dwelt there for a full year, which gave them enough
time to plant and harvest a crop of oats. Oatmeal
was to become a national symbol of these peoples,
and represents something of a milestone in their

nutrition.

This was an important step for them for they
had previously believed that agriculture weakened
their military striking power. Now they were to
learn that, on the contrary, only very small populations can subsist on their herds alone. In the
old days, they had swooped down and stolen the
crops of the settlers in their path. Now they
themselves were the settlers.

It had been calculated that as much as eighty
head of livestock of one sort or another are
necessary to maintain a family of six. Consequently, it was logical for them to turn to agriculture,
even if their instincts rebelled against it. They
were frugal men, and saw quite well that they would
starve in the midst of their victory, if they
attempted to live on herds alone.

Not only that, but they were conquering people,
and as such, they wished and expected to increase
in numbers. It was obvious to them that cattle
raising alone was impractical.

And it is worth noting that the conquests
by the people from the north did not occur all at
once. Some of the most powerful landowners
resisted the nomadic invaders, and withdrew behind
their high castle walls. They continued to live
there, with their newly-assembled armies and atten-
dants, and resisted interference, including the
tax collectors. They developed a certain self-
sufficiency within their walled fortresses, and
many of the invaders continued their nomadic existence, as far as into the eighth century in some
cases. This freed the land outside the fortresses
for use by the invaders. However, this was not to
produce the fine harvests which were needed.

For there were harsh lessons to be learned from
the Roman empire. As early as 300, the clearance
of virgin soil had ceased; the empire was already
beginning to fall in pieces. There was a spread

of "agri deserti", abandoned fields. By 476,
forests, marshes and deserts "grew back". Wild
species of plant and animal were to take over, and
to reconvert the artificial soil communities of
Roman times into natural soil communities.

This may have been an advantage, although at
the time it would look to be disastrous. For Rome
had been the center of the world, the Mediterranean
world. In making its provinces, Rome had demanded
bread from them. As a result, a good deal of
land was being ploughed up in many of their provinces; this was land which was easy to plough,
and as we now know, should not be ploughed. The
semi-arid areas were to become aggravated by the
shift in the depression pattern, as we have just
said. Accordingly within the empire, erosion
had occurred, and good soil had inevitably been
lost.

These weather changes prompted the nomadic
peoples to strike out afresh to find water for
themselves and for their animals. But the forests
of Bavaria, Allemania, Switzerland and the Frank-
ish kingdoms still remained more or less intact.
They knit the soil together, and held the moisture;
and the dampness of the north European climate
helped in this.

This is what assured these peoples of a
steady food supply, which was to include grains,
fruits and vegetables, as well as their accustomed
meat and dairy products.

THE CULTURE OF THE NORDIC PEOPLES

The culture of these peoples was very different from that of the Graeco-Roman world of the
Mediterranean. It was as though they came from
another planet. This is important for our story
because it relates very emphatically to food.

The Nordic peoples were wind-worshippers.
Their chief god, Odin, rode upon an eight-footed
horse. Only men whose great-grandfathers had

never seen a house could believe that the world
was created by a wind-god. The Mediterranean
peoples on the other hand, centered their cultural
base on "house, hearth-fire, and field". It was
as if nothing else existed. Their god of travel,
Hermes, (Mercury in the Latin pantheon) is pictured
as a rather handsom-looking young man, with very
small wings attached to his feet just above the
ankle. Hermes was not very important in the scheme
of things, because the Mediterranean world was
entirely unfamiliar with the tempests that raged
in the seas of northern Europe. The power that
could break rocks and forests was entirely unknown
to them. They had no eyes and no imaginations for
the kingdom of chaos.

But the northern peoples lived in a state
wherein the storm god, Odin; the thunder god,
Thor-Donar; and the cloud goddess, Freya, reigned
supreme. The importance of these dieties is perpetuated in our language as Wednesday, Thursday and
Friday.

It was one of the fundamental beliefs of these
Nordic peoples that free, uncontrolled nature was
much more than mere mortal man. To impose changes
on the earth was therefore sinful and fraught with
danger. They always had to placate their heavenly
foes: Odin, Thor and Freya. Accordingly, they
farmed with a bad conscience.

The Romans had not felt the need for so much
propitiation; but the Nordic peoples tried to make
order our of chaos, if they could. Some tribes
considered a field to be a living creature that
had to be tamed. Consequently, they would ride
horses furiously back and forth across a field,
in order to imitate a storm. They would thereby
command the field to the good graces of Odin. They
would place horses' skulls at the four corner of
a field, in order to placate the anger of the
earth.

They pretended that the plough was an animal
with its own will, so that they might be forgiven

for having injured the earth. The Anglo-Saxons
called the plough: "pig's nose"; the Letts called
it: "bear", and the Rhinelanders: "wolf". This
was done as though to lay the blame on an animal
for having dug up the earth.

After ploughing, came the seeding. The ancient
enemy of seeding is the wind, which thus must be
placated if seeding is to be successful. Whereas
the Bible, the sower, with God's blessing, obtained
that part of the crop that fell "upon good ground",
the Teutonic peoples were more logical. They fully
understood that indeed the wind was stronger. Their
realistic approach attached great importance to
the natural cycle of events.

Accordingly, harvesting became an event which
was developed into a ritual. All sorts of superstitions have since grown up for protecting man's
daily bread. A whole cycle of propitiation led
inevitably to anxiety. The Kelt, Slav and German
had to be sure that their harvests would succeed.
For whereas they felt fairly sure of their animals,
they could not be quite certain of their fields.

CHRISTIANITY

Christian missionaries at this time in history tried to overcome these superstitions. They
attempted to assure these people that no activity
could possibly be evil which had as its ultimate
aim the baking of bread: "Christus paniformis".
But the barbarians could not understand this. The
priests thereupon tried to persuade them of the
Jewish view; namely that the earth was a slave of
man, and that man was God's governor on earth.
Accordingly, there was no need to be apologetic
about ploughing, sowing, harvesting. By these
activities they were taking nothing away from the
earth.

Thus arose a struggle for mastery between the
two cultures, for the northern peoples were more
concerned with propitiation of the wind god than
whether or not bread was "Christus paniformis".

139

Because of these conflicts, the whole Roman
agricultural technique lay neglected. For Columella had written excellent treatises on agriculture
by the year 70. Nordic peoples were either unable,
or unwilling, to study these great writings. Latin
became merely a professional language of the educated, who were mainly the monks. The great mass
of the people could no longer share in the treasury
of the ancient world's knowledge.

We refer to the time when people were having
trouble with their agricultural pursuits as the
Dark Ages. Amid all this struggle between dogma
and superstition, and between "Christus paniformis"
and Odin, the soil was cultivated increasingly
badly, for men were no longer certain of their tasks.

Kuchi "yurt", in
Afghanistan: 1966

The war to decide whether Jesus or the old
gods would guide the plow led to confusion of
the reasoning power of men. They became so ignorant of technical matters, and unable to read
or understand the old work, that they did not
know how to cope with the terrible hygienic perils
of the middle ages. One day the devil really did
come to infect bread, but it was not a theological
devil.

PLANT DISEASES

Because of the loss of the ability to grow
food, and to ensure against deprivation of the
poor, there were instances when a disaster would
supervene, beyond the power of men to control.
One of these disasters was to reveal very clearly
how much of the earlier knowledge of food crops
had been lost of forgotten.

There was a town in Gaul called after the
word "Lem", the early celtic word for stag. Until
the Romans came, the people of that region had
lived like free stags in their forests, eating
their acorn meal. When the Romans came at the
time of Caesar, the forests were cleared to make
way for a town, with markets and an amphitheatre.
Temples were erected to Ceres, the goddess of
food, and of plenty. Later on, monks came to
preach Christianity, and with plows, tore up the
earth and planted crops. After the demise of the
Roman occupation, the land was occupied by Teutons
from the east. The rightful inhabitants of Limoges, for that is its name, fled into caves, and
for centuries lived a precarious existence. As
they gradually returned to their town, there was
no peace or plenty. Grain was poorly sown, and
bread was poorly made. They used acorns to eke
out meager supplies.

In the year 943, frightful things began to
happen. Shrieking, wailing, and writhing men
and women collapsed in the streets of Limoges.
They suffered epileptic fits, and sudden insanity,
crying out, "Fire, I'm burning!" This was something quite different from the plagues and
infections that were common in the Middle Ages.

141

No amount of propitiation of the saints could stem the disease. The Church erected hospitals to care for those sick of the disease, and St. Anthony was invoked as guardian of the hospitals. The disease came to be called "St. Anthony's Fire".

At this time, the people of Limoges noticed a change in the rye bread that they bought from the boulanger. It was wet when cut, and oozed a black, sticky substance. It seemed clear that something bad affected the rye, but the unfortunate people of Limoges did not know what it was.

No farmer in the Roman empire would have threshed such rye. No miller would have milled it, and no baker would have baked it. Why not? Because Columella had long ago instructed the Romans why and how this disease must be fought. It is described in his writings, which provided clear instructions concerning the cleanliness of the grain to be used for milling and subsequent baking.

But the new settlements of Europe had lost the old conscientiousness in the arts of milling and baking. There was as yet no medical research in Europe, and there would not be until Renaissance times. Therefore the people did not know what to do, and the disease had to run its course. We now know that the disease was ergotism, a rye blight; and that ergot contains as many as twenty materials, one of which is lysergic acid diethylamide, or LSD.

In the same tenth century, another source was to reach Europe, this time affecting wheat. The all-conquering Arabs inadvertently carried with them along the northern coast of Africa and up into Spain, a small bush that was to have an effect on the food supplies of Europe. Until the ninth century, the deadly black stem rust, which can lay a whole field of wheat to waste, had been almost unknown in the west. But it had been known in the Middle East in the time of Jesus; "Lay not up for yourselves treasures upon earth, where moth and rust do corrupt."

The small bush is the barberry bush which plays host to the rust during certain stages of its development. The disease began to ravage the wheatfields of Spain. In 915 and again in 929, Spain suffered appalling rust damage. This led inevitably to famine, and ultimately to cannibalism:

> "destitution reached such a pitch at last that men began to devour each other, and the flesh of a son was preferred to his love."

REFERENCES

129   "FUNERAL OF THE WORLD": Edwardes, Michael (1971), from Tannahill, p 105.

129   VISIGOTHS TOOK OVER SPAIN: Vicens, Jaimie; An economic history of Spain; (1969).

130   DEPRESSION TRACK: Tuchman, Barbara; A distant Mirror, p 24 (1979).

130   HUNS: Simkin, C.G.F. The traditional trade of Asia (1968).

131   PARCHING DAYS AND FREEZING NIGHTS: Grousset, Rene; The rise and splendour of the Chinese empire (1952).

132   BLOOD AS FOOD: Davidson, quoted in Tannahill, p 130.

132   DRISHEEN Misson, Henri; Memoirs (1690); tr Odell 1719.

132   BLOOD ENJOINED BY THE KORAN: V. The Table, sura 2.

132   MILK AS FOOD: Fairbank, J.K., Reiscauer, E. and Craig, A.

133   East Asia: The Mongol Empire, chap 7 p 154 (1973).

134   DRIED MILK: Marco Polo; Travels; trans Lathan (1958).

136   CULTURE OF THE NORDIC PEOPLES: Munch, Peter Andreas; Norse Mythology. (1926).

138   STATE OF EUROPE IN THE MIDDLE AGES: Hallam H. (1908).

138   CHRISTUS PANIFORMIS: Jacob, Heinrich H: Six thousand years of bread, p 119 (1944).

140   LIMOGES: Jacob; ibid p 121.

141   DISASTER IN FRANCE: Funck-Brentano: The Middle Ages; national history of France. p 106 (1923).

143   CANNIBALISM: Jacob, ibid p 149.

FOOD BEFORE THE NORMAN CONQUEST

It was reported that before the eleventh century much of the cooking took place out of doors. Contemporary illustrations indicate this. Meat broths and stews containing pot-herbs were concocted in giant cauldrons. Meat was also fried, steamed, or roasted, and brought to the table on long spits.

Winter diets have often been portrayed as consisting of salted-down meat, not very appetising at that. However it should be noted that at this time cattle were not reared primarily for meat. Oxen were used as draught animals, and this would continue until later, when new technology was to bring the horse to the fore in this capacity. Cows were for milk. The diet was largely one of dairy produce, together with game, fish, wild fowl and young animals; cereals and legumes made up the vegetable part of the diet. There were as yet few forest laws and no enclosures. These were to come later.

The average man therefore had access, if he were lucky, to game, fish, fuel and fodder, for the taking. Archbishop Aelfric produced a glossary which yields some insight into the english food at that time. Salt was much used, for without it food was said to taste insipid. Cheese and butter were churned with salt. Fat was valued, and it seems that vegetables were considered better when boiled quite pale: "If you expel me from your company," says the cook, "you shall chew your cabbage green; nor can you have fat broth without my art..."

There were no hot, sweet tea, no coffee or hot chocolate of a later time. Consequently in the chilly climate of northern Europe they would relish sustaining comforting meals, and a heavy diet based upon bread and pulses. Everyone drank ale, sweetened with honey to counteract the sourness in the brewing, and families brewed their own ale.

THE NORMAN PERIOD

There was so much excessive eating in the Norman period by the upper levels of society that laws were even passed to limit it. There were sumptuary laws to prevent excesses at banquets in the reign of Edward III. Statute 10 reads:

"No man, of whatever condition or estate, shall be allowed more than two courses at dinner or supper, or more than two kinds of food in each course; except on principal festivals of the year, when three courses at the utmost are allowed."

These laws were honored in the breach more than in the observance, and in later centuries the excesses were to be far more pronounced as we shall see. Easter, "after brown Lent", was a particularly fine time for excessive feasting.

But these were the few. The peasantry lived, as had their Saxon forebears centuries earlier, on what they could produce from the land and glean from the hedges: herbs, legumes, cereals; gruels and porridges made from oats; coarse breads made from barley, and from wheat if they could get it. Occasionally the history shows a bright glimmer of hope and charity towards the unfortunate. It is refreshing to record that at one time it was customary for estates to be settled in favor of those who contributed something to the community. For example, a man might be required to provide one day's food per year to the poor people. In 958 Aethelryd was to enjoy an estate at a rent of five pounds a year, provided that he contribute 40 sesters' worth of ale, sixty loaves, a wether sheep, a flitch of

146

bacon, two cheeses and four hens. We learn of
attempts to assist the poor people in an otherwise
harsh unyielding world.

For life in the Middle Ages was hard, especially at famine time. Famines and epidemics,
said the Church, were sent down by God as a
punishment for the wickedness of the people.
They should heed warnings and repent. The men
of the middle ages did not suspect that in dealing with famine you must start with proper plowing. Cato had known this a thousand years earlier.
Columella too had felt that the earth had a life
of its own, and said so in his writings. This
great idea was to lie forgotten until 1840, when
Liebig was to rediscover it, and develop it scien-
tifically.

MILLING

Many people blamed the millers for the disastrous famines of the early middle ages, but they
alone were not to blame. There was a breakdown in
understanding the technology of flour making,
with the result that the millers lost the Roman
art of bolting, or sifting, flour. In this case
the sieving off of the branny particles and the
separation of the chaff, which made the flour so
much more desirable, was a technique which was
now forgotten. But it had been known for centuries. In addition, the stones used for grinding
grain, if not properly maintained, and from time
to time replaced, would wear off into the flour.
The townspeople would be consuming as much as
four pounds of stone in the bread made from such
flour. This was unpalatable to say the least;
the bread was "all puffed up with air" according
to one author.

Another aspect of milling is significant at
this time. The milling procedure was sheer
drudgery for man, and for animals walking in their
everlasting circle. The Romans had devised water
mills to do away with this drudgery, because
they understood the power of just a small trickle

of water appropriately diverted onto the blade of
a wheel. The Romans had produced thousands of
these wheels and the northerners had found them
as they went south into the Roman spheres of

Early water-wheels

influence. They hated them and feared them,
believing that it was blasphemous to compel the
spirit of free streams and wild brooks to work
as a slave of the mill. And so they let the mills
rot and decay.

The people of the middle ages came to look
upon the Roman miller of old as a kind of magi-
cian, and his mills, where the water was tortured
upon the wheel were considered to be uncanny
places. And it turned out that the water spirits
were in fact in league with the spirits of fire,
or so people thought, for often the mills exploded.

We know now that the very fineness of flour
can itself cause a dust explosion. But in the
fifth and sixth centuries, particularly, these
habitual mill fires aroused superstitious horror,

and were considered proper punishment for the sin of compelling water to work for man. We still have the phrase: "a millstone around my neck". And yet these Roman machines were not only millstones, but milestones of civilisation. And eventually Christianity came to terms with them. The Church said, simply: "the mills make your bread, and bread is Christ."

Even so the millstone itself was a great problem. Its thundering noise reminded the Germans of the thunder-god, Thor-Donar. Christians tried to counter that sort of belief by introducing St. Verena into the situation. Little idols of Thor-Donar were being put up in the mills of the peasants in order to ward off trouble. St. Verena was able to throw these idols into the stream, thereby gaining great grace. There were many superstitions to overcome in regard to milling, including the one that millstones could speak.

The mill itself was too large to be owned by one individual, and as the years went by it came to belong to the community, and then to the lord. The miller thus became and employee of the lord. Tenants could use only the mill belonging to their lord and no other. They brought their grain to it for grinding. This practice effectively prevented all competition, and promoted a dependency relationship which persisted for centuries. Later peasant revolts were to be based upon this grievance, among others.

When the miller became the vassal, or minion, of the lord, the people felt that he was no longer one of them. Thus arose the common hatred of the miller; in order to live, it was said, he had to steal grain, and cheating was common. "Beside every mill there is a hill of sand", laments an old German proverb. And so bribery, corruption and ill-dealing crept into the miller's operation, and he became an outcast. The townspeople eventually were to banish the miller from their towns, and not alone for his alleged dishonesty. The mill had to use either wind or water, neither or which was available in the early, narrow walled towns. The water that came into the town was used for other civic purposes, and a miller's wheel was not allowed there.

BAKERS

The baker was different; he was a man living in the town, one of the people. Because the miller was banished from the town the miller and baker became separated. Neither the Egyptians nor the Romans had done this. A most vivid illustration of the link between millers and bakers is afforded by the recent restoration of certain frescoes and murals at Pompeii, dated A.D. 79. Revealed to us is the whole process of Roman bread-making, from the unground wheat to the finished round breads. It was all carried out in one place, as a series of single operations carried out in sequence.

As time went one, both millers and bakers, although separate, were to become more and more important members of society. According to a German common-law book of the middle ages, bakers and millers were punishable by a fine three times as much as that given an ordinary malefactor. Later on, in the France of Louis XI, it was decreed that no baker be forced to stand on duty as sentinel. The argument was that they would have no excuse to say, if their bread were bad, that their baking had been interrupted.

RISE OF THE GUILDS

An excellent account of the early guilds is given by Mollat and Wolfe. In 1272, at Nimes in the province of Languedoc, France, there were listed nine categories of occupations. These included such craft occupations as weavers, fullers, and dyers; blacksmiths and "all who work with a hammer"; carpenters and stone-cutters. It also included a group of laborers and brassiers; i.e. those who have only their arms to work with.

From these nine groups it was decreed that representation on the local councils should be fairly allocated. The revolts of the coming years were to center to a large extent on the allegiances of these guilds. Although they were formed in the first place to protect the trades and crafts, membership was strictly limited; eventually they became very powerful and even oppressive.

But we see that six and a half centuries before the full development of trade unions, the average skilled or non-skilled man had representation. All of these activities were instituted in order to improve the lot of the average man and his family, especially in the matter of enabling him to choose his leaders. At that time there was little or no reference to wages. The guilds also became restrictive; a "black founder" (iron), could not be a "yellow founder" (gold or bronze); a tanner of leather must not make shoes. At this time arose the dogma: "where a brewery stands, no bakery may stand." This was plainly retrogressive. An ancient Egyptian painting shows bakers and brewers working in adjoining rooms. Why not? They were both using yeast.

THE LOT OF THE PEASANT

The old system of taxation in the thirteenth century was based on land, and was derived from earlier arrangements such as Danegeld and Scutage. An act of Parliament in 1283 replaced these land-based taxes with a tax on movables (mobilia). The peasant was now to be taxed by a distant and unknown source, instead of by the local baron or lord. Part of the tax was levied as work, called "boon days". This was highly unpopular, because the "week-work" was interfered with, and the peasants' fields were neglected when he had to fulfil his "boon days". A writer of the time laments:

"...thus breedeth many beggars bold,
and our rye is rotted or flat ere we reap;
flat is our rye or rotted in the straw
from wicked weather by brook or by brink;

151

there wakeneth in the world dread and woe
as good to perish at once as so for to
swink..."*

Other demands were made on the unfortunate peasant;
even seed corn might be demanded as a tax.

Throughout time the peasant has been universally looked down upon. For who would practice
agriculture voluntarily? The peasant existed
because of economic need or compulsion. Consequently it was assumed that any man with any
ambition at all would under no circumstances choose
to make a living as a farmer. It was even believed
by some that man created music in order to make
rhythmic work in the fields tolerable. Greek terra-
cotta groups show women kneading dough while flute-
players play to them. Sea shanties, work songs
and slave songs serve the same purpose in a much
later time.

The knightly classes, the priestly classes
and the artisans all looked down upon the village
man (or villanus). In many districts the villanus
was not even allowed into the town, and had to
use a middle man in order to gain access to goods
and services available in the town. The townsman
for his part seldom left the town; indeed because
of the animosity between townsman and countryman
it might not have been safe for him to do so. This
led to difficulties, particularly with tools.
These need repair, but in the middle ages no town
wheelwright or smith would feel safe in entering
a village, for fear of his life. The peasant
likewise would not venture into the town. Consequently he might soon be working, literally, with
his bare hands because of his lack of tools.

Such an impossible situation had never happened in Rome, where there had been a particular
street called "Interfalcarios". In this street
were hundreds of sicklesmiths working for their
rural customers, who brought in their tools for
repair and sharpening.

* swink: to labor, toil.

THE PEOPLE'S FOOD

The European peasants' diet in the eleventh century is recorded as consisting of bread, porridge, herbs and roots. If he owned a pig, perhaps he was able to fatten it on acorns, beechnuts, and chestnuts. A way of estimating the value of woods was sometimes to relate it to pigs; thus we hear of "a wood for two pigs".

Wood for two pigs

His few chickens scavenged where they could. He might hunt for rabbits occasionally, and caught fish if he lived near the coast or close to rivers. The vegetables grown were radishes, turnips, onions, and leeks; the greens were cabbage, spinach and cress.

Animals were at a premium, and winter feeding was as yet unknown. In the late fall they would kill off any animals that they had which seemed too weak to last through the winter. They would salt the meat away, rather than have the animals die of starvation. As a result late winter was often a rather difficult time for the family.

Cooking these foods always presented a problem for the peasant. He could not readily introduce fire into his home, for fuel was always scarce and expensive. The food was plain, with none of the sauces and spices which had played such a part in the Roman cuisine. Most of our information about it is found in administrative archives, inventories and ecclesiastical records.

This plain-living society, common in all of north Europe would in general have as their dinner, "bread, water or ale, and that which goes with the bread: "companaticum". The farm family could have a fire, whereas the early town dwellers could not usually afford this luxury. If there was a fire, it was always furnished with the "pot-au-feu"* or cauldron. Into this cauldron went anything that happened to be available: a rabbit, hen or pigeon would give the broth a good meaty flavor. Except in hard times there would be something filling in the pot; a stew thick with the shreads of past dinners, dumplings or rye flour or a piece of pork or game.

This pot would always be there when company arrived, and served as the companaticum. Savory puddings wrapped in cloth were hung from a hook above the fire, and over the cauldron. Some foods would be boiled in various types of containers. In Scotland the sheep's stomach itself was the container, used for making haggis.

Pease puddings were a vegetable pudding into which everything went: peas, lentils, beans, anything you had.

"Pease pudding hot, pease pudding cold,
pease pudding in the pot, nine days old."

Frumenty was a dish made by soaking husked wheat in hot water for 24 hours. It would sit by the fire in an earthenware crock, and when eaten with milk and honey it formed a very nourishing combination. It could be eaten cold, or re-heated for use with fragments of meat from the stock pot.

* Literally: "pot at the fire".

One has the feeling of wholesome but plain fare. In the case of the poorer people, life would be very hard, and food difficult to manage. Langland draws a pathetic picture of the peasants of his day; no chickens, geese, pork or bacon came their way, but two green cheese, curds and cream and a cake or oats. Two hundred years later the people would have been grateful for such a meal. These comparisons are of a different time from ours; but nowadays we should regard such a diet as a pretty fair one.

Regardless of the level of society, fuel for cooking was always a problem. The Phoenicians, Greeks, Egyptians and Romans had all used wood for shipbuilding, and as an aid in national growth and power. The iron age in Greece and Rome had caused the forests to be swallowed up at an alarming rate, which had a great deal to do with the downfall of these great cultures. The erosion which had desiccated Sumer much earlier, would return to haunt later centuries.

But in the north where the new Teutonic kingdoms were situated, there was no shortage of timber, at least for a time. The forests seemed to be endless. But now the metal-workers had first call on the wood supply to make charcoal needed for the smelting of metals. The metals were used for armour, for the King's pewter goblets, and then for shipbuilding. What wood and twigs remained to be gleaned from the trees on the common lands could be used for cooking. The men were allowed to pull down the branches within reach, "by hook or by crook", a practice which was most detrimental to the trees themselves.

Although wheat for bread had become a necessity in all the civilised world of the time, yet it had difficulty in ripening in some of the northern climates. The use of rye became very significant over a large part of Europe, for it was more reliable as a crop. It was the main crop in countries like Poland, where it was used for everyday bread.

155

Many farmers when planting wheat had found
that rye persisted so that it contaminated the
wheat fields. Rather than attempting to weed
out the rye, it became customary to let them
grow together, and to harvest them together. The
two were threshed, ground, and milled together,
to be baked into bread. Such bread, in fact a
mixed bread, was called "miscelin" bread by the
French (from the latin miscere to mix). This
word was corrupted into maslin by the English.
It found favour in the making of pastry. Rye
flour made a pastry which was too difficult to
handle, and barley flour one that was too brittle.
Maslin flour was just right for pastry, and for a
long time it was used in the more sophisticated
homes and baker shops.

The average family obtained their food locally,
and so the cuisine became rather dull. None of
the Roman "liquamen" flavors could reach the poor
crofter's cottage in what is now Scandinavia or
northern Germany. Some herbs and delicacies grew
within the monastery walls, and we know that the
monks kept bees. Because of abstinence rules
monks also kept vivaria for fresh fish. Rabbits
were kept for many centuries in the past, because
the Church had decreed, at some point, that a new-
born rabbit was "not meat". It is noted here
that the Romans had considered new-born rabbits
a delicacy; evidently some remnant of this cultural preference survived within the walls of the
monasteries, during the centuries that followed
the decline of Rome.

The value of eggs was not lost on the people,
as gifts of the kindly saints, to get them through
the many abstinence days. For Christianity impinged
on every aspect of daily life. Even cooking
instructions recommended boiling an egg for "the
length of time it takes to say a miserere."

THE MANORIAL SYSTEM

The lord of the manor became more and more
important in the scheme of living, because it was

he in the last analysis would be responsible for the fact that the people were fed. The anglo-saxon word for the man who owns the soil is "hlaford.' It also comes to mean the one who is the dispenser of gifts, the one who gives out the bread. From this derivation we get our word lord. His wife was the "hlaefdigge", the kneader of the dough, from which we get our word lady.

Life under the manorial system was hard for the peasants. As Tuchman says, besides paying the hearth tax, a clerical tithe, and aids for the lord's ransom, as well as for the knighting of his son and the marriage of his daughter, the peasant owed fees for everything he used; for grinding his grain in the lord's mill; for baking his bread in the lord's oven; pressing apples on the lord's cider press; and many another fee. At death he owed the heriot; this was the forfeit of his best possession to his lord.

Laws were enacted to favor the rich. The right to a animal's manure was written into a law called Jus faldae. The lord could commandeer the manure of animals not his own, in order to enrich his land. But even then yields of crops were rather low; increases of 3 or 4-fold were customary; in other words, eight bushels by sowing two. In times of dearth this was apt to lead to disaster for the peasant and his family, especially in winter.

Chaucer described the plight of his poor widdowe:

"...no win drank she, neither white nor red; here bord was served most with white and black, milk and brown bred, in which she found no lack; seinde bacon and sometimes an ey or twey...."*

Such were her "slender meles". Dairy produce was known as white meats, and was used extensively in

* singed bacon and perhaps an egg or two

mediaeval times. Two hundred years later, in the
reign of Elizabeth I, the poor widdowe's fare
would have seemed almost a plentiful diet, and
as we now realise it was nutritionally very sound.
Black is the rye bread already referred to. Bacon
was often salted down the previous autumn. This
diet is a very good one compared with that of half
the world today.

ADVANCES IN AGRICULTURE

Many changes were due to erupt in Europe
shortly. These were to bring an end to what we
have called the Dark Period. Although the Islamic world was making great strides forward at this
time, Europe as a whole was without commerce,
without cooperation, and without either love or
devotion to a cause.

One of these changes was introduced by the
Slavs in the east. It was a new heavyweight plow,
which cut very deeply into the soil instead of
merely scratching the surface like the hoe and the
early stick plows.

It was known as the mold-board plow, and it
consisted of three moving parts. A knife blade
called the coulter slashed vertically into the
earth; another knife-blade, the plowshare, at
right angles to the coulter, cut horizontally
through the earth at grassroots level. These
two blades constituted the cutting edge, and
behind them was a shaped board called a moldboard.
The moldboard neatly pushed the furrows to one side
as it turned up the topsoil or turf. This plow
was the main instrument that enabled northern
Europe to move out of the Dark Ages into a more
prominent position. For it was now possible to
plow the heavy clay soils of Germany, Holland,
Scandinavia and England. It became possible to
farm great areas of previously unproductive wasteland.

As the centuries passed, this new plow came
to be widely adopted, although its use was limited

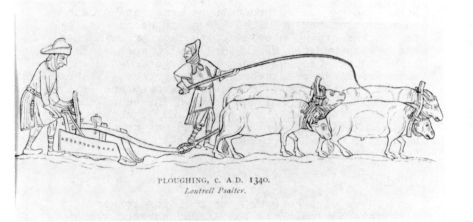

PLOUGHING, c. A.D. 1340.
Loutrell Psalter.

by certain constraints. It was expensive to build
and maintain, and as we have learned in the earlier
description of bovate, as many as eight oxen
might be needed to drag it through those heavy
clay topsoils. It worked well in the wide-open
spaces, but the average farmer could not afford
it. The small landowners came together in a
cooperative way to manage a team jointly, and the
word team came to be used in this connection.
They also merged some of their landholdings. This
meant an entirely new set of relationships, and
led to new social adjustments, and to a sense of
community. That, as much as anything else, lifted
the people out of the chaos that had existed before.

In the times of the Roman empire, crop rotation had been known and practised, every other
year, the land was allowed to lie fallow. However it was several hundred years later before
crop rotation began to be used in Europe. When
it was introduced, the fallow year was practised
one year in three instead of one year in two.
The new system was more productive and yields

increased. Wheat or rye would be planted on one field in the fall; peas, chickpease, lentils, or beans would be planted on a second field in the spring. The third field was left fallow. This arrangement ensured productive farms, and produced more, and better, food. Peas and beans supplemented the grain, providing superior protein that the people had not had before. With such an improved diet, they became more energetic, and in turn, society could become more vigorous. These people, particularly in France, Germany and England, became literally "full of beans." The beans carried the nutrition that grain alone did not supply. The population of Germany in 1100 was reported to be four times what it had been in the days of the Roman empire.

THE HORSE

There were however some problems connected with this agricultural thrust and advance. The team of eight oxen was expensive to maintain. The horse, which had been domesticated on dry lands, and is native to hard, arid areas, was unable to move and function well in muddy areas. As a result it could not pull the new plow, until someone learned to shoe a horse with a heavy iron horseshoe. Then and only then, could he tread in front of the plows of the middle ages. This shoeing of horses had to be done by a smithy, who was already important in the fashioning of farm tools. He understood both the art of shaping a piece of metal, and the physiology of a horse's hoof. It had to be done with a certain amount of tender loving care as well. All of this combined to make the smithy a notable man in those days and for centuries after.

In addition to shoeing horses, the mechanics of pulling a plow was solved when farmers discovered a new kind of collar called a harness. It could be put on the animal so as to take the load off of its throat; it freed the windpipe, and put the strain of pulling the plow back at the shoulders where it belongs. The horse could now

160

show that he was just as effective in
pulling plows as were the oxen, and in addition,
had more endurance.

The horse was also useful because of his
versitility. He could be used for a trip to the
market as well as for pleasure riding. However,
the horse could not thrive on a diet of hay and
grass, as oxen do. And so that third field came
to be planted with oats, which were necessary
for the horse. And after the chores of the day,
the horse could be used for riding and transport.
This helped gregariousness, and the association
of people with one another. This was a very important advance. According to Coulton, the
average village of those days might have contained
400 souls, of all ages. The isolation was so
complete that people would spend their whole lives,
from cradle to grave, in the company of just that
number; apart from a few stray passers-by, there
would be little opportunity to see anybody else.
But the horse provided a new degree of freedom
for the farmer-peasant.

Even if he had the opportunity to go to a
larger town, their location had always been a
problem. For it was a day's walk to market and
a day's walk back, with time wasted in between.
This was now changed, for it was possible to make
the journey much more quickly and therefore much
more often. Whenever the horse could be spared
from the fields, one could use it to go to town.

This in turn led to an increase in the number of customers available to the newly-emerging
towns. Trade expanded, food increased, artisan-
ship spread. The people learned to make many
kinds of implements and tools, as well as articles
of clothing, for commerce. In general the facilities for living were vastly improved.

It was mentioned earlier that during the
Dark Period men were uncertain of their tasks.
One of these tasks was to learn from experience

161

that things could be modified and improved. This
ethos had been in abeyance for centuries.
Now, at last, with the re-emergence of this idea,
society was once again able to thrust forward into
new enterprises.

All advances, however, bring with them certain inevitable disadvantages. The number one
problem in the late middle ages was that of feeding
large numbers of people who could not, or were
not able, to feed themselves. Who was to feed
the smithy, or the tinsmith and his family who
lived in the town? The farmer now had to feed not
only himself and his family, but also increasing
numbers of citizens who were not producing any
food. This was not a new problem. Three thousand
years earlier the Egyptians farmers had succeeded
in producing food for three times their number,
those who were working in hundreds upon those mag-
nificent tombs and buildings.

But it was to be more difficult in the north
to do this. The pressure of population growth on
the limited food supply was to manifest itself in
a number of ways. One of these was a distinct
deterioration in the diet, after 1525 particularly. This will be taken up a little later.

THE TOWNSPEOPLE

What did the townspeople eat? They had to
be content with what they could get that was
brought in from the countryside close by. A
record of the type of fare available to tradesmen
and artisans, dated 1363, has survived. This was
an act which decreed that townspeople be given
meat or fish once a day, and the "offal" of other
victuals* together with milk or cheese, "according to their station." This applied also to the
servants of noblemen. It was certainly a good
diet, except for the lack of vegetables. It was
quite different from anything that the poor vil-
lager was likely to get.

* offal denoted the liver and lights of other
  animals

As for the poorer townspeople, they seldom saw meat, except on important feast days. Bread was, of course, the staff of life, and made up the diet of the poor in both town and village. The bread was coarse, according to one writer: "naturally the villeins have to use flour that is very coarse and made of barley, oats or rye, producing black bread, which makes the noble folk shudder. It is one of the signs of messire's prosperity that all his household are ordinarily fed on white bread..."

The rich had plenty to eat, as many records show; "..the banqueteers have little need of plates. They take loaves lying ready, hack them into thick slices, place the pieces of meat upon them, and cut up the meat while it is resting on the bread"..these tranchoirs would not ordinarily be eaten at the table, but would either go to the great alms basket for the poor, or else would be thrown to the dogs, who seem always to be in attendance at a banquet. Only on special occasions such as wedding feasts would they place pewter or silver plate underneath the bread trenchers. Knives and spoons were used, but forks were as yet unknown. They were not common until much later, the seventeenth century. "God in his wisdom has provided man with natural forks; it is considered impious to substitute them by metallic artificial forks when eating..."

There were many sorts of meat, but no salads, no ices and no confectionery. Soup was much used in those days:

"One cannot stay at the castle long, and not discover the vast importance of soup; one partakes there at least twice a day; dried peas and bacon water; watercress coup; cabbage soup; cheese soup, and poor man's soup. There were fish soups for Lent. All the better soups are spiced with marjoram, sage and sweet basil, if not with the favorite condiment, pepper..."

163

The soup would have one or more sops in it, in proportion to the hosts' generosity.

GROWTH OF THE TOWNS

Those who moved into the new and growing towns had only known life as country peasants. They liked their neat little patches of gardens. But gardens were impossible in the walled town, and they would grow their crops and vegetables there. (This custom persists today in many parts of Europe, where people work their vineyards or other crops outside the town, and return to their homes in town each evening).

The towns themselves were apt to become filthy. The farmer had always lived among his animals, and he continued to do so in the towns inso far as it was possible. The towns thus became thick with mud and manure, and littered with hay, straw and all sorts of refuse. As more and more people swelled the population, these towns became impossibly cramped. Then the newcomers would have to lodge outside the town walls. Dwellings spread farther and farther out, over land that had once grown food. One can see this by noting some of the place names in London: Blackheath, now a suburban area; Smithfield, now in the middle of London; St. Martin's-in-the-Fields, a famous church at Trafalgar Square. This process of suburbanisation has continued until the present day.

MARKETS

As the towns grew so did the markets. These were run originally on a barter basis: for example, people traded apples or day-old chicks, for other goods they needed. As the markets grew, coinage replaced the old barter system. Later still, as people came to desire a wider variety of goods, the markets would supply spices, wines and silks from overseas. Eventually markets became very important trading places. They brought a certain prosperity to the towns, but it was soon evident that some safety precautions would be necessary.

164

Market
Cross,
Chichester
Sussex

Thus developed the "market peace", which sig-
nified an agreement by all concerned "not to mar-
aud, steal, or otherwise corrupt" the operations
of the market. In this new Christian world the
market peace was symbolised by a cross, still
visible in many of the cities of Europe where the
markets used to be, and in some cases still are.
Chichester, Sussex is a notable example. Every
city had its great markets, and ensuring the market
peace was not easy.

Thus it became necessary to regulate the
areas where sales could take place. Different
areas were established where different types of
merchants could set up their wares for sale. This
had long been a practice in Byzantium, and in

parts of Asia where prosperous towns with their bazaars, had existed for centuries. Following the Crusades, the practice was adopted in many of the cities of Europe.

The concept of the itinerant merchant was another idea from the middle east which caught on in Europe after the Crusades. Some merchants, rather than setting up shop in the marketplaces, found it profitable to wander the streets and hawk their wares to householders who had neither the time nor the inclination to go to the market themselves. The powerful guilds, however, resented this free-lance competition, and in 1345 an edict was passed flatly prohibiting, "folks bringing poultry to the city to sell in the lanes, in hostels and elsewhere in secret." The ordinance commanded the out-of-town poulterers to take their fowl "...to Leadenhall, and there sell it and nowhere else." This is the origin of the streetin London called Poultry today, which exists close to Leadenhall. Thus one sees the power of organisation making itself felt to restrain competition, even in 1345.

Just as the merchant guilds knew how to force through those edicts which suited them, so too they knew which they could disregard with impunity. In 1369, for example, Edward III informed the directors of the city of London that he had received grievous complaint from those of his subjects who lived near the shambles (slaughterhouse) of St. Nicholas. The complaint concerned "...the slaughtering of beasts in the said shambles, and the carrying of offal and entrails of the said beasts through the lanes, streets, and places aforesaid, to the bank of the river, where the same entrails and offal are thrown into the water aforesaid." His Majesty said further that grievous filth and corruption had been generated, and he deputized the people to see that it did not continue. Not the slightest attention was paid, despite the King's warnings. Two or three years later, the shambles was still causing "corruption and grievous stenches and abominable sights," and King Edward was still threatening retribution. At the same period, Charles V of France was reporting much the same trouble in Paris.

Not all the cities of Europe suffered such conditions. Florence enacted strict laws regulating the time and place of butchering meat. Smoke nuisances was controlled, and the considerable number of fires from thatched roofs led to the passage of laws requiring the red tile roofs which had been associated with Florence ever since. Furthermore it is recorded that by 1283, Florence had thirty hospitals with more than a thousand beds. Hospitals for the sick, and hospices for travellers were very early combined into one and the same institution. Thus in the fifteenth century, we learn from Tafur, a Moslem traveller in Europe, that "Florence is very clean and well-ordered, its hospitals unequalled in the world..."

And Florence could afford such amenities. There were some eighty banking houses in the city by 1250, and sixty commercial companies by 1300. There was even a postal service which arose out of all this activity. Such was the accumulation of wealth in Italy that the Florentines began to advance large sums of money all over the known world, to kings and to states. They side-stepped the Church law by charging no interest at all on the loan for a specified period, during which time they knew very well that the borrower either could not, or would not, repay the loan. Then they would demand that the whole principal sum be paid up, and assess damages if it were not. Then they would repeat the loan procedure to the same party after a short time.

Not every city was as fortunate as Florence, however. In most cases it was extremely difficult to keep the town clean. As has been mentioned, in the early days, the towndwellers still somehow contrived to keep their own cow,

pigs and chickens. The cows were often shackled,
and the chickens did not wander far. But pigs
would roam the streets and tangle up the early
traffic.

Certain rules were passed; for example,
an early law in Cambridge, England was possibly
the first of its kind. It was enacted in 1388
and stated, quite simply: "He that will have a
pig, let him keep it in his own house." However
the pig was tolerated, because it did provide a
civic function before cities had cleaning depart-
ments.*

"Pigs seem to penetrate everywhere save
into messire and madame's chamber. They
are the general scavengers and apparently
replace plumbing and sewerage systems.
They infest castle courts and the streets
of towns. People tell you that pork
promotes leprosy, but nevertheless they
devour it. Pork is the them the main
substance of those great sausages and
black puddings in which everybody de-
lights, especially at Easter, when
you break your fast with as much heavy
food as possible."

EARLY ATTEMPTS AT FOOD CONTROL

As time went on, the authorities in these
towns began to worry about food quality. One
of the earliest types of food inspection was
carried on in France in the thirteenth and
fourteenth centuries. Official inspectors,
called "langueyeurs"**, were appointed to inspect

* this practice persisted until fairly recently.
  Early accounts of the river settlements that
  became Cincinnati, Ohio, mention that pigs
  would roam the streets of the town. It was,
  no doubt also the case in other early American
  towns and frontier settlements.

** langue, French for tongue

pigs' tongues for ulcers. For ulcers were said to cause leprosy. An old scourge like leprosy, mentioned in the Bible could elicit public support for its control and suppression, because people were afraid of it.

There must have been other and more dire conditions brought about by the state of food brought to the markets of those times. In Venice, the most important trading center of that period, the fish markets came under official scrutiny. The obvious smells arising would certainly attract the attention of the authorities, because it was something that all could agree on.

The guilds insisted that all fish brought in should be taken down to the San Marco and Rialto fish markets for duty payable. The stalls were inspected for stale fish, which, if found, had to be destroyed. But for every offense, it seems, a defense could be found. The use of "fish fags" is an example. In order to outwit authority, one would knock the other down, by pre-arrangement, and a fight ensued. In the general melee, someone picked up a bucket of water, and -- illegally -- sprinkled the fish, which might then pass for fresh. The fish fags would then conveniently disappear into the crowd.

Officials existed to oversee the markets as early as 1319. Sworn warders of the city of London were appointed to "oversee the flesh markets". A record of that time shows them condemning two carcasses of beef for being "putrid and poisonous". The jury afterwards convicted the merchant for "selling bodies that have died of disease".

Punishment was swift, and usually public. William Sperlynge of West Hamme was put into the pillory, and suffered, appropriately enough, the punishment of having the putrid carcasses burnt beneath him. The archives of most European cities of that period are full of instances of

cases being brought against food offenders.
In 1366 one John Russell of Billingsgate was
prosecuted for exposing for sale: "37 pigeons,
putrid, rotten, stinking and abominable to the
human race." He too was duly sentenced to the
pillory, and the offensive pigeons were burnt
beneath him.

Criers would announce when anyone was to be
put in the pillory, and people would assemble
with baskets of bad eggs, decaying vegetables and
rocks, to throw at the offender. Rich prisoners,
and there were some, would pay someone with a
cloth on a long pole to wipe their faces clean,
or else they might suffocate under the wealth
of decomposed matter.

In 1361 Langland in Piers Plowman dealt
with such wrong-doers:

"to punyschen on pillories and pynyng-
stoles brewsteres and bakeris, bochers
and cokes for thise are men on this
molde that moost harme wercheth to the
povere peple.."

Because bread is so important, grain became
a matter of speculation and hoarding in times
of scarcity. In mediaeval times authorities acted
to prevent dealers from going out into the surrounding country to buy up supplies of grain. This
would prevent the available supply from being
displayed before the whole body of consumers
in the public open markets during the prescribed
hours. This practice was known as forestalling.
Forestallers when caught would be brought before
the magistrate, and sentenced to the pillory.
One in Norwich was accused of holding up to 300
quantals of wheat, 60 of rye and 200 of oats.
Punishment was meted out, and it was usually
public.

A number of laws were passed to protect the
purchaser. One of the earliest of these was the

Horttaller and
regrat of markett
and bey res and
vittelars

A FORESTALLER IN THE PILLORY, 1497

First Assize of Bread, enacted in 1261. It regulated the size, weight and price of bread. Most
of the early laws were concerned with quantity
rather than quality. Bread was often seized
as it was brought to market. If short weight
it was confiscated and given to the prisoners at
Newgate prison, a custom that seems to have been
fairly common. It however, the culprit was caught
selling underweight bread, as was quite frequently
the case, the penalty was likewise appropriate.
In London in the fourteenth century a halfpenny
maslin loaf was supposed to weigh 28 shillings.
Records of short weight exist, and the offender
was frequently caught and punished, not only in
the pillory, but:

171

"by being drawn upon a hurdle from the
Guild-Hall to his own house, through the
great streets where there may be the
most people assembled, and through the
streets that are most dirty, with the
faulty loaf hanging from his neck."

For indeed bread was as important as it had
been in Greek times. It had to be baked in com-
munally in ovens in mediaeval times, because nobody could afford an oven in their own home. In
any case, the homes were firetraps, so bread had
to be bought from the bakers. The bakers were
early organised into guilds, which had to approve
all bakehouses. The bread was classified as either
white or brown, and by 1307 there were two bakers'
guilds, one for each type. They were to unite
into one guild two hundred years later.

Long before that time there was to be a
disaster in the world which deferred all thoughts
about man's stuggle for food, merely. He was to
struggle for his own life, even when he had food
enough.

REFERENCES

146   SUMPTUARY LAWS.. Edward III; statute 10.

147   "THE EARTH HAS A LIFE OF ITS OWN.." Columella;
      De Re Rustica. Book II; sections 3 to 7
      (A. D. 70).

147   WATERMILLS: Leeds, E.T. Dark Age Britain (1956).

148   MILLING: Thompson Early History of the Towns,
      English municipal history (1857).

150   LINK BETWEEN MILLERS AND BAKERS: Carpecci,
      A.C. Pompeii 2,000 years ago.

150   THE EARLY GUILDS: Mollat, Michel, and Wolfe,
      Philippe, trans; Lytton-Sells; The popular
      revolutions of the middle ages. (1973).

151 "..THUS BREEDETH MANY BEGGARS BOLD.." Ashley, Sir W. Bread of our forefathers. p 100 (1928).

152 DIFFICULTIES OF THE PEASANTS: Garnier, Russell, Annals of British Peasantry. (1895).

153 "A wood for two pigs.." Vinogradoff, Sir Paul; English Society of the 11th century (1908).

154 COMPANATICUM: Tannahill, Rhey: Food in History; chap 6; The Silent Centuries, p 109 (1975).

156 MASLIN BREAD: Ashley, Sir W; Bread of our forefathers; p 16-20 (1923).

156 RABBITS NOT MEAT. Zeuner, F. E. History of domesticated animals p 412 (1963).

156 "...TO SAY A MISERERE.." Tuchman, Barbara; A distant Mirror, chap 2, p 32 (1979).

157 THE MANORIAL SYSTEM: Bennet, H.S. Life on the English Manor; a study of peasant conditions, 1150-1400, p 184 (1937).

157 HEARTH TAXES AND TITHES: Tuchman, ibid chap 7 p 172.

157 CHAUCER'S POOR WIDDOWE..Chaucer, Geoffrey: Nonnes Priestes Tale (1390).

158 NEW PLOW: White, Lynn; Mediaeval Technology and Social Change, pp 53-54 (1962).

160 "FULL OF BEANS." White, ibid p 72.

160 SHOEING OF HORSES: Derry, T.K. and Williams T; a short history of technology from the earliest times to A.D. 1900. (1960).

161 INCREASED MOBILITY WITH THE HORSE. Mumford, Lewis, The City in History, p 361 (1961).

163 TRENCHERS: from Le Meangier de Paris; translated by Eileen Power; date about 1390 (1928).

163 FORKS AT BANQUETS: Davis, W. Stearns: Life on a mediaeval barony; cookery and mealtimes at St. Aliquis; chap 7 (1877-1930), quoted in Tannahill p 226.

166 SELLING POULTRY.. Riley, H.T. Memorials of London Life, 1276-1419. p 139 (1868).

166 SHAMBLES. 19 Edward III letterbook F, quoted in Riley.

169 "USE OF FISH-FAGS." Athenaeus VI; 5; The Deipnosophists, trans. Gulik.

169 SELLING PUTRID MEAT: 22 Edward III: quoted in Riley.

170 VISION OF PEIRS PLOWMAN, PASSUS III, line 70-84 (1360).

170 PUNISHMENT IN PUBLIC: Langland, William;

171 UNDERWEIGHT BREAD: Carpenter, John, and Whittington, Richard; Liber Albus, (1419); quoted in Riley (1861).

172 BAKERS' GUILDS: Stow, John; A survey of London (1598).

   The population of England in 1086 was said
to be 1.5 million. As the population grew, so did
the villages, both in size and number. Wasteland
was gradually brought into use. By the thirteenth
century a growing number of small tenant farmers
had become independent of the manor. They had purchased their freedom by working for their lord on
a contractual basis for a period of time. The
lord would then cede to them a piece of land, not
to own, but to rent from him. Each farmer could
then work his piece of land in his own way.

   Because of the increase in trade, especially
in wool, the lord needed cash; consequently a
cash system began to replace barter. Service began
to be replaced by cash wages, which the peasant
would remit to his lord in lieu of rent. Thus by
degrees the lord acquired wealth, and the peasant
his freedom.

   This arrangement foreshadowed the end of the
manorial system, and more and more land was disposed of in this way. Thus was formed a group of
independent farmers whom we have called Yeomen,
a new class altogether. The new prosperity ushered in a population surge, such that by 1340 it had
grown to 4 million.

   The fourteenth century did not begin auspic-
iously. The miseries to come were seemingly heralded by early climatic changes. The Baltic sea froze
over in 1303 and again in 1306; storms and high
water in the Caspian sea and intense cold in the
north were evidence of what we now call the Little
Ice Age. Advance of polar glaciers caused effects
which were to last until about 1700. Cultivation
of grain was almost disappearing from Iceland, and
severely curtailed in Scandinavia, affecting adversely the food supplies of settlements. A shorter growing season was disastrous for a growing
population. Soils were not productive and fertilisers were not yet in general use. The result was
that people starved.

In 1315 there was a period of incessant rains, which was compared with the Biblical flood. Crops failed all over Europe, and famine became familiar to all. People who did survive were left vulnerable to hunger and disease.

The misery of the people was compounded by a combination of factors. The Hundred Years' War between France and England, which seemed never to end, entailed staggering costs. Generations of the people had to finance them, in the name of chivalry. The depravity of the knights, their insistance upon crusades and possessions, and their obliviousness to the needs of the time made it worse. Taxation for these enterprises was ruinous. The Church itself, now divided with two popes, one in Avignon, meant allegiances which tore Christians apart. It is no wonder that there had to be a crisis. Its form was not the one expected, although there had been a famine in 1344, and a dearth in 1346. There had also been an outbreak of plague in Florence in 1340, which according to records was to cost the lives of 15,000 out of a population of 80,000. According to Giovanni Villani, the commune in Florence had to assist between 3 and 4 fifths of the population during the famine of 1347. Even so 4,000 died of hunger and the prisons were emptied so as not to have to feed the prisoners. This was at a time when Florence was one of the cleanest and most prosperous cities in the west, as we have already noted.

THE BLACK DEATH

These conditions existed to create a good deal of dissatisfaction at least in Italy and France, before the arrival of the Black Death itself. The descriptions given in Tuchman are vivid, because she gives the story both before and after 1349, so that one is able to trace the events in the context of the arrival of this particular scourge. It is hard to pin down the date at which it all started.

It is said that the plague had already decimated the population of India before arriving in trading ships at Caffa, the port in Europe at which it is reported first. This was a great trading center, and it is recorded that it visited the city in 1346. According to Coulton, it had already done its work, en route. He states: "many galleys were found drifting about the sea with their cargoes, but no living soul on board." The contemporary writer Mattias Neuenburgensis added: "It was the punishment of God."

The results were far-reaching. Since it was spread by rats and then fleas, food certainly played a great part in its occurrence. It spared nobody, and not even the animals. As Boccaccio, in the preface to Decameron has it:

> "the rags that a poor, plague-stricken man had worn were cast into the open street; presently there came two swine, who, according to their wont, first scratched among them with their feet, and then shook them in their jaws. Then they staggered for a while and within a very brief space, as though they had taken poison, both fell to the ground upon those rags among which they had rummaged to their own destruction."

The plague did not spare the well-to-do either, for it had a way of jumping over a castle wall.

Whatever the actual numbers of the dead, and historians differ, it is certain that the world afterwards was a very different place. The population of England is said to have dropped from 4 million in 1340 to 2.5 million in 1377, at which time they took a census.

On the death of William Hastings in 1349, who was Lord of the manor of Benham Valence, the following was quoted:

> "Westbrook is a parcel of the manor, a park with game; there were six customary tenants, all dead now, and their lands

uncultivated."

A later insertion says:

"a sixth part of the pleas and perquisites
of the Court of Newbury, a twelfth part
of the market toll, and a sixth part of
the tan mill; which used before the pestilence to be worth 26/8, but now yields
nothing on account of the deadly pestilence..."

The scarcity of labor itself contributed to
the breakup of the manorial system, and brought an
end to that feudal order of society which had characterised the world for so long. Higher wages were
paid but farming itself suffered a set-back. There
were larger expenditures and less receipts. Servile
tenure came to be replaced by lease-hold, and finally
by freehold tenure. Social changes were however
slower in coming.

The social questions of that period cannot be
understood unless it is remembered that in 1381
more than half of the people in England did not
possess the privileges which Magna Carta had supposedly secured for every freeman over a century
and a half earlier. No wonder the time was ripe
for the Peasants' Revolt, which was led by Walther
the Bricklayer (Wat Tyler to subsequent history),
in 1381. The peasants were still deemed to be serfs,
and looked down upon. They even required their
lord's license in order that their daughter could
marry. But this condition could not last. The
Renaissance was in full vigor on the continent,
and was soon to spread to England.

The labor shortage and the rising prices were
bemoaned by more than one author. In 1375, Gower
wrote:

"the world goeth from bad to worse, when
shepherd and cowherd demand more for their
labor than the masterbailiff was wont to
take in days gone by. Labor is now at so

high a price that he who will order his
business aright must pay 5 or 6 shillings
for what cost him 2 in former times.
Laborers of old were not wont to eat of
wheaten bread and their meat was of coarser corn or beans, and their drink was water
alone. Cheese and milk were a feast to
them, and rarely ate they of other dainties; their dress was of hodden gray...
then was the world ordered aright for
folk of this sort...

Ha! age of ours! whither turnest thou?
for the poor folk who should cleave to
their labor demand to be fed better than
their masters..."

This is an illuminating passage, and serves to
show how the views of people do not change. Much
the same thing was said of the working men and
women in the nineteenth century, when they dared
to raise their voices in protest against intolerable conditions.

According to MacNeil the effects of the Black
Death, and subsequent recurrences (such as the one
in 1385 when a new generation of victims was to be
attacked, whose immunity had not been established),
were severely felt for a long time. It is recorded that the population of 3.7 million in 1340 was
not passed for ten generations, until it reached
3.8 million in 1603.

However that may be, the bubonic plague
(as it has been determined to have been), was to
bring finally to an end a whole society of relationships, and pave the way for new surges forward, as
other discoveries became available.

We shall deal with the importance of the com-
pass to man's food a little later. At present it
is necessary to discuss events closer to home,
which were to have a lasting and detrimental
effect on man's food for centuries to come.

179

WOOL

Of all the changes that were going on at that time, none was more important to the nutrition of the people than the emphasis which came to be placed on the woollen trade.

The production of wool was not a new development in man's history. Weaving as a craft was being carried on in India before the time of Christ. In the old days it was done with abaca, rushes and other kinds of natural fibres. It was in turn based on earlier methods of making baskets, the origin of which is distant and obscure. The Sumerians at any rate were acquainted with this ancient craft.

Weaving cloth was being done by the women in England many centuries ago. When asked what women should be doing as work, Piers Plowman says:

"..An ye wyves that han wolle,
werchath it faste,
Spynneth it spedily,
sparith not your fingris..."

CARDING AND SPINNING, c. 1340.
Loutrell Psalter.

The Flemish wool artisans were famous in Europe during the middle ages. As a result of dissatisfaction at home, partly due to ruinous taxation imposed on Flanders by the French (to whom they were allied by marriage), many of them left Flanders for England, and took with them their advanced methods of carding, spinning and weaving. By 1337 the woollen trade was well established in East Anglia. One result of this was that Norwich grew into a prosperous city, the third in England, after London and York.

In addition to their techniques of weaving, the Dutch also brought with them some advanced methods of gardening, especially of vegetables. They had managed somehow to settle down on their small parcels of land in Holland, and had learned how to derive the very best results from them. They also brought with them the familiar windmills which were to dot the landscape from then on, and were to be a force in the grinding of grain. The long-term results of these changes were to affect the course of people's food supplies in entirely new ways. The effects of these changes are with us today in the twentieth century.

Thus it happened that a very close tie developed between England and Holland, a circumstance which was to be very useful later on when people fled oppression in England and found refuge in Holland, some of them temporarily on their way to America.

WOOL AS A CASH CROP

Advances in the woollen trade heralded the beginnings of a cash crop economy, with its insidious overtones. One of the main reasons for the change was due directly to the effects of the Black Death on the population. Sheep tending needed fewer hands than did other forms of agriculture, and so it was a useful way out of the labor shortage.

The profits from the trade were so tempting
that landowners turned all their available land
over to grazing. Not content to use their own
land, the landowning class requested use of the common

land as well. The Enclosure Acts which were forced through were among the most insidious pieces of legislation ever to be perpetrated on a people. Robert Crowley was to bemoan this situation in 1549:

> "...Cormerantes, gredye gulles; yea men that would eat up menne, women and chyldren are the cause of sedition. They take our house over our heddes, they bye our growndes, they reyse our rentes, enclose our commons..."

Latimer also spoke up strongly from the pulpit against the enclosures.

If the sheep got to the common land first, they could clip the grass very short so that there would be nothing left for the cow. The loss of arable land everywhere caused food shortages and aggravated an already difficult situation. It caused unemployment, and in effect it brought about the downfall of individuality in farming. According to Latimer:

> "...certain causes gathered together, wherein is showed the decays of England, by the great multitude of shepe, to the utter decays of household keeping, maintenance of men, dearth of corn and other notable discommodities..."

Many writers attest to the dire changes that were taking place. In 1581, Stafford wrote his "Discourse on the Common Weal of Englande." In it is this passage:

> "...so that I have known of late a docen plowes within less compasse than 6 myles about me, layde down thes vii yeares; and where xl persons had theyre lyvings, now one and his shepherd hath all."

Sir Thomas More was to say at this time: "the sheep ate up the men, and whole villages were deserted." The common man who lost his grazing land as a result of the Enclosure Acts, also lost his cow; and this was a tragedy indeed:

> "...why sir alasse my Cow is a commonweal to me; for first, sir, she allowes me, my wife and sonne for to banket ourselves withal; butter, whay, curds, cream, sod milk, raw milk, butter milk and sweet milk..."

The effects on people's diets were far-reaching. The diet became low in calcium, vitamin A and fat, as well as in assimilable protein. Present-day analyses clearly show these changes.

The authorities were very half-hearted about the people's complaints in those days. In 1548 Henry VIII did set up a commission to look into the effects of the enclosures since 1485. He died before the commission could report, and his successors did nothing about it.

FOOD OF THE WEALTHY

Inasmuch as standards and norms in food were (and to a certain extent still are) set by the well-to-do, it is necessary to glance briefly at their diets. For the lord of the manor's table, was, after all, to be envied, and emulated if possible.

A certain amount of information has come down to us about the customary meals of the well-to-do and their dependents. In 1470 the household of the Right Excellent Princess Cicill had certain rules to go by in these matters. She was the mother of King Edward the fourth. It states that the Officers of the Household were alone to receive breakfast, and wine with it. The rest of the staff were given no breakfast as such, but instead large amounts of bread and ale. Everybody in the household had dinner and supper. On Sundays, Tuesdays, and Thursdays dinner consisted of beef, mutton and one roast; on Mondays and Wednesdays it was boiled beef and mutton; and on Fridays and Fast Days there was salt fish and two dishes of fried fish. Supper except on Fish days, was to be leyched beef and mutton roast. It is evident that meat was the staple of the diet.

Dated 1512 there is a rather precise list of food in the Household of the Fifth Earl of Northumberland. For breakfast on fast days, my Lord and Lady were served; "furst a loif of bred in trenchers, manchets, a quart of beere, a quart of wine, pieces of salt fish, bacon'd herring; dyshe of sprats." On flesh days the fish was replaced by "half a chyne of mutton; also a chyne of beef boyled." A manchet was a fine wheaten bread rather like a pancake.

It is interesting to note the meals given in the Nurcy of the same house, for "my Lady Margaret and Maister Ingeram Percy. For breakfast a manchet, a quart of bere, a dysche of butter, a pece of saltfish, a dysshe of sproittes, or iii white herryng." This was on fish days; on flesh days iii mutton bonys boyled was given instead of fish dishes. We shall have more to say about the feeding of children.

From another source an Elizabethan dinner at home might consist of; "a piece of bief, a loyne of veal, 2 chickens, oranges and sauce." Oranges were a luxury, and were probably used for flavor, and for marmalade which has been a favorite ever since. In 1597 there is a record of a purchase of two pounds of marmalade for five shillings and twopence. Oranges were sometimes called "portynggales", because they were imported from Portugal.

As we proceed further into the sixteenth century, we find references to the larders of the big manor houses. There were many types of meats; eggs, butter, cheeses and beans; bacon, ling, saltfish, capons, hens, ducks, plovers; mutton, vinegar and wine. Pepper was available although it was still expensive. Occasionally there is mention of a little sugar in these records. There is hardly any reference to fruits and vegetables. But raisins, prunes and currants appear for the first

time. These had been known in the Moslem world for
centuries; gradually the tables of the rich would
begin to reflect the new contacts with the east.

These references reflect the fact that the
people at this level were eating a very high proportion of meat and fish, with an abundance of
protein. By comparison with later days, it seems
affluent indeed. The rich then, as now, were given
to a certain amount of ostentation, as had happened
in Roman times. This extravagance was not just
a matter of state; it was a matter of Church. After
the excesses of the fourteenth century, in which
the Church had participated fully themselves, there
was an effort at reform, if anything promoted by
the secessions in the church itself. These excesses
in the matter of food were supposed to be curbed.
Archbishop Cranmer during the time of Henry VIII
ordained that churchmen at least should have some
limitations placed upon their food. Accordingly
he ordained that an archbishop should have.."not
more than 6 flesh dishes followed by not more than
4 second dishes." Bishopes should be limited
respectively to 5 and 3; deacons 4 and 2, and the
lesser orders 3 and 2. These ordinances followed
the already established hierarchies of the Church;
but it reinforced them by equating office with the
type of food they could get. These types of
lavish meals were for the few. The townsman might
have three meals a day, but more often he would be
limited to two. And they would be on a more modest
scale, without the variety. But what of the ordinary man? He figures so little in many history
books. Yet it is his food and his struggle to get
it which is our subject.

CHANGES IN TUDOR TIMES

The village people were not so well off as
they had been a century earlier. Even the techniques of gardening which had been in use during the
fourteenth century, were allowed to fall into
disuse. One author, who wrote a history of gardening in England, claims that this decline was in
part due to "a still lingering taste for hunting,

186

chivalry and war; by Crusades to the Holy Land, and just as wild expeditions to the Continent." At least a book on Mediaeval Gardens by One Master Ion Gardener, dated about 1440, lists 78 plants suitable, but most of them herbs. He lists the vegetables of importance as "rotys for a gardyne; naming parsnepys, turnepez, karettes and betes; but usually only onions, garlic, leeks, and spinach, cabbage."

The Dutch as we have seen were to teach the English about market gardening all over again when they came into contact over the woollen trade. However, although the peasant had hardly any meat, he sometimes had bacon. Eggs were as a rule plentiful. Hence the development of the very English dish of ham and eggs, which has been a feature of their diets ever since. The doctor in Piers Plowman ate "egges fryed with grece on heighe dees." Andrew Boorde speaks of "collopes and eggs".

Early in the sixteenth century times had been good, as we have learned already. Food was abundant and cheap; two good-sized loaves could be had for a penny, a pound of butter cost twopence, and two chickens the same amount. In 1525 the changes began. Prices rose, accompanied by only a small increase in wages. In 1603 the two chickens cost six pence; a goose which had cost four pence in 1515 cost one shilling and fourpence in 1597; that is four times as much. As a result of the Enclosure Acts, coupled with the emphasis on wool, less and less milk was consumed by the average family. Meat came to be reserved for only special occasions, and then it was apt to be old mutton, a by-product of the woollen trade. More bread and cheese were consumed, and these became staple foods, at least until the nineteenth century.

A grim picture of conditions was drawn by one H. P. Platt, Esq., in 1596, entitled: "Sundrie new and artificiall remedies against famine, written upon the occasion of the present dearth." Those who were short of corn, were recommended to "boile

your beans, peases, beechmast, etc., in fare water..
at the second or third boyling you shall find a
strange alteration in taste; for the water hath
sucked out and imbibed the greatest part of the rank-
ness. Then you must drie them and make bread thereof." One can imagine what kind of bread this was.
And when these sources gave out you did not lose
heart, "for you can make excellent bread of the
rootes of starch of the wild lily from the hedge-
rows."

This description was not exaggerated, as many
other authors have painted similar pictures. There
were always speculators who stored grain in order
to raise prices, beef and mutton even became so
expensive that no poor man could ever afford them.
Sir William Forrest, makes a comment on this point:
"Our english nature cannot live by rotes, herbys
or such beggerybaggage". He insists that one must
give Englishmen "meat after their own usage, beef,
mutton, veal, to cheer their courage." But this
could not happen during the times of the Tudors.
The villagers had to fall back on the simple diet
of much earlier times; bread, peases and beans;
and what they could trap in wood, field, river or
pond. White meats (i.e. milk products) were now
out of the question entirely.

In addition to the woes of the country, there
was considerable debasement of the coinage, ostensibly carried out in order to provide inflated money
for the expeditions against Spain and other compet-
itors. This inflation, unlike some of the other
difficulties we have mentioned, affected those with
money as well as those without. Their investments
were worth less than formerly. This was the price
they had to pay for military aggrandisement. For
this was at the same time as the glorious exploits
of Drake, Hawkins, and Frobisher were being touted
all over the realm.

For the reign of Elizabeth I did indeed bring
about a depression, and a considerable amount of
insecurity. As prices rose so did unemployment.

QUEEN ELIZABETH, A.D. 1558.
the Order of S. Michael and S. George (Public Record

England began again to be overrun with numbers of
rogues and vagabonds, who often had to steal and
commit other crimes in order to keep body and soul
together. Thus began a serious problem which is
still with us today. We can appreciate a piece
called Churchyard's Challenge, dated 1593:

"England was called a librell countrey,
rich that tooke great joy in spending beefe
and bread indeede the day the countrey
spendeth mich, but that expense stands
poore in little stead. For they finde
nought where hawks and hounds are fed

189

but colde, hard posts, to leane at in
great lacke who wants both foods and
clouts to cloth their backe."

Primitive types of poor law legislation were
introduced in the reigns of Henry VIII and Edward
VI. Some of them were to have a lasting influence,
although we might not recognise the one in question.
It seems that while driving around the streets of
London in his carriage, Henry VIII saw poor children running around in rags, and getting in the way
of traffic, ostensibly of his own carriage. He
determined then and there that there should be
places where such children could go to school; as
we know he was no mean scholar himself. Accordingly he founded a school which came to be known as
Christ's Hospital, although it never was a hospital.
It survived in London until, the early twentieth
century, when it was moved down to the country,
near Horsham in Sussex, where it now is. The
aspect of this school which comes down to us from
Henry VIII is that it was always decreed that those
with wealth should not be eligible to go to this
school. This has persisted, and has in fact enabled
a large number of under-privileged boys to get the
training that such a school affords.

A severe dearth occurred in 1587; accordingly
a type of poor relief was instituted. It took the
form of the sale of grain at lower prices, the
grain having been bought up by the Grocers' Company
or other big guilds. For at least ten years after
this there was enormous privation among the poor.
In 1591 the city fathers of Norwich, as we know
one of the wealthiest towns in England, spent 200
pounds to buy rye from Denmark, to be sold, they
said, "at the cheap rate of 4 shillings a bushel."
to the half-starved poor. But 4 shillings a
bushel was far out of their reach, so they still
starved. For this represented 1½ pounds of rye
for a penny. In 1525 they had got two chickens
for a penny. This type of assistance was a far cry
from the annona of Roman times, and less satisfactory for the poor.

In addition to schools, a number of charitable institutions were founded in those days. One such was the House of Correction at Bury. Records show that they had three diets. The following is an excerpt from the rules:

> "Item; it is ordered that every person who is committed to the said house shall have for their diets their portions of meat and drink following, and not above: that at every dinner and supper on flesh days bread made of rye, 8 ounces troy weight with a pint of porridge; a quarter of a pound of flesh and a pint of beer; and every fish day a like quantity of either milk or peas; a third part of a pound of cheese or one good herring, or two white and red according as the keeper of the house shall think meet..."

But at the end there is this disciplinary message: "It is ordered that such persons as will apply their work shall have allowance of beere and a little bread between meals; but they which shall not work shall have no allowance until they conform themselves to the work." This was a very good diet, far better than any of the poor people could possibly afford on their own. Hence arose the desire to get a place in such a house of correction, if only to be fed relatively decently. This is a very early instance of what was later to be called "coddling the poor"; an attitude which is present today when people who are well-to-do decry the emergence of "the welfare state".

191

REFERENCES

175   POPULATION OF ENGLAND; Peake, Harold: The
      English Village: XII. The Decay of the
      Manor (1922).

175   LITTLE ICE AGE: Tuchman, Barbara; A Dis-
      tant Mirror, chap 2 p 24 (1979).

176   MISERY OF THE PEOPLE: Mollat, Michael, and
      Wolfe, Philippe, Popular Revolts of the
      Middle Ages: trans A. Lytton Sells (1973).

176   "BEFORE THE ARRIVAL OF THE BLACK DEATH ITSELF.."
      Tuchman, Barbara. ibid p 119 (1979).

177   ARRIVAL OF THE BLACK DEATH AT CAFFA: Coulton,
      G.G. The Black Death, p 9 (1929).

177   EFFECT ON SWINE: Boccaccio, Giovanni; Tales
      of the Decameron, The First Day, chap I
      p 2.

177   "ALL DEAD NOW AND THEIR LANDS UNCULTIVATED".
      Chanc. Inquisitio post mortem; 23 Edward
      III 37.

178   PEASANT'S REVOLT: Mollat and Wolfe; ibid
      chap 4 pp 184-208.

178   "THE WORLD GOETH FROM BAD TO WORSE." Gower;
      quoted Ashley, Sir W: Manorial and agra-
      rian history during the middle ages (1894).

179   POPULATION CHANGES. McNeil, W. H. Plagues
      and People, p 136 (1976).

180   SPINNING WOOL: Langland, William: The Vis-
      ion of Piers Plowman; passus 6 line 10
      (1362).

181   GARDENING FORM HOLLAND: Crisp, Sir Frank:
      Mediaeval Gardens (1924).

183 "CORMERANTES, GREDYE GULLES.." Crowley,
Robert: The Way to Health; Tudor Economic
Documents (1550).

183 "CERTAIN CAUSES GATHERED TOGETHER.." Latimer,
Master Hugh; Seven Sermons before Edward VI
(1549-50).

183 COMMONWEAL OF ENGLAND: Stafford, William;
Discourse on the Commonweal of England
(1581).

183 "THE SHEEP ATE UP THE MEN." More, Sir Thomas,
quoted in Coulton, ibid p 72.

184 "ALASSE, SIR, MY COW.." Dodge, Thomas and
Greene, Robert, A looking Gasse for London and England (1598).

184 LOSS OF NUTRITION: Drummond J.C. An Englishman's Food p 29 (1939).

184 PRINCESS CICILL'S HOUSEHOLD. Warner, Rev
R. from Antiquitas Culinariae (1791).

185 EARL OF NORTHUMBERLAND, HENRY ALGERNON PERCY:
The regulations and establishment of the
Household, (1512), ed T. Percy (1827).

185 FOOD IN THE NURCY. Drummond and Wilbraham.
ibid p 61.

185 PORTYNGGALES. Diary of Henry Machin (1550-
1564).

185 LARDERS OF THE BIG MANOR; Woolaston Hall,
Nottinghamshire 1587-88; Middleton, Lord;
Historical Mss Commission 1911.

186 "A STILL LINGERING TASTE FOR HUNTING.."
Johnson, G. W. A history of gardening in
England (1829).

187 COLLOPES AND EGGS. Boorde, Andrew; A compendious Regyment, or a Dyetery of Helth
(1542).

187   PRESENT DEARTH. Platt, H.P. Esq., Sundrie
      new and artificial remedies against famine,
      written on the occasion of the present
      dearth (1596).

188   "HERBYS OR SUCH BEGGARYBAGGAGE." Forrest,
      Sir William (1548). The Pleasant Poesye
      of Princelie Practice.

189   "ENGLAND WAS CALLED A LIBRELL COUNTRIE.."
      Churchyard, T: Churchyard's Challenge.
      (1593).

12.   FOOD ASPECTS OF THE NEW MARKET TOWNS

The development of new towns and cities, and
the increase in size of those already in existence,
like Paris and London, brought a new set of problems
to the ordinary people. One was that they had to
buy food rather than grow it. A second was the poor
quality of some of the food exposed for sale. A
third was that there were (and are) always those
who will take advantage of their fellows, by cheating
or otherwise defrauding them of value.

Although as we have seen there were some early
attempts to safeguard the public in matters of food
spoilage, yet the people had to rely on their own
means of protection. One of these was their sense
of smell. Odors are easily discernable in very
small quantities, and since odor was thought to
transmit disease the mediaeval nose was very sensi-
tive to it. But the smell of decay was everywhere.
So how was the average man to be sure of getting
food for his family?

One way out of this was to have the meat or
fish cooked. But the poorer townspeople had no
cooking facilities, as we have already noted. There
was great difficulty in having home fires, at
least until the eighteenth century, with the development of closed ranges for the kitchen.

And so it is a feature of this time that a
number of cookshops appeared in the cities. Such
cookshops were not new. They had existed in
Mesopotamia in the time of Nebuchednezzar. Certainly they had existed in Persia, Afghanistan and the
middle east since the early Islamic times, and
possibly before that. They were a logical necessity
on the overland trade routes between the middle
east and China, when many travellers had need of
them.

And so the cookshops appeared in Europe, and
the poorer townspeople might buy ready-cooked meat
from them. There was such a cookshop in London in

1183, of which it was said:

> "according to the season you may find viands,
> dishes roast, fried or boiled; fish great
> and small; the more delicate for the rich,
> the coarse flesh for the poor..."

It will be noticed again that there is a class
distinction in food. The same passage goes on to
say:

> "if friends weary of travel should of a sudden
> come to any of the citizens, and if it is
> not their pleasure to wait fasting until
> fresh food is brought to them, and cooked;
> then they will hasten to the river bank,
> and there all things desirable are ready
> to their hand..."

This is an early notation of the fast-food
service of our day. But it is quite different from
the companaticum and the pot-au-feu, which was the
way of entertaining guests in the old days, when
they should "of a sudden, arrive".

The use of a fire inside the house was fraught
with danger. In London and other cities, the houses
would have burned down long ago, made as they were
of wood. Gradually houses in towns came to be
made of stone, and later, of brick. In the meantime town dwellers would do without fires and these
cookshops were most essential.

Prices that could be charged were strictly
controlled by the mediaeval scheme of Just Price.
This was a precaution instigated by the Church which
permitted no man to make more than a bare living
from the sale of his produce or merchandise. Cooks
were allowed to charge only a penny for the trouble
of enclosing a capon or a rabbit in a crust. Although prices are not accurately known, it was recorded that a leg of roast mutton cost a penny in
1361; this was one day's wages for an agricultural
laborer. Three whole pigeons were likewise to be
had for a penny. And any customer could have his

own capon baked in a pasty if he paid six-tenths of a penny for "the paste, fire and trouble."

As such cookshops appeared more and more in the cities, the temptation to use tainted meat in the preparation of cheap pies and pasties became correspondingly great. Detection was then almost impossible, because much, if not all, of the odor had been removed during the cooking. What flavor there was left could be covered up, if not eliminated by the use of spices.

The spice trade was to develop greatly following the opening up of the trade routes by sea to India and other spice sources. The popularity of seasonings, especially in the Germanic areas of Europe is undoubtedly due in part to the frequency with which it was necessary to mask taint. And spices added relish to the salted meats which were used during the winter months.

Among the most important spices pepper has a significant place. It has been important ever since 3,000 pounds of it had formed part of Alaric the Goth's ransom for Rome. During the eleventh century, there arose a guild whose purpose was to see to it that valuable food adjuncts were controlled. This guild was called the Worshipful Company of Pepperers, who were given charge of the Great Beam, or Peso Grosso. This was the most accurate scale for weighing known in those days. It was accordingly used for weighing pepper and other valuable spices, which commanded such high prices that they needed correspondingly accurate weighing. The Peso Grosso was supervised by the Freemen of the Mistery of Grocers, as the grossarii came to be called in English. They assumed authority and power of supervision over imported spices, which were now to include sugar, still a luxury item. In Edward I's time sugar was one shilling a pound, as much as a poor man might save in a year. Sugar arrived in Europe from India and Arabia, and only the wealthy could ever buy it. Only when the alternative trade routes to the Orient were opened, after

Vasco da Gama, did the price of sugar begin to drop.

VENICE

It is important at this stage to mention Venice,
which had been a pillar of trade, before, during and
after the Crusades. At these times the Venetians
contrived to placate both the Arab traders and the
Christian crusaders. The Venetians found out how
to improve sea-going vessels, and made ships with
three masts instead of one. The rough northern seas
which had to be traversed in order to satisfy the
trade of the new northern nations required a different kind of ship from those used in the calmer
Mediterranean. The problem of manipulating two or
even three, rows of oars was acute in the rough
seas, and the new ships overcame this.

Venice kept up its trade with Byzantium to
expedite trade with the nations further east. But
Byzantium was often at war with the Arabs, so that
trade routes were frequently disrupted. Two
countries which were very hard hit by this state of
affairs were Spain and Egypt. Many sea routes were
abandoned altogether and much of the Mediterranean
became a backwater. In 1100 and 1200 only Venice
seemed to be thriving. Most of the European trade
that did exist had to go through Venice, out past
Greece and Constantinople and finally overland to
Baghdad. Returning, caravans would proceed from
Baghdad to the Black Sea ports, where the goods would
be transferred to ships and taken to Constantinople
through the Sea of Marmora. Thence they would sail
past Greece and up to Venice, capital of the western trading world.

Pepper, cloves, cinnamon, sugar; medicines of
various kinds prepared fromherbs; costly and exqui-
site silks...all came to Venice. Thence they made
their way up the Po valley to Pavia and over the mountains by various routes to areas now known as Switzerland, Austria and Germany. In return, the northern
states, members of the Hanseatic League, produced
furs, fish, amber, tallow and wood for trade with
the east.

Venice had built its prosperity originally on salt. This vital commodity was obtained from their lagoons, and enabled them to build a strong position in the trading world. Ultimately Venice was to provide food supplies, and engines of war as well. Arms and latest types of siege engines were being made around Venice at the time of the Crusades. They were supplied to the Crusaders, who elected to travel as far as possible by ship in later crusades, after the disaster of the first crusade in 1099.

Thus Venice gradually turned the Arabs out of their dominant position in the spice trade, and the Venetians came to monopolise it. They took such an autocratic grasp of it that other countries were later driven to try to break the Venetian monopoly.

The immediate cause of the changes to come was the fall of Byzantium to the Turks in 1453, followed three years later by the fall of Athens. For four more centuries the Ottoman empire was to rule in Constantinople, and the city became the center of Moslem culture and power. Thus trade routes were blocked to the Christian nations, and enterprising men had to seek other routes.

Price Charles the Navigator, of Portugal discussed these problems with Vasco da Gama, who eventually sought, and found, a route to India and the east around the base of Africa. His objective was to locate the spice islands, both for himself and for Portugal. He arrived at Calicut, India in 1498. In the space of the next twenty-five years Portugal was to hold as firm a grip on the spice trade as the Venetians had held earlier.

In the year 1523 a decree was issued at Nuremburg, complaining that 2,000 tons of pepper had come into Germany from Lisbon alone, and that "the King of Portugal has set prices as he will, for at no manner of dearness will it rest unsold among the Germans."

For spices were valued for their own sake, and were used in many ways, not just for masking odor.

They were used in embalming and in medicines. But
their chief value was that they tickled the palate
and stimulated the thirst of people who lived in
an age without tea, coffee, snuff, tobacco or tropical fruit. They were also useful as a back-up
currency. Even in early days Langland's Piers
Plowman has a reference to it. The tavern-keeper
asks Gluttony: "Hast thou ought in thy pors,?
quoth he, "any hote spices?" "Yea, gossib, I have
pepyr and pyanye, and a pound of garlek, and a farthing worth of fenel for fastyng dayes."

The Dutch began to whittle away at the Portugese monopoly, and by 1599 the price of pepper in
England had risen from 15 to 40 pence a pound. At
that time a group of merchants assembled in London,
seeking ways to overcome the Portuguese and Dutch
monopolies. They formed the East India Company,
heralding a future for the British in India which
could not even be guessed at the time.

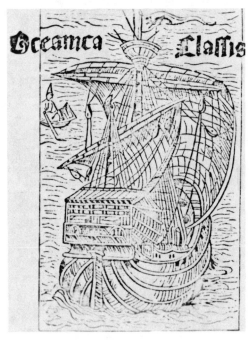

Early ship

And at the same time that Vasco da Gama made his historic trip around Africa, the Spaniard Magellan made his voyage around Cape Horn and finally arrived in the Phillipines. The way was now open for the Spanish to go west for their empire, and this was to have enormous consequences for the world's food.

FISH

Man has used fish as an article of diet from the earliest times. Before the introduction of the bow and arrow, he had attempted either to spear them with a harpoon-like implement, or to club them insensible when occasion permitted it. Fishing had been an individual enterprise, and remained so until fairly recent times.

During the building of overseas empires such as the Greek and Roman fishing became significantly more important. The numerous fishing boats could be used for defence in times of war, and serve also as backup supply boats.*

In the days of overseas explorations to the Americas and Asia the fishing industry was a very large undertaking. No longer an exclusively individual affair, the authorities encouraged fishing, in order to help in the ship-building trade, and to stimulate the training of mariners, "for the maintenance of convenient numbers of seafaring men."

The North Sea, the Baltic Sea and the English Channel were very large resources of sea food of many kinds, especially cod and herring. Herring became a staple of north European diets, and had remained so ever since. In the fourteenth, fifteenth, and sixteenth centuries there were many large centers for the fishing trade: Yarmouth and Scarborough in England and Briel in Holland.

* It is worth noting that the evacuation of thousands of British from Dunkerque in 1940 would not have been possible without the use of every fishing smack available.

Fish was caught in the Thames in those days, even at London Bridge.* The size of the mesh was fixed by law and the punishment for using a net with too small a mesh was appropriate enough:

> "...the xxii day of Marche dyd a woman ryd about Chepesyd and London frr bryngyng young frye of divers kinds unlawful, with a garland upon her hed with stryngges of the small fysse..."

Such exposure to ridicule was much used in those days in order to bring people into line.

SALT

Fish has to be eaten soon after it is caught, for otherwise it quickly develops taint. We have already seen instances of the attempts to control this abuse of the food supply.

Taint was no problem in the old days when man lived by hunting and fishing, because he and his family were always ready to eat what had been caught. But in the periods of exploration food had to be taken on long voyages, thereby necessitating some form of preservation. In addition the growth of new towns gave rise to markets where unsold food would frequently rot, giving rise to many problems of disease and sanitation. When the authorities tried to cope with this issue, fresh fish in particular came under scrutiny, as we have already seen. The procedure of using salt to help to preserve food, especially meat and fish, now becomes very important.

The origins of salting are obscure, but it is known to date back at least to Egyptian times. There arose a cultural connection between the use

* For several centuries it was impossible to catch a live fish in the Thames at London, until the latter part of the twentieth century, when pollution control of water finally rendered the water pure enough for fish.

of salt for embalming the bodies of the dead, and its use in preserving food for the living. In Egypt food was put into the tomb along with the body of the deceased, together with a number of familiar articles, so that the person could continue his activities as he passed over to the other side. The other side refers to the other side of the Nile from Karnak, to the Valley of the Kings where the burial grounds and the tombs were located.

The Egyptians ran a thriving trade in salted and dried fish. Later on fish was salted for use in Spain in the time of Hannibal, as recorded by the historian Strabo. In Roman times Gaul was noted for the excellence of its salted and smoked hams. But the culture of Christianity was to have more to do with the salting business than even the most optimistic Roman tradesman could have foreseen.

FISH AND LENT

The increasing importance of salt as a result of the rules of Christendom led to further developments in the fish trade. For fish was not easy to obtain inland, and the Church's rules had to be obeyed. Even as late as the sixteenth century, failure to abstain from meat on days of fast and abstinence could theoretically lead to a hanging, although this was soon abandoned. The penalties were nevertheless fairly severe, unless you were allowed a dispensation; such a person could be exempted from the rule, but on the following type of condition:

> "...provided also that all persons which by reason of notorious sickness would be forced through recovery of health to eat flesh for the time of their sickness, shall be sufficiently licenced by the Bishop of the diocese or the parson or the curator, where such a person shall be sick..."

This long sentence at least indicated the prevailing idea that you might have to eat meat for your health.

> "...And if by virtue of extreme youth,
> extreme old age or sickness you could
> not fast, then there was no fault in
> you..."

There were other, secular, reasons for keeping
the rules of the Church. The fast days of Lent,
as well as Fridays during the rest of the year
number over twenty percent of all the days of the
year. A proclamation dated 1595 enumerated "the
benefits that grow to this realm by the observation of fish days." It pointed out that by one
days' abstinence from meat per week, "the citie
of London would yield a saving of 135,000 head
of beefe per yeare." Harrison had already in 1557
referred to the eating of fish as a national advantage, "to the end that numbers of cattell may
be better increased, and the abundance of fish
which the sea yieldeth shall become generally
received." For the dearth of meat at that time
had resulted in very high prices.

But even so it was possible in the time of
Elizabeth I to obtain a special license to eat
flesh on fish days:

> "...Lords of Parliament and their wives
> shall pay for a license 26/8 yearly to
> the poor man's box in their parish; knights
> and their wives shall pay 13/4; persons of
> lesser degree 6/8; provided that no lic-
> ense extend to the eating of beefe at any
> time of the yeare, nor of veal between
> Michaelmas and May 1st..."

This special license therefore allowed only
mutton, lamb or pork, thus helping to conserve the
necessary beef.

Ordinary men and women could not afford to buy
such indulgences, but they were however supplied
with liberal advice on how to conduct themselves
with regard to fast and abstinence. Thomas Tusser

is credited with a tract published in 1580 called "Five hundred pointes of good Husbandrie.", setting forth advice for the seasons of Lent, Easter, Midsummer, Michaelmas, Halloween and Christmas.

THE EARLY GUILDS

During this period when fish was becoming increasingly important, the Fishmongers' Company became powerful. Sales were regulated, and pickled herrings, for example, were to be sold at 9 for a penny, and no higher. But when traders were caught selling them to hucksters at 5 for a penny, the offender was fined; the Fishmongers' Company saw to it that the price of 9 for a penny was reinstated and maintained. Instances of this sort illuminate the period for us, as we try to understand how the average man had to struggle to buy food for his family.

As has already been mentioned, the Pepperers became the purveyors of spices, and were entrusted with the function of their accurate weighing. But they were not above sharp practices and were sometimes caught at it, as they sifted and weighed their spices. The Arabic word for sifting is gharbea; in Italian this became garbellare. Hence our word "garbled" for all mixed up. Much of our language is based upon concepts related to food.

In due time the salt and pepper trade became amalgamated, and the Salters' Company, which had been founded in 1394, merged to become the Worshipful Company of Salterers and Pepperers.

MAN'S NEED FOR SALT

To conclude this section it may be well to point out that the need for salt in the diet was known long before its use as a preservative. Man and animals have a craving for salt that has to be satisfied in order to preserve the balance of the body fluids. Hence man and animals have always had to learn how to obtain it, especially in the arid areas of the world where its need is even more pronounced than it is in humid regions.

Early man could find out where salt was located
by watching the animals, which would lick certain
mineral deposits. But the best source for wild
animals is the blood of their prey. As mentioned in
an earlier chapter, an animal after the kill will
suck the blood as long as it flows, after which it
will tear out the liver and spleen, both rich in
blood, and eat them. In this way he protects himself against both salt deprivation and anemia.

After having found salt, early man used it as
a lure in order to entice animals to approach their
camps. This, as we have seen, led eventually to
the domestication of certain animals, the reindeer
particularly.

In historical times salt has been obtained
from salt springs, from mines below the ground,
and by evaporation of sea water. This last method
was used by Venice in the early days, and is still
the method used today on both the east and west
coasts on India. In this latter case, salt would
have to be carried into the interior of the country, where often the important cities were situated; such as Agra, Baghdad, Florence, Madrid, Damascus, Cairo. It was usually carried on the backs
of slaves, and it was frequently possible for a
slave to earn his remission in this way. From
this arose the phrase: "A man is worth his salt."

The meat-eating nations have enough salt as
a result of their diet, but the vegetarian has to
look elsewhere for his salt. But because of his
craving for it, man and animals on the whole get
enough of it. The question nowadays is whether
or not he gets too much salt.

However, it is important to realise that
grains have been, and are still, the basic life
support of the vast majority of the world's
people. It is therefore appropriate to turn our
attention to man's grains before proceeding with
the discoveries of the Renaissance period.

REFERENCES

195 COOKSHOPS IN LONDON: Fitzstephen, William.
A description of London, ca 1183; quoted
from Dodd.

197 "THE PASTE, FIRE AND TROUBLE." Riley, H.T.
Memorials of London Life 1276-1419 (1868).

197 EDWARD I AND SPICES: Salzman, L.F. English
trade in the Middle Ages (1931).

197 GROSSARRII: Drummond and Wilbraham p 37.

201 "FOR THE MAINTENANCE OF CONVENIENT NUMBERS
OF SEAFARING MEN.." William Harrison:
Description of England, 1557.

202 "..WITH STRYNGGES OF THE SMALL FYSSE.."
Diary of Henry Machin 1550-1563.

203 SALTING OF FISH IN SPAIN: Forbes, quoted
in Tannahill p 211.

204 "SAVINGS OF 135,000 HEAD OF BEEFE PER YEARE.."
Drummond and Wilbraham, p 64 (1939).

204 ".LORDS OF PARLIAMENT AND THEIR WIVES..."
Tudor Economic Documents, Vol II #71
ed. Tawney and Power, 1924.

205 FIVE HUNDRED POINTES OF GOOD HUSBANDRIE.."
Thomas Tusser, 1580.

We are becoming increasingly aware in this story that bread has now supplanted meat as man's staple article of diet. In fact it was to be known in later years as the staff of life.

It is therefore not out of place at this stage to review briefly man's grains. The oldest was Father Millet, which fed men and their gods long before the plow. It was used in China and in early India at least as long ago as 2,800 B.C. At the time of established agriculture in India, the time of Moenjodaro, barley assumed great importance. It is said that it was brought down to India from the mountainous regions of the northwest. The Aryans decreed that the food of the subject Indian races, which was rice, was not appropriate for their men; so they brought their own grain.

Barley thus became established in India, so that Vedic literature referred to barley and rice as the "two immortal sons of heaven". Accordingly barley became the diet of strong men, and it deposed millet. Later on Homer's Greeks roasted barley and sprinkled it on their meat. They were contemptuous of the Scythians, who ate oats like their horses did. This difference however illustrates very well the attitudes of the nomadic types as distinct from the settled river civilisations. The former loved and admired their animals, and knew them by name. Under no circumstances would they raise them to eat. Later on, men would come to despise draught animals as servile creatures; and who would wish to eat the same food as they did?

And in addition, oats as a staple crop was unsatisfactory, becoming "wild" too often, and scattered by the wind. Since it was not sown by the hand of man, it came to be despised by him. But it was an excellent livestock feed; and this was to give oats its later place in our lives.

It was left to the Egyptians to make real advances in man's food, namely the discovery of risen

bread. Most of man's early grains had to have a
preliminary toasting on heated floors before they
could be satisfactorily threshed. However this
procedure subjected the crucial proteins to changes
before they were put in contact with yeast, so that
instead of being elastic they were hard, and could
not therefore respond to the leavening action of
yeast.

But when wheats were produced which could be separated into grain and chaff without heat, leavened bread was possible. The actual discovery was possibly accidental. Favorable organisms happened to drift into a dough made of this new wheat. Left to one side, it rose, just a little perhaps, but enough to make the ultimate bread lighter and more appetising than usual. As so often in the ancient world, enquiring minds set about the task of producing deliberately what had been found out by accident. At first they would have skimmed the beer foam for the purpose of providing the yeast; for beer had preceded risen bread by millennia. Sumer at its height had produced eight different kinds of beer. Barley has been called "drink corn" ever since.

Thus it was that in the development of man's food supplies, wheat had already taken a dominant place by Egyptian times. However, not all the Egyptian people had this risen bread; skulls unearthed still show teeth that had been worn down due to the chewing of the old, hard breads.

The whole Roman system was, as we have seen, based upon wheat obtained from Egypt and other parts of their empire. But when the wild grasses, particularly rye and oats, were swept into the wheat fields, it was difficult to separate them from one another. The origin of maslin bread is based upon this fact. By the same token barley and oats were often found together and when they were harvested it was known as "drage", and it was an admirable diet for animals. But this laziness did not commend itself to the Jews. Early on, in Leviticus, it was stated: "Thou shalt not sow they fields with mingled seed." Our language has origins in such food ideas. We have words to denote these mixed grains: mancorn, muncorn or mengcorn. Manmen- or mun- is a Teutonic prefix to denote mingled, or mixed (as in the word "mongrel").

The Romans were contemptuous of the oat-eating Germans of the north, although the physicians of the day knew better, and advocated oats as suitable food.

But an order of the emperor Diocletian, dated 340, to impose price ceilings, did not mention oats as food. This contempt for oats was handed down through the middle ages. But the Irish and the Scotch, who never lived on Roman soil, were fond of oats. Later on Samuel Johnson in his famous English dictionary defined oats as: "food for men in Scotland, for horses in England." The Scottish retort to this was: "England is noted for the excellence of her horses; Scotland for the excellence of her men."

Thus it is that the history of risen bread really revolved around wheat and rye, although barley loaves were used at least until Roman times. Wheat became the preferred bread very early, and rye had to take second place. But rye has certain advantages over wheat; it can flourish on soils that are inhospitable to wheat. It thus became the cultivated plant for bread in the Baltic states, Poland and the members of the Hanseatic league.

But wheat was preferred. As long ago as the thirteenth century a lack of wheat bread was beginning to be a badge of inferiority. Piers Plowman, after a year of scarcity, speaks of himself as living on:

"...an haver cake
a lof of benis and bren ybake for my
faunte..."*

Rye was tolerated by the general public in the early days of the middle ages, but by the sixteenth century wheat came to be favored in the western parts of Europe. And there was a marked difference between the diet of the poorer sort, and that of the rich. Fynes Morrison in his book of travels, says:

"the english husband-man eats barley and
rye brown bread."

* cake of oats, and bread of beans and peas baked for my infants

212

He gives as a reason its "abiding long in the stomach". He continues: "but citizens and gentlemen eat most pure white bread." Even earlier an observant Italian ambassador wrote as follows in 1500:

"the english, being great epicures and
very avaricious by nature, indulge in
the most delicate fare themselves; but
give their households the coarsest bread,
and beer and cold meat baked on Sunday
for the week..."

Rye was considered an inferior grain by most people of those days. In 1596 Sir Edward Coke speaks of "riemell to make bread for the poore." Oats too was looked down upon: "Otmell to make the poore folkes porage."

How much rye was used at that time? It depended on where you were situated and upon the degree of scarcity of grain. As times of dearth became more frequent, in the Tudor era, the government tried to find out how much grain might be available. The preamble to the survey made at the time states:

"The shortages of grain were rendered more
severe by the selfishness of individuals."

It is no different today, it seems. The survey goes on to specify the issuance of corn certificates which stated the amount of grain which could be spared in the public market. In the same survey it is recorded that rye predominated in the area north of the Sherwood Forest, wheat south and west of there. In Kent, nothing but wheat seems to have been grown. This was because of a climatic difference, for wheat has a hard time ripening in the north of England.

Rye was well described at the time. In 1580 Tusser, after an education at Eton College and two university colleges, settled down in the country and wrote a book entitled: "Fiue hundred pointes of good Husbandrie". Under the September

213

section in the book, rye is prominently mentioned:

> "Threshe sede and goe fanne, for the plough
> may not lye, September doth bid to the sow-
> ing of rye, the redges well harrow'd, or
> ever thou strike, is one poynt of husban-
> drie rye land doth like."

In the October section he continues:

> "the rye in the ground, while September
> doth last October for wheat sowing,
> calleth as fast..."

Rye and wheat were therefore "winter corn"
as they were sown in the autumn and reaped the
following summer. Barley and oats, on the other
hand, were "summer corn", sown in the spring and
harvested a few months later. Whereas rye comprised
forty percent of the bread corn in seventeenth
century England, by the eighteenth century it
comprised only five percent. In attempting to
explain how wheat superseded rye in the seventeenth
century, Sir Symond d'Ewees wrote in 1612:

> "the farmers murmured, the poorer sort
> traversed the markets to find out the
> finest wheats, for none else would now
> serve their use, though before they
> were glad of the coarser rye bread. This
> daintiness was soon after punished by the
> high prices of all sorts of grain every-
> where, which never since abated..."

An interesting aside as to the use of the
two grains appears in the records attributed to
the estate of Althorp, Northants, which belonged
to the Lady Penelope Spencer. For most of the year
equal quantities of wheat and rye were allotted to
her baker; wheaten bread for the guests and rye
bread for the servants. Whenever the family were
in residence and entertaining guests of high social
rank, wheaten bread only was baked. This was during
summer, from June 14 until October 18, 1632, according to the records. But as soon as the guests

214

left, evidently nothing but rye bread was baked.

It appears that the folk in northern England and Scotland were accustomed to rye, and quite fond of it. It was also favored by early colonisers in America, many of whom had come from the north of England through the port of Liverpool. A later quote from the period by William Cobbett in his "Journal of a year's residence in America" (1817), illustrates this:

> "I have heard that Mr. Elias Hicks, the famous Quaker preacher, who lives about nine miles from this spot, has this year, at seventy years of age, cradled down (i.e. cut down with a scythe), four acres of rye in a day..."

And four years later Cobbett says:

> "few people on this earth live better than these Long Islanders. Yet nine families out of ten seldom eat wheaten bread. Rye is the flour that they principally make use of..."

But we have already observed that definite class distinctions arose as a result of the desire for, and use of, ever whiter bread. White after all is the symbol of purity in many cultures. For instance, in Farsi, one of the languages of Afghanistan, pak means white, and it also means pure in the ethical and religious sense. National pride and superiority factors crept into the picture, especially when the French and the English seemed to be dividing up the world between them.

And the Church entered into the controversy. In very early days dogma was set down as follows:

> "water can by no means be used in the sacrifice without wine, nor bread except it be of frumentum,"

215

Thus preached Peter Lombard in the twelfth century. St. Thomas Aquinas in the thirteenth century said that the material of the host must be triticum, a more decisive word than frumentum. In 1409 the Council of Florence determined that the host should be "of wheaten bread (panem triticum) and no other." This was surely a little off the mark, for had not Christ himself fed the multitudes on five barley loaves and two small fishes? At the time this was conveniently forgotten. But the discussion left the people of Poland and other rye-producing countries in a quandary. In 1617 Suarez, the Spanish theologian, said:

"as a matter of the host, rye is very doubtful."

What was the poor peasant to do on Sunday mornings? Could he then not be saved?

During the nineteenth century the age-old preference for white bread was to reach its peak in the western countries, with some unfortunate nutritional effects, as we shall see. The countries with large overseas empires, England, France, Spain, Italy were able to gratify their national taste for ever whiter bread from the vast wheatlands of their overseas possessions. These wheat lands would never fail to produce a wheat crop for the mother country: Canada, Tunis, Argentine, Libya.

But it is significant that those countries of the northern part of the western world, Scandinavia, the Baltic states, Poland and Germany retained to a certain extent their liking for rye. For rye was the crop that would ripen when wheat faltered, due especially to a wet summer. It is also noteworthy that these same countries did not possess overseas empires to supply wheat, and thus had to rely, in times of duress and dearth, on the home crop; in this case, rye.

These habits and attachments acquired for certain foods often persist for centuries after the need has been removed. Those new Americans from

the wheat-eating countries could continue to enjoy
white breads and rolls which were important to them
above all else. But the newer immigrants into the
middle west, many of whom came from rye-eating countries, were able to enjoy rye breads as well as
wheat. It is no accident that I had never seen
rye bread until I emigrated from the south of
England to Wisconsin in 1938.

RICE

Unbeknown to the early seekers of wheat and
barley, at least until the early Aryans descended
into the plains of India, were Asiatic peoples who
practiced rice culture. At first this was regarded
by western explorers as a curiosity; later, as
these peoples came under the dominion of the nations
of Europe, rice was said to be inferior as a food.
It was the food of people who had been reduced to
subjection.

Only in recent decades has rice taken its
rightful place as a universal food for all men.
It is particularly significant as a food when baking becomes impossible, or too costly. Its use
lends a satisfying variety to the endless bread,
meat and potatoes syndrome which permeated western
industrial society in the nineteenth century. The
use of and acquantance with rice as a food, has
been facilitated by the sudden availability in
the twentiety century of world travel, whereby
the intermingling of food customs can be realised.
The ethnic restaurant, once set up to satisfy a
particular group of immigrants, is now visited by
all who can afford the price, whatever their origins.

It is however as well to remember that over
ninety percent of the world's people never travel
outside their own region, sometimes not even outside their town or village. In such cases, food
customs change slowly if at all. The grain of
tradition is used, and as a rule it is grown locally.

It is now time to retrace our steps to the
late fifteenth and early sixteenth century, for

the peoples of Europe were to know neither rice
nor maize until the great Renaissance period of
world discovery. The effects of these events on
food and the struggle to get it will be dealt with
in subsequent chapters.

REFERENCES

210 RIVALRY OF THE GRASSES: Jacobs, Heinrich;
Six Thousand Years of Bread; chap 5 p 11
(1944).

211 "MINGLED SEED" Leviticus.

212 DIOCLETIAN: OATS NOT MENTIONED AS FOOD.
Jacobs, ibid. chap 6 p 13.

212 "CAKE OF OATS.." Langland, William; Vision
of Piers Plowman; passus VI, p 282-5.

212 THE ENGLISH HUSBANDMAN EATS BARLEY AND BROWN
BREAD.. Morrison, Fynes.

212 OATS GIVEN TO HORSES..Johnson, Samuel; Dictionary 1st edn 1755.

213 OTMELL TO MAKE POORE FOLKES PORAGE..Coke,
Sir Edmund; Household Book (1596); quoted
in Doods: the Food of London (1856).

214 SEPTEMBER FOR RYE. Tusser, Thomas; Fiue
hundred pointes of good husbandrie. (1573).

214 ".THE FARMERS MURMURED.." Sir Symond d'Ewees
(1612), quoted in Ashley, Sir W; Bread
of our forefathers p 37 (1928).

214 LADY PENELOPE SPENCER.. Ashley, ibid; an
enquiry in economic history.

215 MR. ELIAS HICKS, FAMOUS QUAKER PREACHER..
Cobbett, William; Journal of a year's
residence in America (1817-8).

215   "FEW PEOPLE ON EARTH LIVE BETTER THAN LONG
       ISLANDERS." Cobbett, William; Rural Rides
       (1823).

216   "WHEATEN BREAD AND NO OTHER". Villani, Gio-
       vanni, Chronicle of Florence; trans Rose
       Selfe (1906).

216   "TRITICUM", St. Thomas Aquinas from Jacob
       #67 p 163.

EARLY TIMES IN INDIA

      While the events which had been described in
Egypt, Sumer, and Greece were taking place, there
was a civilization in India which from the first
seems to have grown up with its own roots, with a
character and an intellectual life of its own.
For it was cut off from both west and east by vast
mountain barriers and desert regions. The Aryan
tribes which from time immemorial came down from
the highlands soon lost touch with their beginnings,
and developed along lines of their own.

      The river civilization of the Indus Valley
has been mentioned in Chapter 2. Remains of the
cities of Moenjodaro and Harappa have survived,
to indicate the advanced state of that period.
But these cities disappeared, and a result of the
changing course of the Indus River, because of
plague, or of conquest, or a combination of all
three; this is not known for certain.

      However, the river Ganges and its tributaries
tell another story. The Ganges has continued
throughout the ages and up to the present day to
play a vital part in the life of India. Most of
the rivers that make up the vast Gangetic system
have their sources high up in the everlasting snows
of the Himalaya mountains. Consequently, the
Ganges never dwindles away, even in the hottest
summer. The soils of the Gangetic plain can continue fertile by means of irrigation, practised
there by man since time immemorial; in addition
there is, as in the case of the Nile in Egypt, an
annual deposit of alluvial silt which provides a
top-dressing of inexhaustible fertility.

      And so the early inhabitants of this region
of India, called Dravidians, lived under conditions
which were very different from those which existed
in the north and west of India. Wherever the for-
ested plains around the rivers could be cleared,

221

land was available to all; the prolific soil, almost unasked, gave the people all the food they
needed. There was no further reason for them to
wander -- the crops and the seasons were trust-
worthy. Small wonder that the peoples of this
region came to regard the river, the source of
such abundance, with awe and reverence.

Because of the warm climate, the people
needed little in the way of clothing or housing.
And finally, they had one other advantage which
was not available to the Egyptians: the monsoons,
with their extra rainfall, occurred with reliable
regularity.

The people needed so little that trade with
other cultures remained undeveloped. There was
land for all who desired to cultivate a patch of
it; and a patch was all that was needed. The
social and political life was simple, and comparatively secure. No great conquering powers had,
as yet, arisen in India, and even the well-traveled
Greeks knew little about the subcontinent. India's
natural barriers sufficed to halt the early imper-
ialisms to the east and west of her. Thousands of
comparatively peaceful little villages, republics,
and chieftainships were spread over the land.
There was no sea life, and hence no pirate raiders,
no strange traders. All this went on for hundreds
of years, until the sea-going nature of the Greeks
led them occasionally as far as India.

The history of India, thus, was for many
centuries happier, less fierce and more dreamlike
than the histories of other cultures. The rajahs
(noblemen) hunted; life was made up largely of
love stories and myths. Here and there as maharajah
appeared among the rajahs and built a city, caught
and tamed elephants, slew many tigers, and left a
tradition of splendor and elegance. Yet there was
also much active thought among them. Great epics,
known to us as Upanishads* were composed and handed down by oral tradition. There was, as yet, no
writing, for Sanskrit was still in the future. But

* The word denotes spoken stories with the audience
  sitting down nearby.

there was much philosophical speculation.

THE COMING OF THE ARYANS

When the Aryans, from what is now Afghanistan and beyond, descended into the plains of India they brought their own cattle with them, but a breed native to India already existed there. The Aryans' influence was so great that the native Indians felt themselves threatened -- they regarded it as necessary to protect their own cattle, up to and including the formulation of religious laws. The early Rig-Vedas, which were sacrificial hymns and chants, not even written down at first, noted that goats, sheep, horses, buffalo and barren cows were regarded as food. It must have been clear to these Dravidian people that a cow's milk can feed more people than can its carcass. Similarly, in the case of poultry, hens' eggs were more valuable than their meat. So the Indians kept their cattle and their poultry alive instead of killing them. These customs are said to have been in effect as early as 1500 B.C., a millenium before the Greeks appeared on the Indian scene. By 1000

Hump-backed Zebu Bull, forerunner of the Brahma: and flat-backed primogenius type: Indus Valley seals

B.C., the Atharva-Veda was declaring that to eat meat was to commit an offense against one's forefathers, and even barren cows were forbidden. Cows and cowherds were placed under the protection of the

Hindu god Krishna. But by about 700 B.C., these laws had been relaxed somewhat, and it was acceptable to use cattle for sacrificial purposes. They had to be killed according to a special ritual, however.

ARRIVAL OF THE GREEKS

When the Greeks arrived in India in the fifth century B.C., they described the agriculture of the river valleys with great enthusiasm. Megasthenes wrote as follows:

> "...since there is a double rainfall in the course of each year, the inhabitants of India always gather two harvests annually; one in the winter season, when the sowing of wheat takes place as in other countries; and the second at the time of the summer solstice which is the proper season for growing rice, as well as sesamum and millet..."

As the people began to settle into the alluvial plains, they turned their attention more and more to the growing of crops, which provided more food per acre than did animal herds. As a result, herding became less important then it had been, and the raising of animals tended to be reserved for the sacrifices needed for religious observances.

Society was becoming more and more stratified. There were several classes: the priestly class, or Brahmans; the warrior class; and the vast numbers of hewers of wood and drawers of water. A series of levels, later to be called castes, were specified, largely according to the occupations of the persons involved. Even a level below all the castes were the "untouchables," later to be the cause of much social unrest. The Brahmans were in a position to dominate this system, and did so. These, then, were the circumstances of life when there came upon the Indian scene one who was to have more influence on his fellow creature, and for a longer time, than any other man.

GAUTAMA

This man, born in the northern province of
Kapilavastu under the Himalayan mountains, was
Siddhartha Gautama. He came from a good family
of some consequence, and experienced the ordinary
aristocratic life of his time and region. It
appears that he was good-looking, and a capable
young man who lived rather well. At the age of 19
he married, and continued his life of hunting and
playing in his sunny world of gardens, groves, and
rice fields.

But this life was not satisfying to him intel-
lectually, and at the age of about 29 he was to
undergo a great change. It was then that a great
discontent fell upon him. While traveling about,
he saw a number of ascetics, as well as poor and
diseased people, all searching for a way out of
their predicaments. Gautama wanted to work out
his own destiny, and left home to discover some
deeper reality in life. After many adventures he
decided to divest himself of worldly entanglements,
and tried to search out the truth in the company
of other like-minded people. He had five companions,
and they went about in a spirit of self-mortifica-
tion. But one day Gautama began to realize that
this was not necessarily the way to find truth.

Gautama's fundamental teachings, which are
becoming plainer to us now due to the study of
original sources, are clear and simple. It is
beyond any doubt, claimed H. G. Wells in An Outline of History, that these teachings are the
fruits of one of the most penetrating minds that
the world has ever known. At the base of Gautama's
thinking is the concept that all the miseries and
discontents of life can be traced to man's insat-
iable selfishness. Until man has overcome his
personal desires, his life is trouble and his end
is sorrow. The task confronting all mankind is
to recognize this truth.

Personal human selfishness takes three forms:
the first is the gratification of the senses; the

225

second is the desire for immortality; and the third is the desire for prosperity, or worldliness. All these must be overcome. When a man is no longer living for himself, only then will his life become serene. This serenity of soul is the state of Nirvana, the extinction of those personal aims which are so futile. This lesson has been stated in other religions since that time, but not as simply. This was the first, and it may well be the last, great lesson which man must learn in order to survive.

And so Gautama propounded the rightful path of life, in an eightfold lesson. The primary part of the lesson is Truth, or Right Views. He condemned superstitions, particularly the prevalent belief about the transmigration of souls so important in the Hindu way of thinking at that time. His was primarily a religion of conduct, not of sacrifices and observances. It had, at first, no temples; and since it had no sacrifices it had no priests. It had no theology, even. It neither asserted nor denied the great multiplicity of gods and godlings which adorned the Indian scene at the time.

Gautama was preaching his new doctrines about 534 B.C., at the time of Cyrus the Great of Persia, under which regime an early conquest of India was attempted. The title of Buddha was conferred on Gautama at about this time. At about the same time, another preacher, called Mahavira, founded a sect which was even more opposed to the eating of meat than were the Buddhists. The cult of Jainism, as this group was to be called, has persisted to the present time. Both Buddhists and Jains were, and are, opposed to three things: violence, caste, and animal slaughter.

VEGETARIANISM

Man has always resisted the idea that he must die. Accordingly, he will find various ways of persuading himself that he does not have to die, once and for all. The doctrine of transmigration of souls gave form and substance to even earlier resurrection myths. If one has lived one's life well, one is reincarnated at a higher level; if poorly, at a lower level. These concepts have great bearing on the subject of food, for here we have religious sanction for a vegetarian diet: you are not going to eat your ancestors, who may very well be in animal form. Nor do you want, in your turn, to be eaten by your descendants, if you too are reincarnated at some lower level.

Thus it came about that the Indians of Buddha's time re-instituted the old ban on cow-killing, which had been, in part, abandoned. Cows were being killed more and more frequently for sacrificial purposes, and the people would eat the meat afterwards.

By the time of Julius Caesar, the Indians had fully re-instituted vegetarianism, and they prescribed all sorts of rituals which involved no animal sacrifice at all. The cow was, furthermore, endowed with certain sacred rights. Cows and cowherds were again, as they had been centuries earlier, placed under the protection of the god Krishna, and meat was thus completely eliminated from the diet.

Even pigs, which had been given no special privileges in the hierarchy of animals, were to disappear from the Indian diet at this time, after being used as food for three thousand years. (Evidence at Moenjodaro and Harappa proves the existence of pigs at the time of the Indus River civilizations).

Only vegetable protein was available, together with milk and milk protein. The diet which developed in India around this base has sufficed to enable the people to thrive and to develop in a difficult climate. The strength of this diet lies in the fact that milk protein is superior to all other types of protein, especially grain protein. The custom of drinking milk, and of using milk products, has pervaded the Indian dietary for centuries. Milk was not reserved for children only, as has been customary in parts of the western world.

MEALS

If vegetarianism heralded a meritorious life, it also developed a most distinguished cuisine, especially in the south of India. A meal in a middle-income household two thousand years ago might have consisted of an appetiser of one or two pieces of ginger dusted with salt; this was followed by bean soup, boiled rice and hot butter sauce, then cakes with ghee or fruit. Finally, the meal would end with a piece of suger-cane to chew. What a fabulous diet according to our modern nutritional standards!

A rich man of that time might have different curries, shining white rice, savory dishes of meat (until this was prohibited altogether), sweets, and water perfumed with camphor from Borneo. But a poor Indian, then as now, would have to survive on stale, half-cooked squash with boiled rice, other vegetables, or perhaps a grain porridge, all washed down with a rinse of rice water.

After the repeated Aryan invasions brought permanent settlers southward, wheat and barley became standard foods in the north of the country. The south, however, remained dependent upon rice. Gourds, peas, and lentils were found all over the country. Also available were mango, plantain, and tamarind. Finally, there were sugarcane and pepper.

It is almost impossible to get a true idea of Indian food from a list of the ingredients alone. But at the time of Charlemagne in 774 A.D., both Chinese and European foods were dull in comparison with those of India. Chinese foods scarcely used dairy products at all, and Europe was highly suspicious of fruit, as we shall see in a later chapter. Indian diets, both before and since, have made liberal use of both dairy products and fruit.

POLLUTION

As the cow became progressively more sacred, its products came to assume more than their face value. For the higher castes in society were always living in fear of lower reincarnations, and thus became very concerned about ritual pollution. In this matter, ghee came to the rescue, because anything cooked in it was automatically purified.

This is very interesting in the light of modern nutrition. Butter is an emulsion containing up to 20% of water; thus it is subject to action by the enzyme lipase, and the rancidity arising from this action. Ghee, on the other hand, is butter from which the water has been separated. Thus ghee is in fact more stable than the butter from which it is made, because lipase enzymes have to operate from a water base, which is lacking in ghee. This feature of ghee was recognized by the Indians centuries ago, without, of course, the accompanying explanation, which is a twentieth-century finding.

Eventually, a whole list of foods were specified as unclean in the Indian culture: meat cut with a sword; meat which had died by itself; locusts, camels, and hairless animals; ready-made food from the market; food sniffed at by a dog, cat or human -- all these were regarded as unfit for eating by both the Brahman and the warrior castes.

The lower castes were permitted to eat a rabbit, hen, or chicken, or something that had been killed. The lowest caste of all, or untouchables (harijans), as they were later to be called, were likely to eat animals as they died, although the slaughter of animals, as such, was forbidden.

Preoccupation with hygiene extended to dishes. An earthenware dish had to be broken and discarded after one use. Most Indians learned to sidestep this law by using large plantains or other leaves as plates. Even tables were constructed of interlaced leaves and fibres, and after the meal, they were thrown into the river to float away.

During the evolution of Indian history, Sanskrit writings appear, and other languages slowly

developed. In reading these, historians have discovered certain prescriptions about eating. Indians
were supposed to be satisfied, it seems, with two
meals a day, each containing just thirty-two mouth-
fuls. It was believed that the human stomach held
four compartments, two for solid food, one for
liquids -- and the fourth was left empty for the
passage of wind. This seems a sensible arrangement.

It would be difficult to overestimate the importance of Indian cultural attitudes towards food.
It is certainly true to say that mankind as a whole
has been influenced by customs and taboos which
had their origins in the India of long ago. Buddhists and Hindus have comprised over a quarter of
the human race in recent times. The constraints
of food habits and religious custom have affected
agriculture and animal husbandry throughout the
world, and still do.

In concluding this section, it is useful to
note that although Christianity reached India in
the first century, and missions were established
soon after, it did not take hold of the imagination of the indigenous population in the way
that Islam was to do a thousand years later.
Therefore we turn next to a discussion of the
origin and development of Islam, and its impact
on both East and West.

REFERENCES

223 "..BARREN COWS.." Prakash. Om; Food and drinks in Ancient India; Delhi p 18 (1961).

223 "AN OFFENCE AGAINST ONE'S FOREFATHERS." ibid p 15.

224 USE OF CATTLE FOR RITUAL PURPOSES: Kautilya, A.A. Manual of Administration; ca 1st century A.D. ed Kayle (1960-65).

224 ARRIVAL OF THE GREEKS: Bose, Atindranath; Social and Ruria Economy of northern India (1961).

224 IMPOSITIONS OF CASTE: Kosambi. D.D. Introduction to a study of Indian History; p 157-8 (1956).

229 USE OF GHEE FOR PURIFICATION OF FOOD: Tannahill, R; Food in History; chap 9 p 158-60 (1973).

229 UNCLEAN FOOD: Prakash. Om ibid p 148-9.

FOUNDATIONS OF ISLAM

The peoples on the peninsula between the Red
Sea and the Persian Gulf had, during the early
days of Egypt, Greece and Rome, learned the benefits of trade. They had profited greatly from sale
of the incense that they alone were able to produce,
as well as from their role as middlemen in the growing east-west spice trade. There was, however,
continuing friction among these Arab peoples, with
their trading routes and their trading posts.
These Bedouin tribes were semitic peoples, often
bickering and feuding until a unifying factor arose
to put a stop to this internal warfare.

In the year 570 A.D., a baby was born in the
town of Mecca who was to have a most profound
effect and influence on man's affairs. His name
was Muhammad (Mohammed). He was born in considerable povery, and even by desert standards was un-
educated. It is doubtful whether he ever learned
to write. Orphaned at an early age, he was for
some years a shepherd's boy, and then became the
servant of a certain Kadija, the widow of a rich
Meccan merchant. He looked after the camels and
perhaps helped in trading operations. It is said
that he travelled with caravans on trading missions
to Syria and to Yemen.

In the course of time he found favor in
Kadija's eyes, and she married him, still in his
early twenties. Tradition has it that she was
fifteen years older than he, but she was able
nevertheless to bear several children. And so
Muhammad lived in Mecca as the husband of a prosperous wife, until he was forty years of age.

Yet he must have been thinking deeply about
life. He had seen Christian churches in Syria,
and will have known about the coming of Christianity to Abyssinia. He almost certainly knew much

233

about the Jews and their religion. He heard their
scorn for the black stone of the Kaaba, that ruled
over the three hundred-odd tribal gods of Arabia.
He saw the pilgrimage crowds, and noted the in-
sincerity and superstition in the paganism of the
town.

When he was forty he began to express his
feelings about the reality of God, first to his
wife and to a few intimates. He claimed that he
had received certain verses from an angel about
the unity of God. He insisted on a future life,
fear of hell for the evil and the negligent, and
paradise for the true believer. He started to
preach accordingly, saying that he was a witness,
an exhorter, a messenger.

The Meccans went about their trading business
without paying too much attention to him. But
later on, as the movement gathered strength, the
leading men of the town began to fear that he was
aiming at a sort of dictatorship in the town. He
attracted many susceptible and discontented people
to his side, and so the merchants began to institute harassment against him, and all manner of
petty persecutions, in an effort to suppress the
new movement.

Mecca was already a place of pilgrimage for
the sake of the old cults and idols. By tradition, no blood could be shed within its walls.
Nevertheless, things were made extremely disagree-
able for the followers of the new teacher, with
boycott and confiscation. At the end of ten years
of prophesying, Muhammad found himself altogether
unsuccessful in Mecca, and he was already fifty.
Kadija was by now dead, and so were several of
his early followers.

Just when things looked bad, the town of
Medina invited him to come there and rule in the
name of God. The people of Medina had been attracted by his teaching; perhaps he would be able to
settle their feuds.

Accordingly, one day in 622 A.D., Muhammad picked
up his belongings, and accompanied by his faithful follower Abu Bekr, journeyed from Mecca to
Medina. He arrived there on September 20, 622,
which date denoted the end of his probation and
the beginning of his power. The flight from
Mecca was adopted by later generations as the
start of the Moslem calendar; dates are reported
AH.*   In Mecca, he had preached Islam, in Medina
he practiced it. And the records pass from legend
into history.

Muhammad stated for his followers the mission
of the one true faith for mankind. He quickly
gained adherents, and for the next ten crucial
years, he developed a whole array of teachings
about the one true God, whose name was Allah.
Until his death in 632, he continued to lay the
foundations of this new faith. These teachings
have been handed down, by word of mouth originally,
and then recorded in a book which we know as the
Koran.

SPREAD OF ISLAM

When Mohammed's** followers went out to spread
the word of Islam, they roamed far and wide, eventually traveling as far west as Morocco and as
far east as Indonesia. This happened in the space
of a few generations. It is a remarkable story,
by any criterion. How did they achieve it? What
was it that they had to offer? Were they so excellent in the arts of war that they could conquer
everybody in sight?

This is hardly likely. At first they were not
even organized into armies; they were just Bedouin
horsemen riding across the sand-dunes. So they did
not conquer everybody they met by force of arms.
But they conquered their hearts and minds. This
is the feature which has fascinated historians
ever since that time.

What was it that really attracted those people
to Islam? In order to look into this question,

* az hegira: from the flight. The present year
  in Islam is 1358 AH.

** The more usual spelling will be used hereafter.

we must consider the kind of people they were
addressing. What was the world like in 632 A.D.?

CHRISTIANITY

Christianity had become, by then, partially
institutionalized. The fall of Roman authority,
the rise of Byzantium by comparison with Rome,
and the adherence of many rich people and influential people in the Mediterranean world had wrought
certain changes in it. The simplicity of the early
Christians and their church had been changed. The
persecutions had ceased. Among many things which
had occurred were the concepts of church buildings,
church property and holy ground. Another concept
was that of the Sabbath, carried over from ancient
Judaism.

Now the Bedouin tribesman, with his tent, his
horse, his camel and his few herds, would go to
the water-hole on a communal basis; it was largely
a tribal arrangement, not in any way infringing
on the rights of other Bedouins. The small cities
that were really trading posts comprised the
Bedouins' world; his frontier was limited to the
desert itself. How could such a man worship God
in a building? Why would he be concerned with the
day of the week?

These were important questions, because one
of the tenets of Islam is that you can pray to
God at any time and in any place. And furthermore,
that you can attain grace by doing so. And you
can also be buried anywhere in the ground, with
your feet and head in line with Mecca, and have a
graceful burial. The Christian church by 632
would have none of this. Christians were concerned
with church buildings, Sunday and holy ground,
place for burial that had been hallowed. Otherwise
heaven would be denied. Even the wealthier traders
of the spice and silk routes were hardly attuned
to this aspect of Christianity, and so Mohammed's
message fell on willing ears.

THE KORAN

The Koran became a work of such significance and religious import that it was usually regarded as impossible to translate it into any other tongue than its original Arabic, without losing its authority and effect. It became traditional that it should always be transmitted by word of mouth, in the original Arabic. People today in countries like Afghanistan, who are just becoming literate, are encouraged to read the Koran in Arabic if they possibly can, rather than in Persian or Farsi.

The Koran is neither prose nor poetry, but a musical fusion of both, and it has been treasured with great care for over 1300 years. It is very significant that it was not translated even into Latin for the benefit of mediaeval Europe until 1143, well after the First Crusade, which was supposed to be fought against the tenets of Islam. The first English edition was not produced until 1657.

The Koran carried a ringing message that there is no God but God. The verses and various sections of the Koran start with the name of God, followed by a number of epithets, such as the all-compassionate, all-loving, the all-merciful, the all-powerful. There are ninety-nine epithets in all.*

God was not only one God but He was everywhere, and thus could be worshipped in any place. From this simple fact arose the forceful idea that daily prayers, at certain times, if you will, (though not necessarily), could be entered into by oneself, without regard to place or persons. But even so God expects sincerity:

> "It is not piety that you turn your
> faces to the east and to the west.
> True piety is this: to believe in
> God and the last day; the angels, the
> book and the prophets."

* Only the camel knows the hundredth name of God; legend has it that Mohammed whispered it to his camel on a last journey before he died; this is why the camel is such an ornery, supercilious creature.

237

This matter of prayers is very important to the average man in Moslem countries.

The Koran also shows how God enters into the minutest details of daily life. One repeatedly comes across the phrases, "God assuredly knows all that you do", said in a variety of ways. God is terrible in retribution, but at the same time is all-compassionate. For example:

> "...if thou obeyest the most part of those on earth, they will lead thee astray from the path of God. They follow surmise, merely conjecturing. The Lord knows very well who goes astray from his path. He knows very well the right-guided."

And even closer to the individual is this passage:

> "...and on the day when the house is come, upon that day shall be vain-doers lose. And thou shalt see every nation hobbling on their knees, every nation being summoned to its book. Today ye shall be recompensed for what you were doing. This is our Book that speaks against you the truth. We have been registering all that you were doing."

The Koran provided answers to so many of the ordinary facts of life for the humble man; about marriage, divorce, ownership, credit, prayer, and most certainly about food. All of this appealed to the illiterate tribesman who had little use for the abstract points of Christian dogma. Man was exhorted to be a part of nature and not outside it:

> "no creature is there crawling in the earth, no bird flying with its wings, but they are nations like unto your-selves. We have neglected nothing in the book. Then to their Lord shall

238

they be mustered..."

But the Lord gave man a place in the great scheme of things:

"It is God who made for the earth a fixed place, and heaven for an edifice; and
He shaped you and shaped you well, and
provided you with good things..."

However, there is a threat as well as a re-
ward:

"upon the day when the unbelievers
are exposed to the fire, we shall say,
you dissipated your good things in
your present life and you took your
enjoyment in them; therefore today you
shall be recompensed with the chastise-
ment of humiliation, for that you
waxed proud in the earth without right,
and for your ungodliness..."

MATTERS RELATING TO FOOD

In general one finds that we are invited to use God's gifts correctly. "Eat and drink of God's providing, and mischief not in the earth, doing corruption."

"Permitted to you is the game of the
sea, and the food of it, as a provision
for you and for the journeyers."

But there is always a powerful reminder of the wonder and the force of God's works:

"It is God who split the datestone and
the grain, who brings forth the living
from the dead; and He brings forth the
dead too from the living; so that then
is God. How are you perverted?"

A particularly significant passage is the following:

"He splits the sky into dawn and has
made the night for a repose, and the
sun and moon for a reckoning. It is
He that has appointed for you the
stars that by them you might be guided
by land and by sea. We have distinguished signs for a people who know.
It is He who sent down out of heaven
water, and thereby we have brought
forth a shoot out of every plant; and
then we have brought forth a green leaf
of it, bringing forth from it close-
compounded grain, and out of the palm
tree from the spath of it, dates, thick-
clustered, ready to the hand, and gardens
of vines, olives and pomegrantes, like
each to each and each unlike to each.
Look upon their fruits when they ripen.
Surely in all this are signs for a
people who do believe..."

Some things are forbidden to eat. Carrion,
blood and the flesh of swine, what has been hallowed to other than God, these are specifically
enjoined, as follows:

"the beast strangled, the beast gored,
the beast beaten down, the beast fallen to death, and that devoured by
beasts of prey, except that which you
have sacrificed duly. Also enjoined
are things sacrified to idols, and
partition by divining arrows; that is
ungodliness..."

What other assistance is given the Koran which
bears on nutrition? There is an important passage
which relates in a surprisingly up-to-date fashion
to the question of suckling:

"Mothers shall suckle their children for
two years completely, for such as desire
the suckling. It is for the father to
clothe them honorably and to feed them.
No soul is charged to save to its capacity,

and a mother should not be pressed
for her child, nor a father for his
child; but if the couple desire by
mutual consent to wean, then it is no
fault in them. And if you desire to
seek nursing for your children,
it is no fault in you, providing that
you hand over what you have given honorably, and fear God; and know that God
sees the things that you do..."

CONFLICT

Islam has a great deal of common ground with
the Jewish faith. Both believe in the prophets,
the Moslem sacrifice of a sheep at the festival
of Id-el-Fitr is to commemorate Abraham's willing-
ness to do God's will and sacrifice his own son.
All of the prophets were real, and Christ was one
of these prophets, the latest and most important
one. For He too was a messenger. The Koran is
very clear on the subject of Jesus:

"The Messiah, son of Mary was only a
messenger. Messengers there were before
him who passed away. His mother was just
a woman. They both ate food. Behold we
make clear the signs to them..."

And so Christians were to revile Moslems for
being anti-Christ. But why did the Moslems in
their turn object to Christianity? They say that
the Christians parted company with the true God.
They claim that Christians have come to worship
a multiple God, three-in-one. This is unacceptable
to them. "They are unbelievers who say that God
is the Messiah, Mary's son. Verily whosoever
associates with God anything, God shall prohibit
him from entering paradise." And they are definite
about the penalties. "Your refuge shall be the
fire. Wrongdoers shall have no helpers." "They
are unbelievers who say that God is the third of
three. Will they not turn to God and pray for
his forgiveness?"

THE SPREAD OF ISLAM

At Mohammed's death in 632 there was quickly established an arrangement for the succession, whereby there would be an assured head of the newly-founded Islamic faith. This successor was known as the caliph, and the caliphate was first set up in Mecca. In a short time it was moved to Damascus, and then to a new town called Baghdad. Baghdad had been built as a walled city upon the residual remains of Kish, Babylon and Ctesiphon. The year was 763 and Charlemagne reigned in Europe.

Baghdad became the repository of all the teachings of Mohammed, and it was the place where the scholars, the mullahs and the other authorities carried on the work of Islam. Everybody came to Baghdad, not just Arabs, Greeks, Parthians, Sassanids, Persians, Syrians, and Turks. Everybody from the known world came, and the Bedouins, the people of the dusty desert, were particularly enchanted with Baghdad. They took back to their land seeds of citrus and almond; they obtained sugar-cane cuttings which the Persians had introduced from India.

Innumerable caravans came and went, especially those which travelled the silk route to China through what is now Afghanistan. They brought back cinnamon and rhubarb; they brought grapes from Bactria, honey from Isfahan; apples and quinces. And they brought salt from wherever it could be found. Thus was the diet of the people enriched, as these exchanges took place. A greater variety of food was possible than ever before. The Arabs who once had lived on mutton, dates and sheeps' milk, enjoyed the plenty and variety of the marvelous dishes and foods from Baghdad.

In the golden age of the caliphate, many cookbooks were written, not only by princes of the blood, but by philosophers as well. They used meat prodigally at that time, the tenderest parts in slices or chunks. This gave rise to the kebab, originally held in the fire to cook on a sword.

242

They used great quantities of almonds, walnuts and pistachios to thicken savory or sweet dishes. They used juices of lemons or pomegranates. Sweet-sour sauces were a feature of their cuisine, which they learnt about through their contacts with China.

Partly as a result of this type of plenty, self-indulgence, regarded by Mohammed as a sin, ceased to be regarded as such. As the heirs of Islam extended their influence and power, they became less sincere about their observance of the month of fasting (Ramadan).

And so an important Islamic empire was formed on the remnants of the old Persian empire, which was falling apart at that time. Baghdad reached its height, and became a prime city of the world. It was to remain so for some time afterwards. The palaces and the gorgeous silks and cottons learnt about from China, were so fabulous as to engender a spirit of wonder if not envy in those not so fortunate.

The desert peoples were particularly entranced with the canal systems; they took back with them ideas of Paradise, which in Arab literature had often been pictured as a garden under which eternal waters flow. Baths, irrigation and general matters of hygiene were to be used and practiced for the first time. There was great progress in the arts and letters, incidentally kept carefully in libraries, one of the most famous of which was in Alexandria. Astronomy made great strides in this period.

All this was the world of the infidel, the world into which the Crusaders were to barge their way in 1099. To the citizens of the Islamic world, these Crusaders appeared as rough and unruly brigands. Their behaviour in the Holy Land was despicable; they ravaged and plundered in the name of Christ. To the Arabs, they appeared simply barbarous.

243

ISLAM AND INDIA

When Islam reached India in the eighth century, it was faced with an already highly developed culture and life-style, as noted in the previous chapter. The faith was introduced into India in isolated places, but it did not come to conquer at that time.

But the impact of Islam on India was to persist, and it became extremely important in the fifteenth and sixteenth centuries. An invasion, like so many before from over the high mountains to the northwest, was carried out by Babur the Tiger, in 1521. He established the Moghul* dynasty in the northwestern part of India. Babur was an Afghan chieftain who had spent much of his life in what is now Samarkhand, USSR. At the appropriate time, he gathered his forces together and marched southeast to take up his residence as a conqueror. He established himself in Agra and in Delhi. As a result, Islam became strongly organized in that part of India, and was to dominate it until the present time. The Hindus continued to live their ordered lives in the east and south of the country.

The history of modern India may be said to have begun with Babur. The British arrived, in the shape of the East India Company, during the reign of Akbar, Babur's grandson, at the height of Moghul power and influence. The consequences of this are well known. A camaraderie of sorts was to evolve between the British and the Moslems, which the Hindus did not share. Much of this was due to the food habits of the Hindus, which the British did not understand.

The balance of power exerted by the British was in fact made possible by the innate conflicts between the Hindus and Moslems. The issues dividing them were deep ones, based on the value systems and cultural forces, which are very powerful. The cult of vegetarianism that generations of Hindus had come to adope directly challenged the habits of the meat-eating Moslems, as well as those of the

* Moghul, derived from Mongol.

beef-loving British.

The importance of Hinduism, Buddhism, and
Islam in world affairs has tended to be overlooked
when we start to open up a new world across the
Atlantic. It is as well to remember that these
cultures were in place long before the days of
the western colonial empires.

Their food customs and taboos have featured
in some of the wars and quarrels which are an
element of the imperial scene. Only recently have
these same peoples reached a type of independence
which enables them to vindicate their own beliefs
in matters of food. The impact of this has yet to
be felt.

REFERENCES

All references in this chapter are taken from
The Koran Interpreted, by Arthur J. Arberry,
Oxford University Press 1964. s denotes sura;
v denotes verse.

237   "..IT IS NOT PIETY... The Cow s 2 v 171.

238   "..HE KNOWS VERY WELL THE RIGHT-GUIDED.."
        Cattle s 5 v 116.

238   "..UPON THAT DAY SHALL THE VAIN-DOERS LOSE.."
        Hobbling s 45 v 27.

238   "NO CREATURE IS THERE CRAWLING IN THE EARTH.."
        Hobbling s 45 v 11.

239   "THE EARTH A FIXED PLACE.." Sand-Dunes
        s 46 v 19.

239   "..YOU DISSIPATED YOUR GOOD THINGS.."
        Cattle, s 6 v 38.

239   "..EAT AND DRINK OF GOD'S PROVIDING.." The
        Cow s 2 v 57.

239   ".PERMITTED TO YOU IS THE GAME OF THE SEA.."
        The Table s 5 v 95.

239   "IT IS GOD WHO SPLIT THE DATESTONE.." Cattle,
        s 6 v 95.

240   "..HE SPLITS THE SKY INTO DAWN.." The Cow
        s 2 v 167.

240   "..THE BEAST STRANGLED, THE BEAST GORED.."
        The Table s 5 v 4.

240   "MOTHERS SHALL SUCKLE THEIR CHILDREN..."
        The Cow s 2 v 233.

241   "THE MESSIAH, SON OF MARY.." The Table
        s 1 v 79.

241   "ENTERING PARADISE.." The Table s 5 v 26.

241   "..WRONGDOERS SHALL HAVE NO HELPERS.." The House of Imram s 3 v 188.

241   "..THEY ARE UNBELIEVERS WHO SAY THAT GOD IS THE THIRD OF THREE." The Table s 5 v 78.

The Middle Ages came to an end for a variety
of reasons. Among these were the voyages of discovery, the Black Death, new thinking about astronomy and the place of the earth in the solar system,
and a growing resistance to the doctrines of the
Church.

There were many schisms in the Church by the
late Middle Ages. One of these had to do with
bread and its transubstantiation. For instance,
what is the host actually made of? When is it
changed from bread into the body of Christ? And
what does the body of Christ consist of? What
happened in the rye-consuming countries that did
not have any wheat -- were they to be damned forever, though they were Christians? Could the host
be stolen or not? What were the punishments for
stealing it? To whom does the host belong? These
questions had exercised churchmen for a long time.
Peter Lombard, who died in 1164, had said that
"water can by no means be used in the sacrifice
without wine, nor bread except it be of frumentum."
St. Thomas Aquinas, in the thirteenth century, said
that the material of the host must be triticum,
a more decisive word than frumentum. The Council
of Florence in 1409 concurred, saying that it is
to be wheaten bread (panem triticum) "...and no
other." Suarez, a Spanish theologian of the sixteenth century, said that "as a matter of the Host,
rye is very doubtful." Scores of knotty questions
were being asked during this period of history.

Other developments which helped bring the
Middle Ages to an end include the deeper plow, and
the new farming techniques resulting from its use.
Farmers could now practice rotation of one fallow
field out of three instead of one out of two. One
field was left fallow, one was used for the cash
crop, and the third was used to plant oats for the
work horses.

But it was the opening-up of the New World that really moved western civilization into a new era. This development was to give confused Christianity the means to continue its life by opening up vast new lands for cultivation. It included the discovery of new cereals, new tubers and other foods not known in Europe before the fifteenth century.

COLUMBUS

In the late 1400's a certain Genoese, Christopher Columbus, began to think seriously about what seems to us a very obvious and natural enterprise, but which strained the fifteenth century imagination to the utmost -- a voyage west across the Atlantic. At that time, nobody knew of the existence of America as a separate continent. Columbus knew that the world was a sphere, but he underestimated its size. The travels of Marco Polo had given him an exaggerated idea of the size of Asia, and he supposed therefore the Cipangu (Japan) lay across the Atlantic in about the position of Mexico. He had made various voyages in the Atlantic; he had been to Iceland and had perhaps heard of "vinland," which must have greatly encouraged his ideas. This prospect of sailing into the sunset became the ruling purpose of his life.

Columbus was a penniless man, stranded in Portugal, and the only way for him to secure a ship was to get someone to entrust him with a command. He went first to King John II of Portugal, who listened to him and his ideas, and then surreptitiously arranged for a purely Portugese expedition to start without Columbus' knowledge. This scheme failed, the crew became mutinous, the captain lost heart and the ship returned in 1483.

Columbus then went to the court of Spain. At first, he could get no ship and no powers, for Spain was involved in attacking Granada, the last foothold of the Moslems in Europe. Most of Spain had been recovered by the Christians between the eleventh and the thirteenth centuries, except the far south. Now, all of Christian Spain was united by the marriage of Ferdinand of Aragon and Isabella of Castile. They set about the completion of the Christian conquest.

Despairing of Spanish help, Columbus sent his brother Bartholomew to Henry VII of England, but the adventure did not attract the English monarch. Finally, in 1492, Granada fell to the Christians, which afforded some slight compensation for the fall of Constantinople to the Moslems some forty years earlier.

Then, helped by some merchants from the town of Palos, Columbus got three ships, of which only one, the 100-ton Santa Maria, was decked. The other two were open boats of half that tonnage. The little expedition, consisting altogether of eighty-eight men, went south to the Canaries and then stood out across the unknown seas, in beautiful weather and with a helpful wind. The crew were full of doubts, for they feared that they might sail on forever. But they were comforted by seeing some birds, and later they found a pole worked with tools floating by the side of their ship.

Early on the morning of October 12, 1492, land was sighted and while the day was still young Columbus landed on the shores of the new world, richly apparelled and wearing the royal banner of Spain. They were not, however, in Japan. They were in Santo Domingo, in what is now known as the West Indies.

Columbus and his men had thought that they would reach the Orient. They had set off for India where they expected to find, among other things, spices and rice; for these had been known to grow in India. But upon landing on the new continent, they found no rice, nor did they find the traditional spices which had so stimulated the earlier voyages of discovery. But they did find something they had never seen before. It was a plant larger than any grain that they had ever seen or heard of. It grew, not in tufts or pannicles like wheat or oats, but on huge ears, protected from the sun by long leaves. It was maize.

Columbus first mentioned the maize plant in his log on November 1, 1492. The natives, whom the explorers called the Indians, had told Columbus that these plants would grow in ninety days. But the Spaniards were very diffident about the new plant, and at first rejected it, although they saw how devoted to it the natives were.

The maize fields were cultivated differently in native America. Here the plow was unknown and unnecessary. Draft animals, therefore, were not needed. The native Americans knew that the plants needed fertilizing, because they used bats' droppings and wood ash for this purpose, dropping them into the hole along with the seeds. Carletti reported that "maize is gathered four or five times a year."

The origin of maize is unknown. As far as can be ascertained, nobody has ever seen wild maize. Pollen grains of the maize plants have been found in some excavations dating back as far as 50,000 years ago, before the last Ice Age. Maize evidently grew wild then, but the transition from being wild to its domestication is not traceable.

Columbus took maize home as a botanical curiosity, and showed it to Ferdinand and Isabella. It was subsequently planted in Spain, but used only as cattle feed. One of the reasons why it was rejected as unfit for humans was that meat-eaters found it distasteful -- they could not stomach the roasted corn flavor. Another reason was that the Emperor Charles V decreed that maize was not a food fit for either Christians or conquerors; that is, it was not appropriate that Europeans should eat the same food as those they had conquered, for doing so would seem to put them on the same level with the subjected, and therefore inferior, peoples. For another thing, Spaniards were told that wheat was the eucharistic bread of the Lord and that they were forbidden to use maize instead.

As a result of these orders, bounties were
paid to the settlers, to encourage them to plant
wheat in the New World. Wheat was considered
necessary so that the settlers would not be cut
off from taking communion in the proper way. This
strategy, however, did not succeed, because wheat
was alien to America and remained so for a very long
time.

But maize fairly leapt into the Mediterranean
world. It traveled in Spanish, and Greek ships,
and soon reached the Middle Eastern nations of
the Levant and Syria. It took hold especially well
in Turkey, where the Ottoman Empire had become
established in 1453. As traditional enemies of the
Christian world, the Turks had no scruples about
eating maize instead of wheat. And so maize became
very well accepted in Islamic countries, and even
reached Java and China, although it never did supplant rice in those two countries.

Maize also became well entrenched in southern
Europe, and is still used in traditional dishes of
that region today. For when wheat fields were
stubborn and you could not plow them up, you could
plant maize instead. If there were a dry period
in the spring, the winds came and took other seed
as well as the soil; but maize never seemed to fail.

Whenever we read of the reactions of travellers
to this new-found crop, they are always intriguing.
Such an account of it is given by Purchas, in his
memorable book "Purchas his pilgrimage" or "relations of the world and their religions: America.
The eighth booke (1625 or 6)":

"...for their Seeds and Graines, Mays is
principall, of which they make their
bread; which our English ground brings
forth but hardly will ripen...it grows,
as it were, on a Reed, and multiplieth
beyond comparison; they gather 300 measures
for one..."

However, it was soon found that when maize was ground up, the meal did not make the type of bread that was desired. In the final analysis, despite its many good qualities, maize could not be used as a substitute for wheat in the making of bread. Consequently it was eaten in a different form, as polenta, a kind of porridge.

As time went on, the colonists in the New World observed the native custom in the cultivation of maize. For example, they learned to interplant other vegetables between the rows of corn; in this way, the broad leaves of the corn plants could give the vegetables some protection from the hot sun.

The colonists also observed the ways in which the natives prepared the maize for eating. First they softened the maize with lime water, and then took the softened kernels and cooked them to a paste. After that, they would take the paste and form flat cakes which they called tortillas. Having made these attractive tortillas, the natives added red peppers, sweet peppers, kidney beans, squash meal, fish, nuts, maple syrup, and other foods, making a wide variety of nutritious meals. The Spaniards did not at first adopt this native cuisine, but in later years, as the two cultures mingled, they did. However Carletti was quick to appreciate tortillas.

Before the Europeans arrived, the natives of America were eating a balanced and varied diet, with peppers and various kinds of beans, which provided necessary protein and vitamins. The beans were eaten either fresh or boiled. A tortilla with a savory stuffing was called a tamale, and was a complete one-dish meal capable of endless variations, some of which we have only lately come to know and appreciate.

It is interesting to note at this stage that the disease called pellagra did not touch the Amerindians, as we learned four hundred years later when it became so rampant in the southern United States. But as we now appreciate the methods which they used for preparing their foods retained the available niacin, to protect them against it. This was noted by MacNeill. But both European and African populations who took to the corn culture were to suffer severe pellagra, due to incorrect methods of preparation, as noted by D. A. Roe in "A plague of corn: the social history of pellagra 1973 (pp. 15-30). It was noted by Casal in northwest Spain in 1730 as a new disease.

The natives of the Americas also used another vegetable which was entirely unknown to the Europeans, called a tomato. Tomatoes appear to have arisen as weeds in the maize fields, but at some point, when the natives found that they were edible, they were cultivated and improved. This had happened long before the arrival of the Spaniards and, as is true of the domestication of so many plants throughout history, no records survive to give us a clue as to exactly how it was done.

Thin shavings of unripe tomatoes are used in all sorts of Mexican dishes today, to dress up the blandness of the beans. We have mentioned pepper and spices from the Orient which were used in part to cover up taint in meat and to enliven the food. But in the tomato there is something that is pure flavor, not used to cover up anything, but simply to add relish and delight to the meal.

Early in 1493, Columbus returned to Europe, bringing cotton, maize, some strange beasts and birds, and two native Americans. It was thought that he had not found Japan, but India. The islands he had found were therefore called the West Indies. Before 1493 was over, Columbus sailed for the New World again with a great expedition of 17 ships and 1500 men, and with the express permission of the Pope to take possession of the new lands for the Spanish crown, and of course, for the Catholic church.

CORTEZ

Truly, when Cortez and his Spaniards arrived
in Mexico from Hispaniola in 1519, he wrote back
to Spain, "Nobody is hungry here." By that time,
the Spanish soil had become so denuded that it could
no longer feed the Spanish population. The Islamic
occupation of Spain had just come to an end. When
the Moslems left, the Spaniards gradually went down-
hill, agriculturally speaking, because they were not
paying attention to the known requirements of the
soil, as laid down over a thousand years earlier in
the writings of Columella. The Spaniards were
thinking rather of crusading, chivalry, and honour.
For these reasons, the population pressure from
Spain and from other European countries as well
was a very important factor in the search for new
lands. The people who went there were energetic,
and had a certain type of courage to face the unknown. A better life in those days meant enough
to eat, first of all. And, in the New World --
especially in Central America -- enough to eat was
both a promise and a reality. Afterwards one could
get riches -- clothing, property, and land.

And what did the Old World contribute to the
New? It contributed cattle, the source of meat,
milk, and cheese. The native Americans had been
using none of these, because although they did have
game, fish (when they were close enough to water)
and (used as food) dogs, they had no cattle. Nevertheless, their diet had been fairly rich in protein,
fat, and most of the vitamins.

An important creature in the New World was the
turkey. The turkey has an interesting place in our
cultural life, although it may not be an important
source of diet. Apparently the turkey (Mexican:
Uexolotl) appreared in Turkey as a result of the
activity of Turkish merchants in the eastern Mediterranean. Vague as to its origin, the French when
they came across it dubbed it "coq de l'Inde", on
the mistaken supposition that it came from India.
This was ultimately corrupted to "dindon". It was

also known to theFrench as "galle d'India", and
to the Germans as "indianische henn". But the
turkey was not Indian at all. The Turkish merchants
had brought it along with maize and other products
from the west. Nobody seemed to know where it came
from. It certainly was a strange bird, which the
east Indians disclaimed altogether. It did come
from the new world, for Bernal de Diaz, Cortez'
chronicles, described it for the first time. In
meat dishes "the turkey meat was put on top, and
the dog underneath, to make it seem more."

IMPROVEMENTS ON SHIPPING

None of these voyages of discovery would have
been possible without the advances in shipping
which preceded them. Rudders came into use for
the first time, and vessels as a whole improved.
In the fifteenth century, shipbuilders started to
build ships with three masts instead of one, and
to include the movable boom which meant that the
sails could be moved around to catch the wind from
any direction. Longer, more strenuous voyages could
at last be undertaken.

The age of exploration produced various kinds
of new knowledge -- knowledge about the stars,
planets and the earth; knowledge that the seas
join together and are all one, so that you can
reach "anywhere"; knowledge about other races and
peoples, and other places; other birds, animals, and
plants; and knowledge about other food.

But sailing was a risky business. It was accounted a good return if only half the seamen survived.
Famines and epidemics on land had always accounted
for many deaths. Perhaps that is why people were
prepared for such a high mortality rate at sea; and
in any case the average age or life span in Europe
at that time was only about thirty years.

Why did they take such risks? To get rich,
ostensibly, although not everybody did. It is
calculated that Vasco da Gama arrived back from

his second journey to the Orient with spices worth sixty times what it cost Portugal to outfit his 13 vessels.

In addition, as noted previously, there was population pressure. Restless and competitive cities and states were all vying for overseas empires. Nobody wanted to be left behind in this restless surge of exploration.

And finally, the New World was a source of metals which Europe now needed to make coins: copper, silver and gold were especially needed in southern Europe. Florence, for example, had begun minting gold florins and silver ducats as early as 1253.

It is always interesting to note the relative power of countries in the matter of trade. Spain and Portugal were intensely competitive in explorations, so much so that an arrangement was made to share the wealth. In 1494, Pope Alexander Borgia drew a line from north to south through the Atlantic Ocean. He awarded to Portugal all lands east of that line, and to Spain went all lands west of the line. Thus it was that Portugal acquired the African colonies and Brazil, while Spain got all the lands of central and South America, except for Brazil.

SUGAR

As a result of the Pope's decree, Portugal was able to corner both ends of the African slave trade: the source of slaves in West Africa, and Brazil, where they were to be sent. The Portugese did this with a clear conscience, for Pope Nicholas V had authorized them to "attack, subject, and reduce to perpetual slavery the Saracens, pagans and other enemies of Christ southward, including all of the coast of Guinea." As it turned out, the kings and the merchants of the African Gold Coast were only too willing to part with slaves in exchange for European cloth, hardware, spirits and firearms.

In 1550 there were five sugar plantations in Brazil, and in 1623, just 73 years later, there were 350. Consequently, more and more slaves were needed. The Dutch also took a hand in the slave trade, and then other nations followed. Under slavery, sugar was produced profitably.

It had been estimated that fewer than one million blacks were landed in the Americas before 1600. By 1700 the figure was 2.75 million; and by 1800 it was 7 million. They were put to work not only on sugar plantations but in cotton and tobacco fields as well.

Sugar became profitable, common and cheap, and replaced honey. It was discovered that fruit could be preserved in sugar, and jam made from it, so that by 1730 these commodities were in use all over Europe. The influence of jam on our culture is unmistakable, especially in England. Sugar became so important that in 1670 the Dutch were willing to yield New York to England in return for the captured islands of Surinam. In 1764, France was prepared to agree to the terms of a treaty with England following the Seven Years' War, provided that England would return Guadaloupe to France as part of the deal.

On Hispaniola the natives had shown the Spaniards what has been called cassava bread. This is made from the manioc root, which when squeezed yields a liquid. When boiled, this juice produces a sediment known as tapioca. The pulp was shaped into flat cakes and cooked slowly on a griddle to form cassava bread. It would keep for years. The Spaniards are said to have developed quite a liking for this bread.

The Americas contributed a long list of foods to the old world: maize, the tomato, turkeys, sugar, green and red peppers, avocados, pineapples, lima beans, chocolate, peanuts, papayas, sweet potatoes, and finally the potato, which will be dealt with in the following chapter.

PERU

When the Spaniards got to Peru, they could
scarcely believe the things they saw there. Irrigation was practised, and water was impounded in
reservoirs made with primitive tools. Maize grew
there, too, and the Peruvians had a myth to account
for the origin of maize in their land.

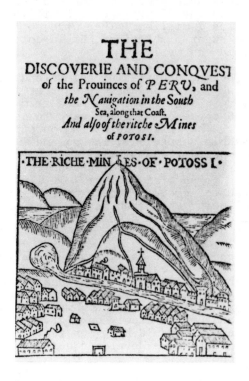

THE
DISCOVERIE AND CONQVEST
of the Prouinces of *PERV*, and
the *Nauigation in the South*
Sea, along that Coaft.
And alfo of the ritche Mines
of *POTOSI.*

·THE·RICHE·MINES·OF·POTOSSI·

It was believed that:

"...after the deluge, the god of the earthfires
had created men out of glazed clay from the
depths of the earth. He breathed life into

260

them and put ears of corn in the hollow
of their right arms. Then he sent them
out of a crater near Lake Titicaca. There
were four brothers and four sisters, and
they began at once to sow the maize.
And so maize was sown all over South and
Central America by the hand of man,
long before Columbus came.

It was the food of the laborers who
built the roads and the stone walls of
South America, and of the workmen who
constructed the lovely limestone temples
and palaces of Central America."

A surplus of maize gave the leisure necessary
for artists to create the beautiful tapestries and
pottery of Peru, and for scientists to build up
the astonishing knowledge of mathematics which was
current in Guatemala and the Yucatan at the same
time that the Romans were trying to civilize the
barbarians of Europe and Great Britain. "Far
more than any other food, maize supported the
great population that America had, before the coming
of the white man."

REFERENCES

249 ..THE HOST..WHEATEN BREAD AND NO OTHER.."
St. Thomas Aquinas; quoted in Jacobs, p 163.

250 COLUMBUS' ATTEMPTS TO GET HIS VOYAGE SPONSORED.
Columbus, Ferdinand: The Life of the Admir-
al Christopher Columbus; trans Benjamin
Keen (1959).

252 "..MAIZE IS GATHERED FOUR OR FIVE TIMES A
YEAR." Carletti, Francesco: Ragionamienti:
my voyage around the world: 1596-1606.
H. Weinstock. (1964).

253 "..MAYS IS THE PRINCIPALL.." Purchas his
pilgrimage: Relations of the world and
their religions: America; The eighth
booke (1625-1626).

254 TORTILLAS..VERY PLEASING TO THE TASTE. Carletti, ibid p 7.

255 PELLAGRA DID NOT TOUCH THE AMERINDIANS.
MacNeill, William H. Plagues and Peoples;
p 179 (1976).

255 PELLAGRA A SCOURGE IN AFRICA AND OTHER PARTS
OF THE WORLD. Roe, Daphne A; A Plague
of Corn: the social history of pellagra.
pp 15-30 (1973).

256 "..NOBODY IS HUNGRY HERE.." Prescott, W. H.
The Conquest of Mexico; Vo- I. p 186 (1843).

256 MEXICO: NEW SPAIN. Diaz, Bernal de: The
Conquest of New Spain (1517); trans. 1963.

256 USE OF TURKEY AND DOG IN THE SAME DISH.
Historia general de las cosas de nueva
Espanan; trans. Cohen (1963).

258   "..ATTACK, SUBJECT AND REDUCE TO PERPETUAL
       SLAVERY.." Pope Nicholas V: The Atlantic
       and Slavery: Wyndham, H.A. (1935).

259   EARLY SUGAR PLANTATIONS IN BRAZIL.   La
       Santa Casa de Misericordia de Bahia
       1550=1775;   Russell-Wood (1968).

259   SLAVE POPULATION IN THE AMERICAS: Oliver.
       T and Fage J. A short history of Africa
       p 120 (1962).

261   "FAR MORE THAN ANY OTHER FOOD." Mason. G;
       Columbus came late; (1931); quoted in
       Jacobs; ibid p 201.

When the Spaniards came to Peru in 1531 they
found extensive vegetable gardens in the uplands.
These gardens had a plant that was lovingly tended
by the natives; it showed white, pink and pale
mauve flowers with five-pointed calyces. These
plants which had green squarish stems were planted
at unusually wide intervals from each other. What
was even more odd was that the natives heaped up
earth around each plant. "...As much of the stem
as possible must be married to the earth," they
were to tell the Spaniards. But the newcomers
could not understand this, because it was not the
stem, but the roots which the earth fed, and the
roots were already in the ground.

The ripening fruit was a green, fleshy berry.
When a Spaniard placed one in his mouth to taste
it, a native, knowing no Spanish, rushed towards
him, wringing his hands in despair. The gardener
tried to explain his anguish by lying down on the
ground and playing dead, indicating to the Spaniard
that he must spit the berry out of his mouth. So
the berry was poisonous!

Now the Spaniards already knew that these sav-
age peoples poisoned their arrows; and they needed
poison also to catch fish, for with it they stunned
the fish and then were able to catch them with
their bare hands. One might expect then that the
savages would raise poison. But miles and miles of
garden devoted solely to the raising of poison!
This was hard to believe. With so much poison,
the natives could wipe out the whole vice-kingdom
of New Spain.

Later on that month, so the chronicler has it,
women and children weeded up the plants of the gardens and the white strangers could not believe
their eyes. All the bounty of the gardens was gone.
But attached to the underground stems of these
plants were knobs, enormous ulcerous growths upon
the roots. So these were what the harvesters were

seeking. It was these swollen knobs that were precious to them. All that grew above ground was burned.

"What is that called?", they asked.

"Pappa", the natives replied.

"What is it used for?"

The natives pointed to their mouths. To the Spaniards it seemed fantastic that a beautiful plant which was apparently poisonous was burned while its ugliest part was kept for food. This was first published in a description by Pedro Cieza in 1553.

But later the Spaniards were to eat these curious knobs, cut in slices and fried, or boiled whole in water. They found the taste rather monotonous, but the food was singularly filling. Some of the Spaniards were high-born, and had been used to a whole array of fine foods at home. It would be well to be sparing of these tubers, because whenever they ate them, they left room for little else.

In 1540, this plant was known only in the uplands of the Andes, and the Inca population was very artistic in cultivating it. When the woolly llamas brought in the harvest, baskets full of potatoes to the farmstead, the gardeners sat there and selected the specimens that would serve for the next sowing. For these strange plants were not perpetuated by seed at all, but from these tubers, which were chosen carefully to reproduce their kind. This was a fantastic procedure; nobody had seen it before, and it was reported very carefully by the explorers.

And the newcomers were often fond of the new food, "a dainty dish, even for a Spaniard", writes Juan de Castellanos. Later in the century, when Carletti made his famous voyage around the world, he has excellent descriptions of it.

"With those rafts they take to the ships
that pass there various supplies of the
region, such as fish, hens, pigs, sheep,
and many fruits of the region; and in
particular certain roots called patatas,
white in color. These when boiled, or
roasted under embers have a better, more
delicate and agreeable flavor than our
chestnuts, and can be served instead of
bread..."

LEGEND

The Spaniards saw these native gardeners
operating on these tubers with sharp stone knives
before they replaced them in the ground to produce
the next crop. They may have thought of the surgeons operating on the heads of people. And indeed
these early Peruvians did believe in the connection
between heads and potatoes, for they were also expert surgeons. A most frequent and perhaps the
most dangerous wound in those days would have been
a head wound, inflicted by the clubs in use at the
time. They developed skills in head surgery; they
learned especially how to open skulls to relieve
the pressure caused by bleeding underneath the
skull and the resulting inflammation. This is
proved by the number of skulls that show this operation to have been performed; a window is made in
the skull, which later heals by growing over the
opening. This operation, known only later to
Europeans, is now known as "trepanning". The Peruvians had a proud and serious regard for such skills
and operations.

As Jacobs had suggested, a naive and myster-
ious faith which so often occurs, may have linked
this operation with the plant world, and the benefits accruing by changing the shape of a human
head, especially when injured. Now the potato can
resemble a human head. They were convinced that
each time a new and successful operation on the
potato was made, the result was a new and more
beautiful potato.

267

Needless to say, the Spanish conquistadores were utterly contemptuous of the whole story; but no matter how much they railed against it, the primitive religion and the magic were never wholly eliminated. The potato was a living thing. The natives were stone-worshippers. They buried stones shaped like potatoes in the ground in order to get good harvests. In 1621, a Jesuit, Father Arriaga, noted the superstition of the potato mothers. These are potato twins (axomotl); when potatoes are found thus to grow together in pairs, it was regarded as a good sign. They were kept and hung on posts at the head of the field, so that other plants should follow their example and be fruitful.

The priests stormed but to no avail. They tried to uproot these beliefs (extirpacion de la idolatria), often with great cruelty. But to this day, twin potatoes are hung over the fields in Bolivia and Peru, although now they are hung upon a cross. Thus the old faith and the new faith are stronger than one faith alone.

There is an interesting sequel to this account. When the Spaniards came back to Europe and introduced the potato there, they were at the same time introducing some of those ancient superstitions that they had so vehemently condemned. For the invisible underground roots of the native American beliefs were brought over also at the same time. They were to crop up in Europe in places that had never even heard of the native Americans! The peasant in northern Sweden, for example, placed the same homeopathic stones in the potato field as a magic invitation to fertility. Some of the Baltic peoples to this day believe that there is a connection between human heads and potatoes. When a family eats its first early potatoes in the spring, and rejoice about the success of these early potatoes, it is the custom that those sitting at the table should vigorously pull one another's hair. Hair is the symbol of the long roots attached to the potato. The significance of the act is that one should smart a little before one's teeth chew upon the delicious potato, which after all is a sacred and precious thing.

ARCHAEOLOGY

The earliest remains of the potato have come
from the archaeological sites at Chiripa on the
shores of Lake Titicaca, the ruins at Tiachuanaco
in northern Bolivia, and at Pachacamac near Lima.
These remains date from about 400 B.C. to 1,000 A.D.,
and consist of dried potato tubers or chuno.

According to Thompson, the process of making
chuno is an age-old one dating back into antiquity.
It is a process of freeze-drying. The potatoes are
spread on the ground in a thin layer in the higher
places in the uplands, at heights of between 10,000
and 14,000 feet above sea level. Heavy night frosts
freeze them and in the day they thaw out. This produces a rupture of the cells, such that it is possible to trample out the water. The native Americans would do this, producing the fore-runner of
what we now know as a freeze-dried product. The
winds complete the drying process, such that the
potatoes can now be stored for indefinite periods
of time. A white-colored chuno is obtained by
washing the tubers in a stream for a specified period of time after trampling. This is a superior
product and was much sought after in soups in the
Andes highlands. They were a great standby in years
of failure of other crops.

The potato was probably under cultivation long
before these times, but no remains have been found
to prove it. It is believed that man reached the
Andes from Asia about 10,000 B.C. He migrated
across the land strip now known as the Behring
Straits. The tubers of a wild species may have
been the first plant foods of these early hunters.
The nomadic wanderings of these people may have
marked the beginning of the cultivated potato.
It has been reasoned that wild species gathered at
various sites may have been brought together, and
evolved as mongrels or weedy hybrid forms. The
kitchen middens, or trash-heaps surrounding the
campsites may have received the imperfect or badly
sprouted tubers, which then naturally crossed.

As man became domesticated his first gardens
will have been similar to the early kitchen middens,
containing both desirable and undesirable types.
In time he began to select the more desirable cul-
tivars and probably by pre-Incan times he already
had a large array of potato types. Work on the
history of the potato has been conducted at the
International Potato Institute at Lima, who pub-
lish regular bulletins.

The Inca peoples did not claim to have discovered their potato on their own. According to legend,
the gods gave them seed that produced beautiful
plants, which their invading armies ate, and became
sick. The gods then told the natives to dig up the
roots and to eat them. On doing so they became
strong, and had no difficulty in repelling their
enemies.

THE POTATO IN EUROPE

The potato seems to have remained in the high-
land parts of South America for centuries. The
Mexicans, for example, never knew of its existence,
which had been the Andean food for so long, until
it was brought there by Hernando Cortez, according
to Prescott. The principal food of the Mexicans
was maize, and has continued to be so. But the potato could grow higher up on the slopes of the
Cordillera mountains, beyond the limits of maize.

We have no date on which the first potatoes
arrived in Spain. The Spaniards were quick to
realize that here was a food for all the people;
it was not a delicacy, but for actual survival in
times of dearth. Potatoes quickly became an item
in all Spanish ships' stores, and by 1573, enough
potatoes were grown in Spain to use as dietaries
in some of the hospitals. Salaman notes that the
Hospital de la Sangre in Sevilla was using potatoes
regularly. By 1601, potatoes had spread to Italy,
where they were so commonly used that they were put
into stews.

The second introduction of the potato in Europe

was mentioned by John Gerard in his Herbal of 1597.
"The roote is thick, fat, and tuberous". He
stated erroneously, as it turns out, that the potato came from Virginia. The genetisist Vavilov
in 1926 disproved this theory. Now it is generally agreed that the more likely story is that
Sir Francis Drake collected potatoes in Columbia
in 1586 to take back with him to England. On
his way back he made a side-journey in order to
pick up the stragglers of an unsuccessful colony
in Virginia, and take them back to England. Another story is that he ransacked a Spanish ship and
took the potatoes from it. In any event, those
starving Englishmen in Virginia were the first
Englishmen ever to have seen a potato.

Accordingly, they presented a described
specimen of the potato to a botanical garden in
London, and it was described in an English botany
book as follows:

"...the rootes thereof are not so great
or long, some of them as round as a ball,
some ovall or egg fashion, some longer
and others shorter; which knobbie rootes
are fastened into the stalks with an
infinite number of threddie stringes..."

It was not long before Londoners were to be
quite used to the potato; they were something that
could be eaten, were easy to cultivate, and grew
rapidly.

Shakespeare refers to potatoes in The Merry
Wives of Windsor, written in 1599. At one point,
Falstaff rushes in to exclaim:

"Let the sky rain potatoes...I will
shelter me here..."

Londoners attending the Globe Theatre must
have been acquainted with it, for Shakespeare
would hardly have referred to a greenhouse rarity.

The reference is parallel to the manna from heaven as described in Exodus. The enormous and clumsy potato, "like a stone thrown from a catapult", is being compared with the small and delicate manna that the Jews found in the wilderness, and which sustained them for forty days and nights. Thus potatoes were already being regarded, in the hands of the master, as a substitute for bread, useful in times of crisis.

The people of England as we have already noted, were frequently to suffer want and scarcity, especially in the latter half of the sixteenth century. They had recourse to stretching out their flour with beans, peas, oats and acorns, baking these into their bread. In William Harrison's "Description of England", published in 1577, potato flour is not mentioned. There is reason to believe that it was not known as early as that. However, in the course of a very few years, by 1590, it is said to have taken hold quite widely. Could they not then have stretched their flour with potato flour?

In 1596, after several years of good harvests, in which grain was even exported from England to France, there was a sudden famine and grain had to be sent to England from Russia to relieve it. In a letter dated July 11, 1597, we read:

"...on Thursday a bowle of rye was sold for 32 shillings in Newcastle; and if by the good providence of God, the Hollanders had not come in with corn on Friday following, what it would have grown into the Lord only knoweth; many not having tasted bread in twenty days before, by credible report, and sundry starving and dying in our streets and in the fields of want of bread..."

The potato was readily accepted in England, although some effects were noted. According to Dr. Thomas Venner, "it is very substantial, good and restorative, though somewhat windy". William Salmon claimed that it stopped "fluxes of the bowels", was full of nutrients and arrested consumption. And in its favor was the following:

> "being boiled, baked or roasted, potatoes are eaten with good butter, salt, juice of oranges or lemons, and double refined sugar...they increase seed and provoke lust, causing fruitfulness in both sexes..."

This latter property was very important if you were building an empire overseas. The life-span in those days was about thirty years. The hazards of living in Europe were many, but if you are going to lose at least two sons overseas, one going and one coming back, then large families were necessary. And if a third son was killed by the natives, or died of disease in the colonies, it was a tragedy that one family might not be able to withstand and survive.

CHANGES IN SPAIN

Spain herself had suffered reverses in that same century. They were afflicted by hunger, more than most other countries. The Moslems had been driven out about eighty years before this time, but the soil was suffering the consequences. Spain had been the garden of the Roman provinces, and later when the Moslems came there, they did so in order to farm. It was the preferred place to be in the Moslem world at that time. And they made splendid farmers. In those Saracen courts there were scholars, too. One ruler is said to have had a library of 600,000 volumes. The great classics of Greek and Roman literature, arts and science had been translated into Arabic. And the scholarship was carried out into practice. The Arabs established universities quite early all over the Moslem world. And at these universities their students were taught how to farm according to Columella's teachings in the second century. They read Cato, Xenophon and Plato.

The Arabs came from the desert originally.
Who better than they would understand the importance of conservation of water? The first element
in successful agriculture is water. In describing
Spain in those Moslem times, Prescott has written:

> "...at the foot of this fabric of genii
> lay the cultivated plain. The Arabs ex-
> hausted upon it all their powers of ela-
> borate cultivation. They distributed
> through it the waters of Xenil which flows
> through it into a thousand channels for
> its more perfect irrigation. A constant
> succession of fruits and crops was obtained
> throughout the year. The products of the
> most opposite latitudes were transplanted
> there with success..."

He was speaking of Granada. But when the
Christian Spaniards took Spain from the Moors,
they allowed these irrigation systems to decay.
Great droughts were the result of this ignorance,
because irrigation from where the mountainous
waters were had been allowed to deteriorate. Soon
the "gardens of the west", as they had been called,
looked like the rest of Spain, like the land of
Don Quixote, "where nothing grows but folly and
poverty". The grandees possessed the land, and
they used it for pasturing goats and raising
horses. The towns were too hostile towards the
peasant to relieve this crisis, and thus it was
that Spain could not feed its people when Columbus
left it in 1489.

Ferdinand and Isabella were quite desperate
for some sort of outside activity that would take
people's minds off their misery. How eagerly
those property-less peasants who had no land at
all must have welcomed a plant that needed neither
plow nor draught animals for its cultivation.

SPREAD IN EUROPE

From Spain, the cultivation of potatoes spread
to Italy, Austria and the Netherlands. It did not

at first get very far because it ran up against a
number of psychological obstacles which proved
difficult to overcome. In 1619, the potato was
banned in Burgundy because people were persuaded
that "too frequent use of them causes leprosy".
The Swiss blamed potatoes for scrofula and the
Germans also at first resisted them. It is reported that as late as 1774, the citizens of Kohlberg
in Germany refused to touch potatoes even when
Frederick the Great sent a wagonload to relieve
famine.

But it was soon adopted in most countries.
By 1664, one John Forster wrote a tract with the
interesting title:"England's Happiness increased,
or a Sure and Easie Remedy against all succeeding
Dear Years, by a Plantation of the Roots called
Potatoes". He pointed out how easily the tubers
could be grown by the poor people so that when corn
was dear they would have a good, cheap substitute
from which to prepare both bread and cakes "at
reasonable rates". He waxed lyrical about potatoes,
and continued:

"...But when these roots shall once come
into use, People will live more happily
and plentifully, Trading will flourish,
and much Glory will redound to Almighty
God, for discovering so profitable a
secret..."

He mentioned that the Irish seemed to have
adopted potatoes rather completely, and exhorted
the English to follow their example.

And indeed the Irish had quickly adopted it.
Ever since 1580, they had realized that the potato
was not ruined when battle raged over the ground
on which it grew. This was important, because the
Irish were living in fear of the English; their
peasant homes were being raided by English soldiers,
and the potatoes remained safe under the ground,
hidden away somewhere. A tiny cottage plot could
produce enough potatoes to feed a man, his wife

and six children, even a cow and a pig.

But this Irish taste for the potato hardly
recommended it to the English, who hated the Irish
for being troublemakers, and for being collabora-
tors with France as sources of invasion of England.

If a nation's standard of living is low, then
the food which it offers and chooses is held to
be low, also. Taste, like fashion, follows the
aristocrats. In the England of the seventeenth
century, it had already become a strong prejudice
among the well-to-do that the potato was something
for poor people. And it was cattle feed. At this
same time, sophisticated tastes were used to
spices, which were expensive, and entirely out of
reach of poor people. This included nearly all
the Irish. It is no wonder that the Irish liked
the potato. They liked its mild taste. But the
English had palates which had by now become almost
insensitive to milder tastes. In a book called
Hunger and History, by Parmelee, a Dr. Thomas
Muffett is said to have written as early as the
seventeenth century:

> "...melons, pears, apples are insipid,
> and taste of nothing..."

And so the charm of the potato was lost on the
overspiced English taste, and it was used only as
an accompaniment to meat dishes. But there it
held its own, and it still does. It was soon to
become an almost indispensible part of the meal,
not as a substitute for bread, but as an extender
for meat.

Several books on gardening of that period
make no mention of the potato, but in 1726, Bradley,
in his general Treatise of Husbandry and Gardening,
draws attention to the merits of the potato, and
wonders at the scant use made of them.

In the days before the potato, as we have
seen, banquets and feasts of record show that great
quantities of meat were the norm. When sometimes

very large slices of bread, "tranchoirs", in English, "trenchers", were put under the helping of meat, it had the important property of "sopping up" the gravy; these "tranches" were not eaten, however, but "thrown to the dogs", who were pictured as being present at all such banquets, if the artists of the time are to be believed. Thus the dogs got the benefit of the gravy, containing blood and therefore iron. But with the potato, here was a culturally satisfactory method of getting the gravy as well, especially when the potatoes were mashed.

And soon England was to adhere firmly to the "joint and 2 veg" of the burgeoning middle class. One of the veges was potato; the other usually boiled over and insipid cabbage. Such a meal was aspired to by all the lower economic orders by the nineteenth century, even if it were only once a week. But meat became increasingly difficult to get as the industrial revolution took hold. The ordinary people had to be content with potatoes and cabbage without the meat. That mixture came to be known as "Bubble and Squeak", and it is recorded in Mrs. Beaton's Cookery Book of the Nineteenth Century.

Table manners became a powerful cultural force also, in the nineteenth century. One can only remember the difficult transition from spoon of childhood to knife and fork. But potatoes saved the day here, for it is entirely possible to convey a potato-gravy mixture to an adolescent mouth on the convex side of the fork, the only culturally permissible method at the time. But should one, in an off moment, wipe up the excess gravy with a piece of bread and eat it, the culture forbad it. It was a no-no because, centuries before, that had been "thrown to the dogs".

FRANCE

What was happening in Europe? The French scientist Parmentier, while a prisoner in Germany during the Seven Years' War, had noted that Frederick the Great had forced his subjects to eat potatoes, and that nobody had suffered. He claimed that they were nourishing, and required so little equipment to raise.

However, potatoes were not at first accepted in France, for physicians said that they were poisonous. As late as 1771, the French government asked the medical faculty of the University of Paris about the ill-reputed potatoes, and they replied that they were in fact safe to use. But it was by now in the eighties and the French revolution was at hand. Parmentier won the Besancon Academy prize for the "replacement of grain in case of famine". King Louis XVI sent for Parmentier and awarded him fifty acres of land for experimental planting of potatoes. It is said that Parmentier mounted an armed guard over the potato plots that he had planted on the land obtained from Louis. But he would remove the guards in the evening, so as to enable curious neighbours to sample its "valuable treasure".

And finally potato flowers were seen at court, sported in the buttonholes of the King and his retainers. Not only this, but the nobility also planted potatoes in their gardens, and were careful to be seen by the peasants as they ate them. The King said to Parmentier, "France will not forget that you found food for the poor". And in truth he had, and it was called, aptly, "pomme de terre". What a compliment from the country that had resisted the potato for so long!

And when old Parmentier died, potatoes were planted all around his grave. But his tract, "Traite sur la culture et usage de pommes de terre" had been published in 1789, when the world was thinking of other things besides potatoes. For when the dam burst, who was going to think of potatoes then? And so old Parmentier was disregarded by the new regimes of 1790 on. Napoleon, however, brought him out of retirement, set him up in office, and empowered him to sow potatoes all over France. Millions of lives were to be saved.

And so France did an about-face. Delicious cold
potato and leek soup, called Vichysoisse, is
served in fancy French restaurants to this day.

The potato was to be accepted into Norway,
and as early as 1750, it had transformed the agriculture of the country. But there were still oppo-
nents. The Presbyterian clergy in Scotland are
said to have opposed to use of potatoes as food,
because they were not mentioned in the Bible, and
were therefore not safe to eat.

IRELAND

But to the Irish, the potato became the national destiny. There arose the circumstance that
there was a correlation between the number of
heads on the island of Ireland and the number of
tubers in the ground. As long as the potato remained faithful to the farmer, the Irish could
continue. This happened for ten or eleven generations, until the potato betrayed the Irish for
the first time.

As early as 1822, a poor crop of potatoes
had been realized in Ireland, and from time to
time there had been other years where it was not
so good. But now a new enemy appeared; this was
potato blight, and it is not clear whence it so
suddenly sprang. Scientists have argued that
asexual methods of reproduction weakened the stock
so that it could not resist disease.

In the forties it was struck down suddenly
by what has since been called Late Blight. Whatever the name of the fungus, which was native to
Peru, the effect was the same. It spread even
to Belgium, the Netherlands, and in the Danube
valley. Only in Ireland, however, did it transform a rich crop into a heap of rotting plants.
And this was in just a few days. On July 26, 1846,
a Father Mathew was riding from Cork to Dublin,
and all along the road he saw potatoes in full
bloom. On his return a week later it was all
decaying.

So the Irish must starve and they must die.
For they had planted nothing else. England sent
an emergency shipment of maize from London to help
relieve the want. But the population resisted the
gift, for it had become folk myth that men turned
black from eating maize. Suspiciously and defiant-
ly, they asked, "Shall we eat Peel's brimstone?",
for Robert Peel was England's Prime Minister at
the time. But hunger drove them to eat it.

What should have been done was to plant large
quantities of oats and rye in Ireland, but they
did not do this. The English government imported
large quantities of maize from abroad. But the
Irish did not have the mills to grind it, nor the
vessels to cook it in. Numbers of brass pots for
the purpose were even brought over from England.
It did not help, and famine stalked the land, followed by influenza. In five years nearly a million
Irish died, one fifth of the population.

And then there arose, for the first time in
Irish history, an intense desire, a mass impulse,
to leave. To leave the land of their forefathers.
Irish had been emigrating to America for two
hundred years, and had introduced their beloved
potato there. But this was different. For wasn't
life more important? Farms had been destroyed
absolutely. And so with the opening of possibilities of sea voyages in 1847, nearly a million
Irish landed in Liverpool from Ireland. Nearly
one third went on towards America in yet other
ships, taking the return journey that their beloved
potato had taken centuries before. Not by any
means all of those who sailed completed the journey. For in those days shipping lines were not
obligated to feed their passengers, so many died
on board.

This account of the potato has spanned over
three hundred years, but the account would not
be complete without a short reference to events
in America when the Irish arrived. It was not a
very satisfactory journey for them; but landing in
America was everything. They disembarked at

Battery Park and looked around them.

They no longer trusted the soil of their
homeland; in fact they did not trust any soil.
They did not, as did the Germans and Scandanavians
who landed during the same years, go west to settle in Wisconsin and Minnesota. On the contrary,
they settled in New York, Boston and Philadelphia.
They became city folk.

They had no money to buy farms, no money to
buy tools, they could not do anything but were
not going to wait. So they stayed there and took
root, rather like potatoes. They multiplied exceedingly on the soil of America, but it was city
soil. By 1858, out of 25 million United States
inhabitants, over one million were Irish.

They clung together in the face of hostile
Americans of British descent. Everywhere there were
Irish quarters in the cities, where at least they
had mutual protection, their church, and their
priests. In a short time, the Irish quarters became centers of political power. And the Irish
never forgot their potatoes, nor the consoling
drink made from them. Thus they became important
merchants of alcohol, and they kept saloons. These
too became centers of political activity. In
New York, Tammany Hall became the Irish-dominated
political machine, and it was not to be subdued
until a little Italian named La Guardia did so in
the nineteen thirties.

The Irish in America therefore became important people in their own right. They were able
to carry on without being dominated, just as they
had done for centuries in their own country.

And to conclude this section, it is a part of
our food culture today that makes Irish stew a
commonplace wherever English-speaking cooking goes
on. It contains well-cooked mutton from the sheep
whose wool makes those fine Irish tweeds. It contains any number and kinds of vegetables; but
whatever else is in that stew, there are always
potatoes.

And so the distant land of the Incas had
produced a food which altered the whole subsequent
history of food. It was to include a failure which
wrought such changes in America that it had a major
influence on our life and times.

REFERENCES

265   "..AS MUCH OF THE STEM AS POSSIBLE MUST BE
      MARRIED TO THE EARTH.." Jacobs, H.E. Six
      thousand years of bread; chap 83, p 208
      (1944).

266   ITS UGLIEST PART WAS KEPT FOR FOOD: Cieza
      de Leon, Pedro, Cronica del Peru; Sevilla
      (1553).

266   "..A DAINTY DISH EVEN FOR A SPANIARD.."
      Castellanos, Juan de; from Tannahill;
      ibid p 256.

267   "..AND IN PARTICULAR CERTAIN ROOTS CALLED
      PATATAS.." Carletti, Francesco; Ragiona-
      mienti; my voyage around the world, 1596-
      1606; trans Weinstock 1964.

267   TREPANNING. Flournoy, Bertrand: World of
      the Incas p 163 (1958).

267   "THE POTATO CAN RESEMBLE A HUMAN HEAD."
      Jacobs, H.E. ibid p 211.

269   EARLIEST REMAINS OF THE POTATO: McIntosh,
      T.P. The Potato: its history, varieties,
      culture and diseases; (1927).

269   REMAINS OF CHUNO: Flournoy, B. ibid p 101;
      Ugent. D. Potato Science, 170, 1161,
      Dec 11 1970.

269   FREEZE-DRYING: Thompson, N.R. Potato: gift
      of the Gods; Los Angeles Times, IA, Novem-
      ber 16 1979.

269   POTATOES A STANDBY IN YEARS OF FAILURE OF
      OTHER CROPS. Adamany, Lynette: History
      of the Potato; Seminar series; University
      of Wisconsin-Green Bay, 1977.

269   POTATO BROUGHT TO MEXICO FROM PERU: Prescott, W.H. Conquest of Peru, $\underline{V}$, 65, 1844.

270   POTATOES IN SEVILLE HOSPITALS: Salaman, Redcliffe. N. History and social influence of the potato. (1949).

271   POTATO IN EUROPE: Gerard, John: Herbal (1597).

271   POTATO NOT FROM VIRGINIA: Vavilov, N.I. Bulletin of Applied Botany, $\underline{XVI}$, 139 (1926)

271   "THREDDIE STRINGES." Gerard, John, ibid.

271   "..LET THE SKY RAIN POTATOES.." Shakespeare, William; Merry Wives of Windsor; Act V, Scene V, (1599).

272   "IT IS VERY SUBSTANTIAL GOOD AND RESTORA-TIVE..." Venner, Dr. Tobias; from Sala-man, ibid; Heiser, C.B. jr. Seed to Civil-isation; chap 7; p 138 (1973).

273   "FRUITFULNESS IN BOTH SEXES.." Tannahill, R. ibid p 259.

275   "TOO FREQUENT USE OF THEM CAUSES LEPROSY.." Jacobs. H.E. ibid p 144.

275   "..SO PROFITABLE A SECRET.." Forster, John; England's Happiness increased by the plantation of the roots called potatoes, (1664); quoted in Drummond and Wilbraham, p 94 (1939).

276   MERITS OF THE POTATO: Bradley, R. A dictionary of Plants 1747.

279   POTATO LATE BLIGHT. McNeill, W. H. Plagues and Peoples. chap VI. p 229 (1976).

SCURVY

The condition known as scurvy became particularly noticable during the voyages of discovery.
Out of 160 men on Vasco da Gama's first trip to
the east, only 100 returned, and many of the rest
were lost because of scurvy. The crews of Fer-
nandez Magellan's ships which went around Cape
Horn to Asia and the Phillipines were very badly
affected. According to an early chronicle:

> "...by reason of this famine, and the
> unclean feeding, some of their gummes
> grew so over their teeth that they
> died miserably for hunger..."

They actually starved because they were unable to bite the hard tack and ship's biscuit.

This condition was not new, however. It had
been described by Hippocrates about 370 B.C., and
Pliny later mentioned that the disease was troublesome to the Roman armies in the first century A.D.
It was known to occur during the long siege of a
city. Early Dutch writings speak of scurvy among
the Romans crossing the Rhine. One of the remedies
used by the Dutch for centuries was to eat "lepelblader", (spoon leaves), and this was regularly
practiced by the country people. This is an instance of sound practice being followed without
any detailed foreknowledge of the conditions.

The English learned about scurvy from the
Dutch, and recognized the swollen joints, the dark
haemorrhagic blotches, the foul mouth and the
bleeding ulcerated gums. On the other side of the
world, the Chinese had learned 500 years earlier
to carry on board their vessels fresh ginger growing in pots. By the fourteenth century, the Chinese had arrived at an understanding of the role
that certain types of food could play in preventing
or curing the disease. The Dutch very early on
became associated with the Chinese-influenced areas
of Asia, and they may have learned the importance

of greenstuffs and citrus fruits from them.

Why did scurvy appear with such regularity in the fifteenth and sixteenth centuries? There are two possible reasons: the first one is that Vasco da Gama, Magellan and their crews came from sunny Portugal and Spain, where fruit was eaten all the year round. They were not so likely to have recognized the possibility of scurvy among their men. For in Vasco da Gama's case, it was possible to put in at various ports and inlets to take on fresh food and water as they sailed around Africa. They did not, however, at first recognize the necessity of doing this.

In 1601, ships bound for India for the newly-found East India Company would regularly stop at the island of Madagascar, there "to gather oranges and lemons of which we made good store of juice, which is the best remedy against scurvy". And by 1617, it was well described by John Woodall as follows:

> "...Further the Chirurgion or his Mate must not fail to persuade the Governor or Purser in all places where they touch in the Indies and may have it, to provide themselves of juice of oranges, limes, or lemons..."

Woodall further instructs in the use of it:

> "...the use of lemons is a precious medicine and well tried, being sound and good; let it have chief place, for it will deserve it, the use whereof is: It is to be taken each morning, two or three spoonfuls and fast after it two hours, and if you add one spoonful of Aqua vitae thereto to a cold stomach, it is the better...Some Chirurgions also give this juice daily to the men in health as a preservative, which course is good if they have store, or otherwise it were best to keep it for need..."

This is an early reference to preventative medicine.

The second reason, and the more significant one, was that the sea voyagers who set off across the Atlantic were likely to be out of sight of land for a long time. If you prepared to "sail upon the Dogstar", you could provision your ships with fresh food from the spring harvests at home, and be off by July 15th. The plan was to arrive in the New World by September, hurricanes permitting. The food taken on board, therefore, had to last at least from July until September.

As so many accounts of sea voyages related the presence of scurvy, the disease became known as sea-scurvy. Sir Richard Hawkins knew of the disease in the reign of Elizabeth I. He identified it as:

"...the swelling of the gums, and by denting of the flesh of the legs with a man's fingers, the pit remains without filling up in a good space."

Others, he said, show it by their laziness. He knew of the curative action of "soure oranges and lemons", but he did not put them first on his list of antidotes:

"...the principall of all is the Ayre of the Land; for the Sea is naturall for Fishes, and the land for men..."

CARTIER

Of especial interest to us is the remarkable voyage of Jacques Cartier. In contrast to other explorers so far mentioned, he was not looking for spices or for gold, but for furs, and the possibility of opening up the fur trade for France. He left records of his voyages in a remarkable set of memoirs, beautifully written and in detail. These have been well reported in a recent (1924) paper in the Public Archives of Canada.

Cartier sailed from St. Malo in France in 1535. He reached Newfoundland and spent the winter there, at Stadacona; his description is worth quoting verbatim:

"...in the month of December wee understood that the pestilence was come among the people of Stadacona, in such sorte that before we knew of it, there were according to their confession, dead above 50...

and albeit that we had driven them from us, the said unknown sickness began to spread itself amongst us after the strangest sorte that was ever heard or seen; insomuch as some did lose all of their strength and could not stand on their feete; then did their legges swell, their sinnowes shrank as black as any cole. Also others had all their skin spotted with spots of blood of a purple color; then did it ascend up to their ankles, knees, thighs, shoulders, armes and necke. Their mouth became stinking, their gummes so rotten that all the flesh did fall off, even to the rootes of their teeth which did also almost fall out... with such infection did this sickness spread itself in our three ships that about the middle of February of a hundred and tenne persons that we were, there were not tenne whole..."

There has not been a better description of acute scurvy than this. By mid-March, there had been twenty-five deaths, and an autopsy of Philip Rougement, the first to die, had revealed nothing to cause it. Observation finally saved them. Seeing a native alive and well who had but recently been sick with the disease, they questioned him. Cartier learned that the leaves of a certain tree were an effective remedy. In native language, this was Ameda (Henneda?), possibly sassafras.

The native women taught the explorers how to make concoctions of it from the bark and the leaves:

> "...it wrought so wel that if all the physicians of Montpelier and Lorraine had been there, with all the drugs of Alexandria, they would not have done so much in one year as that tree did in six days..."

Spruce leaf tips may have been used, since young pine needles are an excellent anti-scorbutic treatment. Cartier's notes state specifically that the "Indians" had to wait for the leaves to appear in the spring. In writings on scurvy there is frequent mention of the need for "purifying the blood in springtime". Many remedies are mentioned, including extracts and teas of green herbs, fresh strawberry leaves and other extracts of fruit, such as gooseberries.

As the sixteenth century came to an end, ships' captains began to take precautions to prevent scurvy in their crews. In 1600, Master James Lancaster sailed with four ships to form the East India Company. The ships sailed on February 16, and on July 24 crossed the Tropic of Capricorn, having last touched at the Canary Islands.

> "...very many of our men fallen sick of the scurvy in all of our ships save one ship, the Commander's which had very few cases..."

The Commander's men stood in better health than the men of the other three ships because the Commander had brought to sea with him certain bottles of the juice of lemons, giving each one of his men three spoonfuls every morning as long as the supply would last. "...not suffering them to eate anythinge after it until noone..." The record continues:

> "this juice worketh such the better if

the parties keep a short diet, and
wholly refrain from salte meate, which
salte meate, and long being at sea, is
the only cause of the breeding of the
disease..."

This excellent observation led to the adoption, by the East India Company, of a supply of
lemon water on all of its ships. But it was not
accepted immediately; it was much later on that
the British Navy was to distribute lime juice to
its sailors. To this day, the term "limey" has
been applied to English people, and sailors in
particular.

By 1696, there was published an important
paper about scurvy. It was called "An account
of the Nature, causes and symptoms and cure of
the distempers that are incident to seafaring
people", by William Cockburn. In it he had recorded the following about scurvy, called in this instance, the Plague:

"...the common practice among the Turks
as I was informed by very honest merchants,
unlearned indeed but truly rational, and
most natural for the cure of the Plague
itself, the greatest of all Malignant
Fevers...is by the juice of lemons largely drunk in Broath, by constant eating
of confected Limon Peel and by a drink
much used amongst them called Sherbet...
and in plain English by nothing else than
a cool Diet:....is it any wonder that the
Plague (so terrible to the English Man),
makes no great harvest among them?...

Sour fruits seemed to be the best for preventing and for curing scurvy. The belief thereby
arose that the curative value lay not in the fruit
but in the acidity. Because fruit juices were
difficult to keep in hot climates, other acid
drinks were sometimes used instead: vinegar, and
even elixir of vitriol.* These were, however,
ineffective in curing scurvy.

* mediaeval term for sulphuric acid.

As an understanding developed that the need
was for fruit juices, the idea became entrenched
that it was the juice and not the fruit which was
effective. The Salerno doctrine helped to rein-
force this view, and the distaste for fruit itself
carried on through, until quite recent times. It
is the author's view that our emphasis on juice
today, rather than on whole fruit, may have arisen
because of these early attitudes.

OCCURRENCE OF SCURVY ON LAND

It has been mentioned that scurvy was early
on known to occur during prolonged sieges of cities,
even in Greek and Roman times. But in the north
of Europe the possibility of mild scurvy exists
in nearly all poor people, in town and in country
alike. We shall later come to the existence of
scurvy even in the middle class in Europe, such
as at Christs' Hospital School in England during
the eighteenth and nineteenth centuries.

The country people in particular knew of
certain remedies which they had learned about in
the course of time. Popular among them were:

"...parsley, chervil, lettuce, purslane,
winter rocket and strawberries, good to
fasten loose teeth and to heal spongy,
foul gummes..."

Robert Boyle, known for other scientific
advances, gave a recipe based upon an infusion of
barley and lemon rind, which he recommended for
"scorbutick cholick". Sorrel, so-called scurvy
grass was a popular remedy:

"...the leaves of the scurvy grass are
to be boiled in milk; also in beer,
whey, ale, wine or water; if the leaves
of the scurvy grass are to be used by
themselves, they ought not to be boiled
long...lest the volatile salt be quite
vanished away..."

This is an interesting early reference to the instability of the anti-scorbutic principle.

LIND'S WORK ON SCURVY

In 1753, Dr. James Lind, who was a ship's doctor, wrote an excellent treatise on scurvy. He brought up to date all the findings of the previous 200 years, described scurvy accurately, and realized that good, substantial evidence as to the causes of the disease was still lacking.

There were many folk remedies still in use in those days and Lind proposed to test them methodically. So he performed an experiment, as follows: he selected twelve sailors with the scurvy, and put them together on the ship "Salisbury" so that they were in contact with one another. At first he fed them as usual on the ship's diet. Then he made the following changes: he divided them into six groups of two each: the first two received the ship's diet and nothing else; to the five other pairs he fed, respectively, the ship's diet plus a quart of cider a day; twenty-five drops of sulphuric acid a day; two spoonfuls of vinegar a day; a pint of sea water a day; two oranges and a lemon a day until the supply ran out.

One of the men who received the citrus fruit returned to work in six days and the other soon after; those who drank the cider showed a slight improvement. The other six showed no improvement at all. This is said to be the first controlled experiment in medicine that has been recorded. The Royal Society laughed at the simplicity of Lind's results. They would not believe that a disease could be cured simply by a change in diet.

By now, it began to be realized that all fresh foods are to some extent beneficial in controlling the onset of scurvy. It was the use of hard tack, the ship's biscuit, and salt pork in combination which was so devastating. Northern cities were not able to supply fresh food for so much of the year that expeditions setting out from the north of Europe were not likely to have much in the way of protective foods to load on board.

Another important finding which was not interpreted for three centuries was that animals, when they were taken on long voyages, did not suffer from scurvy in the same way as the sailors did. It is only now that we know that animals can supply their own sources of vitamin C, and therefore do not need any dietary source of this essential nutrient.*

SCURVY IN RECENT TIMES

Two hundred years after the East India Company ships began to use citrus fruits on a regular basis, scurvy began to appear in other parts of the world. One of these occasions was the Gold Rush of 1849 to 1851. The deaths in the mining camps arising from scurvy are hard to document, but have been set at as many as thousands. The last part of the trail to California is marked with the graves of those who died.

In the Civil War, there are reports of 30,714 cases of scurvy, although only 338 deaths. In the Franco-Prussian War of 1871, the besieged city of Paris suffered badly from scurvy. Likewise in the Russo-Japanese War of 1905, half of the garrison stationed at Port Arthur suffered from scurvy during the siege. Even in World War I, thousands of soldiers were incapacitated with scurvy. The troops from India fighting with the British in Mesopotamia had 7,500 cases of scurvy in an eighteen month period.

FUNCTIONS OF ASCORBIC ACID

At the risk of getting ahead of our story, the recent findings will be mentioned here. We have learned much in the last fifty years about the cause and remedy for scurvy. Research has shown that a major function of ascorbic acid is as a co-factor in one of the steps in the synthesis

* an exception is the guinea pig, which needs exogenous vitamin C; it is therefore used in research on scurvy.

of collagen, the connective-tissue protein. Collagen is thought of as nature's glue, because it holds groups of cells together. Lack of collagen results in failure to form mesenchymatous interstitial cells and tissue. This in turn, causes haemorrhages, because collagen is required as a part of the walls of blood vessels. If these rupture too easily, haemorrhage occurs. This is particularly true of the gums, which are subjected to a good deal of pressure and stress.

So we can understand some of the problems faced by pioneers, sailors and soldiers. Poor wound-healing was a serious matter indeed in the days of swash-buckling sailors, fighting with swords. And holding teeth in their sockets is another role of collagen. In previous centuries the smiling young sailor who left port with gleaming white teeth might return months later with no teeth at all.

REFERENCES

285 "..THEY DIED MISERABLY FOR HUNGER.." Lind, James; Treatise on the scurvy, (1753).

285 LEPELBLADER: van Ardel, M.A. (1927), quoted in Drummond and Wilbraham.ibid p 134 (1939).

286 "..STOP AT THE ISLAND OF MADAGASCAR.." Tannahill, R; Food in History, p 272.

286 "THE USE OF LEMONS IS A PRECIOUS MEDICINE.." Woodall, John; Hiss Book: The Surgeon's Mate pp 160-188 (1612).

287 SWELLING OF THE GUMS. Hawkins, Sir Richard, (1588); from Drummond and Wilbraham ibid p 138.

287 CARTIER'S TRAVELS: Biggar. A. Public Archives of Canada, 11, 204 (1924)

289 "VERY MANY OF OUR MEN FALLEN SICK OF THE SCURVY.." Drummond and Wilbraham ibid p 139.

290   DISTEMPERS INCIDENT TO SEAFARING PEOPLE.
      Cockburn, William; An account of the na-
      ture, causes, symptoms and cure of the
      distempers that are incident to seafaring
      people.   (1696).

291   "..TO FASTEN LOOSE TEETH.." Culpeper,
      Nicholas; The English Physician enlarged.
      (1653).

291   SCURVY GRASS..SORREL. Boyle, Robert:
      Medicinal experiments; a collection of
      choice and safe remedies.   (1692-94).

291   "QUITE VANISHED AWAY." Mollinbrochius,
      A.V. (in Latine); englished by Theo
      Shirley (1676).

291   DE SCORBUTO: DISSERTATIO EPISTOLICA:
      Kramer. J.G. Nuernberg. (1737).

"Mistress of the Seas"

After the reign of Elizabeth I, great though
it had been in so many ways, the people were suffering first as regards to their freedoms. For
with the advent of the Stuarts there was much oppression. This was noted by John Milton who in
addition to such works as "Paradise Lost" and
Paradise Regained", wrote tracts setting forth his
rationale as to why the King was guilty and should
be tried.

Secondly the people were suffering as regards
to their food. Good records are difficult to get,
but the diet of an average man in 1610 might be
2 pounds of bread, 3½ ounces of cheese and 9
ounces of pease daily. The milk and the whey have
disappeared. It is possible to get information
from institutional diets, such as those prescribed
for orphanages, boarding schools, and what were
euphemistically called "workhouses" for the down-
and-out. Prison diets are on record, as well as
those for the Navy.

In the early seventeenth century, people
were all planning to go down to the sea in ships;
speculation, trading and adventures overseas were
all the rage. In order to learn about the types
of diet recommended by the authorities on an official basis, it is useful to follow up an idea
proposed by an anonymous writer in 1615, because
it describes in some detail the food regarded as
suitable for the average man.

The idea was to set up a great herring-catch-
ing enterprise off the east coast of England,
centered on Yarmouth. The promoters of the scheme
described it in a tract called: "A computation of
the charge of a Busse, a herring fishing ship."
Such ships, Britain's Busses, were to be outfitted
for as much as a sixteen week outing. A crew of
fifteen men and a boy were to be supplied as
follows:

297

Beer, per day per person, one gallon
Biscuit one pound a day
Pease porridge or oatmeal one gallon a day
Two pounds of bacon in a week
Butter to allow every man and boy to butter
   his fish or otherwise to eat as they like,
   a quarter of a pound per day;
Half a pound of Holland cheese a day.
Also some honey, ginger, sugar, nutmeg and
   vinegar

"They may take daily out of the sea as much
fresh fish as they can eat."

This was an excellent diet except that there
were hardly any vegetables and no fruit. But this
was characteristic of those times even among well-
fed folk in the manor houses on the mainland.
Modern calculations of this diet have yielded a
calorific value of 5,800 per day. This amount
would have been needed, for working on the herring
fleet was indeed a chilly job, and involved much
physical effort. The rations contained 150 grams
of protein and 250 grams of fat per day, over double
what we regard as a recommended daily allowance.
The calcium and phosphorus were ample, with the
ratio between the two excellent. All the vitamins
save vitamin C are in ample supply in such a diet.

What kinds of people manned these herring
boats? They were the average working men, who could
be commandeered, or who would volunteer to go out
on such expeditions.

Another very interesting record is that of
the army in Tangier in 1660.

"The private soldiers live there better
than in any part of the world, for they
have fresh and wholesome quarters with
small gardens. Coals they have for dressing their provisions, out of the stores
at the King's charge. Every Monday
morning each man receives one piece of
beef, one piece of pork, 7 pounds of

bread, a quart of peas, and a pint of oatmeal, besides butter and cheese for his week's allowance."

Any doubt about the size of the pieces of meat is overshadowed by the fact that in Tangier they had gardens, and vitamin C was available in the form of citrus and other fruits.

In 1670, the allowance per day for an ordinary soldier at home was 2 pounds of bread, a pound of meat or an equal weight of cheese, one bottle of wine or two bottles of beer. This has been calculated to yield 3,800 calories, but is quite inferior to the diet at Tangier.

It is instructive to look at a hospital diet. St. Bartholomew's Hospital was founded in London in 1180 by the monk Rahere. Many of the early hospitals did not provide food for the inmates, that being the duty of the patient's relatives. But by 1687, times had changed and the "dyett" prescribed for patients was as follows:

"...every day they had ten ounces of bread; on Sundays and Thursdays they had in addition six ounces of beef boiled without bones; one and a half pints of beef broth, one pint of ale, 3 pints of shilling beer. On Mondays they had a pint of milk porridge and on Tuesday a pound of boiled mutton, with three pints of mutton broth. Wednesdays, Fridays and Saturdays were days of partial abstinence, and they had four ounces of cheese and two ounces of butter besides the bread; the beer was was provided every day..."

This diet had been calculated by modern methods, and it works out to be worth at least 2,200 calories a day on an average. It is a fair diet, with 70 grams of protein and 80 grams of fat daily. The calcium is rather low, the iron is borderline, and again vitamin C is deficient.

In those days people did not know what was good for themselves and their families, except what they learned from the accumulation of experience; and a lot of lore and custom developed around this very question. Fruit, for example, was so often lacking in Britain, as compared with other countries. Visitors from abroad noted this with amazement. According to M. Misson, a French visitor in 1690:

> "The dessert they never dream of, unless it be a piece of cheese. Fruit is brought only to the tables of the great, and of a small number even among them..."

FOOD FOR THE TOWNS

In the seventeenth century large numbers of cattle were sent to the towns for slaughter. This caused many problems, not the least of which was the grime and filth in the streets.

> "The streets of London are so dirty that the women are forced to raise themselves on Pattins, or Galoshes of Iron, to keep themselves out of the dirt and Wet."

writes Monsieur Misson.

There were milk cows in the towns, wandering about the streets with their milkmaids in attendance. They were milked on the spot, in spite of the weather. The milk was at least warm from the cow, and you saw what you were getting.

Attempts were made to organise the cattle trade for the benefit of health. In 1647 the Lord Mayor and Aldermen issued a series of Orders in London. Among these were:

> "Fifth. No poulteress shall deceivably occupy the market to sell any stale victual, or such as the poulterers in this City do stand in strange clothing to do; under pain

of forty s and forfeiture of such
victual (e.g. 13 turkeys, 40 geese
8 lambs)

Eighth.   No butcher or his servant shall use
to drive any oxe or oxen atrot in
the streets, but peacably. And if
any oxe happen to let go when he
is prepared for slaughter, the
butcher shall forfeit two s, besides
recompense if any person be hurt
thereby."

Meat-eating had be now become more prevalent
among larger numbers of townspeople. They observed
how in the country the gentry ate quantities of
meat; they wanted to copy this in the towns, as
much as possible. As the cities grew all over
Europe, people went to them from the country, as
they had in Roman times. In many cases therefore
the land which these people left was adopted to
make the estates larger than ever. These estates
immediately began to produce cattle for slaughter,
as well as for milk products.

The civil authorities tried their best to
regulate by constant inspection the kinds of cattle
that were slaughtered, in order to prevent if they
could the sale of bad meat. But the amount of
illness and the number of deaths caused by food
poisoning must have been appalling. During these
times only half of the children born reached the
age of five. A number of contemporary authors
attest to the frightful conditions of children.
Such a one was a tract by Walter Harris in 1689:
"Tractatus de morbis acutis infantum." (An exact
inquiry into, and the cure of the acute diseases
of infants; englished by W. Cockburn 1693)

Some of the meat that was slaughtered never
reached the tables of the townspeople, but was sent
to the cookshops. It was a temptation to the unscrupulous to use tainted meat, and to cover the
whole thing up so that the customer did not know
what he was getting. Covered meat pies date from

301

this time. A number of seasonings were developed
as a result of the pie business. Whatever the
origin and the state of the meat, a very tasty meal
was to be had at these cookshops, as Monsieur Misson
notes with relish:

> "generally four Spits one over another, carry
> around 5 or 6 pieces of meat each; butchers'
> meat, mutton, beef, pork and lamb. You
> have what Quantity you please cut off; fat,
> lean, much or little done. With this, and
> a little salt and mustard on the side of
> a plate, a bottle of beer and a roll, and
> there is your whole Feast."

The same author notes however that fish was
not cheap, in spite of the thriving trade of the
fishing fleets. "Fish, in proportion, is dearer
than any other belly-timber in London."

The townspeople were beginning to demand more
and more white bread, in the south of England
particularly. In France they favored white bread
already, using at least three siftings to get the
flour as white as possible. The English were giving up the idea of dark rye and bran breads altogether, except in times of shortage.

The regulation of the cost of bread had been
in effect since the First Assize of Bread in 1180.
A second Assize of Bread was enacted in 1608, such
that during the seventeenth century a loaf of
bread was sold at the same price, but differed in
weight.

In spite of attempts to control the quality
of bread, the poor people fared miserably, for
they could not afford fancy wheat breads. Both
rye and later oats were to be used in the poor man's
diet. "...riemell to make bread for the poore",
as recorded by Sir Edward Coke. The use of oats
for porridge developed quite early. "Otmell to
make the poore folkes porage." Later on oats
were to become popular with seamen: "oats boiled
till they burst plus butter." This dish was dubbed
"loblolly".

With the increase in the size of farms, grain was taken to town and milled for trade. The purchase of a sack of flour was beyond the reach of a poor man's pocket; hence he had to develop credit, giving rise to the chandler's shops, forerunner of the corner grocer. We shall see later how the sufferings of the poor became intolerable, and how this eventually led to forced improvement.

Butter became used much more by the working people in the seventeenth century, but it was used by the rich only for cooking. Cheese was more generally eaten, due to the large increase in the population of milch cows on the big estates. The Country people themselves got less cheese; the butter and cheese were sent to the towns; the whey and buttermilk were fed to the pigs.

Sugar became plentiful during this period, as the Brazilian and West Indian plantations developed. The price fell to one third of what it had been before. People were able to indulge in more in the way of sweet candies, sweet puddings, syrups, and candied fruit, if the fruit was available. Various kinds of fruit pies and tarts became popular, especially made with gooseberries and red currants; these needed large quantities of sugar to be edible. Jams of all kinds were developed, and used on bread.

However along with plentiful supplies of sugar, there were also those who were disposed to cheat. According to Dodd, a member of the Grocers' Company was charged "before the wardynes of the misdemeanours in minglinge starches with the sugar and such other thinges as be not tolerated nor suffered; and the said Mr. King having now in his place a goode quantitie of comfytes made with corse stuffe, and mingled as aforesaid with starche and suchlike; it was ordered that the comfytes should be put into a tub of water and so consumed and poured out." It was further ordered that "everie of the comfyte makers shall be made to enter into bondes in 20/-, that they shall not hereafter make any biskitts but with clere sugar only."

VEGETABLES

At this time there was considerable advancement in food production all over Europe. This was
particularly true in Holland where market gardens
were well established. New vegetables were introduced affording more variety to the food. A
real interest in improving crops developed, and
as a result what we might call a balanced diet
came to be possible. The introduction of the
potato was a keynote event of this period, already
dealt with in Chapter 17.

The market gardens which supplied the big
cities of Europe were of necessity situated outside the cities. The farmers and the merchants
had to come quite a distance with their produce.
For centuries in London, one of the main areas for
this produce to be sold was close by St. Paul's
Cathedral. In the Cromwellian period there
were so many disturbances around these markets that
the merchants would spread out all over the surrounding area, and even into St. Paul's churchyard itself. The Market Peace, initiated during the early
Middle Ages, was re-enacted to limit these quarrels,
although it was often difficult to do so. The
King himself was supposed to intervene, but during
the period 1649 to 1660 there was no King, and the
Market Peace was not enforced. If there was serious trouble people would run into the church itself for sanctuary. It was generally agreed that
the people should not be selling their produce
on holy ground. Accordingly, the Lord Mayor restricted the sale of garden produce to certain areas,
and in particular he set aside one area for this
purpose; it was called Covent Garden, established
in 1650, and it has served as London's produce market ever since.

Whereas gardening made great progress in the
seventeenth century, meat production made very
little improvement. Only a few of the more progressive farmers bothered with breeding, or with
the quality of stock. In practically all cases,
approaching winter was a time for slaughtering the

old and weakly animals. The meat was salted down for keeping. Beef was often "powdered" with dry salt, giving rise to so-called corned beef. Thomas Muffett said of such meat:

> "...it is tough, hard, heavy and of ill-nourishment, requiring rather the stomach of another Hercules than of any ordinary and common ploughman..."

Only late in the seventeenth century was this problem of autumn slaughtering resolved. This was due chiefly to the realisation that turnips and other root crops could be used as fodder to carry livestock through the winter. From this advance arose the provision of fresh meat in winter for the first time.

Pigeons were still an important standby in winter, although some blamed them for stealing grain; however they did provide valuable manure. In the country one could poach wild game, if one could get away with it. For by 1659 the laws against poaching were being tightened up. Rabbits, small birds and even deer were possible sources of meat. Various methods of trapping and snaring were fully described in 1629 by Gervase Markham. He compiled his book, as he put it, "especially for the benefit of all the most worth and noble Lords, Knights, Gentlemen and Merchants, Counsellors and Adventurers for the Blessed Plantation of Virginia." It is not stated whether this was to enable those same Lords to catch poachers, and to excel in the art of trapping themselves.

FOOD OF THE POOR

The condition of the poor people was appalling. In 1615 they city of Sheffield had 725 "begging pore" out of a population of 2,027. The begging pore were usually children, who were used for this purpose to elicit pity. Charles Dickens and others were to have a lot more to say about this condition in the nineteenth century.

The villagers were very poorly fed compared with their ancestors of one hundred years earlier, in 1515. The Enclosure Acts and their consequences particularly caused this. The damage which was inflicted on the nutrition of the people by the surrender of the family cow have been mentioned already. The villagers had maybe a pig and a few chickens, but the price of milk went up to 4 and 6 pence a gallon by 1654. This was a whole days' wages for a common laborer, so that his children had to do without milk entirely. The people were short of dairy products other than milk as well; and all that most of them could expect was a little cheese. They fed as a rule on "broth and beans, salted meat, bread, a little bacon, and what they could trap or snare."

There were many poor harvests and several dearths in this same century. One of these lasted for eight years, from 1630 to 1637. Meat became impossible to obtain at any price, and whole generations of people never had meat of any kind. Bread and cheese became the so-called targets against death by starvation, as stated by Thomas Muffett.

During a particular shortage in 1697 the English writer Locke was making a report to the Board of Trade about the state of the people. He reported that: "what children under 3 years of age can have at home from their parents is seldom more than bread and water, and that very scanty too." Bread and water became equated with the punishment for being poor.

Gregory King has written a history about prices. He made a careful study of them during those periods in the seventeenth century. He found that when the harvest was one tenth below expectations, prices rose three tenths. When the yield of the harvest was only 50%, prices went up as much as four and a half times. It is instructive to compare the above with the price increases in oil in 1979.

The working class in the towns had bread, beer
and cheese. Meat eating was out of their reach,
and became related almost exactly to the standard
of living. Meat for the average person had to
give way to broths made of vegetables and beans,
or perhaps a little cheese for the tanginess imparted
to the dish. In better times, those people who
had earlier been suffering so severely in the
dearths, would immediately crave meat. As a direct
consequence of this, vegetables came to be despised
by the townspeople, although vegetables were well
grown, and more varied than before. The association
of vegetables with poverty was to persist until
the twentieth century.

In those days, as now, there was not much
sympathy with the poor. However, a book written
"upon the occasion of the present dearth", at the
turn of the seventeenth century has this to say:

> "I cannot want good will to wish though
> I have no authority to command, that
> the very food of the earth, even the
> blessings of the Lord, should be no long-
> er subject to this copyhold and slavish
> tenure, of such base and unmerciful lords,
> who upon every rumour of foreign scarci-
> ties, upon every petit transportation,
> yea of transportation onely, upon faire
> weather, or foul weather, or any weather
> if they list, can make the same finable
> ad voluntatem domini, and set what
> price they list upon the bushel...."

He continues:

> "Is there no Court of Chancery, neither in
> heaven nor upon earth, to bridle these
> covetous and unmerciful Lords?", "for
> why should the rich man feast when the
> poore are ready to famish?"

This same author goes on to describe how to
prevent starvation using "beechmast, acorns, aaron-
rootes, beans and pease when there is no bread"..

MIDDLE AND UPPER CLASSES

The artisans who did various jobs in the new cities and towns, the entrepreneurs, and the increasing numbers of educated people who ran schools and colleges had a better scale of feeding. Breakfast for them was a good meal, consisting of cold meats, fish, cheese and beer or ale. Herrings, either fresh or kippered,* appeared regularly on breakfast tables.

The Puritan ethic did not permit excesses, at least in theory, and sometimes the table would be set sparely, as in the illustration. Dinner was at midday, but this was changing because or an entirely new development in food habits which was pervading the upper classes. The change of dinner time occurred as social usage changed: in

* kippered: slit open, salted and smoked.

308

Henry VIII's time, it was a 10 am; in Elizabeth's reign it was at 11 am. in the seventeenth century, the so-called merchants' era, it would be at 12 noon, or even later.

One of the reasons was the advent of the new drinks of tea, coffee and particularly chocolate, the latter brought over from the New World by the Spaniards. These delayed the mid-day meal because it became de rigueur to have a cup of beverage in the middle of the morning. They also became accustomed to having these new drinks in the middle of the afternoon; this led to the custom of having something to eat at what was later to become "teatime". Accordingly meals changed somewhat, especially because both sexes partook of this new activity of tea and coffee drinking. Previously there had been a complete separation of the sexes; the men had been wont to go out to their favorite cookhouses at midday, after they had been to their offices; the women would have this new tea at home. Now there was more of a mingling of the sexes, and people enjoyed this new arrangement.

As is usual in a stratified society, affluence feeds on itself. There were excesses among the rich, and ostentation. A midday meal for well-to-do people is recorded as being, for example:

hot shoulder of mutton
good pie baked of a leg of mutton
cold chine of beef
good dishe of roasted chickens

all eaten with bread, cheese, and ale or wine.

For special occasions, there would be much more than this. In April 1654 one week's purchases for the Woburn household of the Earl of Bedford, included a predominating amount of meat:

On bullock of 68 stone; 2 sheet, i calf, a quarter of mutton, a side of veal, 10 stone four pound of pork; i pig; 2 calves'

heads; 4 capons, 12 pigeons, 20 pounds
of butter; eggs; crayfish, a peck and a half
of apples; bread; 2 pecks of oatmeal; six
bushels of fine flour.

Again, according to the inimitable Monsieur
Misson,

> "...the English eat a great deal at dinner,
> they rest awhile, and to it again, until
> they have quite stuffed their paunch. Their
> supper is moderate. Gluttons at noon,
> and abstinent at night."

The wedding dinner of John Verney, for seven
people dining out at an inn, consisted of the
following:

Beer-Ayle	3-0
Wine	11-0
Onings	1-0
A dish of fish	1-0-0
2 geese	8-6
4 fatt chickens	8-0
2 rabets	3-0
A dish of pease	6-0
8 hartey chokes	5-0
A dish of strabreys	6-0
A dish of Cherys	5-6

This took place in May. The fruit was quite
special for that time. But for the greater part
of the year, the price of fruit was such that it
was completely out of the reach of working people.
This was so even in June when it should be plentiful. In 1663, 8 lb. of cherries showed a cost of
5s 6d, which was five days' pay for a labouring
man.. Just two quarts of gooseberries cost 6d,
when even a skilled craftsman was earning only
2 shillings a day.

Misson again the observant visitor notes that
vegetables were at last beginning to be used in
situations other than in soups and broths; namely
as an accompaniment to meat:

"...Another time they will have a piece
of boil'd beef; and then they salt it
some days beforehand, and besiege it
with five of six heaps of cabbage, carrots,
turnips or some other herbs and roots
well peppered and salted and swimming in
butter..."

And the advent of puddings of all sorts is
hailed:

"...One of the good English customs
on the Sabbath Day is to feast as nobly
as possible, and especially not to forget
the Pudding..."

"Blessed is he that invented Pudding,
for it is a Manna that hits the palates
of all Sortes of people..."

TRAVEL

By the seventeenth century a certain amount
of travel was occurring in Europe and elsewhere
in the world. For one thing there was a great deal
of improvement in travel arrangements for the
safety of those going on journeys. For another
thing the incredible surge of book printing and
dissemination of knowledge thereby, assisted in
stimulating the curiosity of scholars and others
to travel to distant places.

Large numbers of people were making the trip
to Rome. This situation immediately brought about
greater dissemination of knowledge about food and
about food customs. Comments occur frequently: an
Englishman named Peter Beckford went to Rome in
order to see the Coliseum, the Catacombs and St.
Peter's. He reported: "raw hams, bologna sausage,
figs and melons but nothing of any substance.
No boiled leg of pork, no pease pudding, no bubble-
and squeak." Small wonder that Mr. Beckford felt
hungry and ill-fed.

311

Distinctive cuisines began to appear; these followed patterns set by the changing times. Before the days of the ages of discovery, Venice was the center of trading between the Arab world and the main part of Europe, as stated earlier. This was especially true for spices, which became part of the Venetian trade pattern. But by 1453 the Turks and the Ottoman Empire were threatening Europe from Constantinople, so that spices became scarce and thus expensive.

Accordingly the Italian cuisine had to adapt itself to do without spices. With no sauces or or hot spices, the Italians developed dishes in which they substituted cheese of various kinds. By 1570 even Pope Pius Vth's guests had a comparatively spice-free meal. They also used game that had been hung for three days, and thus had acquired a taste of its own. Many different dishes arose that were dependent for their interest and variety on what the materials were, rather than by dressing them up with spices.

Ultimately there is the national Italian dish called pasta. One idea as to its origin is that it was brought back from China by Marco Polo, as he had experienced Chinese noodles on his visit. Alternatively it may have been introduced into the great cities of Venice, Florence and Genoa through their trading contacts with China; it could have been spread throughout Italy as early as the eleventh century by domestic servants. These might have included Mongols, who certainly would have known about noodles. In any event it appears that in the Arab countries, in Turkey and in India people were eating noodles long before this time.

The work "sevika" is an Indian word which means a thread; "rishta" is the Arabic word for thread. These are both used to denote the thread-like product made from the pasta in those countries. The word "spago" in Italian means string, and the word spaghetti is derived in this way. There is a history of Italian literature by Wilkins which describes a coarse, rough pudding made of flour, cheese, and butter; it was livened up with many kinds of cheese: mazzarola, gorgonzola.

The pilgrims who went to Rome for the first time met with this Italian food and were suitably impressed by it. The Italians were quite proud of their cuisine. When Catherine de Medici, a member of one of the chief families, left Florence to go and marry the Dauphin of France in 1533 (he was later Prince Henry the IVth of Navarre), she took with her a number of Italian chefs and pastrycooks. They took with them to France the Italian style of cooking, and also introduced various kinds of vegetables, hitherto unknown to the French: artichokes, broccoli and cabbages. French food at the time that Catherine went to marry Henry was loaded with meat, just like the English meals were. They had meals four or five times a day, with little bread or fruit. In 1577 the Venetian ambassador to Paris said: "They ruin their stomachs and their bowels by eating too much, just as the Germans and the Poles do by drinking too much."

But a special kind of French cooking was now to evolve, and 100 years after that time Paris and France generally appear to have developed their own style of cooking, based on those earlier Italian imports. This was codified by a notable Parisian chef called Varenne. He published his famous book in 1655, called "Le patissier francais", which is an important milestone in French cooking. He treated vegetables in their own right for the first time; he made use of the global artichoke, and of mushrooms in many guises. But he frowned upon spices, and recommended the use of sauces that were made of drippings of meat rather than from spices imported from the east. For in France too they found it difficult to get spices, inasmuch as the Portuguese held on to the monopoly that they had wrested from the Venetians. The French would use vinegar, lemon juice and meat drippings to liven up the flavor.

There is a great deal written about the food of the rich of those days, but very little about the

meals of the bourgoisie, the ordinary common folk
or the peasantry. In the great days of Louis XIVth
in the seventeenth century, it was claimed that the
ordinary bourgoisie could "eat like princes if they
had the proper pots and pans, went to market every
day and knew how to make good bouillon." It was
hardly a fair statement, but it was a new depart-
ure for France even to acknowledge the existence
of the bourgeoisie.

But from about 1660 France arrogated to herself
the idea of becoming the national self-assured
culinary experts that she has been ever since.
Not every dish was French, however; when they
used an avowedly English dish, they coined a word
for it to appear on their menus: rosbif, for
example, and that peculiar aberration rosbif d'
agneau. The Europeans as a whole, including the
French, were to become quite nationalistic about
their cooking, and not many of them had a good
word to say about the cooking of other countries.

The food of Spain holds a special place in
the history of foods, because of the voyages of
discovery westwards to find new worlds. The centuries-old connection with Rome was one influence.
Another was the fact that the Moslems lived in
Spain for over 450 years. The food of Spain has
become a mirror of these conquests. Trade over
the centuries has shown this tie.

Consequently olive oil, which came from the
eastern Mediterranean long before the time of
Christ, formed the basis of the Spanish diet. Salt
fish dates from Roman times; mutton came into the
diet as a sequel to the invasions of the Nordic
peoples who liked to eat mutton, and as an accompanying development of the woollen trade. All
these contributed to a varied Spanish diet. Rice
from the Arabs, and the typically Moslem marzipan
and nougat from Baghdad, and finally Turkish
delight, all form a part of what makes up Spanish
diets. Thus it embraced many more cultures than
most other countries, and Spanish foods still
reflect this mixture.

In addition, Spain had colonised all or almost all the lands where the cacao tree could
grow. This tree was confined to the Spanish
conquests in the western hemisphere, and so the
Spanish developed the use of chocolate, which became an important adjunct to the diet. It was
used almost entirely as a drink for 250 years
before it was ever made in solid form to eat.

In between the years 1594 and 1606 a certain
Francesco Carletti recorded his impressions of
of his trip around the world. He observed chocolate being drunk by the people when he was in
Mexico: "they gulped it down in one swallow with
admirable pleasure and satisfaction of the bodily
nature, to which it gives strength, nourishment
and vigor in such a way that those that are accustomed to drinking it cannot remain robust without
it even if they eat other substantial things.
They appear to diminish if they do not have that
drink." By 1631 the preparation of chocolate
in Spain had become a major operation, and numerous chocolate houses existed. The chocolate
paste was subsequently exported to Flanders and
to Italy, but for almost 300 years, the Spanish
adhered to it as a drink.

At the other end of the world, travel had
brought the Dutch into Asia. They had formed an
East India Company of their own. They began to
cultivate as many exotic fruits as they could in
what is now Indonesia. They were past masters
at gardening, and enjoyed the things that a garden could bring. So they decided to bring back
to Holland new and different kinds of seeds. By
1636 in Antwerp you could get exotic fruits of
many and rare kinds: "large plums, various kinds
of peaches, cherries, orange, and lemons, grapes
and other things in a finer condition and in a
state of ripeness to draw from life." Dutch
painters and still-life artists have been famous
ever since. But they also learned to eat the
fruit.

The diets of the Goths, Vandals, and other
Nordic peoples from Scandanavia were ample, as
earlier mentioned. And so it comes as no surprise
that a thousand years later, by the seventeenth
century, they were living a life of robust solidity.
As one chef expresses it: "as substantial and
wholesome plenty."

Although many northern aristocrats were to
send their cooks to France to learn something
(quelquechose) about cooking, they returned feeling that what they had in fact learned (kickshaws)
was a paltry substitute for real food. In what
was later to become Germany the staples of the diet
were: pork and sausage; cabbage (sauerkraut),
lentils, rye bread and beer. A thick hearty soup
appeared on the table at almost every meal; a
fruit-stuffed goose was there for high days and
holidays.

Poland and Hungary, which had borne most of the
nomadic invasions from the east, also reflected
this in their cuisines. Veal, fermented milks
and pickled cabbage occurred as regular articles
of diet. And so did maize, which was brought by
the nomadic Turks, after they had received it from
Mexico in the Spanish era.

Vienna was to become a clearing-house for
many foreign influences, in food as well as in
music and art, sculpture and the style of living
of the Hapsburgs. Viennese food included dishes
from all over the known world, and Vienna became
synonymous with good taste in many areas of life.

COFFEE

It seems that coffee probably originated
not in India or Persia but in Ethiopia. It was
mentioned in the eleventh century by Abdul-y-Sina
(Avicenna), who was a natural philosopher of the
early Moslem world. He dealt with many topics
related to health and medicine. Coffee did not
spread until about the fifteenth century, when it
reached places like Mecca, Damascus, and Baghdad.

It became a favorite Turkish drink, taken very
strong.

By 1554 there was mention of a coffee house in
Constantinople. Travellers there were treated to
delicious coffee, and cool sherbets made of water,
honey, and sugar. The guests were honored chiefly
by being served "a cup of coffa, made from a kind
of seed called caliva, and of a blackish color,
which they drink as hot as they possibly can."
Such was the report of a traveller who went there
in 1632. Pietro della Valle in 1643 recorded that
"it prevents those who consume it from feeling
drowsy. For that reason students who wish to read
into the late hours are fond of it." In 1620
Sir Thomas Herbert in writing about Persia mentions
a drink imitating "that of a Stygian lake, thick,
black and bitter." He was no doubt referring to
coffee.

In Oxford the first coffee houses were opened
in 1650, to emulate those that the students had
seen abroad. People flocked to the coffee-houses,
they wanted to try to new, hot, non-intoxicating
drink that was coffee. The word cafe, imposed by
the French, was where you sat down to have a cup
of coffee.

Later on in the seventeenth century the near-
eastern peoples began to find that their trade
through Mocha, Aden and Saudi Arabia slipped away
from them, including that in coffee. For the Dutch
just as much as the Portuguese wished to open up
trade routes that by-passed these areas. The
Dutch soon found out that their new empire in Java
was absolutely ideal for growing coffee. From then
on the Dutch made Java into one large coffee plantation, just as the British were to make Ceylon into
one large tea plantation. Although the British
tried to develop coffee growing in the West Indies,
it did not succeed there. More suitable for
coffee were the uplands of Colombia and Brazil,
which took almost all the coffee trade for the
western hemisphere, and for a large part of Europe
as well.

These additions to the diet were not exactly
necessary for nutrition, but they certainly introduced an element of pleasurable variety into an
otherwise monotonous diet. It must however be
remembered that they were luxuries and thus unavailable to the poor who comprised the majority
of the peoples of the world. Transportation costs,
plus the duties imposed on coffee and tea by govern-
ments made it impossible for the average person
to indulge. Another century would pass before it
would become possible for the poor man to have his
tea.

DRINKING

Foods that are heavy in carbohydrates and fat,
as most northern European foods were at that time,
have to be washed down with plenty of liquids.
This may account for the reputation which accrues
to Poles, Germans, Dutch and English as heavy
drinkers, especially of beer, ale, stout, lager
and other brewed drinks. This was possible because
there was land enough, so that grain for brewing
could be spared from the food supply. In Italy,
Spain and Greece, as we have seen earlier, beer
drinking had been forced to give way to wine
drinking, because land had become overused, eroded,
and therefore unavailable for the cultivation of
the necessary grain. Vines, on the other hand,
could cling to the steep hillsides, and thrive
where grain crops could not.

Thus it was that the Mediterranean peoples
had become attuned to wine a thousand years before
this time. France, Italy and Spain had long since
established wine growing areas with traditions
of excellence. Chablis, Bordeaux, Burgundy, Madeira
and Malmsey became known throughout the European
world of the time. At Jerez in Spain a type of
wine was developed to become the favorite for
centuries, as sherry. The clear, pale, rose' wines
of France were drunk, as claret, when only a few
weeks old; other wines would be aged for months
or years.

But the northern peoples were to favor beer and its varieties for a long time. A certain machismo developed around beer drinking. As we shall see schoolboys up to and including the days of Charles Dickens' nineteenth century were raised on beer.

Beer of many kinds was known to the Sumerians 4,000 years ago. It had a number of features which are important in our story. One is that it was limited as to the amount of alcohol it contained. Usually it was not more than 6 or 7%, later to drop to 3 and 4%. Another feature is that it had all the nutrients which had been elaborated by the yeast in the course of the brewing operation. We have only recently learned that this contained many of the B vitamins, as well as some soluble protein.

An advance which occurred in the seventeenth century was to change the attitudes towards drinking, and the social implications of the custom markedly. This was the art of distillation. It had been found out as early as 100 A.D. that distillation could be applied in order to separate liquids from solids. But the separation of two liquids from one another did not occur until the end of the middle ages, and it found its application during the period we are discussing. This advance enabled the separation of alcohol and water from mixtures of the two. When conditions are adjusted correctly, almost pure alcohol can be obtained. This was ironically called "aqua vitae" (water of life). In Nordic it was called "uisge" from which arises our word whiskey. When they started with wine rather than with a brewed grain mash, it was called "gebrannte wein", from which derives brandy.

The physical effects of taking this distillate were unpredictable and subtle. It is possible to absorb and to burn alcohol in our system at a certain slow rate, without ill effects; for it does not reach the blood stream to be conveyed as such to the brain; but in the case of these distillates,

the concentration of alcohol is such that it can
be readily absorbed into the blood stream at too
high a rate for the body to metabolise it at once.
Not only that, but the distillates contained,
besides alcohol, a number of volatile substances
called esters, which are detrimental if absorbed in
large amounts. These may even be found to enter
the blood stream through the cribriform plate, just
above the nasal passages, thus providing a ready
and rapid passage to the brain.

Ways to minimise the effects include the
avoidance of strong alcohol on an empty stomach;
sipping slowly, and general moderation. But the
social effects of these discoveries were devastating; and they are with us still. Unhappiness and
unnatural environments may lead to pain, which
can be assuaged with alcohol. And it was not long
before drunkenness on a scale not before witnessed,
occurred in Europe.

As these early distilled drinks became
available, counter movements arose to arrest their
effects arose. Long before any temperance movements
as such, there were enacted in London rules about
drinking. In the period 1641 to 1649 we read
the following:

    1641   Recd of the Vintner of the Catt in Queen
            Street, for permitting of tippling on
            the Lord's day   1 10 0
    1644   Recd of 3 poor men for drinking on the
            Sabbath Day at Tottenham Court
                              0 4 0
    1655   Recd of a maid taken in Mrs. Jackson's
            alehouse on the Sabbath 0 5 0

These were quite stiff penalties. But you
will notice that the sin was to be drinking on the
Sabbath, not for drinking as such.

Alcoholism as such was being noticed in strange
places. For example, in the great days of the
British Raj in India a good many Europeans literally
gorged themselves to death. Sitting down to dine

at one or two o'clock, and spending three hours at
dinner, they would wash it all down with 5 or 6
glasses of Madeira wine. One army contingent at
a later time than this chapter, in 1756, lost 87
out of 848 men, "not from epidemics, nor malignant
disorders, but from irreparable damage to the
liver resulting from overeating and alcoholism."
This had always been excused because the water was
so often unfit to drink, according to records of
that time. But now they had tea and coffee to
drink, which necessitated the boiling of the water,
with at least that amount of protection from disease.

A similar problem of water was to face the
early settlers in America, especially when they
were near the sea coast and fresh water was hard
to come by. Rivers like the Chesapeake had tides
that extended four miles upstream. As the pioneers
went across the country, the idea took hold that
water could be, and often was, contaminated. This
was later reinforced by Pasteur's findings.

Therefore, the people of those times drank beer
as a beverage; not so much for its alcoholic content but because it no longer had pathogenic
organisms in it. Then the early American still
made rye whiskey, and later a type of corn liquor
that Americans have liked ever since. It was made
in Bourbon County, Kentucky. The early Americans
made cider with apples, wine with grapes. They grew
hops, and barley for beer, and apples for cider.

But rum seems to have had a special place in
American history. About 200 years ago, three
imperial gallons of rum per year, per person were
consumed in the colonies as a whole. The Molasses
Act of 1733 was enacted to assure that all the molasses had to go to England to be made into rum
there; none of it was to come directly to the
colonies.

It was sold from England and the money was
used to buy slaves on the African coast; rum running and slave running comprise an explosive mis-
ture. The colonists were not averse to the slave

trade as such, because in fact they bought the
slaves for hard cash when they arrived in Baltimore.
But the Molasses Act was a large bone of contention
at the time, and it raised the whole question of
self-determination, about which the American colonists felt so strongly.

GREEN SICKNESS

During the seventeenth century a number of works
were published having to do with women's problems.
Foremost among these is one called "Child-Birth
or the Happy Deliverie of Women, by Jacques Guillmeau
in 1612.

He said for example that women should expect
to need more food during pregnancy: "the quantity
of her Dyet must be sufficient both for her selfe
and for her child, and therefore they are to be
dispensed from fasting at any time." He recommended milk, and, interestingly enough noted what the
Mongols had practised for centuries, the value of
mare's milk; "for the woman cow milke and the
milk of an Asse are verie much commended"

In a chapter on nursing, he suggests that she
should avoid spices, and "shee shall refrain from
all kinds of raw fruits." This is followed quickly by an emphasis on avoiding constipation; "her
belly must be always loose and if it chance to be
found, she may take a clister. Let her use broths
prunes and apples well-sodden that she may keepe
her selfe soluble."

In 1621 there was a book written by R. Burton
called the Anatomy of Melancholy...He mentions
a sign of "love melancholy" as he calls it, "the
green sickness therefore often happens to young
women". Thus we see the Salerno doctrine still
significant in the thinking of that time. He
pointed out that since the mind is distracting
the spirits, the liver is unable to play its
part in turning food into blood. This condition,
later to be called chlorosis, is a dietary anaemia.
It is very prevalent, particularly at certain times.

322

It was treated either with herbs or with iron preparations. It had been known that certain chaly-
beate springs, containing iron, would be beneficial. Wine, especially port wine was said to be
good for this affliction.

Burton, who recognised it accurately in 1621,
goes on to say: "the Tartars eat raw meat, and
most commonly horse flesh, drink milk and blood,
as the Nomades of old...they scoff at our Europeans
for eating bread, which they call tops of weeds;
and yet Scalinger accounts them a sound and witty
nation, living an hundred years.."

But why did chlorosis appear in the seventeenth
century? It was not unknown before that time, but
suddenly it appeared to be more general. It had
been shown that the diet of the timehad been composed largely of bread, meat, fish, and cheese.
Milk, and therefore cheese are very poor sources
of iron.

The middling folk would get their iron from
wholemeal bread, oatmeal and other components of
the average poor man's diet. Even the 3 mg of iron
per 100 grams of wholemeal bread gives us a fifth
of the daily requirement. It is fair to assume that
these poor people, peasants and workers alike did
not suffer from chlorosis. But the better-off,
who used less bread and more fish, which contains
very little iron, might have suffered. These same
people started to eat poultry to a greater extent,
and this too is low in iron. There is a strong
probability that these people suffered from anaemia.

The iron available to the foetus is transmitted to it across the placental wall and is present
there as a start for the infant. Iron does not go
through the milk, so that the iron that the new
born infant has in its liver is its initial supply,
good for possibly six months after birth. If then
there is no supplement, childhood anaemia appears.
The poor people would give their child a crust of
bread to chew early on, and so iron would be supplied. The better-off people, however, had a

323

difficult time in combating this disorder.

The wholemeal bread which the poor people were
eating supplied not only the iron, but also the
roughage necessary for good functioning of the
bowels. Thomas Cogan had already attested to the
virtue of this:

> "Browne bread...having moche branne, fylleth
> the belly with excrements, and shortly
> descendeth from the stomache..."

But in the seventeenth century the better-off
people would eat as much meat as they could get
hold of. Meat, being wholly digested is therefore
constipating, causing sluggishness of the bowels.

Most of the meat-eating tribes of the world
that have been located, are subject to constipation,
and they were accustomed to relieve this condition
by a dose of what was called "May butter", in this
case rancid fat. This was much used in the sixteenth and seventeenth centuries as an "opening
medicine". Vegetable remedies like senna, rhubarb
and paragoric were added to the pharmacopeia of
the time.

We suffer today from this affliction, if we
eat a high meat diet, with white bread, and a lack
of vegetables and fruit. Even the use of fruit
juices instead of whole fruit has contributed to
the onset of constipation. Apples, pears, peaches
and plums should be eaten fresh, with their skins,
to keep oneself "soluble."

These changes lead us gradually into the
beginning of the eighteenth century, with the world-
shaking events which were to occur, and which were
to affect the people's food in ways not even dream-
ed of at the time.

REFERENCES

297   BRITAIN'S BUSSES..Drummond and Wilbraham:
        The Englishman's Food, p. 1U2 (1939).

298   ARMY AT TANGIER..Thacker, R.A. History of
        the British standing army; ed. Walton 1894.

299   ST. BARTHOLOMEW'S HOSPITAL. Moore, Sir
        Norman, A History of St. Bartholomew's Hos-
        pital (1918).

300   "FRUIT IS BROUGHT ONLY TO THE TABLES OF THE
        GREAT." Misson, Henri de Valbourg; Mem-
        oirs and Observations in his travels over
        England (1690); trans. Ozell (1719).

300   "THE STREETS OF LONDON ARE SO DIRTY.."Dodd,
        George, The Food of London (1856).

302   "BELLY-TIMBER IN LONDON". Misson, ibid p 81.

302   "RIEMELL FOR THE POORE." Coke, Sir Edward.
        Houshold Book (1596).

302   OATS BOILED TILL THEY BURST. Dodd, ibid
        (1856).

304   "A BALANCED DIET BECAME POSSIBLE." Markham,
        Gervase, (1620), quoted in Drummon, ibid
        p 92.

305   "THE STOMACH OF ANOTHER HERCULES." Muffett,
        Thomas Health Improvement, (1655).

305   TRAPPING AND SNARING. Markham, Gervase;
        Hunger's prevention, or the whole art of
        fowling by water and land. (1621).

305   "BEGGING PORE." Fussel, B.E.; Social and
        agricultural background of the Pilgrim
        fathers; Agricultural History, Vol. VII
        (1933).

305   RABBITS, CONNIES. Muffett, ibid p 98.

306 PRICES UP FOUR AND A HALF TIMES. Tooke, Thomas; A History of Prices (1838).

307 "WHY SHOULD THE RICH MAN FEAST WHEN THE POORE ARE READY TO FAMISH?" Platt, Sir Hugh, Esq., "Upon the occasion of this present dearth." (1596).

307 TO PREVENT STARVATION. Platt; a smaller edition of the above was produced in 1683 for Wm. Cooper, and is now in the British Museum (1033 d 15).

309 PURCHASES FOR THE HOUSEHOLD OF WOBURN: Thomas, G. Scott; Life in a noble Household, 1641-1700 (1937).

310 "GLUTTONS AT NOON AND ABSTINENT AT NIGHT.." Misson ibid p 313.

310 VERNEY FAMILY. Memoirs of the Verney family, IV, (1892-99).

311 "SWIMMING IN BUTTER.. Misson, ibid p 301.

311 "..NO BUBBLE AND SQUEAK." Beckford, Peter; Letters for Italy to a friend in England

312 POPE'S SPICE-FREE MEALS. Scappi, Batholomeo, Venice (1570) quoted in Tannahill, chap 15, p 278.

313 VENETIAN AMBASSADOR TO PARIS. Lipponano, G; Viaggio, (1577).

315 TRIP AROUND THE WORLD. Carletti, Francesco; Ragionamienti; my voyage around the world, (trans 1964) p 53.

316 VIENNESE FOOD. Lamb, Patrick. Royal Cookery; London 1710.

317 "A CUP OF COFFA". Lithgow, William (1632).

317 "STUDENTS ARE FOND OF IT." Pietro della Valle; Viaggi (1614-1629).

319   AQUA VITAE..Morrison, Fyne.   Itinerary 1617;
         ed. Furnivall 1878.

322   GUILLEMEAU'S BOOK IS IN THE BRITISH MUSEUM
         as 1177 d 40.

322   MILKE OF AN ASSE VERY MUCH COMMENDED..
         Guillemeau, ibid 5, p 42 (1612).

322   GREEN SICKNESS. Burton, R; The Anatomy of
         Melancholy (1621).

324   "BROWNE BREAD, HAVING MOCHE BRANNE.."
         Cogan, Thomas: The Haven of Health (1584).

20

AVITAMINOSIS A

As we have described earlier the peasant had
to give up his cow in the sixteenth century, and
in the reign of Elizabeth I the inflation was so
severe that he was unable to get milk or eggs at
all.

As time went on, in the seventeenth century,
the large estates raised more cattle, and not just
horses. The country people had much less milk
because it was all sent to the towns; there was
less butter to eat. The farmers in the country
who were running these dairy herds in behalf of
the big estates always fed the townspeople rather
than themselves.

Vitamin A occurs only in animal tissues;
but its precursor, B-carotene, is found in all
green leafy vegetables, associated with other
pigments such as the xanthophylls and chlorophyll.
A diet supplying little fat, or fat obtained only
from cereal sources, should therefore be supplemented with green vegetables, or salads which
provide the precursor. There are many races today
living almost exclusively on vegetable foods,
whose people are virile and healthy. They obtain
their vitamin A almost entirely from vegetables.

It must be appreciated that vitamin A passes
into the milk or egg yolk only if the diet of the
cow or hen contains ample supplies of B-carotene.
The vitamin A of dairy produce is highest when the
cows are out at pasture and the hens are running
loose. Cows on stall in winter and fed on dried
hay yield a milk which becomes progressively
poorer in vitamin A. Thus the deficiency tended
to appear in early spring.

If however insufficient green vegetables are
eaten a proper intake of animal fat becomes essential in order to ensure a sufficiency of the
vitamin. This is probably what happended to the
peasants of the sixteenth century, who has only

recently been deprived of their cow.

VITAMIN A DEPRIVATION

What is the result of vitamin-A-poor diets?

A mild degree of deprivation shows itself in
a curious manner. The sufferer becomes what is
known as "night-blind". Passing from a bright to
a dim light, he is unable to see properly. It had
for centuries been a very common disorder in
countries of the east where people lived on cereal diets of low vitamin A content.

A greater degree of deprivation causes other
and more serious eye disorders. The lids become
swollen and sore and the surface of the eyeball
dry. There may be ulceration of the cornea and
the development of opaque areas; eventually such
cases become blind. This disorder which is common in Afghanistan, Egypt, Ceylon, India and Pakistan, and used to be prevalent in China, is
called xerophthalmia.

What is the treatment for this disease? The
earliest references to the use of liver in the
treatment of eye diseases is to be found in an
Egyptian papyrus dated about 1,600 B.C. It is
known as the Ebers Papyrus and now resides in the
Leipzig Museum. The significant passage has been
deciphered by egyptologists who are skilled in
hieroglyphics. It reads as follows:

"Another prescription for the eyes;
liver of ox roasted and pressed, give
for it. Very excellent."

There is little doubt that the eye disease
referred to was night-blindness, or nyctalopia.
Hippocrates and Galen knew it well, the former
advising ox-liver in honey as a remedy. The same
advice is found in Roman medical writings. Definite proof that this same treatment was brought
to Europe is to be found in a verse by the four-

teenth century Dutch poet, Jacob van Maerland:

"He who can not see at night, must eat
the liver of the goat; then he can see
all right."

Drummond stated that long-continued deprivation of vitamin A is dangerous in other ways. It leads to a weakening of the defenses of the body against invasion by bacteria and other disease-producing organisms. One of the main defenses against disease lies in the layer of cells covering all surfaces of the body; these include the skin, the mucous membrane of the nose and throat; the cells lining the digestive tract, and other such areas. It is this line of defense which also becomes weakened when vitamin A is lacking. There is a tendency to localised infection, which appears as abscesses and ulcers. When the deficiency is more marked, the skin may become thickened and dry. The latter condition is common in the far east where it has been known as toad skin.

By the seventeenth century in England the condition was common. There are many references to the use of herbs such as fennel and parsley for "mists and films over the eyes." Rue and eyebright were also used. The condition was known also in France, and the famous French physician Guillemeau, in addition to the inevitable bleeding, prescribed liver, for he knew the value of it.

In England, Muffett's "Healths Improvement", a tract published in 1655, said that liver was wholesome, because it would:

"please the taste, clear the eyesight,
agree with the stomach and increase
bloud."

But even before this, Walter Bayly, onetime physician to Queen Elizabeth I, wrote a treatise on the relation of diet to the state of the eyes, in which he classified a large number of foods according to whether they impaired or benefitted the sight. He said:

> "Albeit few raw herbs in common use for sallets are commended, except fennel, eiebright, yoonge sage, terragone."

There are many references to the condition. Peg, the daughter of Lady Verney Gardiner was with

> "Ill eyelids, falling away of the hayre, a spott on the pupill, and corrupt fistula in the corner of her eye toward her nose."

She was taken to a famous oculist of Sarum (Salisbury) in 1715 for examination. Why was this? Since the wealthy did not eat green vegetables or butter, it is likely that she, as well as other children of wealthy parents did suffer. For butter was despised by the rich at this time, and was used only for cooking. But it was eaten in large amounts by the working classes whenever they could afford it.

Doctors at the time disapproved of butter except for growing children:

> "It is also best for children while they are growing, and for old men when they are declining; but very unwholesome betwixt these two ages, because through the heat of the young stomachs, it is forthwith converted into choler."

Muffett notes a very significant passage, when he was reading the Latin author Pliny. "Only I wonder with him that Africa and other barbarous countries esteem it a gentleman's dish, where here and in Holland it is the chief food of the poorer sort." He is referring to butter.

REQUIREMENTS FOR VITAMIN A

When vitamin A was first studied in a systematic way, and isolated, the quantities were too small to allow for weighing on the balances of that time. Accordingly the International Unit was devised, which later was to represent three tenths of a gamma, or as later, a microgram of the pure vitamin.

Modern vitamin technology has established requirements of about 2,500 I.U. are needed per day per person. This is from animal sources. This is 5,000 I.U. if vegetable sources are the main sources.

If we look back, and assume that a diet of bread, vegetable soup, and an ounce or two of cheese was supplemented by a pint of summer milk, then the peasant of early days would be getting about 2,000 I.U.; but in winter the same diet would have yielded about 1,000 I.U., a deficient amount.

It is important to note that the viscera of animals especially the liver and kidneys, are rich in vitamin A, much more so than the flesh. Rabbits and other game, of which everything edible was eaten, would provide good additional sources. If the winter was sparse, it is to be recalled that vitamin A can be stored for long periods in the liver, provided that the organ is healthy. The signs of vitamin A deficiency do not develop rapidly.

Although vitamin A deficiency has been reduced in Europe and America during this century, it is almost endemic in certain parts of the world. It is a real scourge in India and parts of Africa. It is particularly vicious as a childhood disease. Work is in progress in India, under Dr. Gopalan at the Institute of Nutrition in Hyderabad, to assess the possibilities of using massive doses of vitamin A for children inasmuch as it is stored for long periods in the liver. They would come to the clinic every six months for such a dose.

One instance of vitamin A deficiency in
Europe occurred in Denmark during the 1914-1918
war. Denmark was then receiving such high prices
for its butter, especially from Britain, that it
almost disappeared from the home markets. At
that time margarine had made its appearance, but
it could not then be fortified with vitamin
A as it might be today, because it was not yet
known what vitamin A was. It had not yet been
isolated and identified, let alone synthesised.

The poor people of Denmark were therefore
subjected to a greater degree of deprivation of
A than they were in normal times, and hundreds of
cases of xerophthalmia occurred mostly in young
children. To remedy the situation in Denmark the
Government found it necessary to limit the expor-
tation of butter, thereby increasing its consumption within the country. You will recall that in
764 A.D., Charlemagne did the same thing with
grain.

All improved markedly when the butter was
restored to their diet, or when cod liver oil was
administered.

The respiratory mucosa is so much affected
by vitamin A deprivation, that it explains the
frequency, severity and persistance of the pneu-
monias, that have been in very many instances
responsible for death in vitamin A deficient infants.

There is yet another aspect of vitamin A
deficiency to be considered. Stones of the bladder and urinary tract seem to have been very common in England centuries ago. The trouble was
usually ascribed to gluttony and luxurious living.
William Bullein wrote in 1595:

"it cometh of hote wines, spices, long
banquets, repletions, fulness, costive-
ness, warme keeping of the backe, salte

meates, etc..."

This is a remarkable passage, but it is not a full explanation, if for no other reason than that quite young children suffered from the stone. Although the causes are still somewhat uncertain, animal experiments at the hands of Osborne and Mendel in 1917, leave no doubt but that a faulty diet can cause calculi in animals, especially if the diet is high in calcium and low in vitamin A. Milk stands out as predominantly the best curative food.

Chronic chortages of vitamin A induce degenerative changes in the epithelium covering the papillae of the kidney. These are little projections from which the urine flows to be collected in the pelvis of the kidney, and thence passed by the ureters to the bladder.

If conditions are right for the formation of little plaques of calcified matter, these may break away, and either in the pelvis of the kidney, or after passing into the bladder, serve as nuclei around which urinary salts collect. Thus is made possible the gradual accumulation of the deposits, and growth of the stone. Infections of the bladder are also apt to encourage the formation of stones, thus the resistance to infection mentioned above is impaired, and the connection with vitamin A is made.

Studies of human diets are illuminating. African blacks rarely suffered from stone troubles. In 1937 a study revealed only one case in a million hospital admissions, but in South African whites, one in 460. The blacks' diets were found to be relatively rich in vitamin A but low in calcium. By comparison the whites' diets were reversed, high in calcium and low in vitamin A or carotene.

THE DISCOVERY AND ISOLATION OF VITAMIN A

The first systematic work was done by E. V.

McCollum at the University of Wisconsin in the early twentieth century. He came there as a young instructor from Yale in 1907, and set about studies of nutrition of farm animals.

McCollum began by covering all the pertinent literature but he could find very little of any help in the study of farm animals. One paper indicated that a diet of pure fat, carbohydrate and protein was inadequate for mice, but that they got along quite well on milk. He decided that rats would be a big improvement, as an experimental animal, because cattle are too big, and need too much feed, and grow too slowly.

Professor Hart at that time was proud of his cattle experiments, and Wisconsin after all was a dairy state. He was astonished that McCollum should want to change to rats. After he vetoed the young scientist's plans, McCollum went to Babcock, already well known for his milk tests, and received his support. But the Dean would not hear of it. But because Babcock was so highly honored at the University, McCollum got a grudging acquiescence for his project, but no money to carry it out.

Thus it happens that often in man's struggle for food, money and support for new work and the searching out of new findings is withheld, and delays in progress occur. However nothing daunted, McCollum went out and caught some rats, and put them in cages that he had made himself out of boxes, and two dollars' worth of wire netting paid for out of his own pocket. The rats turned out to be so wild that he gave them up and bought some domesticated white rats. He prepared their diets and was assisted by Marguerite Davis, a young assistant who had just graduated from the University of California. The two collaborated and the first of many papers was published in 1913. It reported the observation that when they added butter fat or the fat of egg yolk to the basic deficient diets, the rats grew and seemed

336

to be in good health. But if lard or olive oil were used the rats failed to grow, acquired a bad eye disease and finally became blind. This nutrient present in butter fat and egg yolk fat, but absent in lard or olive oil, they named Fat Soluble A. When they used commercial lactose instead of milk, the rats failed to thrive. Obviously milk contained a water-soluble substance which was also essential to proper nutrition of these rats. This they called Water Soluble B. They had no idea as to the chemical nature of these substances, nor would this be known for a long time yet.

In 1917 McCollum moved with most of his rats to Johns Hopkins University in Baltimore, to continue research work for another thirty years. It was in 1920 that Jack Drummond in London suggested that these two nutrient factors be called vitamin A and vitamin B.

Such small quantities of these factors were involved, that there was developed a system of International units to denote amounts and dosages. The vitamin occurs only in animal tissues or products. Fish livers are the most available source. Cod liver oil has 1,000 I.U. per gram; halibut and tuna are rated at 50,000 and 100,000 I.U. respectively. It was used widely in these forms until 1941 when wartime conditions resulted in synthesis of the vitamin.

It was then found that vitamin A is an alcohol, a pale yellow crystalline solid; chemical tests gave a fairly accurate analysis and the International unit is equivalent to 0.3 microgram. The body can make the vitamin from a plant precursor, this is carotene, the yellow pigment so prominent in carrots. It is prevalent along with other pigments in green leafy vegetables, where it is masked by the colour of chlorophyll. One International Unit of B-carotene is 0.5 microgram, from which the body can make one unit of vitamin A.

EFFECTS ON THE RETINA

Vitamin A deficiency affects the eyes in two
entirely different ways, depending on severity.
If the degree of deficiency is mild, it is the
retina which is affected. If severe and prolonged,
an entirely different kind of damage occurs,
mainly in the cornea and the outer part of the eye.

The rods of the retina, as distinct from the
cones, contain visual pigments which consist of
vitamin A linked to specific proteins. These are
bleached in the presence of light, and return to
normal when light is absent. This alternate
bleaching and recoloring stimulates nerves which
carry impulses to the brain. The vitamin A
needed to re-form the complex must come from the
blood. Lythgoe and Lythgoe in London were making
these discoveries about visual purple in the thirties. It was to be very useful during World War
II. This was because the British Air Force undertook the night bombing missions, whereas the
Americans were more instrumental in daylight raids.
The knowledge acquired enabled the bombing squad-
rons to be well supplied with additional vitamin
A or carotene for these raids.

For any slight deficiency slows down the
rate of regeneration of the visual pigments and
results in nyctalopia or night-blindness, as
mentioned earlier. It does not however impair
the ability to respond to bright light, because
that is a function associated with the retinal
cones which do not require vitamin A in the same
fashion as the rods.

If the deficiency is prolonged, the tear
ducts become blocked, due to epithelial damage,
and the cornea thereby becomes dry. This is the
condition of xerophthalmia, mentioned earlier.
This signals total and irreversible blindness,
common in many parts of the world. As a result
of this condition, many other secondary infections
occur, one of which is trachoma. The latter

condition can be saved by a little sulfa ointment applied regularly. But no amount of ointment will reverse the relentless course of vitamin A deficiency.

And yet were we listening? In the early days, Paracelsus said that the Dutch were less troubled by stone than other nations because they ate more butter. He might have added too that the Dutch ate far more liberally of green garden vegetables. As we now know, the highest sources other than liver, milk and butter, are spinach, collards, kale, beet greens, broccoli and carrots. And yet even today how many people throw away the beet greens and use the relatively useless beets?

Are things any better today? A study in Louisiana in 1968 - 9 on 3,346 persons of all ages, showed plasma vitamin A levels at unacceptably low values in 45% of the 645 children from 0 to 6 years old; 40% of the 1,200 between 7 and 17.

The data showed that it was not a question of income levels. Unacceptable values were recorded in 37% of the males and 28% of the females below the poverty level. But the figures for those above the poverty level were, respectively, still substantial, 20% and 17%.

But when we look at the foods which are lacking in carotene and vitamin A, or very low in it, we find the foods that poor people eat: potatoes, onions, beets, turnips, beans, cabbage, cucumbers, bananas, bread, pork, chicken. So the struggle for food goes on, even in the United States today.

330   .."LIVER OF OX..." Van Leersum; Nederlandsche Tydschrift, III (1924).

330   OX LIVER IN HONEY..Opera Medicorum Graecorum ed. Kuhn III, 46, (1927).

331   "HE WHO CAN NOT SEE AT NIGHT.." Van Meerland, Jacob; from Drummond p 81.

331   "FOR MISTS AND FILMS OVER THE EYES." Guillemeau, Jacques; Traite' des Maladies de l'oeil; (1585).

331   "PLEASE THE TASTE, CLEAR THE EYESIGHT ..." Muffett, Thomas, Health's Improvement (1655).

332   "..EXCEPT FENNEL, EIEBRIGHT, YONGE SAGE..." Bayly. W; A brief treatise touching the preservation of the eiesight consisting partly in good order of diet." (1586).

332   "ILL EYELIDS, FALLING AWAY OF THE HAYRE.." Verney, Margaret; Memoirs of the Verney Family. IV, (1899).

332   USE OF BUTTER: Muffett, Thomas; ibid.

333   MASSIVE DOSES OF VITAMIN A: Gopalan, C; A simple method for evaluating the massive dose of vitamin A prophylaxis program. National Institute of Nutrition, Hyderabad, India. Annual Report; 11; 4, p 156 (1975).

334   DEFICIENCY IN DENMARK: Bloch. C.E. Ungeskrift F. Laeger, 79, 349, (1917); cited in J. Amer. Med. Ass. 68, 1516 (1917).

334   IMPROVEMENT WITH BUTTER OR COD LIVER OIL: Bloch, C.E. Jour. of Hygience; 19, 283. (1921).

335   BLADDER STONE: Osborne, T.B. and Mendel L.B.
       J. Amer. Med Ass. 69, 32. (1917).

336   EARLY WORK WITH RATS: McCollum, E.V. and
       Davis, Marguerite; J. Biological Chemistry,
       15, 167-75 (1913).

336   EYE DISORDERS STUDIED OVER A PERIOD OF FOUR
       YEARS: McCollum, E.V. and Simmonds, N.J.
       Biological Chemistry, 29, 341 (1917).

337   NOMENCLATURE FOR VITAMIN A AND B: Drummond,
       J.C. Biochemical Journal, XIV, 660 (1920).

338   VITAMIN A AND THE RETINA: Tansley, K;
       Journal of Physiology; 71, 442 (1931);
       Lythgoe and Lythgoe; ibid, (1933)

21

THE EIGHTEENTH CENTURY

When Queen Anne came to the throne of England in 1702, the long struggle for ascendency was nearly over. With Portugal and Spain out of the way, and the Dutch and French being to a certain extent outmanouvred on the trade routes, fortune smiled on England for a while, and especially on her merchants. For almost fifty years good rains and harvests kept dearth away, and almost all the staple foods were abundant and cheap.

At the end of Elizabeth the first's reign, wages were between sixpence and ninepence a day, or about four shillings a week. By 1730 wages for less skilled laborers and workmen has risen to as much as nine shillings a week; this represented a very real improvement, because food became cheaper at the same time.

Meat which had been five or six pence a pound was now two or three pence; cheese which had been over two pence a pound was now to be had for a penny; a chicken cost about three pence and butter was five or six pence a pound. One penny bought a large wheaten loaf. Wages went further than they had before, and the ordinary man was beginning to look upward to a better life.

New industries of a minor sort were beginning to reach the market, and the culture of the people could take up these new inventions with some success when they were able to afford them. For example, candles, which had been the province of the priesthood, and made by them in their monasteries for centuries, now became available and were made in large quantities. The ordinary man could light himself on the way to bed. This was a great delight to him and his family. Oil lamps, which had been in use for centuries in India and the middle east had not yet reached Europe, and were still in the future for average people.

Cheaper fabrics appeared, and cotton was woven in different ways. These fabrics were now within the reach of the ordinary man and his family.

So things looked rather good for a while as there was plenty of work both on the land and in the towns. Also as people moved to the towns, those left on the land found their lot vastly improved from what it had been before. They were assured of work, and food was so cheap that they could afford meat several times a week.

Some of the villagers of that period were even able to afford a cow again, as well as a pig or two. These they had not been able to afford since the enclosures began in 1525. Vegetables were grown, which included new varieties which had been completely unknown to peasants of earlier times. These improvements in turn wrought an upturn in the population, and England seemed like an opulent country, a phrase which had not been used before in any society.

Because of the increasing population more food was needed. People were no longer content to eat the dark rye bread, as this was considered to be a poorer sort of diet, such as was used by the population of eastern Europe. There were increased demands on the available wheat supply. The new wheaten loaves were generally made in London, and shipped out again into the country. People also turned away from salt meat, and demanded only fresh.

IMPROVEMENTS IN AGRICULTURE

The Reformation caused people to enquire into the nature of things. As a result, in scarcely more than a century, farming methods advanced from a state not far removed from that of the middle ages, to something not greatly inferior to today's. There was hardly a year in this period that was not marked by some useful invention, the introduction of a new crop, or an improved breed of livestock.

It was a remarkable period for agricultural enterprise.

Such advances were fostered from high places. In England there was a Society for the Encouragement of the Arts, Manufactures and Commerce. It later became known as the Royal Society and still exists today. It published treatises of all kinds, including those concerning innumerable crop experiments, land drainage schemes and afforestation programs. The latter were fostered primarily because of a fear that timber was in short supply for the Navy. The authorities encouraged people to plant trees. Valuable prizes were offered by the government for these advances, an early instance of government intervention to influence advances and discoveries.

What were some of these improvements? Undoubtedly the first was the impressive rise of wheat growth. At the beginning of the eighteenth century the south of England grew only sixty percent of its crop as wheat, the rest being in coarse grains: barley, rye and oats. By the end of the century the ratio was 80 to 20%. The north of England was still growing coarse grains, because wheat does not thrive that far north. Even East Anglia where wheat was said not to grow well was converted over to wheat.

In spite of this increased acreage, as well as larger yields, the population grew as such a rapid pace that supplies could not keep up with demand, and with the increasing numbers to be fed, England ceased to be a wheat-exporting country. At the end of the century, when things had suffered a sharp decline, the average per capita consumption was to drop to two thirds of what it had been at the beginning.

But the Englishman and his family were now at least able to have more things than just wheat to fill their bellies. The popularity of root crops grew rapidly in this century. For example,

345

turnips were to be extensively cultivated; the yields were raised due to the practice of allowing sheep to nibble at the turnip tops, at the same time as they fertilised the fields. Defoe remarked on his tour of England how turnips were being used more and more, as a cattle feed, as well as for human use.

A treatise by William Ellis speaks of the value of various forms of fodder. The Dutch were understood to be ahead of other nations in this matter, as so often was the case. The following passage written in 1742 attests to this:

> "...we usually feed cattle with straw in racks in the yard, but in Holland they do thus; for the winter provision they lay in not only hay but also grain, which they buy in summer and bury in the ground; also rapeseed cakes; and they sow turnips not only for themselves but for their cows also. They slice the turnips and their tops, and with rapeseed cakes and grain they make mashes for their cows, and give it to them warm, which the cows will slop up like hogs, and by this means they give much milk..."

For a long time turnips were the only root crops grown in England for cattle feeding. They seemed to provide a complete solution for a winter pablum.

Another discovery made by Dutch farmers was that cattle would thrive on the residues left after the oil had been expressed from crushed rapeseed. Oil was used in Holland as an illuminant and was even better than candles.

In 1783 the Royal Society for the Arts offered a prize for the best method of extracting oil from cottonseed in such a way that the press-cake left was suitable for winter feeding of animals. The word fodder became added to the English lan-

guage at this point. Not long after this, flax-
seed was subjected to crushing and pressing. The
linseed cake so obtained proved to be a success
as fodder, although the oil was not suitable as
an illuninant, burning as it did with a smoky
flame. However the linseed oil, so inferior as
an illuminant, quickly found favor with the paint
arts and crafts, and was adapted for use there.
The animals did not mind the bitter taste of the
linseed cake.

The increasing amounts of cotton which were
arriving from India and Egypt at the port of Liverpool made the use of cottonseed oil a natural.
By the end of the century a considerable number
of farmers were using the new concentrates. The
popularity of the turnip paved the way for the
introduction of other root crops. The swede
was brought to England, not from Sweden but from
Holland, and it quickly became popular.

But the potato, which has been discussed
before did not at the time become popular in
England as it had already in Ireland. At the
beginning of the century it was not grown extensively anywhere in Britain. Several books of the
period make no mention of the potato, but in
1726 Bradley drew attention to the merits of the
tuber, and to the scant use made of it. Twenty
years later the same author was to remark:

> "they are cultivated pretty plentifully
> about London, but are not, I think, got
> enough into the notion of our country
> people, considering their profit.."

People were not yet used to thinking in terms
of potatoes. In many places they were regarded
with a good deal of prejudice, because white bread
was the superior food. It is odd how the feeling
against potatoes was so strong in southern England.
Eventually people learned from the Irish that
cattle and pigs could be fed the imperfect and
small potatoes. Coke saw their value in fattening

cattle, and he exercised his influence and sponsored them for the farmers. He had seen how the Irish peasants fattened their hogs on half-boiled potatoes, together with cabbage leaves and hay.

Another advance at this time was the realisation of the value of clover. Clover was known to Columella in 200 A.D., but farmers did not come around to its general use in Europe until about 1770, when one of the contemporary writers spoke of clover as a pillar of good husbandry. Cabbages also became popular, especially in Germany.

Slowly prejudices against vegetables came to be broken down. Market gardens began to flourish around all the big cities of Europe, and venders would go in and out to sell their produce. Peas, beans, carrots, celery, cabbage and cauliflower were all grown regularly. Many sorts of fruit, heretofore very little used, made their appearance: pears, apples, plums and currants. According to Weston:

> "...some old men in Surrey, where it flourishes very much at present, report that they knew the first gardeners that came into these parts to plant cabbages and cauliflowers, and to sow turnips, carrots and parsnips; to sow raith, rape and pease; all of which at that time were great rarities, we having none or few in England, but what came from Holland or Flanders..."

This was in 1742. And by 1772 there were some enterprising Irishmen who came to settle near London and cultivated potatoes for the London market. They rented farms at Ilford, east of London:

> "...it was once very common to have all the potato grounds belonging to them, but of late the farmers have got pretty much into the culture themselves..."

Arthur Young was impressed with the idea of growing garden crops as field crops. These were then grown in larger quantities, more as we see them today.

It is interesting that food always seems to exert strong ethnic ties and attractions. An excellent vegetable market existed in Liverpool by 1756, because of the influx of French-Canadians after the end of the Seven Years' War. They demanded cheap vegetables for their soups and bouillons. The development of market gardening in this period also led to the emergence of rhubarb; the Society of Arts presented a number of prizes and medals to encourage its cultivation and improvement. People were quick to note its laxative uses.

Thus there were some very real advances during this period. Interest in the new inventions, crops and seeds, as well as the design of drills, reapers and other kinds of farm equipment grew, and became the subject of intense competition. These may be summarised as follows:

--a specialised dairy industry was developed by the Dutch

--regular collection of, and use of, organic fertilisers was practised in Holland

--a seven course system of crop rotation also spread from Holland, involving wheat, turnips barley and clover

--pulping and chopping of animal feedstuffs for use as winter feed

--Jethro Tull's seed drill increased yields

--gears were for the first time introduced into the machinery, reducing seed waste

--improvements in cast iron helped the farmers' implements greatly by enhancing their cutting edges

349

THE TURN OF THE TIDE

These improvements might have continued to
sustain almost unlimited growth had it not been
for a series of natural disasters which super-
vened in the latter half of the eighteenth century.
A series of wet seasons and bad harvests took
place between the years 1764 and 1775. The grain
could not ripen and many times it was too wet to
harvest. There was no recourse in those days,
for there were no ovens whereby you might rescue
a crop by drying it out. Accordingly the price
of wheat soared. Prices of other foods followed
suit. In 1776 the price of a quartern loaf of
bread reached the unprecedented figure of one
shilling and sixpence, just four times what it
had been fifty years earlier. This price rise
encouraged those few who owned land to increase
the acreage under wheat, as well as the size of
their flocks and herds. The farmer-owner also
found that his land was worth more. He found
himself frozen out by other people who had more
money than he did, and who bought his land from
him at a price he could not turn down. Thus
the few rich became richer.

The increase in the price of cattle brought
about another disastrous wave of enclosures.
The amount of land enclosed in the first fifty
years of the century, had not been large. In
the whole of Queen Anne's reign, 1702 to 1714,
a mere 15,000 acres had been taken. From 1760
onwards to the end of the century, more than
three million acres were filched from the people.

All that the landowner had to do was to
submit a petition for the land's enclosure and
get it legalised, before his neighbours, rich or
poor, had heard a word about it. This was not
hard to do. Even when an appeal was lodged, (and
there are many of these pitiful petitions on
record in the British Museum), the childlike
pleas and arguments of the simple country folk
stood no chance against the artifices of the wily

lawyers representing a governing class which was
cynically indifferent to the rights of the poor
man.

The only prosperous people at that particular
period were the big farmers and the big landowners
who were reaping the benefits of abnormally high
prices. In 1793 when there were both poor crops
and an acute financial crisis, the position deteriorated even farther. By the end of the century
a large part of the population was facing dearth,
depression and distress. Small wonder that these
same people were listening with longing to the
propositions of Washington, Jefferson and Adams.

There were others too who furthered the
enclosure movement; it was not just the greedy
landowners alone. There were some who purported
to have the welfare of the people at heart, but
who nevertheless saw in the movement for increasing
the size of farms a change for the better, as far
as the good of the country as a whole was concerned.
Quite a few influential people felt that the only
way to increase production of food was to expand
the estates. These should be farmed, they claimed,
by men with both capital and enterprise. Sir
John Sinclair, the first president of the newly-
created Board of Agriculture said in a speech in
1795:

> "...the idea of having lands in common, it
> has been justly remarked, is to be derived
> from that barbarous state of society, when
> men were strangers to any higher occupation
> than those of shepherds or hunters, or had
> only just tasted the advantages to be
> reaped from the cultivation of the earth..."

In other words, let the big landowner have his way.
Even Young thought that the small farmer should be
eliminated. In Yorkshire he noted that:

> "...the small farmers are a poor and
> wretched set of people, and their hus-
> bandry is universally bad..."

And then this quite extraordinary paragraph:

> "...if it be demanded how such ill courses
> are to be stopped, I answer: Raise their
> rents. First with moderation, and if that
> does not bring forth industry, double
> them; but if you would have a vigorous cul-
> ture go forwards, throw 15 or 20 of these
> farms into one, as fast as the present
> occupiers drop off. This is the only means
> in such cases to improve husbandry, and
> consequently to promote population..."

We have to be aware of the rapid changes that
were taking place in Europe at the beginning of
the industrial era. As the eighteenth century wore
on, the whole structure and nature of society
changed. From a fabric where the threads of town
and country life wove harmoniously and closely
together, it wore to a loose pattern, rubbed in
certain places into holes. Industry was removed
from cottages and villages to urban factories;
village life was left like a piece of knitting
with the stitches dropped where the arts and
crafts had been. Where the village tailor, carpenter, brewer, miller and harness-maker had been,
there was nothing, no occupation. No longer did
the housewife spin; her spindle was silent.

No longer was each shire to be left in isolation,
each hamlet with its own tradition, interests and
character, its ghosts and its gossip. New indus-
trialists set up factories, mills and businesses on
money derived from farming.

DETERIORATION IN FOOD

As has already been noted, the condition of the
working classes deteriorated after 1750. But it
was uneven. In the south the staples were bread,
butter, and cheese, with a little meat perhaps
once or twice a week. In the north they ate little
meat, but drank more milk, and by now were used to
potatoes. By 1795 the poorest laborer in the north
enjoyed a variety of food unknown in the south.

His diet contained both milk and vegetables.

In commenting upon the south in "The State of the Poor", Sir Frederick Eden says:

> "...it is not to be expected that milk
> should ever form a considerable part of
> the diet of laborers in the south of
> England until the practice of keeping
> cows becomes more general among cottagers
> than it is at present...in the vicinity
> of the large towns the value of grassland
> is much too high to enable laborers to rent
> it to advantage..."

The system of enclosures, well described by Hammond had taken away the farmer's pasturage as well as the land where he had been able to collect fuel for cooking his hot meals. At Cobham in Kent it was reported:

> "the usual diet of laborers is bread, but-
> ter, cheese, pickled pork and a little
> butcher's meat...milk is very scarce..."

And so the larger farms took everything to town, and the small man who could not afford to buy large quantities at a time, had to have recourse to the chandler's credit shop. The social revolution had swept away the small man's possession, and the industrial revolution was to sweep away his family's earnings. The average man's independence had been destroyed by 1795.

Housewives' revolts and food riots occurred in the same year all over the land. People were beginning to be restive and resentful. Laborers rejected soup, even from a rich man's table. "This is washy stuff that affords no nourishment. We will not be fed on meal and chopped potatoes like hogs..." As Hammond says:

> "...these riots are a rising of the poor
> against the increasing pressure of want,

353

and the forces that were driving down
their standard of life. They mark a
stage in the history of the poor; to the
rich they were a signal of danger; thus
fear and pity are united to sharpen the
wits of the rich and to turn their minds
to the distresses of the poor..."

And so in spite of the very real improvement
in English agriculture, the cost was desolation
in the villages. Everything was lost; the arable
land, the grazing land for the cows, even the scrub
where they collected their winter fuel; and sometimes even their little garden plots. Their plight
has been immortalised in various pieces of literature, such as Oliver Goldsmith's "The Deserted
Village," written in 1769. It seems that forces
greater than the individual were now beginning
to take hold of society.

Food so often reflects the time we live in.
At this time in the latter part of the eighteenth
century there was a connection between the misery
that the village people were suffering and the type
of food they ate. For some time a certain type
of beetroot, called mangold, had been grown in
Germany. In the terrible 1780's this was one of
the few foods that the starving French peasants
could get. There arose a confusion between the
world mangold (beet) and mangel (dearth). This
led to its being named by the French racine de
disette (root of famine); thus they had inadver-
tantly brought the word Mangel-wurzel into the
English list of vegetables. Later on this vegetable
was fed to cattle, for whom it was intended. But
the false name stuck, and in my day in England you
could buy a mangel-wurzel at the greengrocer's
shop.

It was not only the country people who suffered. The new factory workers in the towns also
found the price of provisions so high that riots
ensued. But at first there was little sympathy for
them. Young glibly dismissed them by saying that
sober and industrious workers never riot. He

354

continues:

>"...in all occupations there will be idle,
>drunken, unsettled and disorderly persons;
>a few of these getting together and talk-
>ing over the dearness of provisions (which
>presently becomes a cant term among them),
>inflame each other..."

THE FOOD ITSELF

Transportation

Transportation was so bad and poorly organised
that food supplies to the various towns in Europe
were inadequate. Nobody had foreseen the growth
of towns at this rate, and the industrial revolution was not yet under way.

Poultry waddled in to London on foot from
as far away as Norfolk and Suffolk. Arriving in
the London area thoroughly exhausted, they had
to be killed the same day. There was, and still
is, an area in London called Poultry, where this
large market was located. It is nor far from St.
Paul's Cathedral. Meat came slowly and wearily
on hoof from Wales and from Yorkshire. Grain
creaked in laboriously in heavy carts.

In order to expedite matters, George III introduced the idea of a turnpike, so called because
a soldier stood with his pike lowered across the
road. Upon payment of a fee to get on this road,
the soldier would turn himself and his pike at
right angles, to allow passage. The money was
supposed to enhance the development of better
roads. They were in fact improved, but the sur-
facing was very poor, and the cart wheels inferior.

Later on the idea of canals was borrowed from
the Dutch. They had been very ingenious in hand-
ling their environment. Due to the low-lying
nature of their country they had been forced to
build dykes in order to keep out the North Sea.
As a result of this they had a system of canals

which they used for commerce and for pleasure.
By 1758 there was such a good system of canals
in Holland that one traveller said: "an inhab-
itant of Rotterdam may hereby breakfast at
Delft or at the Hague, and dine at Leyden; he
may sup at Amsterdam and return home again before
night." Later other countries copied Holland and
built their own systems of canals.

Food Quality

But even with the turnpikes and canals, the
food that did reach the towns was often unfit for
human consumption. We have mentioned food taint,
and the attempts to mask it by the use of spices,
two hundred years before this.

There is indisputable evidence that a marked
deterioration in food quality occurred in the
eighteenth century. The new towns were perfect
places for the commercialist to exploit. They were
not slow to see that there was money to be made
by adulterating food. The food in question was that
which was likely to be bought by the poor people.
This evil was accentuated in the latter half of
the century when the shortages already referred to
offered temptations to the unscrupulous. The poor
people could only have what was left over; for the
servants of the rich went out very early every
morning in order to pick over carefully what was
for sale, and to select the best.

Bread

When shortages develop, more flour can be
obtained, and thus more bread, by increasing the
percentage extraction of the wheat. This in turn
produces a darker bread because colored elements
in the outer layers of the wheat get into the flour,
as well as more bran. Parliament ordered that
such a loaf should be the standard loaf of the
time, and be marked with an S. This loaf was
rather dull-looking, a dun color, whereas the
people wanted white bread. They had wanted white
bread in Roman times and they wanted it now, even
when it was a penny dearer.

In order to counter this difficulty, alum was added to the flour. In addition to whitening the flour, alum also does improve slightly the loaf volume as well as its texture. But the whitening was just what the millers and the bakers wanted. People fell for this adulteration and bought this new whiter bread. However some suspected this new-found whiteness. And with some justification. For chalk was cheaper than alum and readily available to whiten flour. Its addition to flour became rampant by 1757. An anonymous pamphlet was then published, entitled: "Poison detected; or frightful truths, and alarming to the British metropolis." It dealt mainly with the adulteration of bread with alum, lime, chalk and worse:

> "...it is averred by very credible authority that sacks of unground bones are not infrequently used by some bakers amongst other impurities, to increase the quantity and to injure the quality of flour and bread. The charnel houses of the dead are raked to add filthiness to the food of the living..."

A spirited counter-attack by the bakers and millers followed in 1758, resulting in a clear and concise essay on Bread. It showed that chalk will not help the bread, and that bone ash actually reduced the size of the loaf, so that it would not do the bakers and the millers any good even if it were added. But the controversy dragged on for a number of years. The public did not know the actual size of their loaves, being conscious only of the whiteness. A characteristic passage by Smollett in 1771 is as follows:

> "...the bread which I eat in London is a deleterious paste, mixed up with chalk, alum and bone ashes, insipid to the taste and destructive to the constitution. The good people are not ignorant of this adulteration, but they prefer it to wholesome bread, because it is whiter than the meal of "corn". Thus they sacrifice their taste

and health, and the lives of their tender infants to a most absurd gratification of a mis-
judging eye, and the miller and baker is ob-
liged to poison them and their families in order to live by his profession..."

This is an interesting passage because it places
the first responsibility on the parents, who apparently knew of the adulteration yet still bought the
bread for their families. We shall have occasion
to look into the problems of flour in the twentieth
century. Things have not changed much in 200 years.

Meat and Fish

Smithfield just outside London had a fair in
the reign of Richard II, 400 years earlier. It
was permitted royal grant, "such that valid transactions could be made there." But it became a
nuisance and in 1380 butchers petitioned Parliament
prayering that: "slaughterers may not throw blood
and offal into the River Fleet, but do their work
at Knyghtsbrygge or elsewhere."

In the eighteenth century Smithfield was
still a famous market, but no longer a field. It
was in the heart of London city, and the main meat
market of the realm. For all roads led to London.
The cattle walked all the way, even from Anglesea,
which meant that they had to swim the Menai straits.
By the time many of these meats reached the plate
they must have been thin, tough and gristly. They
would surely have been vastly inferior to the mediaeval meat, which had spent the summer quietly
fattening before being locally slaughtered around
Michaelmas.

Meat can live on the hoof until time for slaughter, but fish once caught becomes rotten very quickly. Even when fast-trotting horses brought the
fish up from the coast, it would often arrive, as
Smollett said, "in such a state as to turn a Dutchman's stomach." Before the days of refrigeration,
the fish markets at Billingsgate on the Thames became a byword for stenches. It was probably because

mackerel went bad so quickly that one was allowed to "cry it on the streets of London on Sundays before 9 a.m. and after 4 p.m. This was a great concession of the churches because no markets were ever open on Sundays in those times.

Vegetables

The canal system which was developed in England at this time permitted the transport of fruits and vegetables by barge into the cities. The barges would return with night soil to the country, where it fertilised the same plots from whence the produce came.

Country people were warned in various graphic passages not to trust the fruit and vegetables in London. People were advised by a Dr. Trusler to make their own arrangements with a market gardener directly, or else go to Covent Garden where the prices were high but the produce was on the whole satisfactory.

For oranges, lemons and other fruits were by now being sold in the streets from "movable shops that run on wheels, attended by ill-looking fellows," according to a book called "The London Spy." These costermongers were coming onto the scene and a quotation of that time indicates that you had to look out for yourselves then, as now:

"It was but yesterday that I saw a dirty barrow bunter in the street, cleaning her dusty fruit with her own spittel; and who knows but some fine lady at St. James' parish might admit into a delicate mouth those very cherries that had been rolled and moistened between the filthy and perhaps ulcerated chops of a St. Charles' huckster."

Dr. Trusler emphasised that, to arrive fresh in the city, fruit and vegetables must have been raised close by within easy travelling distance. Even then according to one author, everything seemed

359

to be impregnated with the smoke of sea-coal.

Milk

The supply of milk to the towns was almost always indescribably bad. Most of it was provided by cows kept in the towns. The wretched beasts were herded together in dark hovels, standing ankle-deep in filth, and poorly fed on little besides hay and brewers' grains (this incidentally is quite a good diet, although they did not know it at the time the comments were written).

Sometimes the cows were driven round the streets and the milk sold straight from the udder, a practice which was popular in the west end of London because it reduced the risk of getting watered milk. This practice of watering milk was almost inevitable if one dealt with the milk-women, according to the same Dr. Trusler in his London Advisor and Guide.

The best milk in London was that obtained from the cows grazing in St. James' Park, right near Buckingham Palace, according to a traveller from Switzerland.

But the quality of milk hawked in the streets of London as a whole must have been appalling, and there is no reason to think that Smollett was exaggerating when he wrote as follows in 1771:

"...but the milk itself should not pass unanalysed; the produce of faded cabbage leaves and sour draff, lowered with hot water, frothed with bruised snails; carried through the streets in open pails, exposed to foul rinsings discharged from doors and windows; spittle, snot and tobacco quids from foot passengers; overflowings from mud carts, spatterings from coach wheels; dirt and trash chucked into it by roguish boys for the joke's sake; the spewing of infants, who have slabbered into the tin measure, which is thrown back in that condition among the

milk, for the benefit of the next
customer; and finally the vermin
that drops from the rags of the nas-
ty drab that vends this precious
mixture, under the respectable denom-
ination of milkmaid."

THE FEEDING OF INFANTS IN THE EIGHTEENTH CENTURY

The foregoing description of conditions in the
eighteenth century prepares the reader for the
appalling statistics on infant mortality. The
topic was briefly touched upon in the seventeenth
century chapter. In England only one in three would
reach a year, and a further third would die before
the age of five; these conditions were worse than
those reported a century earlier, when half of the
children would reach the age of five.

It was not to be until after Pasteur that a
realisation of the effects of hygiene was to be
developed, and even then it was to be a slow business of education before real and extensive improvements were achieved. This was a hundred years into
the future.

The picture was painted in 1767 by Jonas Hanway, and a grim one it is. In "Letters on the
importance of the rising generation," he noted that
orphaned infants were handed over to the tender
mercies of the parish nurse. In one parish 11 out
of a total of 174 survived for two months. In
another parish, out of a total of 3,000 all but 40
died before they could be placed out as apprentices.

Why had things taken such a desperate turn?
It seems to me that the most important reason for
such conditions was to be found in the very severe
culture shock experienced by these people. They
had moved from the comparative security and certain-
ty of village life into the growing cities. It was
the first culture shock of its kind, and was bred
out of the early days of the industrial revolution.
Hundreds of women, to say nothing of children, were
working long hours in factories in fearful conditions.

COLLIERY.

COLLIERY
1806

These unnatural circumstances would lead naturally to various types of behaviour: moroseness, tears, and above all, drinking.

Some of the infant mortality was undoubtedly due to the carelessness shown by those said to be in charge. There was a great deal of spirit-drinking in the towns, especially after 1742 with the availability of cheap gin. Wet nurses to whom the infants were often entrusted were too often gin-tipplers themselves, and the practice of giving spirits to children to quieten them was quite general. William Forster in 1738 speaks of the "mad and imprudent fondness of many mothers, who do often permit their infants to sip up ale, wine and many other strong and spirituous liquors." And in the second half of the century as we have already noted, dearth and high prices added to the misery of existence.

The Governors of the Foundling Hospital apparently decided to rear some of the infants in the hospital itself. Good records were kept by Thomas Cram of the hospital. In 1747 these records show that orphanages and foundling hospitals as a whole would serve a breakfast of broth, gruel and porridge alternately. Dinner would consist of roast pork, or boiled mutton and potatoes, or hasty pudding and dumplings. Supper would be bread with either milk or cheese. This was not at all a bad diet, and far superior to anything that the working people could command. By the end of the century it deteriorated somewhat.

The Governors decided to send a good many foundlings out to wet nurses in various parts of the country. These so-called baby farms in some cases were a terrible scandal, and only a few of the infants could survive more than a few months' care by their foster-parents. Frequently the infants were entrusted to any rogue who might take them. Accordingly the appalling infant mortality figures were forced upon the notice of the public. And by 1740 the Governors of the Foundling Hospital were addressing themselves to the following types of questions:

363

- should wet nurses be abandoned wherever possible?

- should one then bring children up by hand, "all such as will so feed"?

- and suckle only those that will not so feed?

- how long ought a child to continue to suck?

These were new problems, brought about by the age and the times. Wet nurses had been used for centuries, presumably ever since man began, when the mother might die for whatever cause. But the mass existence of orphans was something else again.

But the last question had been addressed in the Koran a thousand years earlier:

"Mothers shall suckle their children two
years completely, for such as desire to
fulfill the suckling..
But if the couple desire by mutual consent
and consultation to wean, then it is no
fault in them..
And if you desire to seek nursing for your
children, it is no fault in you, provided
that you hand over what you have given honorably.."

As mentioned in the chapter on Islam, Europeans were denied access to the wisdom of the Koran for many centuries. There is no doubt from this passage that there is an inherent tolerance for the problem. But Christian instruction books contained no such advice.

There is no record of the Foundling Hospital trying artificial feeding. Perhaps the College of Physicians had reported adversely on it. For although various feeding devices for feeding infants had been developed in mediaeval times, and even before that, it was not widely practised in England until 1750. The first dispensary for sick children was founded in London in 1769, and it appears that by then they were aware of artificial feeding.

When it was at length adopted, use was made of
a number of devices. They made a gruel or pap. It
was thinner than porridge and was made up of bread
or flour, mixed with water or milk, and slightly
sweetened. This panada as it was known was placed
in a cloth sucking bag with a hole at one end of it.
They would squeeze the panada through this sucking
bag into the child's mouth. An enormous amount of
infection would thereby be communicated to the child,
for these devices were veritable breeding grounds for
bacteria.

Various enquiries were made into the causes and
symptoms of the many childhood diseases rampant at
the time. However at this time people were too busy
with other concerns: both the French and the American
Revolutions were imminent.

Once in a while a pioneer arises and recommends
revolutionary changes. One such was an eminent
physician named Dr. W. Cadogan. He wrote his views
to the Foundling Hospital, and they were interested
enough to get them published. At that time babies
were heavily swaddled to keep them from chills, and
to straighten their limbs. The leading physicians
of the day recommended that they be kept from direct
sunlight lest it damage their eyes. Not so Cadogan.
He insisted that children were not "hotbed plants",
and that the lighter and looser the clothing the
better off the child would be. He even said that
swaddling was more likely to cause deformities than
to cure them.

To compound the heresy he completely rejected
the age-old idea that fruit and vegetables were
dangerous for children. He said that as soon as they
were able to live on bread and butter and a little
meat, he wanted them also to have raw, baked or stew-
ed fruit, and "all the produce of the kitchen garden,"
Cadogan was nearly 200 years ahead of his time. He
also insisted that nurses should be prevented from
giving opiates of any kind, and especially not in the
Foundling Hospital.

Another eminent physician of that time, Dr.
William Fordyce, made an enquiry in 1773 into the

365

nature and performance of some of the nurseries
where infant feeding was going on. He had some
strong things to say about them. He wrote: "they
are fed on meat before they have got their teeth;
and what is worse, on biscuits not fermented, or
buttered rolls or tough muffins floating in oiled
butter, or cows' feet jellies or strong broth;
all yet more calculated to load their powers of
digestion."

Recommendations were made from time to time
by forward-looking people. Conditions of over-
indulgence in matters of food are common, and
were then. These were in numerous cases recorded
by artists and cartoonists. They attest to such
excesses as give rise swollen limbs, bulging cheeks
and pendulous paunches:

"Tis amazing how the voluptuous, the lazy
people of delicate constitutions should
think themselves able to carry off such
loads of highly seasoned food and inflammatory liquors without injury or pain."

The same author continues, in Materia Medica:

"A large quantity of vegetables should be
constantly mixed with animal fat to take
off its putrescency, and to prevent it
from corrupting while it continue in the
stomach...in short we should eat in great
moderation, and make vegetables the principall part of our food."

Doctors at that time frequently attested
to instances where men and woman had benefitted
from adopting a sparse diet. Such are the first
early suggestions about the use of discretion in
the eating of food, and in its amounts and kind.
These ideas came at a time when excesses were rampant among the well-to-do.

DRINKING

The problems of drinking were to become acute
in this century. We have mentioned already the

culture shock brought about by the Industrial Revolution, and in particular referred to the unnatural conditions suddenly forced upon people's lives.

The sale of beer and ale had been under control in European countries from as far back as 1550. A license was required to sell beer, and by 1700 it was enforced and binding. A fine of twenty shillings was exacted in England for selling beer, ale or cider except at such licensed houses.

But there were no constraints on the selling of spirits, and thus gin shops sprang up all over the country. The duty on these drinks was minute: twopence a gallon. Between 1700 and 1750 gin consumption in England alone rose tenfold, from half a million gallons to five million gallons. The authorities became concerned and tried to control it but by then the habit was well ingrained. Gin Lane by Hogarth is not exaggerated; he was saying in his paintings many of the things that Dickens was to say in his books a century later.

Raw economics entered the picture at this point. The dearths previously mentioned after 1750 sent to price of grain higher, so that in some years there was a threefold increase. You could not afford to make gin cheaply any more. By 1758 gin was three times its former price, and people began to turn to other drinks, especially beer. The brewers got into the picture again, and a number of world-famous breweries, Meux for example, got started at that time. But the brewer too found that the price of grain was high, so they attempted to circumvent this by making a simple kind of beer with only two or three percent alcohol in it, instead of the usual four or five percent. They anxiously brewed this small beer, or near beer, in the hopes that it could compete with tea, which by now had become available and very cheap.

Unscrupulous people are always ready to adulterate food, as has been mentioned before. And so with beer and other drinks. Various ingredients such as pepsicum, a type of red pepper, made the beer sharper; coriander seeds and various berries were used to impart certain flavors to beer. Nor did wine escape such adulteration. It was apt to turn sour after a time, and in order to counteract this they would use a basic lead acetate, the so-called sugar of lead. How many died as a result of this particular practice will never be known. Reliable chemical and physical tests for detecting these additives had to await the next century before realisation.

However the main, and long-practised fraud as regards beverages was watering down. It therefore represented a great advance when in 1729 Clark described his hydrometer. For if water had in fact been added to alcoholic beverages, the result was that the product was heavier.

The instrument used then was rather similar to the one in use today, except that it was made of copper. It bore on its stem three marks: one mark represented the depth to which the stem of the instrument would sink in "proof" spirit; a second mark was ten percent above that level; and a third mark ten percent below it. With this device you had to prove in front of the inspector that your alcohol was not watered. The word "proof" is still on the bottle, as it relates to whiskey, gin, rum, vodka and other distilled drinks.

Thus the people in their struggle for food always had to fight against fraud. It was to be another hundred years before the Food and Drug Administration was to be set up to take some of the risks out of food and beverages.

TEA

As mentioned earlier tea was becoming available, and cheap. Tea plantations in India and Ceylon were expanded at a great rate in the eighteenth century. And so tea became one of the chief beverages of that time, and it has persisted ever since.

The amount of tea drunk expanded enormously during this period. After the year 1700, tea consumption in England trebled in the ten years, from 10,000 pounds to 30,000 pounds. But this was a mere trickle. By 1760 duty was paid on five million pounds, and by 1800 it was 20 million pounds.

Not everybody was keen about all this tea drinking which became a craze and then a habit. Some thought that it was a pernicious custom. "When will this evil stop?" asks Jonas Hanway: "your very chambermaids have lost their bloom; I suppose by sipping tea." After an equally violent attack on gin, he added: "What an army have gin and tea destroyed!"

But there were others who believed that tea, because it was an infusion, must have medicinal properties. Indeed it had been in use for centuries in the east as a beverage. According to Galen's writings nearly 2,000 years earlier, any infusion of herbs was beneficial, or at least useful. It was said by one author of that time:

> "with the drinking of tea only, and regular living, the distemper of England, occasioned by our too much feeding upon flesh, may be cured."

The distemper of England, according to that writer, was scurvy.

SUGAR

As the consumption of tea rose so too did that of sugar. Sugar ceased to be a luxury as trade with the West Indies developed. It has already been noted how rapidly the Portuguese developed the sugar plantations of Brazil a century earlier.

The English and French islands in the West Indies became sugar plantations also, and these in turn gave rise to the rum business already referred to.

369

Later in the eighteenth century, at least by 1780, there was a great deal of talk in Europe about using the roots of carrots and of beets to get sugar. This was particularly true of the Germanic and Scandinavian peoples, who were denied direct access to the sugar lands of the tropics. Germany, Holland and Belgium were most interested in this possibility. Margraf, a Dutchman, discovered and developed beet sugar, and larger scale production was achieved by Claproth in 1798.

The popularity and abundance of tea and sugar brought about a sharp decline in the sale of coffee, cocoa and chocolate, all of which were a good deal more expensive than tea. Towards the end of the eighteenth century many of the once-famous coffee houses had disappeared. The affluence of the twentieth century was to bring coffee to the fore once again.

THE FOOD PEOPLE ATE

There are at least two ways to search for information about the food available to the people. One is to study the records of institutional feeding. In this case the food to be eaten was allocated by the authorities; it gives insights into what was regarded by them as being adequate for the purpose. The other is to look at actual budgets of people who had to buy their food. This is more difficult.

Records are available for orphanages and foundling hospitals, for the workhouse population and for the British Navy. It is instructive to look at these.

At the lowest level is the workhouse. As reported by Cary in 1714, three meals were provided:

for breakfast: bread and cheese, or broth, alternately

for dinner: boiled beef and suet pudding, or cold leftovers, alternately

for supper: bread and cheese

Again it will be noticed that the quantities were not given. The presence of milk in the diet might have been an improvement over what was available at home in a poor family.

Of considerable interest are the rations for the Navy, recorded in 1745. These were compared with those of 1811. It is to be seen that there was a very marked deterioration in the diet of sailors by the end of the Napoleonic wars. We are indebted to Drummond for giving an approximate breakdown of these two diets, calculated in 1939 from nutritional analyses by then available.

1745 (per week)	1811 (per day)
12 oz. cheese	13/4 oz. cheese
2 lb. salt pork	2¼ oz. pork
4 lb. salt beef	4¼ oz. beef
8 oz. butter	7/8 oz. butter
2 lb. biscuit	¼ oz. suet
2½ lb. oatmeal	7/8 oz. sugar
2 qt. pease	1 lb. bread
7 gallon beer	3 oz. flour
	1 quart beer

You will notice the very great deterioration in the quantity of food allocated; only a quarter of the beer, for example; less than half the meat; no oatmeal and no pease. This is a telling reminder of the dietary problems which were to supervene during the nineteenth century.

The calorific value of the first diet is 5,500 per day, a necessary amount for the chilly job of manning ships on the high seas, especially in the northern climates. The second diet is worth about 2,900 calories, which would have been entirely inadequate. Cutting the ration of beer did not help the morale either. According to calculations made by Drummond, these two diets had approximately the following constituent amounts, per day in each case were:

protein	160 and	80	grams
fat	180 and	100	grams
calcium	1.9 and	0.7	grams
phosphorus	3.7 and	1.9	grams
iron	36 and	18	milligrams
vitamin A	1,750 and	1,450	International units
thiamin	2.6 and	1.6	milligrams
niacin	100 and	46	milligrams
riboflavin	4.0 and	1.5	milligrams
vitamin D	26 and	27	International units

It will readily be seen that, even with these rather approximate figures, the diet of British sailors, even in 1811, did in fact contain essential nutrients in amounts consistent with health. The diet was sparse, though, and the calorific value hardly enough to carry on the day's work.

These figures will be remembered as we approach the changed conditions of the nineteenth century, when the food of average people was to take a turn for the worse.

When we come to the ordinary man and his family, we are able to get an insight into what the people as a whole might be eating. We have already referred to the difference between the south of England and the north. This applies both to the kinds of food eaten and to the amounts.

We shall consider two budgets: the first represents the amount spent on food in one year by a laborer with a wife and four children. They lived at Streatley in the county of Berkshire, one of the poorer regions of south England in the eighteenth century. The total income of this family was 46 pounds a year. They consumed per week as follows:

8 half peck loaves
2 pounds of cheese
2 pounds of butter
2 pounds of sugar
2 ounces of tea

½ ounce of oatmeal
½ pound bacon
2 pennyworth of milk (2 pints)

This cost at that time about a pound a week,
of 50 pounds a year, more than their total wages.
They could rarely eat meat, and seldom afford
potatoes. The diet included hardly any milk.

The second budget is that of a laborer, his
wife, and three children who lived in Kendal, West-
moreland. Their income was less than that of the
southern family, namely just under thirty pounds
a year. But they ate as follows:

75 stone (14 pounds a stone) oatmeal per year
12 pounds of butchers' meat   per week
1½ quarts of milk   per day
tea and sugar regularly
potatoes (4 quarters/3d)   per year
butter (40 pounds/9d)   per year
treacle

Oatmeal was cheap, 2d a pound. They had milk
every day and potatoes in plenty as well as butter.
This was a good diet, and yet it cost them only
just over 20 pounds a year; less than half what
the southern family had to spend. The situation
in southern England at the close of this century
was in fact rather bad. Few people, and certainly
none of the poor people, ever had meat from one
end of the year to the other.

How did people manage? It seems impossible
that the population could survive under such poor
dietary conditions. And there were few people in
those days who had any regard for the sufferings
of the poor. They seemed obsessed with the idea
that all the needy required were nourishing soups.
It does not seem to have occurred to these well-
meaning people that the poor could not afford hot
meals of any kind, as there was no way as yet of
internalising a fire in the tiny houses in the
towns. The range fire was in the future.

But the setting up of soup kitchens to feed the poor did begin at this time. To this day soup is not a popular dish in England, as it is associated with pauperism. A soup kitchen existed for the poor, the down-and-out, who know no other kind of kitchen.

And so the poorer people knew very hard times in the latter part of the eighteenth century. Whenever dearths and scarcities appeared, even necessities became dear. This led, understandably, to food riots and lawlessness. Pressures built up on the Government to do something, to act, in these situations, and sometimes they did. They might take steps to relieve a dearth, as they did in 1796. They allowed Carolina rice into the country, duty-free. But the British people were not about to eat rice, and the move proved rather unpopular.

Much of the discontent was due to the fact that the working people in the towns had become accustomed to eating plenty of butter and cheese and even some meat in the more prosperous years. Those who were comfortably off thought that the poor were being spoiled by getting ideas into their heads. A quotation from one Josiah Tucker in 1751 points up this situation:

> "the palates of the poor are become nice and sickly...they are not able to purchase dainties, and they cannot touch what is coarse and ordinary. Hence the great dealers of flesh meat have justly complained of late years that they have no purchasers for the coarser parts of meat, which formerly used to be sold to the poorest at a low price; but now must be buried or thrown upon a dunghill..."

Such an attitude is typical of a person who is well off, and made uncomfortable by the consideration of the plight of the unfortunate.

However there were some benefits even from this privation. Various people who were ahead of their time prescribed how you might have a very good meal if you extended the meat with vegetables. As James Hanway said in 1767:

> "with the addition of legumes, roots and vegetables 5 lb. of meat with go as far as we generally make 10 or 15, and the consumer will be free of the scurvy, and not less fit for the laborious offices of life..."

This was an entirely new statement to make, for meat was supposed to be for the well-to-do, and vegetables for the poor. Here was a recommendation that such a diet would enable a man to carry out the hard work of life, even with additional vegetables and less meat.

At this time other important changes affected poor families. They suffered because nobody seemed to understand at that time that a growing child needed more food. The rations in schools and institutions were seldom sufficient in quantity, let alone quality. For example the ration provided for the poor in one parish in 1782 may have been fairly good in a qualitative sense. It consisted of bread, cheese broths, a bowl of vegetables twice a week; meat once a week and milk five times a week. In addition some beer was allotted. But it was too little. The amount for a grown man only afforded him 2,000 calories a day, meaning a steady loss of weight. And the "working" children were even worse off. They were allotted only 1,500 - 1,800 calories a day. For them it meant starvation. It never occurred to the authorities in those days that growing boy of 15 needs as much as a grown man. Consequently they become stunted, malnourished, and "old before their time".

It was at the end of this century that the children were beginning to work in the mills and down in the coal mines, always in deference to the great God, Progress. In the early part of the century the towns were not yet centered around

coal, for the age of industrial coal had not yet
quite arrived. Large towns were appearing everywhere, engaged in all kinds of craft work, such
as the smelting of iron, tin-smithing, furniture-
making, woodworking, pottery of all kinds and the
development of china and glassware. These activities were going on all over Europe. In England
they began to concentrate in the south because
London was there. Later on they went to the north
as well.

The age of coal now began in earnest, and this
took place in the north, because there is no coal
south of Birmingham, except in south Wales. These
developments gave rise to the Black Country, as
it was called; black from soot.

And so the struggle for food became even more
acute. Although the people in the north had, as
we have seen, a better diet than the southerners,
which was soon to deteriorate as well. In the
vicinity of the large towns, the value of grass
lands became so high that laborers could not afford
to rent it; as the towns grew, the cows had to
go, one by one. Thus milk went out of the diet.
The north was still better off than the south, because the towns were fewer and far between, so that
some land was available for grazing.

There are other interesting records about the
diet at this time. Christs' Hospital was founded,
as mentioned earlier by Henry VIII, as a place
where boys might go to get educated, occupied and
also off the streets. At the beginning of the
eighteenth century the school was already 160
years old, and famous. Records for the school show
that in 1704 the following was purchased for the
boys at the school: cheese and bread, butter, beef,
oatmeal and dried pease. There was no mention of
vegetables. Each boy also got a quart of small
beer a day.

Records of scurvy appeared at Christs' Hospital, but about 1770 they added potatoes to the
diet and the scurvy disappeared. In 1845 potatoes
were

to disappear everywhere, including England; then scurvy reappeared all over again.

A famous pupil at Christs' Hospital, who was there from 1782 to 1789 has left us a memorable description of the food, which is worth quoting:

> "while were were battening on a quarter
> of a penny loaf, our crug was moistened
> with attenuated small beer in wooden
> piggins, smacking of the pitched leathern
> jack it was poured from. Our Monday's
> milk porritch, blue and tasteless, and
> the pease soup of Saturday, coarse and
> choking; the Wednesday's mess of millet,
> somewhat less repugnant; our half-pickled
> Sundays or quite fresh boiled beef on
> Thursdays (strong as caro equina), with
> detestable marigolds floating in the pail
> to poison our broth..our scanty mutton
> scrags on Fridays, and rather more savoury,
> but grudging portions of the same flesh,
> rotten-roasted, or rare, on the Tuesdays..."

Charles Lamb (1789)

FOOD OF THE WELL-TO-DO

On the other hand the big landowners lived exceedingly well in this century. Their farms, orchards and kitchen gardens supplied them with a wealth of food, to which they added costly wines and other luxuries from abroad.

Breakfast was usually a light meal, taken at nine or ten, and consisted of tea or coffee or chocolate, with rusks or cakes. An hour or two later a glass of sherry and a biscuit followed. Dinner was the main meal of the day, taken at about two o'clock. Later in the century it occurred about four o'clock.

There are records which attest to the fact that well-to-do were prodigious eaters and often sat over dinner for several hours. Supper was

377

seldom eaten before ten o'clock in the evening.
It consisted primarily of cold meats. These
people ate a lot of meat and correspondingly little
bread. It is recorded that Parson Woodford, a
middle-class landowner, had a household of three
mean, three women and a boy. These seven, at least
five of the engaged in manual work, consumed a
mere 13 pounds of flour a week, an amount that
would have lasted a laborer's family at most two
days. Thus the household servants would benefit
from the standards of the master of the house.

Wealthy towndwellers also indulged in
extravagant living. With dinner getting later
a rearrangement of mealtimes occurred. Afternoon
tea at five filled in the time between dinner
and supper. It was this custom that revived the
use of bread. Only it was now cut very thin, lest
it be confused with the diet of poor people. It
was buttered or toasted, and a contemporary writer
has said: "it is now cut so thin that it does
as much honor to the address of the person who
cuts it as to the sharpness of the knife."

French cooking was becoming popular with some
of the well-to-do, although there were those
whowould prefer to return to the diet of their
forefathers. Vegetables and fruits were now eaten
at almost all the tables of the rich. And last but
not least, the French customs introduced table
manners to the English, who were heretofore pretty
uncouth in such matters.

At this stage it is time to take a look at
the situtation in France during the eighteenth
century, in order better to appreciate the earth-
shattering events which were to supervene in
the next hundred years.

REFERENCES

343   WAGES HIGHER BY 1730; Tooke, Thomas A History of Prices (1838)

343   COSTS OF FOOD LOWER: Halliwell, J.O; A collection of bills, accounts and inventories (1852).

344   ENGLAND AN OPULENT COUNTRY: Wallace, R. Characteristics of the Present Political State of Great Britain;

346   INCREASED USE OF TURNIPS: Defoe, Daniel; A Tour thro' the Whole Island of Great Britain (1724-1727).

346   VARIOUS FORMS OF FOODER: A treatise by William Ellis (1733).

346   ."WE USUALLY FEED CATTLE WITH STRAW.." Weston, Sir Richard; a treatise concerning the Husbandry and Natural History of England. (1742).

348   "CLOVER AS A PILLAR OF GOOD HUSBANDRY" Young, Arthur; A six weeks' Tour thrugh the east of England; (1771).

348   MERITS OF THE POTATO. Bradley, R; A Dictionary of Plants (1747).

348   GARDENING IN SURREY: Weston, ibid (1726).

351   COMMON LANDS DECRIED: Sinclair, Sir John; Cultivation and improvement of the waste lands of the Kingdom (1795).

351   "SMALL FARMERS ARE A WRETCHED SET OF PEOPLE". Young, Arthur. A Six months' tour through the north of England (1771).

352 STRUCTURE OF SOCIETY CHANGED. Pullar, P. The Industrial Revolution; chapter 7: Corporate Greed.

353 DIETS IN THE SOUTH: Eden, Sir Frederick; The State of the Poor (1797).

353 ENCLOSURES: Hammond, John le Breton; The Village Laborer; pp 97-119 (1760-1837).

353 "WE WILL NOT BE FED LIKE HOGS.." Eden, ibid (1797)

354 RIOTS OF THE POOR. Hammond, ibid p 110.

354 RACINE DE DISETTE: Parkyns, Boothby; Journal of the Society of Arts, Vol II. (1787).

355 "IN ALL OCCUPATIONS.." Young, Arthur; ibid (1772).

355 POULTRY TRAVELLED ON FOOT..Defoe, Daniel; A Tour through the Whole Island of Great Britain (1724-1727)

356 TRAVEL BY CANALIN HOLLAND: Phillips, John; A History of inland navigation (1792).

357 CHARNEL HOUSES OF THE DEAD..from an anonymous pamphlet entitled Poison detected; or frightful truths; and alarming to the British Metropolis (1757); from Drummond and Wilbraham. ibid p 188.

357 "BREAD A DELETERIOUS PASTE.." Smollett, T. The Expedition of Humphrey Clinker (1771).

358 SMITHFIELD MARKET: Dodd, George; The Food of London. p 30 (1856).

359 WARNING ABOUT VEGETABLES. Trusler, Rev Dr; The London Advisor and Guide. (1786).

359 "MOVABLE SHOPS ON WHEELS.." Ward, E; The London Spy; (1703).

359 "DIRTY BARROW BUNTER.." Smollet. T. ibid (1771).

360 MILK SOLD DOOR TO DOOR: Bayne-Powell, R; Eighteenth Century London (1937)

360 COWS IN ST JAMES' PARK. Moritz. C.P. A journey to England (1782)

361 ORPHANED INFANTS. Hanway, Jonas; Letters on the importance of the rising generation (1757)

363 "MAD AND IMPRUDENT FONDNESS OF MANY MOTHERS.." Forster, William: A compendious discourse on the Diseases of Children. (1738)

363 FOUNDLING HOSPITAL: Nichols, R.H. and Wray, F.A. The Governors of the Foundling Hospital (1935).

364 "MOTHERS SHALL SUCKLE THEIR CHILDREN..." The Koran sura 2, The Cow, stanza 233.

365 FEEDING CHILDREN BY HAND: Armstrong, G; An account of the diseases most incident to Children from their birth till the age of puberty (1772).

365 FRUIT AND VEGETABLES FOR CHILDREN: Cadogan. W. Essay on Nursing and Management of Children (1750).

366 "THEY ARE FED ON MEAT..." Fordyce, Sir William; A new enquiry into the causes, symptoms and care of inflammatory fevers. (1773).

366 "'TIS AMAZING HOW THE VOLUPTUOUS..." Cullen, William Materia Medica. (1773).

369 WHAT AN ARMY HATH GIN AND TEA DESTROYED.." Hanway, Jonas; An Essay on Tea. (1757).

369 THE DISTEMPER OF ENGLAND: PECHLINUS. J.N. A treatise on the inherent qualities of the tea-herb; from the Laton. (1750)

370 USE OF BEETS FOR SUGAR: Claproth, Journ. Natural Philosophy and the Arts; ed. W. Nicholson (1797-1802).

370 WORKHOUSE FOOD: Cary; reported by Eden, Sir Frederick; The State of the Poor (1797).

371 NAVY DIETS IN 1745 and 1811; Admiralty Regulations; Drummong and Wilbraham; ibid p 263 (1939); and Appendix p 465 (1954)

374 "THE PALATE THE POOR ARE.." Tucker, Josiah. Bristol (1751).

375 ADDITION OF LEGUMES AND FRUITS." Hanway, J. ibid (1767).

376 CHRIST'S HOSPITAL: Pearce, E.H. Annals of Christ's Hospital (1901).

377 "WHILE WE WERE BATTENING ON A QUARTER OF A PENNY LOAF." Lamb, Charles; Essays of Elia (1823).

378 USE OF TOAST. Moritz, C. P. A Journey to England (1772).

The early days of this century were also fairly affluent in France. The nation had turned its
attention to plays, literature and the arts generally. The righteous king, Henry IV had wished to
give to every Frenchman his chicken in the pot.
But Louis XIV succeeded Henry, and was considered
a pharoah by some and a despot by others.

However conditions in France steadily deteriorated as Louis' radiant court impervished the
country by means of war and taxes. Here is one
bitter description:

> "certain savage-looking beings, male and
> female are seen in the country, black,
> livid and sunburnt, and belonging to the
> soil which they dig and grub with invinci-
> ble stubbornness. They seem to be capable
> of articulation, and when the stand erect,
> they display human lineaments. They are
> in fact men. They retire at night to
> their dens where they live on black bread,
> water and roots..."

The French peasantry at the height of Louis
Quatorze's glory were seen in the neighbourhood of
Blois eating nettles and carrion. Women and children were found lying dead by the roadside, their
mouths stuffed with inedible weeds. Madmen crouch-
ed over graves in cemeteries, sucking and gnawing
at bones. In 1683 bread was being made with ferns,
and most of those who ate it repeatedly, died. In
1698 various governors began to suspect that France
as a country was dying of starvation. Famine
swept over it unchecked. Around 1715, according
to Taine, a third of the population, about six
million, had died. Such was the opening of the
eighteenth century, said by some to be France's
greatest and one of the greatest in the world's
history.

"The first King in Europe", Saint Simon wrote of Louis VI, "is great simply by being king over beggars of all conditions, and by turning his kingdom into one vast hospital of dying people, from whom their all is being taken without a murmur on their part."

"Before, men turned to eating grass like sheep, and died like so many flies," wrote the Bishop of Chartres. "They tried to hide the rest of their grain, or to pawn their Sunday clothes and pillows, if they had any." It did not help. The tax collectors, preceded by the village blacksmith, forced their way through locked doors, and seized their tables, chairs, linens and tools. These peasant then became a stream of beggars, armies of uprooted vagabonds who infested France from north to south.

A huge police force that cost a fortune to maintain was set against these criminals, if criminals they were. In one day it was reported that 50,000 were arrested. The prisons were not large enough, so they built other ones. They filled hospitals. Many were insane from starvation, and for these they built reformatories. The government vouchsafed to them bread, water, and an ounce or two of lard, which cost the treasury only five sous a day per person. When the records claim that the king expended annually a full five million francs on the "care" of the poor, we can imagine how many of these poor wretches were crammed into those reformatories.

And yet the greater part of these people had once been productive, if not prosperous, peasants. It was not quite correct of Saint Simon to say that there was not a murmur. 250 years after the discovery of America it was no longer possible for mediaeval conditions to exist as a matter of course, because people had changed. They had begun to reflect on things, especially in the city of Paris, where most of the alert minds were. People began to read. Voltaire was there, and he noted the people suddenly ceased to think about love and the theatre only, but they began to think about the shortage of grain and food.

SEEDS OF REVOLUTION

The first philosopher at that time who began to bring about some new thinking as regards society was Quesnay, who preached as follows:

> "Industry does not increase wealth; the farmers alone are the productive class. All citizens engaged in occupations other than agriculture constitute the sterile class."

Benjamin Franklin was in France at the time, and as he listened to Quesnay he became a supporter of his. Franklin enthusiastically endorsed Quesnay's ideas, which were not new, except for those times. Solon had advanced the same ideas to his Athenian audiences over 2,000 years earlier.

Quesnay demanded that the lot of the poorest farmers, who were by far the majority, be alleviated by the granting of credit, so long as they remained farmers. He considered that famine existed because these numberless poor possessed neither animals nor ploughs. Their beasts had long since been slaughtered and their ploughs had fallen to pieces. The laboring class were working literally with their bare hands. No wonder yields were so poor.

But many people, including Voltaire, mocked at Quesnay. Voltaire sensed the importance of farming but was bored by it and preferred craftsmanship and industry. But Quesnay's writings piqued and stimulated the interest of society. Interest in nature revived. The rich who had owned land, but never really visited it, because of the puddles and the misery, now became adherents of the pastoral life. Le Societe d'Agriculture was founded, and several model farms were established. Swamps were drained and roads improved.

Nevertheless grain prices continued to rise, mounting steadily from 1705. Wheat and oats had risen a fourth in price, barley half. And taxes continued to rob the peasant of, not fifty percent but seventy-five to eighty percent of his produce. Leaflets began to flutter, and people began to read them.

Quesnay's adherents were known as physiocrats, and they believed that physics ruled all man's relationships with nature. Alongside the physiocrats, another group arose who worked to try to obtain cheaper bread for France. These were people like Lavoisier, the chemists and the natural scientists. Lavoisier wanted to find the cause of all this misery. Why was agriculture at a standstill? Why could the land no longer feed the people? He examined the taxes and the internal tariffs, but in addition he blamed "le banalité' des moulins." As a scientist he was concerned with the wretched state of the French mills, which were ancient and crippled. Why was this?

As we have already seen in the Middle Ages, people hated the miller. He was suspected of adulterating the flour, mixing sand and sawdust with it, according to popular thinking. He was also an outcast because he had to operate his mill outside the town boundaries, for the wind and/or water to run his mill. But it was not the millers' fault alone. It was the fault of the mills themselves which had hardly been improved since their invention.

The very first millers used their teeth for grinding their food, once having torn it. The first mechanical mills were based upon this principle. Through all the centuries since before Egypt, millers complained about their millstones. They were too soft, and had to be changed too often. Men searched for a long time for a stone which would be harder than all other stones,

and so outlast them. The French came to think that
they had found the answer in their flint quarries,
but the tough wheat ruined even these stones.

The difficulty with the mill, and with the
mouth, is the same. Both are made to break up
the food, to comminute it, grind it up. But this
fails with grains, which remain hard, and in the
end, break both millstones and teeth. Skulls
with teeth still in place can be observed to have
suffered with this problem. Before the time of
cooking grains, they were eaten raw, before fire
was in general use. Skulls from that time often
contain broken teeth.

Even when the mill was operating to break up
the grain as finely as possible, the art of flour-
making remained as it had been in Egyptian times.
The Egyptians had learned how to separate the
bran from the flour 3,000 years earlier. The
French, however, ground their grain in such a way
that the bran was distributed finely throughout
the flour, and could not be separated by sifting.
Consequently the loaf produced was imperfect, to
say the least.

This problem exercised the mind of a Parisian
by the name of Malisset. He reasoned as follows:
what would happen if you were not to grind the
wheat, but gradually to reduce it in size in a
series of steps? and then separate the various
end-products according to size? this is what Malisset did in Paris in 1760. The millstones were
held at, first flour, then three and then two
millimetres apart, in a series of "breaks". The
germ and the coarser parts of the grain were removed at the first step, and not sent on with the
flour. The medium-sized particles were held at
the "second break". Only the final close grinding produced the actual flour.

This was a significant innovation, but it
was not adopted at the time. 95% of the French
flour mills continued to grind wheat ineffectively.

Lavoisier in 1785 saw this as a danger signal.
Benjamin Franklin, in Paris the same year, commented on the milling process and said; "there must be a better way." He reported in a depressed state of mind on the condition of nutrition and feeding in France.

PARMENTIER

A significant contribution was made by the army apothecary, Parmentier, who recognised that the "husks and woody parts of plants were not intended to form part of our food." The art of the miller, he said, should consist in removing this husk from the grain, because it contains no meal. "This must be done without pulverising it in such a way that it can no longer be sifted out. Close grinding is therefore harmful", he said. He reported his results to his officer-superior, Marshal du Muy, France's War Minister.

Parmentier was the first to state this great fact, which was to alter the history of man's food from then on. He set straight the misconception that because bran was heavier it was the more nourishing. In reality it was eaten without being digested, thus deceiving the stomach. It left a man as hungry as before.

We now know that you can go too far in the other direction, eliminating much of the nutrition of the wheat by taking the final break alone by itself. You cannot live and thrive on that alone either. But this was not appreciated for another 150 years. At that time France wanted bread, and the whiter the better.

Parmentier also encouraged the use of the potato as noted earlier. It was not a popular food; France had refused the potato long before this time, and in fact was the very last major nation to adopt it. In 1700 when potatoes were imported into France from Switzerland, they were regarded as poisonous. Other members of the solanaceae family are poisonous or at least narcotic: such as the leaves of the tobacco and capsicum (deadly nightshade). However the poisonous properties are in the leaves, not in the roots. Frederick the Great of Prussia had forced his subjects to eat the potatoes, and Parmentier reported that no one there had died from eating them. He recommended potatoes to the Franch not only because they were nourishing, but also because they needed so little equipment to raise, neither animals nor ploughs.

When the Besancon Academy offered a prize for suggestions as to how the food supply of France might be improved, especially in replacements for grain, Parmentier won the prize. It was ostensibly awarded for a food that could at once replace grain "in case of famine". King Louis sent for him, and graciously granted him fifty acres of land for experimental planting of potatoes. Afterwards potato flowers were to be seen at court, sported by the King and his retainers in their buttonholes. Potatoes were frequently served at the royal table. The King tried to realise what Parmentier wanted, which was to introduce potatoes, not as a vegetable but as a source of bread, to extend the flour. The King said to him: "France will not forget that you found food for the poor."

In 1780 a school for bakers was opened, largely as a result of Parmentier's work. It was to make experimental breads, including those made with potato flour. Benjamin Franklin was often present on these occasions. As a matter of fact, Franklin very much liked corn, but did not care for potatoes. In fact, Boston, Massachusetts had a city ordinance which specified that apprentices to city jobs were not to be fed potatoes at any time.

So Parmentier tried hard to get the people to eat potatoes, but during his lifetime they would have none of it. When his epoch-making book, "Traité' sur la culture et usage de pomme de terre"

was published in 1789, it was already too late.
Other events were pressing. The storm broke.
Who then cared about potatoes?

1789

In the months before the storming of the
Bastille, the people of Paris were wont to greet
one another with the forbidden greeting of the
Jacquirie: "le pain se lève" But what bread?
There was no bread, only the vision of bread.
The hand of destiny was once more at work, knead-
ing the dough, opening the great oven.

The people, the "oï polloi", the plebs, they
are the amorphous dough. Every popular leader from
then until now knows that yeast is needed before
dought will rise. And only a little yeast is
needed. This yeast is composed of ideas, prefer-
ably a single idea. A fact or a rumor which gains
the ear of the multitude breeds revolt even in
the most sluggish mind.

A rumor existed and no one knew from whence
it had sprung, but most people in France at that
time believed that the lack of bread was due to
a conspiracy: that their hunger was something
unnatural and not necessary. They had farms and
worked those farms. What then had been happening
for the past ten, twenty, thirty years?

They thought that some people must have made
up their minds to exterminate the French nation,
by starving the people. Now there is no doubt
that grain speculators were at work, as they are
at work today, but the unique factor in the unrest
was this feeling, this delusion, if you will,
about extermination. It was powerful medicine
indeed.

Advocates and journalists spread the notion
that there had existed for seventy years a secret
society, a band of traders who had concluded a
"pacte de famine": an agreement to create an

390

artificial famine. And that was why there was no grain. It was said that Louis XV had already earned ten million pounds by this murderous conspiracy. The society was alleged to be buying cheaply all the grain in France, secretly exporting it, buying it again from abroad, and importing it back into France at tenfold the original price.

The fact was that this was not true. The export of all grain from France had been forbidden for the past one hundred years; but the rumor-mongers had an answer to that one: "The King himself is in this business", they said. "All he has to do is gather all the grain in the warehouses, and send it to the border under military guard."

Nobody knows how the tale got started, but everyone seems to have believed it. It was spread abroad that on August 28, 1765, four men had gathered in Paris to discuss once more their technique for starving an entire generation. These men were said to have sent all the grain abroad, with the approval of the King. It was stored in vast granaries on the islands of Jersey and Guernsey, whence it would be re-imported into France, to bear frightful tariffs. Now the fact is that the price of bread did triple in September 1765. But was it true? Where were the ships? Nobody seems ever to have found the ships that took it there.

Some years later the police located a man who was responsible for the story; he had seen the books recording the profits. This man's name was Prevost de Beaumont. He was immediately sent to the Bastille and retained there incommunicado for twenty years. A trial was not afforded to such people. A "lettre de cachet" was sufficient to cause a man to vanish from the midst of Paris. It stated that you had to be hidden away in the lowest dungeon of the Bastille, so that nobody would ever find you.

There was danger to people who might speak loosely in the streets of Paris. They had to think twice before they spoke of a "pacte de famine"; but they whispered about it all the more. One of the four men supposedly implicated was Malisset, the same who had earlier suggested improvements in the arts of milling. He was shunned like a leper, and branded as a scoundrel and an enemy of the people. For 30,000 pounds a year he was said to have sold France. He finally died, having earlier lost his mind. What happened to his grain profits?

So on July 14, 1789 the people, enraged by the grain plot, rose up. They stormed the Bastille, where honorable men like Prevost had been incarcerated, released them and demolished the hated fortress. For a thousand years the masses had battered futilely against a closed door. Now it opened, and partly of itself. In just one assembly in August, 1789 the nobles surrendered their property and the clergy their tithes. But this was not the question:

"Il ne s'agit pas de ca, coquins"
(that is not the point, you scoundrels!)

and the gallery roared in chorus: "Nous voulons du pain."

The Bastille contained a number of poor devils who had been sealed up for years, but no bread. But again it seemed that the hand of God intervened. That same August, 1789 brought a terrible drought. The streams dried up and the mills would not run. Windmills in the north could manage to operate, but there were none in the middle or south of France. Now the little grain that there was could not be ground. Horse-drawn mills were ordered but this took time. In September prices rose shamelessly again. The King and Queen and their nobles with their silver-buckled shoes, they had bread. "On to the Palace...on to Versailles!"

So, early in the morning of October 5, 1789, Paris spewed out her human torrent onto the streets. They marched with their pikes and their

scythes, in rags and barefoot. Surrounding the
core of men marched women and children, 50,000 of
them, someone said. But nobody counted them.
"On to Versailles!" the monarchy would be crushed.

When they arrived there after the eighteen
mile walk, they were tired and dusty. There was
the Park, but it was not at all as they expected.
they had heard about it from others, from their
fathers and grandfathers, perhaps, but had had
no occasion to go there until now. Where were
all the fountains that they had been told about?
Weeks earlier the King had ordered all the
fountains turned off, because the little water was
needed for running the mills. A small amount of
grain was being ground, for a little bread.

So, interestingly enough, it occurred to
the marchers that the King did not have bread
either, although he had gold and jewels enough.
And so they actually took the King and Queen with
them back to Paris, without at first harming them.
The people of the suburbs, seeing the returning
procession late that evening, recognised the
fat face of the King within the coach, and that
is when they cried the famous words:

"Voila' le boulanger; voila' la boulan-
gière; et le petit mitron"
(there is the baker; there is the baker's
wife, and the little fellow)

But the point that they realised perfectly
well was that Louis XVI could not conjure up
any bread either. Everything was decaying in
France: roads, means of transportation, ploughs,
animals and the minds of the people. And on the
frontiers of the country the speculators lurked,
and caused prices to mount. Countries like
England, Germany and the Netherlands were anxiously watching France, ready to pounce.

The men of the Revolution could not get bread.
They knew nothing of trade. Parisians had been
accustomed to good bread, and they would not touch

macaroni, the Italian invention which was so
economical and so filling. They did not like the
smell of maize flour, and oats was for horses.
All they wanted was wheat bread and there was not
enough. The new National Assembly and the Administration knew that, kingdom or republic, the
people would hang all those in authority who did
not solve the bread problem. While the Assembly
in Paris were debating the Declaration of the Rights
of Man, and the abolition of aristocratic prive-
leges, the market women of Paris were demonstrating
their disapproval of the fact that a quartern loaf
cost 14½ sous, when a day's wages were 18 sous.

Food crises and food riots were to bedevil
the plan of revolutionaries and their successors
throughout the 1790's. It was a real question
as to whether the revolution could be sustained.
France had to go to war in 1792 to secure her
borders, so bread had to be commandeered for the
army, causing more trouble. The Revolutionary
authorities had to tell the people that the war
in 1792 was against all Europe, and that supplies
of what there was would have to go to the gallant
soldiers who were defending the revolution against
the dreadful plots of the Royalists. Even the
army's own generals were likely to spirit bread
away for sale elsewhere. So one's own revolutionary people could do the same, and it would
mean the end of the revolution. Accordingly,
the idea of the pact de famine again reared its
ugly head, this time from among the people.
All the guilty men were executed, but their
followers were legion. The army must have bread.

Various peoples wanted to surround France
and subdue the Revolution, and accordingly France
found herself at war with Holland, the Germanic
states, Austria and eventually with England. She
took care of everybody on her borders so that
about 1800 there was peace for about five years.
Then in 1805 France went to war with England.

NAPOLEON

The five years of peace at last permitted the
French people to return to their fields. France
had won the war and she would win the peace by
cultivating her fields and gardens. If the crops
in France were insufficient, there were the inexhaustible fields of Russia. Ukrainian grain
travelled up the Danube through Austria to Stras-
bourg to feed the French. North Russian wheat was
shipped from Danzig to le Havre. Napoleon had
been able to make favorable arrangements for himself and for France as he marched over Europe.

Where had France obtained all the money to
do this after such a devastating war? It came not
only from the treasures seized by the armies of
the Republic from Holland, the Rhineland, Austria
and Venice. It came also from a new source of
wealth -- industry. All his life Napoleon had
believed fervently in industry, and not so much in
agriculture. He was in charge of France and of
three quarters of Europe besides. Food he arranged
for quietly and regularly, by trade treaties. It
was always to be delivered punctually, on the spot.

The gods Napoleon worshipped were called
activité' and vitesse. The soil, to be sure was
active, but it had too little esprit; it worked
too slowly. Napoleon said: "let other people till
the soil; we will buy it."

He initiated metalurgical and chemical industries in France. He rewarded inventors hand-
somely, not just through the Société of the Arts,
but the philosophical society as well. Here was
the emperor, personally seeing and rewarding inventors. He caused trees to be planted along the
straight French boulevards, but they were not just
any trees. They were walnut trees. The nuts could
be eaten and the wood was used for gun-barrels.
As a practical man, Napoleon encouraged gardens,
but they were not just any gardens; they were herb
gardens.

When the war came again in 1805, his one objective was to replace English manufactures with French ones. There must be substitutes for the cloth, spices and dyes that the English ships had formerly brought to be sold in France.

As a result of the Seven Year's War in 1756-1763, India and Canada, partly French-occupied or French-influenced, fell to the British. 1763 was a dark year indeed for the French. Now, 45 years later, Napoleon was wondering how he could possibly get back those lands. No wonder that he coveted Egypt for example. The Battle of the Nile was fought because he wanted to have the whole of Egypt, and thus secure for France an east-to-west dominion right across Africa.

Napoleon made the distinction between industry and commerce. Commerce to him was just trading. People had traded for 4,000 years or more, and Napoleon did not think that commerce was what France needed. He well understood that all entrepreneurs could make money off other people. Industry, however, was creating something that did not exist before, a very different thing.

He brought back and put into prominent positions various people, including old Parmentier, whom he empowered to sow potatoes all over France. Nobody would laugh at the old man now. Indeed the mania to sow potatoes was to save the lives of millions. However Napoleon overlooked the real malaise of France's agriculture, and when Alexander I of Russia lined with the Napoleon's enemies, the dream of cheap grain once more faded. Even then he recognised the importance of bread.

At first he needed to take care of England, first on the Nile and then in a sea battle of Trafalgar, off the coast of Spain. The day he set out on his famous march into Russia, hoping to reach Moscow, if not St. Petersburg, he said to his ministers:

"I desire the people to have bread, sufficient bread and good cheap bread...while
I am away from France do not forget, Mr.
Minister, that the first care of the
government is to secure public tranquillity, and food is the chief means of
ensuring this tranquillity."

But what could the poor minister do? The
farmers of France had been conscripted. The last
harvest was very poor and eastern Europe was
closed to the French, Poland as well as Russia.
Did Napoleon know, one wonders, how empty the
Franch granaries were as he marched eastwards?
While his vast armies rolled through Russia,
famine knocked at the door back home.

What was the general situation in 1812? In
that year, France's textile industry alone provided 54% of the French national income. Agriculture included all those inedible products such as
tobacco, wine, hides, etc., and comprised a mere
13.7%. In fact France depended on other countries
for food: Italy, Germany, etc.

The famous battle of Austerlitz in 1812 between
Napoleon's armies and the Austrians heralded the
start of the fabulous march eastwards. All the
grain that France could assemble went eastwards,
following the army: wheat and rye for the soldiers,
and mountains of oats for the horses. The bakers'
ovens glowed through the night before a battle at
dawn, as the soldiers must have bread. The term
"sappeurs blancs" (white engineers) referred to the
bakers in the field. And the French soldier's
bread was better than any other army's bread. It
was remarkably white, with a porous inside and an
attractive crust outside. Malisset had taught the
French to grind their flour three times. But the
Russian bread was very bad. Their loaves were so
wet that a daily ration for a Russian soldier was
3½ pounds, enough to make any man ill.

But even in the field the French proved themselves born bakers. In addition to their excellent

bread, they had biscuits and the twice-baked panes biscocti, or hardtack. This was a French invention of the middle ages which had saved many a sailor's life. The German bread was almost as bad as the Russian, being very heavy, because it had not been sifted and therefore contained lots of bran. And half of it was water. But the French were superior bakers, and being conquerors saw to it that they had the best food. Other previous conquerors did the same thing: (the Aryans for example in Asia millennia previously).

At the beginning of the long march the French had plenty of food, wagon loads of it. But they were eating it up as they went, and hoped to use the food of the land as they marched. All conquerors fed off the land as they passed through. But two things happened. When the march began Napoleon's armies went so fast that cavalry and wagon trains got separated. "Some army corps never saw their bread wagons again", Baron von Richtoven was later to say. The second thing they were not prepared for. They had not reckoned with the scorched earth policy of the Russians.

As the Russians retreated they took every single thing that grew off the land for the winter; and they scorched the rest of it so that there would be no final crop for the French when they arrived. Lack of resistance was planned by the Russians, and the French were thereby encouraged to go ever faster. And this was part of their downfall. When Moscow was finally burned, and Napoleon began his famous retreat into Poland, the greatest bread disaster in the history of warfare began.

At first the soldiers killed and ate their horses which were dying of starvation because there was no oats. They drank the blood while it still flowed. It took them three months to struggle back through snow and ice, even to the populated areas of Poland. The emperor returned swiftly and unharmed by sled, but the hundreds of

398

thousands who were without horses, wagons, blankets or furs, froze on that terrible road. Those that were frozen were eaten by their desparate fellows. One does not need to dwell upon the horrors of that march.

But an empire ended that had depended more on fame and conquest than on the gifts of its own soil. When Napoleon returned home he found a famine-stricken France. He was still able to function as leader, and recalled that a scientist named Benjamin Thompson had devised a poor man's soup of bread fragments, vegetables and bones. He ordered that two million plates of this soup should be distributed daily in France to the poor. This was done for five months, until the next harvest. When the English learned of this they knew that the end of France was near. "The French swallow dirt and bones"; they said. The English themselves had bread. It became apparent that he who had bread had victory.

This was two years before Waterloo. So what had Napoleon really accomplished? He had reduced the number of French bread-eaters by two million dead, and those of his allies and enemies by another six million. And he had fertilised the soil of the continent with corpses.

But Napoleon was such a towering figure that after the battle of Waterloo he was accorded the opportunity to live his life out in exile on the island of St. Helena. In attempting to stage a comeback he was removed and brought to the island of Elba, close to France, where he died in 1821.

REFERENCES

383   "TO EVERY FRENCHMAN HIS CHICKEN IN THE POT."
Jacobs, H.E. Six thousand years of bread.
Book 5 chap 93. p 238 (1944).

383   FAMINE IN FRANCE IN 1715; Derry, T.K. and
Williams T.I.: A short history of technology from the earliest times to A.D.
1900 (1960).

384   "MEN EATING GRASS LIKE SHEEP." Letrosne,
1779, quoted in Jacobs, ibid p 41.

385   "INDUSTRY DOES NOT INCREASE WEALTH."
Quesnay: Philosophie Rurale, 1782.

385   SOLON'S IDEAS. see The Greeks, chapter 5.

386   AGRICULTURE AT A STANDSTILL: Lavoisier,
La banalite des moilins; quoted in Jacobs,
ibid p 241.

388   "THE HUSKS AND WOODY PARTS OF PLANTS ARE
NOT INTENDED TO FORM PART OF OUR FOOD."
Parmentier, Augustin A. (1736-1812);
Experiences et reflexions sur le ble et
les farines.

388   "CLOSE GRINDING IS THEREFORE HARMFUL."
Parmentier, A.A. La fabricationet commerce
du pain, (1778).

390   PACTE DE FAMINE: Jacobs. H.E. ibid chap 97,
p 246-252.

392   "THAT IS NOT THE POINT, YOU SCOUNDRELS!"
reported by one Thomas Blaikie, a Scottish
gardener at the French court at the time.

394   THE REAL QUESTION WAS WHETHER THE REVOLU-
TION COULD BE SUSTAINED: Wells, H.G.
Outline of History pp 898-901.

397   "I DESIRE THE PEOPLE TO HAVE BREAD." Napoleon; quoted in Jacobs, ibid p 257.

The Napoleonic Wars had left all parties
thoroughly exhausted, victors and vanquished alike.
The opening of the nineteenth century had been a
distressing time for everybody except the landowners and the wealthy classes of entrepreneurs,
who had not only survived the wars but had profited
by them. And the Peace of Paris was not a vindic-
tive peace, as far as France was concerned. She
was soon to become a respectable member of the
Industrial Revolution, which was occupying everybody's minds.

The advent of new factories and trading enterprises had created new kinds of jobs which had not
existed before to any large extent: bookkeepers,
sweepers, those who tended and oiled the new machinery, messenger boys, lawyers' assistants. And
the new surge in population came at a time when
education was about to be placed in the public domain, at least in part. Consequently, there were
all sorts of positions for teachers and their helpers in the schools. And there was a spate of
activity as regards new shops for supplying the
needs of people.

The main problems centered around the growth
of towns and cities. For example, in 1800 Manchester had 75,000 inhabitants; by 1850 this had
grown to 400,000; in a century the number of
people living in Vienna had multiplied by five;
in Berlin by nine and in London by four. The fast-
est growing city of all was Dusseldorf, sitting as
it does on the Ruhr coalfields. In 1800 it was a
small town of 10,000 inhabitants; by 1910 it had
grown to 360,000.

This rapid industrialization and urbanization,
which was very erratic and haphazard with little or
no planning brought with it a host of problems.
Being an unnatural occurrence it had unwarranted
and unwanted effects. For almost the first time

in history, mass urban poverty could be observed by all who cared to see. Conditions in these industrial towns were shocking, as recorded by philanthropists as well as by social writers like Engels and Dickens:

> "...and the houses were devitalising and dehumanising; bludgeoned by day by the intolerable clamor of early machinery, which was noisy in the extreme; suffocated by the laden air of the weaving shed..."

The working man or woman went home in the 1830's to a cellar, an overcroweded slum or a flimsy shack thrown up out of half-bricks by some speculative builder. For in order to get people to work in the new factories they had to have houses. These were as often as not put up as company houses, as close to the factory or mine as possible, in the days before any transportation. These houses were simply let out on a rental basis; the nineteenth century factory worker never did own his own home. Cooking facilities were at best sketchy. The water supply was drawn from wells and rivers often contaminated by seepage from cesspools. It was distributed through street standpipes which might be turned on by the authorities for no more than five minutes a day. Sewage systems were a mockery.

Friedrich Engels writes of the stark horror of these hovels when life was as its lowest ebb. In his "The condition of the working class in England", which was published in German in 1844, he describes slums in London:

> "...it is a disorderly collection of tall, three or four-storied houses with narrow crooked filthy streets...the houses are occupied from cellar to attic, filthy within and without, and their appearance such that no human being could possibly wish to live in them; but all this is nothing in comparison with the dwellings

in the narrow courts and alleys between
the streets, entered by covered passages
between the houses, in which the filth
and tottering ruin surpass all description. Scarcely a whole window pane can
be discovered, and walls are crumbling,
door frames and windows loose and broken..."

These conditions could also be seen in the
new industrial towns of France, Germany and other
countries, which were embarking on this course of
industrial life. It is interesting to note that
Engels' book about English factory life was not
to be translated into English until 1892. Dickens'
description of the neighborhood in South London-
walled Southwark, as written in Oliver Twist in
1838 is as grim as anything Engels wrote.

Distress and discontent were rife amount
the laboring classes, and this even spread to
the newly emerging middle class. Thousands were
driven by these desperate conditions to seek almost
any way out, including suicide. And some were
only too glad to endure the long journey to Australia rather than suffer the misery at home.

Hundreds of thousands of children were to
die, not only from the resultant diseases but also
from malnutrition. Engels in describing the diet
of the poor in the northern manufacturing towns,
said:

"...we find animal food reduced to a small
bit of bacon cut up with the potatoes;
lower still even this disappears, and
there remain only bread, cheese, porridge
and potatoes; until on the lowest round
of the ladder, among the Irish, potatoes
form the sole food..."

But there was work even in those dark, Satan-
ic mills in Lancashire and Yorkshire and Staffordshire. The factories were located there because
there was black coal underground.

403

Back-to-back housing

Under such conditions, what types of food
were available to the worker and his family? In
Britain in the 1930's and 1940's a worker might
earn anything from five shillings to two pounds a
week; but what could it buy? Five shillings could
buy six four-pound loaves, just enough to feed a
family of two adults and three children. But it
left nothing to pay the rent with, nothing for
tea, nothing for that little bit of meat, and
hardly anything for cheese. A man with fifteen
shillings a week could manage, besides the loaves
5 pounds of meat and 40 pounds of potatoes; the
potatoes gave the family something filling and
warm, along with the tea. An ounce of sugar, as
well as 2/6 pence for rent; schooling about 3
pence and 2 pence left over. Such a diet was
typical of the semi-skilled worker, but only in

times of good employment. In bad years, the meat would have to go.

And even when the wages were there, the food had to be bought. It is significant to read again what Engels has to say about this:

"...and so he comes to market at 5 or 7 o'clock in the evening, while the buyers of the middle class have had first choice in the morning, when the market teems with the best of everything. But when the workers reach it, the best has vanished, or, if it is still there, they would probably not be able to buy it. The potatoes which the workers buy are usually poor, the vegetables wilted, the cheese old and of poor quality, the bacon rancid, the meat lean, tough, taken from old, often diseased cattle, or such as have died a natural death, and not fresh even then, and often half-decayed... As all shops must close at midnight on Saturday until Monday, things are sold off at any price between 9 and 10 and midnight; but nine-tenths of what is sold at 10 is past using by Sunday morning, yet these are precisely the provisions which make up the Sunday dinner of the poorest class; but having bought it, they must use it..."

Accordingly in the early part of the nineteenth century, the food in the towns consisted mainly of bread, potatoes and strong tea. The following statement appeared in 1824, dealing with the substitution of tea for stronger drink, and not without some misgivings as to its value.

"...We are sorry to remark also, notwithstanding all that we have said so often about, and in favor of, tea; that the use of it with bread and butter solely, by the working classes in the manufacturing towns is a leading cause of the

405

extension of scrofula among the masses of our population; and it hence becomes a question, whether sobriety, which the introduction of tea has promoted, compensated for the loss of vigor of constitution, and powers of body, which have followed its use by that part of the community..."

And indeed tea had taken a very important place in life which it was not to relinquish. By 1871 its consumption had reached its highest level. One expert put his finger on a very real problem when he stated that the consumption of large quantities of hot fluid would supplant the intake of other more nutritious food. A poor person could enjoy quite a deceptive warmth from a hot cup of tea, whereas a cold glass of beer would have given him far more real food value.

There was a tendency for the diet of townspeople to improve somewhat after 1860 because of a rise in wages coupled with a fall in price of some staples. But bread remained the staff of life for the poor. Even as late as 1892, it was reported that the children of Bethnal Green, a suburb of London, had bread only for 17 out of the 21 meals a week. They seldom saw meat, as we have already noted. And when the cattle plague swept the country, meat became out of reach of the ordinary people entirely. But by now elementary canning was being carried out, especially in Australia, and such meats could be sold in England more cheaply than could the fresh article. Imported American bacon also arrived, coarse, fat and not very appetizing.

Milk was bought hardly at all by the average people, because it was too expensive. This was deplored by such far-sighted people as Dr. Wilson, who in 1877 found that if factory children were given milk at breakfast and at supper, they grew four times as fast as if they drank tea and coffee. Nevertheless, it was an undisputed fact that fresh milk was at that time deplorably infected with typhoid, dysentery and tuberculosis organisms.

Not until 1890 did people realise that a measure of protection was to be afforded by boiling the milk. Condensed milks appeared at this time; and then treacle. And finally all sorts of cheap jams made their appearance. And so bread and butter gave way finally to bread and jam.

The skilled workmen fared better, for their wages went further; they were able to make use of the cookshops, to have their joint done for them, or even the whole meal. Sometimes artisans would take their whole family out to a meal at a cheap eating house, where an "ordinary" of hot meat, vegetables, bread cheese and beer cost sixpence to a shilling. Not always were such meals as appetising as this. A quaint piece appeared in 1853, called "The Memoirs of a stomach, written by himself, that all who eat may read," edited by a Minister of the Interior. It went as follows:

> "I have dined at eating-houses, the effluvia of which, steaming up through the iron gratings made me qualmish before eating, and ill the day after...I have groped my way down hypocausts in Fleet Street, and dined in cavern-like taverns, wishing myself a thousand miles away the moment the eternal joint was uncovered..."

The better-paid artisans by now could return to his home to an evening supper of cold pies, cold meat, salmon and, by now, bottled beer. So much for the people in the towns, earning the going wages. But what about the villagers? How were they faring? Their lot at this time was deplorable, according to William Cobbett. In 1830 he explored the country-side, to find a wretched state of affairs:

> "...Here are new enclosures without end;
> The farmhouses have been growing fewer
> and fewer, and it is manifest to every
> man who has eyes to see, that the villagers
> are regularly wasting away...the farmhouses
> are not so many as they were 40 years ago
> by three-fourths."

These smaller farms were being swallowed up by the big estates, and many a cottage with its little garden was being ruthlessly liquidated, continuing a process which, as we have seen, had begun generations earlier. He goes on:

> "...ordinary wages were 8 to 12 shillings a week for a farm laborer which is certainly not much. But that has not increased more than a shilling or two in all the years since Arthur Young made his report in 1760..."

After the Peace of Paris in 1815, the situation deteriorated, for real wages were not going up even if the actual wages were. Unemployment had begun to be a problem by as early as 1825; by 1830 there were riots and incendiarism. Wages continued to fall for the next 20 years.

REFORMERS

Reformers began to appear, such as a notable British nobleman named Sir John Sinclair. He had an idea which he felt would alleviate some of the misery. He envisaged that a plot of land of three acres should be cultivated, and sown with potatoes, barley, oats, wheat, clover and rye grass. The produce of such a plot, together with the possession of a plough, some pigs and poultry, would enable a man to support his family very well. This would certainly have been far better than anything that could conceivably be achieved in the villages or the towns of that period.

Sinclair's report did lead to an unsuccesful attempt to form a protest movement. The fiery leader of the Chartist movement, O'Connor, established a colony called O'Connersville based upon Sinclair's formula, and the cry became: "Three acres and a cow."

But this never happened. And the appalling growth of pauperism went on, with its attendant rise in the incidence of suicide, murder and in-

cendiarism. For in 1819 Peel had revised the
barbarous criminal code, by removing at least 100
crimes which had previously been punishable by
death.

A demand for an increase in wages of 2 to 6
pence a day was made. For at last it was beginning
to dawn on people's minds that the conditions in
the factories were so appalling, and wages so low
that changes must be made.

In 1832 the first of the Factory Acts was
passed, making it illegal to hire a child under 9.
Children from the ages of 9 to 13 were to work only
8 hours a day. Even this move elicited opposition
from the tycoons of industry.

Things were as bad in the country, as we have
already seen. Cobbett wrote in 1830:

> "...I asked a man who was hedging on the
> side of the road how much he got in a day.
> He said one and sixpence, and he added
> that the allowed wages was 7 pence for the
> man, and a gallon loaf for the rest of the
> family; that is to say, 19 ounces of bread
> a day for each of them. This, " says Cob-
> bett, "is rather less than the bread allow-
> ance of the gaols."

PRISON DIETS

It is instructive at this point to take a
look at the gaols of the time. A committee was
requested to report on the state of the prisons,
and to consider the diet of prisoners in the light
of meals required by a free laborer. One of their
statements in interesting:

> "...it is extremely difficult to ascertain
> what the ordinary food of a free laborer
> is...even were it to appear that as a class
> their food is badly chosen, badly cooked
> and insufficient in quantity, it would
> not be incumbent upon us, in framing diets

for prisoners, to imitate their bad example..."

In other words, the report was planning a
better diet for the prisoners than that which they
knew to be current among free laborers. It is
useful therefore to look at a few prison diets.
There are five diets to be considered here;

i.   Gloucester gaol 1815
ii. Prison diet class I (one week or less) 1843
iii. Prison diet class 2 (21 days or 6 weeks, 1843
iv. Prison diet class I..1864
v.   Prison diet class 2..1864

The first three will be considered first;

i per day	ii. per week	iii. per week
beef 3½ ounces	meat 0	meat 6 oz.
cheese 1½ oz.	cheese 0	cheese 0
potatoes 14 oz.	potatoes 0	potatoes 64 oz.
bread 1¼ pound	bread 112 oz.	bread 140 oz.
oatmeal 2 oz.	gruel 14 pts.	gruel 14 pts.
(pease pudding	soup 0	soup 2 pts.
twice a week)		

Drummond and Wilbraham in 1939 made calculations as to the amounts of nutrients in these diets.
The scandalous shortages shown in diets ii and iii
were somewhat alleviated in 1864. The class i
diet was to include potatoes and an Indian meal
pudding, which was not described in any detail.
In the light of modern knowledge these diets are
seen to have been low in calcium, low in ascorbic
acid and vitamin A. Thiamin and iron are adequate
simply because the bread is of the coarse type,
unrefined and therefore it contains certain amounts
of nutrients which later had to be added as forti-
fication. The diets tend to promote scurvy, rickets
and eye conditions. The actual amounts of these
nutrients can be seen by reference to Drummond's
book.

But in spite of the movement in favor of improving the prisons, in diet as well as in other ways, the culture of the nineteenth century said that you might be getting "soft". Although prison reform was called for, it invoked a fear in the people, lest liberality in a prison diet might provoke an outburst of crime. In 1864, a Parliamentary paper made this statement:

> "...if they wished imprisonment to deter from crime, they must cease to supply an excessive diet as to afford temptation to a poor man to commit crime in order to get to prison."

The diets were so bad in the 1840's that when the diets were cut almost in half, 118 out of 850 inmates in one prison were found to have scurvy; almost half had limb deformation.

Later on in the nineteenth century, Dr. Edward Smith was able to prescribe quantitative diets for prisoners using up-to-date information, but the Prison committee would not listen. They could not be convinced that the weight of a prisoner meant that he was underfed. To them, this was merely an inevitable consequence of confinement. Consequently the prison diets of 1864 were incredibly bad, as we have seen, even though the calories reached 2,450.

THE MIDDLE CLASS

How about the emerging middle class? What were they eating in the nineteenth century? The new Victorians like Dickens' Bob Cratchett, for example. The middle classes did increase in numbers, and gradually in power. The great employers of factory labor needed also the services of banks and usurers, insurance people and accountants, clerks by the hundred. They needed shippers, carriers, engineers and managers. More shops, more schools and more medical men were all needed. A knowledge of how they ate when they could exercise choice, is difficult to ascertain.

It is possible to learn something about their eating habits and norms by referring to an institutional diet. There were at that time an increasingly large number of boarding schools where the boys, and later the girls were housed and presumably fed.

We already saw how the boys at Christ's Hospital were fed during the previous century. Conditions were to get, if anything, even worse. For now morality was brought in to excuse the inexcusable. In the "Life of Charlotte Bronte", written in 1857, Mrs. Gaskell tells of the half-starved Bronte girls being lectured, when they pleaded for more to eat, about the sin of caring for carnal things and pampering greedy appetites. Later in the century, Gilbert was to satyrise this attitude for posterity, when he states to the girls at the University, through the mouth of the Professor of Abstract Philosophy:

> "...Hunger I beg to state
> Is highly indelicate;
> This is a fact profoundly true,
> So learn your appetites to subdue..."

The retort to this is rapid and to the point:

> "Madam, your words so wise
> Nobody could despise;
> cursed with an appetite keen I am;
> But I'll subdue it...
> With a cold roast lamb."

Earlier in the century we find another of Christ's Hospital's famous old boys, Henry Field, writing in 1813:

> "...their diet is plain and simple; the allowance of bread is very ample and of best quality; that of animal foods is in quantity moderate and of culinary vegetables but small; but the great quantities of bread allowed to them renders the latter less necessary and thus without material

inconvenience they may be dispensed with."

As one might surmise, these same boys were found in 1816 to be suffering from scurvy. In 1834, the Lancet severely criticised these diets, but the Governors of the school resented such criticism. Nevertheless a few small improvements were effected. They were accorded potatoes at a level of one to two pounds a week each, which tended to clear up the scurvy. However, as has been noted elsewhere, the onset of the potato blight in 1845 soon dispensed with the potatoes, and the boys of Christ's Hospital were to get scurvy again.

In a lurid account of another type of Boys' School, Dickens has this to say about Dotheboys' Hall:

> "...pale and haggard faces, lank and bony figures, children with the countenances of old men, deformities with irons in their limbs, boys of stunted growth and others whose long meagre legs would hardly bear their stooping bodies..."

These boys were fed upon thin porridge, bread, stirabout and potatoes, plus some hard, salt beef. Even at famous schools for the well-to-do vegetables were scarcely ever used, certainly not green leafy vegetables. The author at one such school ate almost no green vegetables and no salads at all from 1925 to 1930 after which a distinct improvement set in. Old habits die hard.

In order to combat rising costs and scarcities which occurred from time to time, the boys' diets would be modified. At Christ's Hospital School, during the later nineteenth century, vegetable soup was introduced twice a week; but at the same time butter was reduced from 4½ to 1½ ounces per week. This reduced the calorific value of the diet from 2,050 to 1,950 per day, scarcely enough to keep a growing boy going. In addition his supply of vitamin A was considerably curtailed leading to eye conditions such as night blindness and xerophthalmia.

His intake of vitamin D was severely limited.

It is now the appropriate time to discuss rickets, because this condition was to become of significant importance during the nineteenth century.

REFERENCES

401   RAPID GROWTH OF CITIES: Briggs, Asa: The Nineteenth Century: The Contradictions of progress. London (1970).

402   BLUDGEONED BY DAY... Tannahill chap 16 p 328.

402   ".IT IS A DISORDERLY COLLECTION OF TALL..." Engels, Friedrich: The Condition of the working class in England p 27 (1844).

403   SOUTHWARK: Dickens, Charles; Oliver Twist: Chap L p 339 (1838).

403   "..POTATOES FORM THE SOLE FOOD.." Engels, Friedrich. ibid p 72.

404   "..BUT IT LEFT NOTHING TO PAY THE RENT WITH.." Burnett, John. A History of the cost of living. Harmondsworth 1969.

405   "..AND SO HE COMES TO MARKET.." Engels, Friedrich; ibid p 68.

405   ".WE ARE SORRY TO REMARK ALSO..." The Family Oracle of Health: edited by Crell and Wallace; Vol II, (1824).

406   CONSUMPTION OF TEA: Pavy, W. A. treatise on food and dietetics. (1875).

406   "..BREAD ONLY FOR 17 OUT OF 21 MEALS A WEEK.." Drummona and Wilbraham ibid p 331 (1939).

407   "..HERE ARE NEW ENCLOSURES WITHOUT END.."
Cobbett, William: Rural Rides, p 390 (1830).

408   RIOTS AND INCENDIARISM: Hammond, J.L.& B.
The Village Labourer- 1760-1832; (1911).

408   "THREE ACRES AND A COW". Drummond and Wilbraham, ibid p 280 (1939).

409   "..I ASKED A MAN WHO WAS HEDGING.." Cobbett,
William: Cottage Economy II. p 82 (1823).

409   "..IT IS EXTREMELY DIFFICULT TO ASCERTAIN.."
Parliamentary Paper xlix, (1864).

410   PRISON DIETS: Drummond and Wilbraham; ibid
Appendix A p 465 (1939).

411   "..IF THEY WISHED IMPRISONMENT TO DETER.."
Smith. E; from Journal of the Society of the
Arts, Vol. XII, 1864.

412   "..PAMPERING GREEDY APPETITES.." Gaskell,
E.C. Life of Charlotte Bronte p 44 (1856).

412   "..HUNGER I BEG TO STATE..." Gilbert, W. S.
Princess Ida, Act II (1882).

412   "THEIR DIET IS PLAIN AND SIMPLE." Field, Henry,
The London Medical Repository, (1813).

413   SCURVY AT CHRISTS' HOSPITAL. Wilson, J. I.
The History of Christs' Hospital. (1824).

413   "PALE AND HAGGARD FACES": Dickens, Charles;
Nicholas Nickleby: p 82 (1839).

413   CALORIES REDUCED FROM 2,050 to 1,950: Friend,
G. E.: The Schoolboy; a study of his nutrition, physical development, and health.
(1935).

It is now important that we take a look at this condition. The nineteenth century did in fact provide a combination of circumstances to make the onset of rickets a common phenomenon. It is not generally known that what we have come to call rickets has been known for a long time.

The disease has undoubtedly existed ever since man began to wear clothes and to live in houses. The Greek historian Herodotus, who lived from 484 to 425 B.C., records that he visited a battlefield where the Persians had defeated the Egyptians more than seventy years previously. He observed, and so reported, that the skulls of the slain Persians were very fragile, whereas those of the slain Egyptians were much stronger. The Egyptians went bare-headed from childhood, whereas the Persians wore turbans to protect their heads from the sun. Research done in rickets in the last hundred years tends to confirm these conclusions. Greek physicians knew about crooked spines and bowlegs. They were later described by Galen in 200 A.D.

The word itself is written in two ways, both derivations of older languages. The word "rickets" is probably derived from early English: "wrikken", to twist. The same root has afforded the words "writhe" and "awry". Another source is the Greek word, $\acute{\rho}\alpha\chi\iota s$, meaning spine. When later, the vitamin found responsible was identified, it was called the anti-rachitic vitamin, from the Greek, "rachis".

One of the earliest references to rickets that has been found is that of Francis Glisson, a professor at Cambridge University. He reported that rickets was known in Leyden and other towns in Holland, where it was thought to be due to infants walking too soon. It was also known in England to such an extent that it became known on the continent as "die englische krankheit".

> "...Somersetshire, a beautiful, clear,
> rural pastoral area where milk, butter,
> eggs, and vegetables were ample...yet
> rickets was prevalent and intense..."

Why was this happening? It was stated earlier that the year 1512 saw the beginning of the deterioration of the diet. At that time, early Tudor diets were good, providing as they did, 3,000 calories daily, including 1½ pints of milk. Such a diet, as we now know, was providing those people with nearly two grams of calcium and three grams of phosphorus daily. But by the end of Elizabeth I's reign in 1603, milk was unobtainable by the poorer sort. For the Enclosure Acts and the beginning of the woollen trade had deprived the people of their lands and their forage; so the cow was given up:

> "Alas, sir, my cow is a commonwealth
> to me; she provides me withal with
> food and drink and medicine..."

As a result, their calcium intake was lowered to one sixth of what it was previously; the ratio of calcium to phosphorus was upset, and rickets could supervene.

It became more prevalent than before. A visitor to Ireland in 1652 mentioned it among the reigning diseases there, and continues:

> "the Rickets, a disease peculiar to
> young children, is so well known to
> everybody in England that it is needless
> to give any description of it".

Various paintings exist, many of them Flemish ones, which show children, particularly babies, with the bowed legs characteristic of rickets. A famous one, Hans Bergmaier's "Virgin and Child" showing the baby Jesus with a clear case of rickets. Artists then, as now, painted from life.

Glisson now began to report that the disease was beginning to appear among the wealthy rather than only among the poor. The wet nurses of the rich were usually poorer country folk who were ignorant; even the peasant's child might occasionally get cows' milk in one form or another. The educated class, on the other hand, were influenced by the mediaeval view that milk was appropriate only for infants and old peole, and the mediaeval view at that time followed this trend. Thus, milk should be discarded after weaning. Consequently, very young children were often put on to bread, soups, and thin gruels.

A letter to John Verney from his wife as early as 1647 probably described rickets:

> "I must give thee some account of our
> own babyes heare. For Jack his leggs
> are most miserable, crooked as ever
> I saw any child's. He is a very fine
> child all but his legges...for they
> let him eat anythinge he hath a mind
> toe, and he keepes a very ill diett..."

It is noteworthy that they in this case are the boy's servants and nurses within that same household, and yet the mother is not in charge. Sir John Verney's reply is just as illuminating:

> "truly the Crookedness of his Leggs
> grieves my very Hart; aske some ad-
> vise about it in London, but doe
> not Tamper with him."

In those days, they would sometimes resort to severe measures such as strait-jacketing. This is what Sir John is warning against.

But the ill diet was perhaps not corrected. It took some time to associate this condition with food. Even Glisson concluded that bad hygiene and a poor home environment were responsible. However, there are certain indications that lead falteringly toward the truth. For example, a year later, Dr. Denton said of the boy Verney:

> "His swelled leggs and great belly looks
> so like a dropsy...it argues a very weak
> liver."

In 1672, a further statement is very much to the point. A letter by Sir Thomas Browne suggests that the country people near Norwich had used the remedy of ravens' liver:

> "Many are killed for their livers, in
> order to the cure of the Rickets."

In the seventeenth century, rickets was quite prevalent, but it declined somewhat in the first half of the eighteenth century, probably because as we have noted, butter was cheap enough and wages were good, jobs plentiful. Later on in the eighteenth century, whole milk, skimmed milk, or even whey disappeared as articles of daily diet. And rickets again began to attract some attention. In 1773, William Farrar wrote "of the unhappy progress that rickets has of late years made among us..."

By that time, the poor could not afford butter at eight pence a pound. A woman living on a diet so poor in calcium is unable to provide her child with milk fully enriched with bone-forming materials. The consequences of this might not become apparent until late in the nursing period, or until the child began to live on the defective diet of its parents. Glisson observantly noted how the disease would so often appear in children from nine to eighteen months old. One must remember that in the seventeenth and eighteenth centuries, the only food that many infants got at weaning was a thin slop made of flour and whey or diluted cow's milk.

In a vague sort of way, improper diet was beginning to be suspected as a cause of rickets. In 1738, William Forster said that the wrong type of food would favor the development of a "Big Belly, the most convenient thing in nature for producing the Rickets, or King's Evil".

However, the general treatment for it remained the use of tonics, remedial exercises, and the wearing of supports for the weakened limbs. The following advertisement appeared in 1748:

> "Mrs. Parsons, Stay-Maker, at the Golden Acorn, James Street, Covent Garden, made for misses that are crooked, or inclined to be so, either by falls, rickets, sickness, etc..."

Only the well-to-do could afford such contraptions.

A beginning of real understanding about rickets came from France in 1793. In the midst of the French Revolution, Citoyen Bonhomme read a paper in which he said that in his opinion phosphate deficiency might be the cause of it. For bones had been analyzed in 1768, and reported to be calcium phosphate. He deduced from this, the importance of both elements. He was far ahead of his time, for he realized the concept of calcium balance, and said that the demands of lactation might cause a drainage of calcium from the bones of the mother.

COD LIVER OIL

Cod liver oil had probably been used as a household remedy, if not an article of diet, from time immemorial, especially in the villages of northern Europe. In Iceland, the people had for centuries eaten a mixture of mutton tallow and fish liver oil, which they called "broedingur". This was highly valued for its health-giving properties. Such oils were also found to be used in Newfoundland. How did the remedy gain such reputation in Europe and elsewhere? Nobody knows for certain, but it is well to remember that one of the oldest remedies for the treatment of a painful

joint or limb was, and is, rubbing with oil.
Could not the oil sometimes have been swallowed?

The primitive method of obtaining the oil was
the frightful process of allowing the livers to
putrify, and skimming off the oil that rose to
the surface. Most people could not stomach this
revolting material. However, it was tried and
used in a first recorded clinical trial at the
Manchester Infirmary in England in 1782. It was
used for "chronic rheumatism", an interesting term.
One of the many prizes offered by the Society of
Arts was one for "the edulcoration of this oil".
Later in the nineteenth century the livers were
steamed to make the product, and the separation
was effected with a more palatable oil.

The idea of eating the liver itself did not
occur to them, even then, because it was to be
used as a food and not as a medicine. And this
was in face of the fact that the country folk in
and around Norwich had used liver as a remedy over
a hundred years earlier.

RICKETS AND THE INDUSTRIAL REVOLUTION

In the early part of the nineteenth century, the
doctors, for some reason, became less and less
interested in rickets. In 1823, the Lancet published a reference to rickets but thirty years
later there was no mention of it. But tuberculosis
was also on the upswing, and many people felt that
this was due to infected milk. But Pasteur was
not yet on the scene, so that if they did not have
the time, or the knowledge, to boil their milk,
they tended to skip it, further aggravating the
situation.

There exists a report from St. Bartholomew's
Hospital, London, stating that in 1868, as many
as one third of all the children who were alive
in cities like Manchester and Glasgow had obvious
rickets, and indeed it was rampant all over the
country by now.

Social writers took it up; for although crooked limbs are often mentioned at this time, these were blamed on the long hours of standing in the factories at looms and other machinery, usually tended by women and children.

One of the results of the Factory Acts of 1832 and 1833 was the creation of the Grainger Children's Employment Commission. It issued reports especially about the use of children in the threading rooms and in the lace-making operations in Nottingham and Leeds. According to the Grainger Commission, the children, in consequence of sitting perpetually bent up, became feeble, narrow-chested, and scrofulous from bad digestion. Disordered functions of the uterus were almost universal amongst girls, so that, as the report said:

"...all the runners can be recognized by their gait."

"In the lace-making factories the children work in small, ill-ventilated, damp rooms, sitting always bent over the lace cushion. To support the body in this wearying position the girls wear stays with a wooden busk, which at the tender age of most of them, when the bones are still very soft, wholly displace the ribs, and make narrow chests universal. They usually die of consumption after suffering the severest forms of digestive disorders, brought on by sedentary work in a bad atmosphere."

In a survey made in 1884 in the Clyde district of Glasgow, almost every single child was affected by rickets. The rickets maps and the industrial map could almost exactly be superimposed. The effects of climate, and of smoke in particular, were not at that time known.

423

THE EFFECTS OF DIET

People cast around for explanations of these dire effects of industrial life. Diets of starch that were lacking in both fat and in milk were suggested as reasons, but they did not mention calcium. And when they did get calcium alone, it did not cure the situation.

The Germans had used cod liver oil in 1822, and the French in 1841; but they did not know why it was effective. One reason was said to be a minute amount of iodine. This theory, although erroneous, was not shown to be so until 1912. X-rays were thirty-five years away, and nobody knew what rickets really was.

ZOOS

In 1860, it was observed that young leopards raised in captivity developed rickets when fed meat without bones. This was the first real evidence that meat was not a complete food. Lions born in captivity were reared, but found to be unfit for display in zoos.

These lions and leopards were an offshoot of the great days of empire. During the nineteenth century, travel to exotic places was undertaken by those with means, and one of the objectives was to "bag" a tiger. The hunter did not spend any time observing his prey, but got in his shot right away. He thereby gained great prestige among his club fellows, and satisfied his wife with a beautiful tiger-skin rug in front of the fireplace in the drawing room.

If they had taken the time to observe the animals while living, they would have noted that when a lion or other animal in the wild kills a gazelle, he drinks the blood as long as it flows, and then rips out the liver and spleen as the tastiest morsels. After he is satisfied, he is to be seen lazily gnawing a bone to get at the

marrow. He does not touch the fleshy muscle meat.
That is left to the carrion crows and other smaller animals. What a wonderful diet! But all this
was before the days of the United States National
Parks and the other wild life refuge areas of the
world since created.

And so it was that when the cubs of the
killed parents were taken home alive, to be reared in the zoos of London, Paris, Berlin, and
Madrid, the zookeepers did not have the slightest
idea of how to feed them. They were expected to
thrive on the wrong diet. Nutritional science
was not yet available to help in this problem.
And so the animals developed not only rickets, but
also various forms of dermatitis and other skin
troubles; for the B vitamins of the liver were also lacking in the diets they gave to the animals.
The cubs so reared looked mangy and hideous.

Other bone conditions such a osteoporosis
and osteomalacia were also noted in these animals,
so that the conditions were all lumped together.
As a result of this confusion, practically all
bone deformities were called rickets.

RESEARCH ON RICKETS

The first attempt to solve these difficulties in
a systematic way was carried out in 1889. Bland-
Sutton fed to zoo animals crushed bone and cod
liver oil. He did not consider the bones important, but regarded the condition as being due
to a fat deficiency. The story was not to be solved until the work of Mellanby in 1917, and of
McCollum two years later.

Mellanby was the first to set up a series of
controlled experiments. He worked with puppies
which were known to suffer from rickets on certain
diets. He arranged four groups of puppies, and
fed them on the following diets:

425

Group I	Group II
whole milk, 200 ml.	whole milk, 175 ml.
rice porridge	white bread
oatmeal porridge	salt, 1-2 gm.
salt, 2 gm.	

Group III	Group IV
separated milk	separated milk, 250 ml.
white bread	white bread
70% extr. linseed oil	70% extr. linseed oil
1 ml.	10 ml.
yeast, 10 gm.	yeast, 5-10 gm.
salt, 1-2 gm.	orange juice, 3 ml.
	salt, 1-2 gm.

The results were as follows:

--all four diets produced rickets in the puppies.

--diets I and II contained the recently-discovered vitamin A; diets III and IV did not.

--diet II produced more severe rickets than did diet I.

--yeast, rich in vitamin B, just at that time discovered, did not prevent rickets.

--orange juice, which prevented scurvy, did not prevent rickets.

These conclusions were very indicative; as a result a second set was developed using especially diet IV. To it were added, systematically, a number of food materials; all diets were assayed on puppies. The following were found to give no relief from rickets; white bread ad lib; oatmeal; up to twenty grams of yeast; babassu oil, hydrogenated fat; tricalcium phosphate; meat protein; milk protein.

The following gave some relief, but it was variable: whole milk up to 500 ml. a day; olive

426

oil; butter; lard; cottonseed oil; meat; suet and
cod liver oil. Of these cod liver oil was superior
to butter, and these two were far superior to all
the rest.

It was plain to Mellanby that rickets was
indeed a dificiency disease. It was distinct from
scurvy, vitamin A deficiency, and all the vitamin
B syndromes. At first the true state of affairs
was not clear, because both cod liver oil and
butter contain vitamin A. It was left to McCollum
and his American group to take the experiments
the necessary step further. They heated cod liver
oil and passed oxygen through it, thus oxidising
all the vitamin A. But the oil so treated still
prevented rickets. They also found that coconut
oil which contains no vitamin A has some affect
in curing rickets (or preventing it). They were
thus able to conclude that there is indeed a
fourth vitamin, separate from the previously designated vitamins A, B, and C, and whose specific
property related to the metabolism of the bones.
This work published in 1922 gave rise to the
naming of the new vitamin as vitamin D.

Various pieces of circumstantial evidence
now begin to fall into place. For example, Mellanby showed that the greater the proportion of
cereal in the diet, the greater the rickets-pro-
ducing tendency. This ties in with the findings
of the poverty-stricken workers of the nineteenth
century, who were reduced to a diet largely of
bread and water. Mellanby designated an unknown
factor as being responsible for this, and said
that it was present in cereals as a harmful ingredient, which he called toxamin. Later on this
turned out to be phytic acid, which insolubilises
calcium as calcium phytate; and this in turn
deprives the bone of needed calcium even when it
is present in the diet.

A second important finding was that cereal
grain diets low in calcium caused xerophthalmia
as well as rickets. Butter fat cured or prevented

this although some rickets occurred unless calcium also was added to the diet. But if cod liver oil replaces butter fat in such diets, both the xerophthalmia and the rickets are cured without added calcium. This proved that whereas both cod liver oil and butter fat were able to prevent the eye symptoms, these same fats were markedly different in their effect on bone development. Biological tests were developed in order to follow the course of bone development. The zone of calcification was identified and measured in what has since become known as the line test.

SUNLIGHT

It is now time to return to the early observation of Herodotus over two thousand years ago. Kessowitz in 1884 noted the rise of rickets during the winter months. Palm in 1880 had concluded that light should be regarded as a therapeutic agent, and ever since that time it had been recommended to send those afflicted with such bone disorders to Switzerland, out of the smoky atmospheres of industrial cities.

In 1906, Hanserman made the observation that children born in the spring and dying the same fall were free from rickets, whereas children born in the fall and dying the following spring showed rickets.

The next step was in 1912, when Rascinski performed experiments with puppies. He kept one group in the dark and the other in the light; after six weeks there was a significant difference in the calcium and phosphorus content of their bones. In 1919, Huldchinsky claimed that it was ultraviolet light which exerted a curative effect. As more understanding about rickets was accumulated, additional tests were developed. X-ray tests were described in 1931, as well as phophatase tests. Already longitudinal sections of the tibiae of experimental animals had been used for study under the microscope, after suitable staining.

Sunlight therapy had been used in 1921 by Shipley, in a series of experiments using the following basal diet: (#3143)

ground whole wheat	33
ground yellow maize	33
gelatin	15
wheat gluten	18
calcium carbonate	3
sodium chloride	1

This diet has a calcium/phosphorus ratio of 4/1. Young rats on such a diet develop rickets in nineteen to twenty-one days. Without the addition of vitamin D, the undersized rats were kept as exposed to the sun as possible. It was discovered that they were free of rickets after sixty-two days. This was indeed a startling discovery. From then on, the search was rapid, and it was soon apparent that this curative action was due to the effect of ultraviolet light on the skin.

It was further shown that the vitamin occurred only in the fat fraction of the liver; that pure fats were not activated by irradiation; and that the fraction responsible for this effect was the sterol fraction of the fat, or oil.

Finally, this exciting story begins to fall into perspective. When Steenbock in his monumental work proved that the ultraviolet irradiation of foods, such as for example whole corn, caused the formation in situ of vitamin D-like materials, the whole story could be substantiated. Nowadays irradiated foods are commonplace, but it can be traced back for a considerable distance in our history.

We now know that those in the sunnier parts of the world, especially in the underdeveloped areas, are not as subject to rickets as those born into an industrial economy. In the northern

429

states, where sunlight is less prevalent anyway,
the beneficial effects of the sun are diluted
or even eliminated by the black smoke of the
chimneys of our modern factories. Smokeless fuels
have done something to alleviate this difficulty
in the modern state, but the re-introduction of
coal in place of petroleum will need to be controlled. Otherwise, we shall see a recurrence of
vitamin D deficiency, much as the shortage of
butter brought it about in the reign of Elizabeth
I. For the majority of the world's people do
not eat the foods which have been fortified with
artificial vitamins, nor do they have access to
irradiated milk.

REFERENCES

417   VISIT TO AN EARLY BATTLEFIELD: Herodotus;
       History; trans Rawlinson, New York 1928
       pp 149-150.

418   SOMERSETSHIRE...Glisson, Francis; The Rick-
       ets Dicitur; tractatus. London, 1650.

418   EARLY RICKETS IN HOLLAND AND IN ENGLAND:
       Glisson, Francis, ibid.

418   "ALAS, SIR, MY COW IS A COMMONWEALTH TO ME.."
       Lodge, Thomas, Gentleman; and Green Robert;
       A looking Glasse for London and England,
       1598.

418   RICKETS IN IRELAND: Boate, Arnold; Ireland's
       Natural History, 1649.

419   MORTALITY RATES: Graunt, John, Citizen of
       London; Natural and Political Observations
       upon the Bills of Mortality; 1662.

419   VERNEY'S LETTERS: Verney, F.P. Memoirs of
       the Verney family II; (1892).

420 ".IT ARGUES A VERY WEAKE LIVER.." Verney,
     Margaret M: Memoirs of the Verney family.
     (1894).

420 USE OF THE RAVENS' LIVER: British Journal of
     Children's Diseases, Vol XXXII. (1935).

420 UNHAPPY PROGRESS OF RICKETS: Farrer, William
     A particular account of the Rickets in
     Children; (1773).

421 BIG BELLY, OR THE KING'S EVIL: Forster, Wil-
     liam; A compendious discourse on the dis-
     eases of children; (1738).

421 STAY-MAKER: The General Advertiser; February
     11, (1748).

421 PHOSPHATE DEFICIENCY: Citoyen Bonhomme;
     Annales de Chimie, August 1793.

421 COD LIVER OIL IN ICELAND: Purchas, S. Life
     and Manners of the Icelanders; Purchas
     his Pilgrimmes. (1625-1626).

421 USE IN NEWFOUNDLAND: Percival, T; Encyclo-
     pedia Brittanica; Rickets. 3, (1797).

422 USE IN MANCHESTER: Percival T, Essays
     Medical, Philosophical and experimental
     (1789).

422 EDULCORATION OF THIS OIL: Wood, Sir Truman;
     History of the Royal Society of the Arts,
     (1913).

422 EATING LIVER NOT A NEW IDEA: Drummond and
     Wilbraham ibid p 159.

422 ST. BARTHOLOMEW'S HOSPITAL: Reports, IV
     (1868).

423 GRAINGER COMMISSION: Engels, Friedrich;
     Condition of the Working Class in England.
     pp 192-3 (1844).

424   "PEOPLE CAST AROUND FOR EXPLANATIONS.."
Garrod, A.B. Lectures on Chemistry, Pathology and Therapeutics. 1848.

424   YOUNG LEOPARDS IN CAPTIVITY: Roll, M.F., Lehrbuch der Pathologie; Die Knockenweiche. (1860).

425   USE OF CRUSHED BONES AND COD LIVER OIL: Bland-Sutton, J. Journ. Comparative Medicine and Surgery, X, 1, (1889).

425   CONTROLLED EXPERIMENTS ON RICKETS: Mellanby, E. Journal of Physiology, 52, xi, (1918).

425   RICKETS INDEED A DEFICIENCY DISEASE..Mellanby, E. Lancet, (London) i, 407 (1919).

427   NEW VITAMIN NAMED VITAMIN D: McCollum, E.V. Journ. Biological Chemistry; 51, 41 (1922); 54, 248 (1922).

428   USE OF X-RAY TECHNIQUES: Biourdillon, et al; Medical Research Council, London, Reports. 158. (1931).

428   LIGHT A THERAPEUTIC AGENT: Palm, T. A. The Geographical Distribution of Rickets; Practitioner, 65, 270 (1890).

428   EXPERIMENTS WITH PUPPIES: Raczynski, J. Comptes Rendus de l'Association Internationale de Pediatrique;. 308 (1913).

428   ULTRA-VIOLET LIGHT THERAPEUTIC: Huldschinsky, K. Deutsch. Med. Wochenscrift; 45, 712, (1919).

429   SUNLIGHT THERAPY: Shipley, P.G. Journ. American. Med. Association 79, 1563, (1921).

429   FACTOR IN THE STEROL FRACTION: Goldblatt, H. and Soames, K.M. Biochemical Journal 17, 446, (1923); Steenbock, Harry and Black A. Journal of Biological Chemistry 61, 405, (1924).

429   PHOSPHATASE TESTS: Kay, H.D. Physiological
        Reviews; 12, 384, (1932).

429   ETIOLOGY OF RICKETS: Harrow, Benjamin:
        Prnciples of Biochemistry 5th edition
        pp 176-186 (1955).

WHEAT VERSUS RYE

What was happening in America during these eventful times? Europe for all its tragic nutritional decline was nevertheless becoming addicted to wheat. Why should America care about this? There was enough to eat, and to spare, on the extensive farms of the new continent. Those farms were occupied by those self-same Europeans, bringing with them their own eating habits. These included the eating of rye as well as wheat.

But why should there be an empire of wheat? Why did America not devote its attention to maize? But Europe needed wheat, or so they thought. The victorious French, at the beginning of the century had convinced all nations that a "master race" ate only wheat. This was not a new concept. The Aryan conquerors, as noted earlier,* brought with them into India from the northwest the barley that they cherished, disdaining the rice of the Dravidian inhabitants. This was about 4,000 years earlier than the time we are talking about. And Charles V of Spain had enjoined his conquistadores not to eat corn, the food of the subject race, but wheat, the food of the conquerors.#

So too with the French. Paris became the ruler of taste in food, just as Rome had been 2,000 years earlier. Even after Napoleon's defeat the French were quickly restored to their place as arbiters in food tastes. There was hardly a restaurant anywhere in the world that did not use French names in its recipes and menus.

Opprobrium was heaped upon every grain but wheat. "Rye is evil-smelling", Galen had said in 200 A.D. Now rye was to come under attack again.

In the middle ages Europeans were very fond of the taste of rye. Some of the Germans called

* Chapter 14

Chapter 16

themselves Rugii, rye-eaters, undoubtedly to dis-
tinguish themselves from the ignoble eaters of oats.
In Anglo-Saxon England August was called Rugern,
the month of the rye harvest. As late as 1700, as
we have seen, rye formed 40% of all English breads.
By 1800 the percentage had dropped far below this.
In 1830 Jasny wrote that there were people in England who had never heard the word rye.

Where rye bread was very firmly established,
in Germany, in Poland and in Russia, it remained
so. Both physicians and farmers insisted that
people who for centuries had eaten the dark bread
of their fathers, bread which gave forth a spicy
fragrance like the soil itself, could not find
the soft white wheat bread filling. And they
pointed to the fine physique of the rye-eating
Germans, Poles and Russians.

The wheat eaters countered with the rejoinder
that rye made those who ate it stupid and dull.
There was invective on both sides. They were accused of being wine drinkers if they ate wheat,
and beer drinkers if they ate rye. The rye-eaters
said that the wheaten bread had no more nutritive
value than air. But the nations who had become
wheat-eaters after 1800 did not agree that wheat
was air. Traditional rye countries like Sweden
and Denmark were converted. In Scotland wheat
bread had long been so rare that only the well-to-
do had it once a week for Sunday dinner. But by
1850 not only the middle classes but the workers
as well ate it habitually. In 1700 Poland exported
three times as much rye as wheat; a hundred years
later this proportion had been reversed.

This metamorphosis in Europe's tastes acted
as a signal to America. In the eighteenth century,
wheat had been of little importance to the young
nation. In 1775 it was harvested for the first
time in Kentucky and Tennessee. George Washington
raised wheat on his farms but it was little more
than a hobby. In 1780 John Adams' wife, when writing of the high prices caused by the war scarcities,
did not even mention wheat because it was not a

food eaten by the people.

EUROPE'S NEED FOR GRAIN

The Europeans who came here to the new world
were interested in raising crops for themselves
and their families; what was left over would be
sold in the nearest town. These new Americans did
not think that they were going to do much in the
way of exporting, and certainly not of food. You
ate the food that was produced here in this country. And you ate it before it spoiled; for there
was as yet no food processing; there were no railroads.

The increasing populations of European cities
as a result of the industrial revolution meant that
food had to be provided. And Europe decided to
feed its increasing city population on American
grain. There was old land in Europe, and a dwin-
dling amount of it; but there was no new land.
New land was in America.

Europe did achieve better yields from its
old land, thanks to the work of Liebig and others,
who pointed out the possibilities of fertilisation
and better crop management. This was a needed
step in the right direction; it was perforce the
European solution to more food. But they did not
yet have the powerful plows that were necessary.
Thus it seemed simpler, as well as cheaper, to
buy bread from abroad. It could be paid for by
exporting European industrial goods. This made
economic sense.

There were other factors also. After the
Peace of Paris, as mentioned before, both sides
were exhausted. It seemed as though there must be
a period of peace, which might last, who knew, for
hundreds of years. A feeling arose among nations
which superseded raw nationalism. The idea was:

"let there be world trade; obviously
the gifts of the soil are not equal

437

everywhere; but the earth is a unit.
One part of this globe, which belongs
to all of us, bears grain; another
factories; let us exchange our products."

Perhaps at last they would beat their swords
into machinery, including the new ploughs that were
needed to till vast areas of the new world.

This was the basis of the big free trade
movement of the nineteenth century, especially popular in England. For she had a start in machine
goods, as well as limitless raw materials from
her empire. But those who wanted protectionism
were still a powerful group in America. They were
protecting grain. The idea was that they wished
to prevent American grain from leaving the country,
and so they clamped duties and tariffs on it.

But the repeal of the tariffs on grain was
finally achieved; and after the potato famine of
1847, the outcry in Europe for cheap bread was
overpowering. And so a torrent of wheat poured
into Europe from America.

But it was hard to understand at first why
England should need it. How could one believe that
an empire spread all over the globe was so poor
that it could not feed its people, and had to buy
American grain? This island seat of empire, which
had until so recently ruled America itself, was it
now at the mercy of the productivity and munificence of the United States? It was hard to grasp
this.

And the Americans could not at first see how
they could possibly have the tools to satiate the
hunger of a country like England; and France too,
by 1860, decided to live by American crops. But
in 1846 America did not have the machines to plough
up the west, as they were to have later.

But what about Germany? Germany was rye land,
and they did not particularly want to buy wheat
from America. Russia was close by; whenever more

food was needed for her new industrial cities
it could be bought there. But America was planting
only wheat.

And soon Germany too was caught up with the
new taste. The self-consciousness of the new cities
brought this about. Great chemical industries were
developing in Germany such as I.G. Farbenendustrie
especially after Perkins' discoveries of the new
coal-tar dyes. These city folk, and the large
new middle classes that developed in Hamburg,
Berlin and Essen soon took to the notion that they
were too fine to eat the dark peasants' bread. The
German industrial worker would look across the
border westward, and determined then and there
that he would eat as well as the Belgian or French
worker. Dusseldorf was a burgeoning city on the
Ruhr coalfields, with large numbers of such workers. They now demanded wheat bread, or at least
bread made with equal parts of wheat and rye.

And so in 1865 the German tariff walls were
removed, and this was a signal for America to
channel her vast river of wheat to Europe as a
whole and not just to France and England. The
German states were in the early part of the century
a number of discrete entities, often at loggerheads.
After the Franco-Prussian War of 1871, they were
unified under Bismarck. They became an important
force in the economy of the whole of Europe and
have remained so ever since.

And so the ships went to Europe, loaded down
with grain. Some of them went to the bottom;
sometimes the boats leaked, and the force of im-
bibition of the grain would literally burst the
ships asunder. But most of it arrived. It was
all wheat, of course. For the Europeans would have
nothing else.

WHEAT AND MAIZE

In order to be exported, wheat had to come
to terms with maize, the older national grain.
Maize was to the Americans, not like rye was to

Europeans, something to be despised, the food of peasants. It was not something to be discarded as soon as you had something better. It was the grain of everybody. It was an economic factor of enormous weight.

It was America's stock feed, the basic fodder of all cattle, hens, turkeys, swine, ducks and geese. Out of the maize plant grew the emporia of the meat trade, and its attendant industries: fats, oils, starches, glue, soaps and candles. But wheat? Wheat was for bread alone. It is understandable then, that in 1861, when 24 million bushels of wheat passed through the Chicago grain mart, the figure for maize was even higher. But animals do not eat bread, so that it was possible for the two cultures to coexist.

And a monoculture of wheat in America would have been disastrous. Naturally wheat would try to thrust maize aside, especially at the boundaries of its domain. But as long as maize remained in the country and was not destined for export, wheat had nothing to fear from its competition. And so in 1864 the empires of wheat and maize dwelt peacably side by side. Indeed, the better that maize could feed the mainland of America, the more easily and securely could wheat conquer international trade.

But how could this be done? You could not do it with just carts. You needed an iron tool of some sort. The iron tool that was to achieve it was the web of railroads that was to arise. In 1840 America had no more than 2500 miles of track, almost all of it in New England and the eastern states. But the locomotive had only been in use anywhere for ten years.

Every single device was used to encourage the building of railroads. In 1848 a law was passed permitting 25 persons to establish a railroad company, if each person could subscribe $1,000 for every mile of track to be built; in actual cash only $100 had to be paid in, a total of $2,500.

Inasmuch as track frequently cost as much as $35,000 per mile to construct, this law permitted debts of several hundred times the actual capital. The banks were glad to supply the necessary credit. They could do this because of the large amounts of capital that were flowing from Europe to America. Since the 1848 disturbances in Europe, those who had money would send it first to London, and then to the new world. So Europe had a hand in building those American railroads. And the workers in Dublin, Dusseldorf, Paris and Birmingham got the cheap bread which they wanted.

There was a fly in the ointment. As the price of bread dropped in 1865, so too did the wages of European workers. Their bosses said that since bread was now cheaper, they did not need such high wages. As always the worker came off poorly, having no voice at that time. Discontent seized the workers, and the rising up of labor leaders dates from about this time.

Meanwhile the situation in America was fantastic. The crops which farmers here had cultivated on a small scale for hundreds of years, going right back into their European backgrounds, were transformed overnight into the stuff of international trade. The Government presented the railroads with vast tracts of land, territories as large as European kingdoms. As unlimited lords over this land the railroads could produce crops on a scale with which the small American farmer could not compete. The railroad companies became deaf to the desires of the government which had enriched them. They did not give a fig for the individual or for the commonweal. Greater profits were the sole aim.

Latifundia was thus born in America, similar to those in Roman times and in the south American states; but these were far larger, far richer. Although they kept no slaves, they nevertheless drove out the small farmer, because small farming had become unprofitable.

Every city that was washed by a river became
paved with gold. Chicago, for instance, was one
of these. When Napoleon was defeated at the
Battle of Waterloo in 1815, Chicago had been a
small village that the native Americans had called
"wild onion place." Since 1833 it had called itself a city, with characteristic mid-western opti-
mism. But even in 1840 it did not have more than
5,000 inhabitants, although it did have a large
number of hogs.

Then in 1847, Cyrus McCormick came into town.
He had seen the crops rotting in the fields of the
northwestern territories, because the sickles and
scythes were too slow, and the hands to wield
them too scarce. He and his brothers founded his
reaper factory on the northwest of town, and was
to make his mechanical harvester the symbol of
the city. Five years later, in 1852, the railroads came to Chicago, and wheat and maize ran on
tracks all the way to the foot of the elevators.

The world price depended upon Chicago; London,
Paris, Berlin and St. Petersburg all listened. Chicago's word was law. And by 1870 Chicago had
300,000 inhabitants, a 60-fold increase only match-
ed by Dusseldorf in Germany. And the hogs were
no longer driven off the streets. They were fattened with maize and slaughtered; the meat was
exported. There were millionaires in wheat,
millionaires in meat, and millionaires in railroads.
In the early days grain arrived at the market in
the bags of the small farmer; now it arrived in
millions of bushels in the freight cars of the
rich. The small farmer, who but a few years earlier had had no trouble in earning his living
from his modest harvests, peered with hands over
his eyes at the freight trains roaring past him.
He could not afford the freight rates, and could
not get his crops to market. Where indeed would
he send it? abroad? World trade, the stock market
were so much gibberish to him. He sat down
wearily on a stone and realised that he was lost.
There was nothing else to do but to sell his land

to the men in power. The wheat which fed whole
nations, and that enriched America's millionaires
could no longer sustain the small farmer.

As a result of this surge in the demand for
wheat and meat, large areas of the middle west
and the plains had been turned into one huge granary by 1870. Between 1860 and 1900 more than 400
million acres of virgin soil were put under the
plow. And there was land in plenty. This had
been evident early in the history of the young
country. At the beginning of the century, Thomas
Jefferson had stated it clearly:

> "In Europe the object is to make the
> most of their land, labor being abun-
> dant; here it is to make the most of
> our labor, land being abundant."

Unwittingly but quite naturally, Jefferson
set the stage for a whole new group of attitudes
which persist even to this day. These center around
wasteful land-use patterns which we are still
trying to control by legislation. Otherwise we
would not have walked into the Oklahoma dustbowl
disaster in the 1930s. It is in a sense a cultural
extravagance which pervades much of our life: an
almost prodigal and even lavish use of resources.

And so, as Tannahill says:

> "...the industrialised nations of Europe
> were never again to go short of the
> materials for their daily bread, although
> meat and dairy products were to be
> luxuries as far as the people were
> concerned..."

This statement was rather sanguine, although
it may have been true at the time. The point was
that this would be the case, only if the Navy kept
the seas open. They were not able to foresee
1914 and 1940.

443

RICE

The empire of wheat now stretched from the
Atlantic to the Pacific. It seemed that the ex-
portable wheat of the United States would conquer
the entire world. But when it reached Asia it
ran into difficulties. For throughout the far
east rice had ruled for thousands of years. The
greater part of the world output of rice came from
Asia. It is eaten where the monsoon lands men
live out their lives in marshes and tropical heat.
Rice prospers in climates where no bread grain could
possibly survive. Climate and soil mould men, and
they shape their customs and their foods accordingly.

And the sense of taste in foods is very difficult to change. A middle-class Japanese un-
accustomed to bread might react to the finest
variety of wheat just as a Roman might have reacted
to rye...he might find it unpleasantly sour, if
not worse. The white man finds the sourness of
bread to be its vital aspect. To Orientals on
the other hand, the bland silken taste of rice
has its own beloved and characteristic qualities.

Good rice is as rich in protein as good
wheat. But there is little similarity between
nations who practice rice monoculture, and those
who eat bread. Eaters of bread who are suddenly
shifted to a diet of rice may resist the change.
After the capture of Manila in 1942, a neutral
offical pointed out to the Japanese that they should
feed their prisoners better. The Japanese retorted
that this request was unreasonable, for the prisoners received the same rations as did the Japanese
soldiers. But this did not suffice to solve the
problem. Men whose basic food for hundreds of
years has been bread, meat and coffee find it
difficult to enter the other food triangle of
rice, fish and tea.

An Indian professor, Dr. Rahdakamal Muker-
dshi, has compared wheat and rice. He called the
grain of the west: "the grain of capitalism; its
inhuman and acquisitive tendency favors the creation

of large estates." He pointed out that this had
occurred in Rome, in Latin America, and now in
North America. Rice, on the other hand, he called
the "friend of the small farmer". This is because
its cultivation is limited to gardens, terraces
and swamps. It is not entirely fair, it seems to
me, to blame wheat for its far-reaching social
effects in a detrimental fashion. Rice, too, has
become an important accumulator of capital. This
was the case especially when rice began to be
grown on non-rice lands, by means of subsequent
irrigation.

In addition it is important to consider the
by-products. Wheat straw is not as long-lasting
as rice straw. In a culture where roofs, aprons,
hats, mats, sandals, and every kind of basket are
prepared in the home, the more adaptable material
was naturally preferred; in this case rice straw.
But not all of Asia was rice-producing. In the
northern Chinese cities wheat was grown, and had
been for 4,000 years. They also practised crop
rotation. The same fields were sown to winter
wheat and to summer rice, alternating with melons
and soybeans.

After the exciting overland adventures which
led to the settlement of California, it was not
long before trade began across the Pacific. About
1867 the first ships were sent westwards, with
grain for north China; for there the people were
used to the taste of wheat.

It was said that every grain of wheat in the
United States belonged to the big four: Marc
Hopkins, Charles Crocker, Leland Stanford, and Col-
lis P. Huntingdon. It was also said that of every
three raindrops that fell on California, Huntingdon
owned two. And so he set out to recoup what he
had invested. But when prices rose in response,
the Chinese said that they could go back to eating
rice, which they did; and the price of wheat fell
precipitously.

But many Chinese at the ports of Shanghai
and elsewhere, seeing the grain ships, saw also
the sailors, smokestacks and the free and easy
life on board. They became interested in America,
and the wanderlust siezed them. When the steamers
returned from China many bland smiling men came
too, and settled down to be laundry workers,
longshoremen, and restaurant workers. They were
happy to live in beautiful San Francisco.

But after death, they wanted to repose only
in the soil of China. When they died in America,
undertakers carefully cleansed the body; bones and
skulls were dipped in brandy and packed in boxes
for the journey. These Chinese coffins, carefully
addressed to their native towns, sailed with every
shipment of wheat that crossed the Pacific to feed
the living Chinese. Men and grain sailed together.
Thus arose between the empire of wheat and the
north Chinese provinces a permanent grain trade.
The two nations had become acquainted.

REFERENCES

437   INCREASED ACREAGE FOR FOOD: Derry, T.K. and
       Williamson T.I., A short history of techno-
       logy from the earliest times to A.D. 1900.
       (1960).

440   VALUE OF MACHINERY: Jones P d'A; The Consumer
       Society: History of American Capitalism
       (1963).

442   USE OF HORSES: Hurst. W.M. and Church L.M.
       USDA Misc. Pub 157 (1933).

442   GROWTH OF CHICAGO: Tannahill, R; Food in
       History, p 356 (1973).

443   USE OF SCARCE LABOR: Jefferson, Thomas;
       quoted in Tannahill p 350.

443   "THE INDUSTRIALISED NATIONS OF EUROPE..."
       Tannahill; ibid p 353 chap 17.

446   CHINESE IN CALIFORNIA: Jacob; H.E. "Six
       thousand years of bread. (1944).

The enormous progress in the quantity of food grown, and the machinery for harvesting and transporting it represent real advances. But at the same time the century saw a decline in many features of nutrition.

For the culture of the time was a factory culture; you were forced to obey a new master, the factory whistle. One to go to work by, one for lunch break, one for quitting time. And there were very few safety measures in those early factories, or the whistle would have been sounding at all hours of the day to summon the workers out. But the factory whistle meant jobs. These demands were demeaning to human life, because the factory dominated the whole framework of one's thinking.

One of the important features of nineteenth century life was the decline in home life which the factory demanded; for women and children worked also in the most harsh circumstances. It is not surprising to find that one of the consequences of this kind of life was the increase in the bottle-feeding of children. This occurred not only among the working classes of the towns, but also in the more prosperous classes as well. Wet nurses went out of fashion, and were replaced by the bottle.

Children were not well cared for in any sense at the beginning of the nineteenth century. In 1817 there was practically no attention of a medical nature available for mothers and young children. Many hospitals would not admit a child under the age of two. Dr. Davies carefully recorded the fate of children who had attended his "Universal Dispensary for Children", over a period of fifteen years. 178 out of 413 died before the age of twelve. He regarded improper feeding after weaning as the chief cause. Many were given bad potatoes and half-cooked vegetables by their poverty-stricken, ignorant mothers.

It was customary to use cows' milk and water, or skimmed milk and a little arrowroot, possibly diluted with barley water, according to Dr. Andrew Ure. The feeding bottle was stoutly recommended, and since absolutely nothing was known about sterilisation, it is hard to believe that it was not a death trap. The Lancet of 1838 recorded that one of the French hospitals tried feeding its orphans with bottles. 297 out of 378 died before they were a year old. Other practices, such as giving children opiates to keep them quiet, as well as the custom of chewing food ahead of the baby were to be condemned later, but they were culturally accepted at the time.

Many formulae evolved as a counterpart to mother's milk. Pea flour, cooked wheat flour, sugar, bicarbonate of potash, starch, malted flour and other such ingredients were all used at times. These were responsible for an appalling amount of sickness, deficient as they were not only in the amount of protein and fat, but in vitamins as well.

The children of the more prosperous classes, whose family status enabled them to receive such preparations, suffered greatly also. Although they did sometimes put on weight, they were pale and flabby. They were apt to develop mild rickets, and in later life their teeth were badly affected. They were sometimes afflicted with scurvy. In 1889 all of this was reported by Cheadle and Barlow; they were convinced that the occurrence of scurvy in children who already had rickets was due to an essential factor that was lacking in their food.

About this time condensed milk came onto the market in large quantities; this was made by evaporating skimmed milk to which sugar had been added. It was thus defective in fat, and in vitamins A and D. This was noted by Cheadle and Barlow, and in 1894 a Commission ruled that a label should appear on the cans to indicate that

450

condensed milk was not suitable to feed to infants or young children.

Another advance at this time was based upon the work of Pasteur. His findings were slow to be adopted; but when they were accepted, it was fashionable to see micro-organisms, or microbes as they were called, as being responsible for just about everything in the way of sickness. Sterilisation became the order of the day; water must be boiled, milk scalded and all due precautions taken for baby's bottle. These were important steps forward, especially among children and infants of the well-to-do during the last decade of the century.

It is rare to find scurvy among children fed upon the breast. A woman's milk contains up to three milligrams per ounce of ascorbic acid, of course depending on the diet of the mother. But a cows' milk contains very little, so that a child who is bottle-fed needs additional vitamin C; but this knowledge was as yet incomplete, and so the children suffered. Any small amount of the vitamin present in cows' milk was in any case almost completely lost on boiling the milk. Thus it was that fruit juices were first recommended by Cheadle in 1889.

In a study by Holt in 1900 it was found that 214 out of 379 cases of infantile scurvy which were studied could be traced to the use of proprietary infant foods. And the centuries-old belief that fruit and vegetables were bad for you lingered on from the past. Only after 1900 did the summer diarrhoea and other such complaints get attributed to the correct sources, namely to disseases of bacterial origin. After that the use of fruit could assume its rightful place in the diet of the people.

WHITE BREAD

The other feature of nutrition at this time concerned bread. In 1830 there was another very

significant advance in the technology of milling.
The early ideas of Malisset, mentioned previously
that the stones should be set apart at different
distances was adapted to a new approach. It was
conceived by a Swiss engineer named Mueller, who
thought that if only the grain could be compressed
until it burst, the whole process would be improved and revolutionised. This could be done with
iron rollers running counter to one another.

The idea attracted Swiss bankers who backed
Mueller's concepts, but the first mills failed.
Jacob Sulzberger developed the technique further
and these modifications proved successful. The
mills were five stories high, and the grain started at the top, finishing with the final break at
ground level. At each floor the iron rolls were
set closer to one another. Mueller's first mill
ground too slowly, but Bulzberger's later mills
were arranged so that the rollers were placed,
two pairs in an iron frame, one above the other.
Each set of rollers were driven separately. This
worked, and the Sulzberger mills became famous.

Mountainous Switzerland was too small to exploit such machines. Almost immediately Hungary,
where wheat had long been important, and which was
the granary of the Hapsburg empire, saw its opportunity. Thanks to the Swiss invention the milling industry in Hungary became the most important
on the whole of the continent of Europe, and Hungarian flour became a most desirable article for
export.

The point of the new flour was that it was
white. We have learned that for thousands of
years men have desired white flour. A Greek
writer named Archestratus wrote a book about cooking in the fourth century B.C. He related that
on the island of Lesbos the flour was so white
that the Greek gods sent Hermes to buy some for
them. Very white flour is, as we know today,
flour which has been all too thoroughly ground
and sifted; and we also know today that it does
not provide the best of nourishment. But it

pleases the eye and flatters the sense of aris-
tocracy. And so because of this, Hungary's largest miller, County Stephen Szechenyi (1791-1860)
set out to conquer the world market. And he did,
for a while.

The agrarian part of the Hapsburg empire
ruled Austria, for a change. And Vienna was the
first great customer for Hungarian flour, which
was so much finer ground and sifted than French
or English flour. Thus arose the "imperial roll",
which became as famous as Strauss' music. At
the Vienna World's Fair in 1873 Americans tasted
these products of the Viennese bakers' art for the
first time, and they enquired about the flour.
For Americans also were interested in white bread
for themselves, although they exported no flour,
only grain. This was the beginning of the end for
the triumphant leadership of Hungarian flour. For
the plains of Minnesota were far more expansive
than those of Hungary. In 1879 Washburn, then
Governor of Minnesota, sent for Hungarian engineers, and soon roller mills appeared all over
Minnesota. The tenacious Scandanavian-Americans
took the matter in hand, and began writing another
chapter in food history.

THE END OF THE CENTURY

And so when Queen Victoria's reign came to an
end, the progress was measured in terms of empire
and riches, in return for a few casualties in
campaigns. Few troubled to look deeper. The
country was to pay for it. For its remarkable
expansion in the commercial realm was accompanied
by a marked deterioration in health and in physique. It is no exaggeration to say that the year
1900 saw malnutrition more prevalent in Europe
than it had been since the great dearths of the
middle ages. Author after author attests to this.

There were reformers who wished to draw attention to the sorry state of affairs. In 1901 a
report was published by Rowntree about the city of
York. It was mainly concerned with housing and

sanitation. But relatively little was known about
the effects of bad diet on health. Rowntree noted
that practically all families lived on bread, and
by now, of course, it was mainly white bread.
Nine out of ten suffered from sheer poverty.

But there was a good deal of callous indiff-
erence, until war came. The Inspector of Recruit-
ing for the South African Boer War of 1899 reported difficulty in getting the requisite number of
men with satisfactory physique. Rejections were
as high as sixty percent in some areas, and forty
percent for the country as a whole. This really
was news. The chief grounds for rejection were
bad teeth, heart afflictions, poor sight or hearing, and deformities. So serious was this that
the minimum height for recruits, which had already
been lowered in 1883 from 5 feet 6 to 5 feet 3
inches, was now decreased a further 3 inches to
5 feet. What did these miserable specimens look
like when they were set alongside the famous Sikh
regiments of the Indian army?

Of course this was all there to be seen had
they chosen; but nobody went up to Manchester, to
see where the real England was; it was the second
city in the realm, yet the conditions had changed
very little from those described by Engels in 1844.
A joint committee of the College of Physicians
and Surgeons was set up in 1904 to look into the
matter, and reported that nothing that Rowntree
had said in his reports was in the least exaggerated. A report in 1907 by Watt Smyth noted:

> "the public which had rejoiced vicarious-
> ly in the triumphs of the football field
> and cycle track were discouraged to learn
> that of those who wished to serve their
> country in her hour of need and her day
> of trial, a startling number were found
> physically unfit to carry a rifle..."

LIFE IN THE SLUMS

We have already drawn attention to the appalling conditions of factory life. Witness after

witness was to testify to the horrors of "back-to back" housing, unpaved courts filled with filth and excrement, half-starved children in ragged clothing, with pitiable pallid faces and deformed limbs. It was realised that indeed Engels had not exaggerated in 1844, because the reports of such conditions now refer to the year 1904. There were areas at the end of the nineteenth century where infant mortality was 250 out of every 1,000.

Meals were by now bread and tea only. But even when the food shortages were known, the committee report stressed such factors as overcrowding, bad sanitation, alcoholism, factory conditions and ignorance; three of the five of these were said to be the fault of the people themselves. But not nearly enough mention was made of the condition of semi-starvation due to near- or actual poverty. The doctors of that time were completely obsessed with the quantitative approach to dietary problems; this was just calories and grams of protein. Consequently the diet itself was often overlooked as causative of these conditions of ill-health.

One medical witness assured the committee that, "White bread made properly was as rich in nutritive value as any form of brown bread." Nearly twenty-five more years were to elapse before the deficiencies of the modern types of bread were to be recognised. And even then brown bread was to be made from white flour to which bran had been added. This was nothing at all like the old coarse wholemeal flour, a rough but nutritious food. Reference has already been made elsewhere to the fetish surrounding white bread; this was to reach its peak in the twentieth century, when bread reached its lowest nutritional level ever.

But slowly attention began to be paid to the feeding of children. It had reached its lowest possible level due to badly fed mothers who could lactate only poorly. Nothing is worse than to read about the women of the factory towns. They went to work in the morning with a cup of strong,

black tea..no time for anything else perhaps.
Bread and jam and tea at midday. At night, too
tired and/or too poor to cook, they paid a visit
to the fish-and-chip shop on the way home. A
kipper, maybe a few cheap sausages made some semblance of an evening meal. Such working routines
left many with chronic digestive troubles, bad
teeth, anaemia and general debility.

Now it is known that such women may produce
children not much below normal weight, but the
trouble is that they cannot feed them. By the sacrifice of her own flesh and blood, so to speak, a
woman living under such conditions may produce a
near-normal child, who, given an optimum diet
might be little the worse for a poor start. But
in nine cases out of ten her milk dried up; she
bought for her infant the cheapest food possible,
which was sweetened, condensed milk in cans.

A survey in 1900 in the city of Sheffield
showed that over sixty percent of the working
class women of that city were feeding their babies
wholly unsuitable food. Results are not hard
to deduce. Sixty percent of the children of the
city of Leeds had carious teeth in 1902.

Not all of the people abandoned their traditional food habits for the exigences of factory
life. The Jews for example provide an interesting facet of this. The incidence of poor nutrition amongst the Jews was much less than the norm.
For one thing, they were breast-fed; for another
they have a sense of good living, and used fat
in their diets and dishes. And they love fruit
and did then, according to Drummond.

It is a very sad story, to come to the year
1900 with such incredible deterioration in the
people's lives. Factories in developing countries,
based originally on the cottage industry patterns,
were just as bad, if not worse. The advances
which we look for in vain were not to happen for
another fifty years, because World Wars I and II
were to intervene. But real progress in nutrition-

456

al knowledge was to be made in these years, only awaiting the time for application. We are eighty years towards the twenty-first century, and yet we have to achieve food security for the people of the world.

REFERENCES

449 ..INCREASE IN THE BOTTLE FEEDING OF CHILD-
REN..Drummond, J.C. and Wilbraham A.
ibid, xxii p 373.

449 "UNIVERSAL DISPENSARY FOR CHILDREN." Davies,
J.B. A cursory enquiry into some of the
Principal Causes of Mortality among
Children. (1817).

450 ARROWROOT AND BARLEY WATER. Ure, Andrew:
A practical compendium adapted to the
treatment of diseases of Children. (1839).

450 "OPIATES TO KEEP THEM QUIET." Family Oracle
of Health Vol I, (1824).

450 COUNTERPART TO MOTHER'S MILK. Liebig, Justus
von; A food for infants: a complete substitute for that provided by Nature. (1867).

451 SCURVY IN CHILDREN: Cheadle, W.B. and Barlow, Thomas; The artificial Feeding and
Food Disorders of Infants (1889).

451 "CONDENSED MILK NOT SUITABLE TO FEED TO IN-
FANTS OR YOUNG CHILDREN." Lancet, ii (1894).

451 "WATER MUST BE BOILED, MILK SCALDED." according to Pasteur; Drummond and Wilbraham;
ibid p 378.

451 INFANTILE SCURVY IN 1900; Holt, L.E. Diseases of infancy and childhood. (1900).

453   THE CITY OF YORK: Rowntree, B. Seebohm;
        Poverty: a study in town life.   (1901).

454   "..UNFIT TO CARRY A RIFLE.." Smyth, A Watt;
        Physical deterioration; its Causes and
        Cure.   (1907).

454   "BACK-TO-BACK HOUSING..."   Drummond and
        Wilbraham, ibid p 405.

456   SHEFFIELD: "Wholly unsuitable food" J.C.
        Drummond, p. 405.

Food preservation has been practised for centuries. Thousands of years ago the countries around the Mediterranean Sea were used to catching fish, which they would slit open, flaying it in order to dry it in the sun. They also knew enough about putrefaction to cut their meat very thin in order to dry it; otherwise it would get mushy and putrid on the inside. Rubbing salt into the fish was also beneficial.

The practice of salting down meat has been carried out over the centuries, in order to meat for some time after the fall kill. Bacon and ham are the results of this practice.

We now know that the purtrifying bacteria find it osmotically impossible to live on dried foods, from which water has been removed to below a certain level. They did not know this in those far-off days; but by a series of deductions which we can only call primitive logic, they carried out this practice for preserving foods, and observed with pleasure the results.

But now we are to be concerned for the first time with the shipping of food from overseas for long distances, and in slow ships. Grain would travel well, as it had indeed since the Roman fleets brought it from the overseas Roman empire. But what about perishable foods?

CANNING

The first "canning", developed after Nicholas Appert's prize-winning discovery in 1806, was in glass bottles. These were subjected to heat and carefully sealed. The essential leap from breakable bottles to unbreakable "tins" was taken in England by Bryan-Donkin. By 1812 he had already set up a factory which would coat metal cans with tin. This process of tinning led to the tin can which was to play such a vital part in food supplies for over a hundred years. Donkin's factory turned out especially "corned" beef, again a salted product.

By 1818 boiled beef, carrots, soups, vegetable stews and mutton were all available in tinned cans. At first these were expensive, and bought only by explorers and other special people to whom such preserved foods were of vital importance. The early cans were the 2 pound and the 6 pound cans. The producers believed, as did the scientists at the time, that it was the expulsion of air before sealing that contributed the preserving effect. As we now know, the heating, which was designed to drive out the air, had the very much more important effect of killing off the harmful bacteria. This was well before Pasteur's time.

Accordingly, when they decided to use larger cans, namely 16 pound cans, the heating which was effective for the smaller cans was not sufficient

for the larger ones. The result was that most of
the bacteria were left viable in the interior of the
meat, causing the whole thing to putrify. This was
a good case of the fallacy of the doctrine of
bigger is better, which we have still not entirely
learned. In 1850 it is recorded that 111,000
pounds of meat had to be discarded as unfit for
human consumption. And so canned meat got a bad
reputation, at least for a time.

The quality of canned mutton received from
Australia during the next twenty years did not
enhance the same reputation either. The meat was
coarse and stringy; each can contained a lump of
overdone and tasteless flesh, flanked on one side
by a wad of unappetising fat, and surrounded by a
great deal of gravy. The experienced cook learned
to discard the fat, make the gravy into soup and
cut the meat into pieces that somehow could be
made into an appetising dish. The poor urban housewife, however, merely served the meat as it was,
with bread and potatoes on the side. It cost
less than half the price of fresh meat in England,
the price of which soared after outbreaks of rinder-
pest in 1863 and 1865. And so the poor families
had no choice but to eat this unappetising food;
and the imports of such canned meats rose from
16,000 pounds in 1866 to 22 million pounds by 1871.

Canning factories had been established in the
United States as early as 1817, but until the Civil
War had come and gone, Australia led in the matter
of canned meats. Rapid developments brought about
the canning of other foods, notably fish, vegetables
and fruits. Giant canning concerns grew up, each
the result of a chain reaction. For example, peas
could not be canned economically in quantity as
long as they had to be harvested by hand to prepare
them for canning. So by the end of the century,
a mechanical gathering and shelling device had
been put into operation. At the same time as these
advances, the work of Pasteur had shown the part
that microorganisms played not only in disease
but in fermentation and in putrefaction as well.

Thus the canning of meats and other foods was a very important and progressive step. It eliminated some of the spurious practices which had crept into the food industry. For example, burning sulphur in the room where the meat was hanging; soaking the meat in sulphites; adding salt plus nitre; adding iron filings to absorb oxygen; adding calcined charcoal to absorb any offensive smell that might develop. They even began to infuse the animal, just before death, with preserving fluids containing salt, sugar, nitre, phosphoric acid, and even vinegar. Even though some of these were purely experimental, canned meats nevertheless gained a bad reputation, especially after a Government report on the topic in 1852. This report gave rise to the phrase "Sweet Fanny Adams".*

REFRIGERATION

Until refrigeration arrived the true preservation of foods, as we know it, could not really occur. The cost of ice was prhibitive, and it required the development of the science of thermodynamics and kinetic theory to solve the problems. And this too occurred in the nineteenth century.

But we must remember that the use of ice for preserving food was known to the Chinese at least by 800 B.C. It had been collected in late winter from the mountains, and stored under insulation for use in the summer. The blocks of ice hidden under straw in American homes in the nineteenth century were a direct follow-up of this practice. The idea that water cools by evaporation had not escaped observers in other societies. By 1820 in Allahabad, India evaporation pans for water to make ice were in operation, known not to the British but to the Indians.

Early refrigeration was based upon observation. Ether, recently discovered, "froze" tissues as well as anaesthetised them. A patent by Perkins in 1834 used this principle of cooling by evaporation, and furthermore regenerated the ether by compression. Carre, in France, discovered that

462

ammonia was excellent as a refrigerant, and in 1861,
in Sydney, Australia a plant was turning out 8,000
pounds of ice a day using ammonia as a refrigerant.
James Harrison, a Scottish emigrant, developed the
idea further, and exhibited an "ice-house" at the
Melbourne Exhibition in 1872. He kept sides of
beef and carcasses of sheep in the ice house for
several months. They were in good condition, and
a year later some of the meat was eaten at a
public banquet in Melbourne, and found to be in
excellent condition.

By 1873, it was possible to ship frozen meat
to England, but in crossing over the tropics the
ice melted and the meat putrified in three months.
By 1880 however, it could be done successfully,
both for Australia and the Argentine. Whereas
the meat had cost the producers and shippers 1½
to 2 pence a pound, it was sold at Smithfield
Market for 5½ pence a pound. And so there was a
boom in cattle farming and ranching generally,
between 1870 and 1890. In 1881 the Prairie Cattle
Company of Edinburgh was able to declare a divi-
dend of 28%.

OTHER DEVELOPMENTS

There were other advances in the food field
during the nineteenth century, which were to have
far-reaching effects, both cultural and geo-
political:

   --1801 heralded the discovery of sugar beets;
     by 1840 there were 58 factories in France
     alone. This was to affect the course of
     wars later.

   --Hydrogenated oils were applied to the
     making of margarine by hardening plant oils
     such as cottonseed oil and corn oil.

   --Development of entirely new and rather good
     cooking equipment, which was adjustable
     and safe indoors.

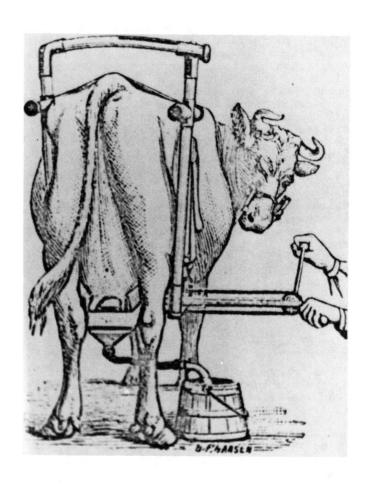

464

--Development by small farmers of truck
farming and dairies, when the large enterprises had pushed them out of grain entirely.

--Development of coal by-products, especially
after Perkin's discovery of the aniline
dyes.

--Use of electricity, although this was not
widespread until 1920.

--The use of coal gas and coke.

--Publication of numerous cookbooks. This
began in 1845 with a book by Eliza Acton
called: "Modern Cookery for Private Families". This was followed by Isabella
Beaton's "Book of Household Management",
which included first attempts to make cost
estimates and preparation times.

--And in America particularly moralists entered the kitchen. Said Mrs. Horace Mann, in
"Christianity in the Kitchen"(1861):

"there is no more prolific cause of bad
morals than abuses of diet..."

THE SCIENCE OF NUTRITION

Even before 1800, and long before vitamins,
there was a beginning in the science of nutrition.
A primitive first attempt was made to draw up a list
of foods in order of their nutritive value, in a
curious tract published in London in 1812. It
was called Nutriology. It listed the following:

butter 4,000; animal fat and cheese 2,000;
beans and pease 900; fruits 250-500; cabbages and greens 100-250.

These figures had no known units and were
empirical guesswork. But they are not greatly at
variance with modern calorific values.

465

The scientific progress which was to come was brought about by the work of Magendie and particularly of Liebig in 1840. Physiologists were working on digestion and its "ferments", later known as enzymes. Liebig was the one who analysed foods. The evaluation of some of his findings was faulty. Liebig equated muscular work with the actual using up of muscular tissue; and this required meat for its regeneration. Such conclusions led to all sorts of excesses. It was not until 1889 that two Swiss scientists, Fisk and Wislicenus climbed the Faulhorn in the Bernese Oberland without consuming any nitrogenous food. This led to the modern view of muscles as machinery that uses up carbohydrates for its daily work. Even athletes until recent times were supposed to do better on excessive meat diets, especially red meat. There is even reference to this in the diets prescribed for the Berlin Olympic Games of 1936.

In spite of these advances the food of the average man was not improved, possible not even maintained, at a level compatible with these advances. Nutritional knowledge was slow in coming, slower in application.

We are still attempting to find a way to feed the world's people, and this can only be treated rather briefly in the concluding chapter.

REFERENCES

460   APPERT'S PRIZE-WINNING DISCOVERY: Appert, Nicholas, Le livre de tous de Menages ou l'art de conserver pendant Plusieurs Annees toutes les substances. (1810).

460   UNBREAKABLE TINS: Donkin, B: Official Reports: Hall & Gamble's Preserved Provisions (1817).

460   .BOUGHT ONLY BY EXPLORERS..Admiralty Purchases in 1818.

460   FROM ONE FACTORY. Goldner's factory in Galatz, Moldavia.

461   ..A WAD OF UNAPPETISING FAT..Drummond and Wilbraham, p 322.

463   COOLING BY EVAPORATION. Perkins, Jacob. British Patent #6662 (1834).

465   FOOD ANALYSIS: Liebig, Justus von; Anneles Chemie, 39, 129, (1841).

As noted in the chapter on rickets, great advances were made in the early twentieth century in the new science of nutrition. New instruments for measurement and new chemical techniques gave the spur to these developments.

At this point it is appropriate to consider an old scourge which was prevalent in the East, but which somehow had so far escaped the west.

ASIATIC BACKGROUND OF BERI-BERI

During the years when scurvy was occupying the thoughts of western explorers, there was a disease in the Orient which the West knew nothing about. In Chinese writings of the third century and later there are references to a disease called Kak-ke'. It was first described by a European in 1642 when a Dutch physician named Jacobus Bontius was sent to Batavia with the Dutch East India Company. He made careful observations of all he saw, and recorded it at the time. It was later translated into English. He wrote the following:

"The inhabitants of the East Indies are much afflicted with a troublesome disorder which they call beri-beri."

He described the disease as producing a loss of sensation in the feet and hands, a peculiar way of walking, and sometimes a trembling of the whole body.

Beri-beri, although well understood now, still recurs in many parts of the world. The cause is unknown; the cure and prevention are known. But this disease provides an interesting example of how food habits and customs have a stronger influence in people's lives than does scientific knowledge.

From 1859 reports appeared about the occurrence of ber-beri in the Dutch navy. It was suggested that food had some effect but nothing was done about this. In Japan, it was a serious problem, especially in the Navy where there were several hundred cases a year. A Japanese medical officer named Kanchino Takaki entered the Navy in 1872, and in three years he saw hundreds of cases of beri-beri. He was determined to learn all he could about it and went to England for medical study. On his return home he was made Director of the Tokyo Naval Hospital.

Takaki systematically studied the disease; he found out, for example, that it was more common in large towns than in small; it occurred most severely amongst soldiers, sailors, policemen, students and shop boys. However it occurred without any relation to clothing or the kind of living quarters. He calculated the food that they ate; it appeared that carbohydrate food, notably of course rice, was very high in the diets of those afflicted. He noted that there was not enough protein food to make up for the body's loss of nitrogen. He also noted that the higher the ratio of carbohydrate to protein in their diets, the higher the incidence of beri-beri, and the greater the severity.

He proposed some changes in the diets but these were not accepted. Thereupon he undertook some experiments, and these show his careful and able thinking. Two naval ships were to be sent on the same long voyage across the Equator and into the South Pacific, so that differences in climate could be observed. The only difference between the two ships was in the ration that was issued to the sailors.

The Riujo with 276 aboard was sent to Wellington, New Zealand, and then on to ports in Chile and Peru. It returned home via Honolulu. With the customary naval ration there were 160 cases of beri-beri and 25 deaths. The second ship, the Tsukuba followed the same course; however the ration was

improved by increasing the amount of meat, fish
and vegetables, as well as the inclusion of some
condensed milk. The amount of rice was decreased.
Out of a crew of 287 there were no deaths, and only
10 cases of beri-beri. These ten had not, it was
reported, eaten all of the parts of the new ration.
As a result of this clear-cut test the Japanese
Navy substituted a little barley for part of the
rice. By 1882 beri-beri had been completely eliminated from the Japanese navy. These results were
published in Japanese at the time (1385), but
escaped the notice of European workers. At this
time everybody was so preoccupied with diseases of
bacterial origin that beri-beri also was thought to
be due to an infection.

At about the same time that the Japanese navy
were being cleared of beri-beri due to Takaki's
work, the Dutch were having trouble with the disease
in their East Indian colonies. Soldiers in barracks
and inmates of prisons were dying of the disease
after a few months' residence. In 1886 the Dutch
government sent a Commission to investigate the
health situation in the East. Attached to this
commission was a young army surgeon who was destined
to become famous, with his name in every subsequent
book of Biochemistry. His name was Dr Christian
Eijkmann.

The bacteriologist on the commission thought
that a microbe caused the disease, and so reported,
recommending disinfection of the barracks. But
Eijkmann was not so sure, and the Government at his
suggestion gave the go-ahead for an experimental
program to be carried out by him in the military
hospital in Batavia.

Eijkmann's first experiments were to inoculate
chickens with fluids from the bodies of beri-beri
patients, but these experiments were inconclusive.
He then initiated some experimental research on
fowl. In order to economise on their diets,
because they have such voracious appetites, he
used scraps of food from the wards of the hospital.

On these diets the fowls developed a form of
paralysis, and a neck-withdrawal syndrome called
opisthotonus. The new director of the hospital
was not impressed with these findings. Eijkmann
then used raw rice in the rations, and on this the
birds recovered. And on changing the diet to white
rice, the birds became affected with this paralysis.
It was a severe form of polyneuritis. This condition, similar in many ways to beri-beri in man,
was reported in Dutch medical journals in 1890; but
other western investigators were no more able to
read Dutch than they had been to read Takaki's
work in Japanese. So it was not read by others.

Eijkmann still thought that there was a nerve
poison in white rice, and that the outer coatings
of rice contained an antidote to that poison.
He returned home to Holland with the problem still
unsolved, and his health failing. It was left to
another Dutchman, Grijns, to interpret Eijkmann's
results correctly, namely that there is an essential
ingredient in the outer layer of rice, which is
removed by polishing. Such substances he called
"protective substances." All of this was checked
out with human beri-beri in institutions; in every
case where raw or unpolished rice was used, beri-
beri did not occur. As a result by 1898 Vorderman
had eradicated beri-beri from the prisons of Batavia by the use of whole rice.

Further experiments showed that the "protective"
substances could be extracted from the outer layers
of the rice with water or with alcohol. In addition
it was soon found out that if polished rice from
other countries was used, the results were the same.
The birds all died. The addition of olive oil, salt
mixtures or minerals to the diets did not help.
Meat extracted with water, and dried, gave no
protection; neither did potato starch or lactose.
This follow-up work by Grijns was published in 1901.

It had been noted that Indians on the whole did
not suffer from beri-beri. The reason becomes apparent; Indians are accustomed to parboiling their
rice. In this process the rice is soaked, steamed

and then dried. The protective substances are thereby drawn into the grain, rather than being extracted from it. This has protected Indians from beri-beri. Observations made elsewhere have tended to confirm these findings. For example, in Malaya, a British physician named Braddon had been astute enough to notice the difference in the incidence of beri-beri between the Malays, the Tamils and the Chinese, all of whom lived in the Federated Malay States of that time. The Malays used home-pounded and unpolished rice; the Tamils parboiled theirs; the Chinese used imported white rice. The Chinese groups were very prone to get beri-beri, whereas the other two groups avoided it. Europeans, who hardly ever ate rice at all (being conquerors) likewise did not get beri-beri.

Various field experiments were carried out to substantiate these findings and were reported by Stanton and Fraser in 1910. They found once and for all that no toxic substances are present in rice, whether parboiled or not. It was found that parboiled rice on long extraction with hot alcohol no longer protected fowls from beri-ber; but if the alcoholic extract were added back again to a diet of white rice, the birds were protected from it.

Another significant fact can be gained by considering the situation in the Phillipines. These islands came under American protection in 1898, after the Spanish-American War. There the American habit of refining grains, especially wheat, and later rice, became fashionable. It was adopted enthusiastically as a part of the gifts of the conquerors. We need to learn a lesson from this to help us in 1980. For a great deal of beri-beri took hold in the Phillipines, where it had rarely been seen before 1850. The Americans there did not get it. Even then they were used to a wide variety of foods, which would provide coverage for a large number of nutrients. Food was plentiful in the new country. to Americans of that time the idea of a monotonous diet was not envisaged. But the Filopinos would never be able to afford such a diet, and so beri-beri became common there; and the answer was simply to eat raw rice.

VITAMIN(E)S*

In 1912 Funk propounded the theory that beri-beri, scurvy, pellagra and possibly rickets were caused by a lack in the diet of "special substances which are of the nature of organic amines, which we will call "vitamins". In the same year Suzuki and coworkers isolated from rice bran the anti-neuritic principle in the form of a crystalline dervative. It was extracted from rice polishings, and from yeast as well. By 1926 a preparation had been made that was 100 times more potent than the yeast itself. Jansen and Donath finally obrained from yeast a small amount of crystalline material which they analysed. This was purified further in 1934 by Windaus and Williams, and its synthesis was achieved in 1937. It was the first vitamin to be used in flour enrichment, and was introduced into the flour sent to Britain from Canada by 1942. For by this time Britain wanted flour for the first time, rather than wheat. For the flour mills located at Plymouth, Liverpool and other ports had been damaged by bombing.

THIAMIN(E)

Thiamin, or Vitamin B1, has been found to relate to the proper functioning of carbohydrate metabolism. The lack of it has severe consequences, as we have seen. Kinnersley and Peters found an accumulation of pyruvic acid and of lactic acid in the brain of a thiamin-deficient pigeon; the uptake of oxygen was impeded, but restored to normal by addition of thiamin. Therefore the thigher the intake of foods high in carbohydrate, the greater the need for thiamin. It follows then that those doing active work will get beri-beri on a diet that might conceivably be sufficient for a sedentary student. Stress, pregnancy and lactation all incrase the need for thiamin. When lactating mothers are deficient in thiamin, beri-beri can occur in their infants.

* subsequently, the "e" in vitamine and in thiamine was dropped.

Thiamin is not stored in the body and must be consumed daily, being very different from vitamins A and D in this respect. It is unstable at high temperatures, such as baking temperatures; How much of a threat is beri-beri? it is not still present to any extent in our country, although there can be insufficiency. Beri-beri is a very acute condition; what about a chronic, long-term insufficiency?

It is not so long ago that there was a very real shortage of thiamin in Europe. An experiment was started in 1931 in an attempt to throw some light on this. The results were most illuminating. Over 1,000 young rats were divided into two groups; one group was fed what was thought to be a complete diet; while the other group was fed a food mixture resembling the poverty diet of the thirties. In effect this turned out to be a study of the nutritive value of wholemeal and unfortified white breads. The rats were observed throughout their whole lives, and a very thorough post-mortem examination was made on each animal at death.

It was found that those fed a deficient diet were stunted. They failed to propagate in a normal manner, tended to contract illnesses and die at an early age. This was not unexpected. But what was striking in these findings was that a very large proportion of their ill-health was traceable to disorders of the stomach and digestive tract. But on the other hand, infections of the lungs, disorders of the blood system, kidney affections, skin complaints and even cancer were the same in the two groups. The incidence of dilated stomachs, ulcers, and inflamed conditions of the caecum were found to be much more prevalent in the badly nourished colony than in the other group.

We cannot extrapolate these results to those earlier nineteenth century diets which were mentioned, because we do not know how prevalent these complaints were at the time. But we do know that they are common complaints now, as they were forty years ago. It was these results which led directly to the decision in 1940 to fortify white flour with thiamin; as soon as the synthetic vitamin was available it was added to flour.

In 1958 the World Health Organisation reported a spread in the use of small rice mills in Burma, Thailand and Vietnam; beri-beri also remained serious in those countries. Just after World War II, a young biochemist from Chicago named Williams undertook a study of people in the Bataan peninsula in the Phillipines. A survey had shown that over 12% of the people had clearly identifiable beri-beri. He set up a large field experiment wich enriched and plain white bread; within a year of this had positive results.

So we see that beri-beri is in fact an example of a disease of civilisation. The use of synthetic vitamins added to refined foods has done much to alleviate these shortages. But such additions are expensive, and out of the reach of the world's poor. We must see to it that the diets can be adequate without costly supplements. They have to be indigenous, and not imported.

REFERENCES

470   OBSERVATIONS ON THE JAPANESE NAVY: Takaki, Kanchino; Lancet, ii 86, (1887).

471   PROTECTIVE SUBSTANCES IN RICE POLISHINGS: Eijkmann, Christian and Grijns, G; Arch; Hygiene, 58, 150 (1896).

472   ERADICATION OF BERI-BERI FROM PRISONS IN BATAVIA: Vorderman, A.G. Geneeks. Tjidschr, v Ned. Ind (1898).

472   PROTECTIVE SUBSTANCES IN RICE ISOLATED: Grijns, G; Geneesk, Tjidschr, v Ned Ind. (1901).

472   PARBOILED RICE: Fraser, H. and Stanton A.T. Collected Papers on beri-beri, No 17.   Federated Malay States (1924).

474   VITAMINES: Funk, C. Jounr. State Medicine, 20, 341-368 (1912).

474   ISOLATION OF ANTI-NEURITIC SUBSTANCE: Suzuki, U, Shinamura, T and Chdaka, S.Biochem, Zeitschrift, 43, 89-153 (1912).

474   ACCUMULATION OF PYRUVIC ACID: Kinnersley, H.W. and Peters, R, Biochem. Journal. 23, 1126 (1919).

474   CRYSTALLINE MATERIAL FROM YEAST: Jansen, B.C.P. and Donath, W.P. Proc. Konikl Akad. Amsterdam, 29, 1390-1400.

475   STUDY OF THE BATAAN PENINSULA: Williams. R.R.: (1926). Journ. Amer. Chem. Soc. 56, 1187-91 (1934).

475   SYNTHESIS OF VITAMIN B1: Cline, J.K. Williams, R.R. and Finkelstein, J.J. Journ. Amer. Chem. Soc. 59, 1052-95 (1937).

476   DECISION TO FORTIFY WHITE FLOUR: Drummond, J.C. et al; Journ. of Hygiene. XXXVIII, 356 (1938).

WORLD WAR I

There was an attempt, albeit a very slight one, to use the findings of science in the feeding of the people. But it took the advances of the twenties, the Great Depression, and the second World War to apply the accumulated knowledge of the previous forty years. In 1914 nobody really suspected that it was possible that an island, least of all Britain, could be starved into capitulation.

Germany was the first to suffer. After one year of war signs of malnourishment began to appear in the towns. Even the middle-class Germans began to lose weight, and became more susceptible to colds and influenza. By the autumn of 1916 the German position was desperate, and they were on the verge of capitulation. When their lightning conquest of Rumania brought relief from the grain shortages, the war was to last two more long years. By the same fall of 1916 2 million tons of shipping had been sent to the bottom, and the plight of Britain herself was extemely grave. A Ministry of Food was set up in Britain, but not until February 1918 was food rationing introduced.

After World War I meat rationing ended in December 1919; butter rationing in May 1920 and sugar rationing by November 1920. The control of flour milling was lifted in March 1921. Following these years the lessons that had been learned ushered in a great era of nutritional research, as well as a spate of surveys.

VITAMINS

Scurvy, rickets, and beri-beri have been discussed already. The new concepts of vitamins had a hard time being accepted, even by some scientists. A Committee on Accessory Food Factors was held in Vienna in 1919, and brought to light a number of important findings concerning edema, scurvy, rickets and other conditions. But the Austrian doctors knew nothing of the discoveries in these areas. Professor von Pirquet, a leading authority on the feeding of children, said of that conference:

> "..at that time I was of the opinion
> that a vitamin deficiency in an or-
> dinary diet was a very exceptional
> occurrence....with regard to the
> etiology of rickets, I held the view
> that it was an infectious disease,
> widely prevalent in this part of
> Europe."

Active research in vitamins was pursued in universities all over the world, so that by 1939 at least nine were well identified, if not isolated: vitamin A and carotene; thiamin, riboflavin, niacin, pantothenic acid and pyridoxin; ascorbic acid, the vitamins D and vitamin E.

But there were difficulties with this new-found knowledge. Foods high in the new food factors, the so-called "protective foods," were too expensive for the poor workers to afford. And they were completely out of reach for the unemployed every-where. And by the 1930s the unemployed numbered in the tens of millions in the industrial nations. As a result the diets of ordinary people reverted back to the worst days of Queen Victoria's reign: white bread, jam, margarine and tea; fresh milk was hardly ever seen.

THE NEEDS OF THE PEOPLE

In 1931 the Minister of Health in Britain received from an Advistory Committee on Nutrition a statement as to how a satisfactory diet might be achieved. It would have to comprise milk, cheese and fruit, as well as the usual fuel principles of bread and potatoes. By the most conservative estimates of the day this worked out to cost between tenpence and a shilling per head per day.

This was equated in 1933 to about 6 shillings per
week per man. When it was realised that as little
as one shilling and sevenpence was spent by an unemployed man for a week's food; and furthermore
that those that did work had no more than 4 shillings a week to spend for food, then it was realised
in official Britain, for the first time, that the
English people could not in any way feed themselves.
Other countries had already found out the same thing.

By this time the League of Nations was
becoming concerned about the problems of nations.
The French government suggested to the League
a minimal diet as follows:

per week per person: 2 pounds of cabbage,
1 pound of carrots, 8 ounces of apples,
8 ounces of herring; 6 ounces of cheese,
5 pints of milk, plus enough bread, and
some meat to make 2,500 calories a day.

This was one of the very earliest such recommendations. This diet worked out to cost the
equivalent of 9½ pence per day, again out of the
reach of the poor people.

A study of English diets in 1935 produced
the alarming information that the poorest, and by
far the largest group in the country consumed
milk only in the amount of 1.1 pint per week.
This was less than a quarter of the amount recommended by the League of Nations.

This milk was almost entirely taken with the
tea, and milk as a beverage was unknown. Even
the smallest and richest group in England consumed
only 5.4 pints per week. Half of the population
was getting insufficient fruit and vegetables.
And yet at this time only the milk was entirely
home-produced. Tea, sugar, bacon, flour, cheese,
meat, and fats were largely imported. It is
important to realise how vulnerable a nation is
that relies too heavily on imports.

An analysis was presented to the Government in 1936 by Sir John Boyd-Orr, describing the national food picture. Of those whose income was 45 shillings a week or over, there was a surplus of all dietary constituents considered: namely, calories, protein, calcium iron and vitamins A and C. All the others, that is to say, 40 million in Britain alone, were deficient in calcium; 22 million were low in vitamin A. The poorest, 4½ million in Britain were deficient in all categories. The shortage of milk, (the white meats referred to in the middle ages) was most pronounced, and gave rise to the calcium deficiency noted.

As for thiamin, discussed in the previous chapter, the average poor diet in Britain in 1938 contained only .3 milligrams out of the needed one milligram. This was provided only if the subject ate 18 ounces of bread a day. Such was the condition of the diet on the eve of World War II. The findings of Drummond in regard to the needs of the people were to lead to notable advances for the country when he was named Minister of Food in 1939. Largely as a result of his efforts and influence, the Second World War found some awareness of the situation. The newer nutrition led him to recommend and to put into operation some enlightened practices:

> vitamins A and D were added to margarine
> steps were taken to increase milk consumption
> imports of cheese and dried skim milk were increased
> milk drinking schemes were introduced for schools, adolescents and adults
> 85% extraction flour for all
> Calcium carbonate added to flour
> consumption of green vegetables and carrots enhanced
> communal meals advocated and used
> workers fed on the job
> school meals service expanded
> importation of sugar halved
> dehydrated eggs introduced

482

removal of "patriotic duty" to eat as
little as possible, a stigma left
over from World War I.

TODAY'S PROBLEMS

Now that we are approaching the twenty-first
century, it is essential to take a long, hard look
at the food practices that have grown up in the last
forty years.

Perhaps the most significant changes which
affect all of us are in the realm of food packaging.
The achievements in this area are very real ones;
for now it is possible to send food all over the
world in a condition fit for eating, clean and
free from the contaminating diseases which were
so prevalent in the nineteenth century and before.

But as is so common in the history of food,
there are accompanying disadvantages. A barrier
has now been set up between the consumer/buyer
and the food which is bought. There is a definite
advantage in picking out one's own fruit and
vegetables before they are packaged. This is rapidly
being lost, with unfortunate results. What happens
is that a problem of the 17th and 18th centuries,
which we have already mentioned, now rears its
ugly head again. There was then a definite temptation to mask taint; today this is no less
real, although the word taint may be too strong;
perhaps inferior is a better word to use.

A second temptation arises in the need for
storage of food for long periods of time. In the
case of fresh produce, such as meat, fish and dairy
products, there is often a date placed on the
package, which denotes the time and by which the
food has theoretically to be sold. When this
date has passed, with the goods not sold, a new and
later date is put on the label, and the food reduced
in price. This is plain deception, for it is
not clear whether the food is spoiled by the date
first specified, or merely questionable. But the
poor, having to buy the cheaper product, must use it.

A third temptation, also very real today, is to package the same, or essentially the same product in a new package, and to sell it as a new product. It is stated with pride by the food industry that there were in 1979 5,000 products on the market which were not there in 1972. This is at best a misleading statement; twenty years ago there were cereals every bit as good as those of today, and made by the same companies. But the craze for newness overrides every other consideration. And so the poor consumer, who may not have the education to combat these spurious statements, is led to believe that we are making progress, when in fact this is not necessarily the case.

In other words, it is not just a question of food for the poor, but of poor food. This affects affluent peoples everywhere. A recent significant article by Julian Armstrong of Montreal points this out very vividly. In a survey carried out by behaviour scientists at the University of Montreal and Ste Justone Hospital, teenagers of the middle class were seen to be endangering their health with poor eating habits. They develop very early an addiction to junk foods, which becomes a life-long affliction, with untold adverse consequences.

This particular set of problems becomes acute at this time in history. For the conscience of the west is beginning to revolt at the exporting to poor countries of poor eating habits, as well as poor types of food. These go to the southern tier of poor countries, often in the name of humanity. In no instance is this more evident than in the ideas about the feeding of infants.

THE FEEDING OF INFANTS

The age-old controversy about breast feeding has arisen again in the present decade. An article on this subject appeared in the Wall Street Journal on March 21, 1980. It speaks about the virtues of breast feeding as though this was a new idea, when in point of fact it has been a normal situation throughout man's existence. As we have seen in

484

an earlier chapter, tradition had it that a wet nurse was to be summoned, whenever, as was often the case, the mother had died, or was otherwise unable to feed her infant. This is soundly based on experience over time. It is handed down as a legacy of the past and like other legacies we should treat it with respect.

A further point was raised in the same article: "research shows that nursing mothers transmit to their suckling infants antibodies, that protect the infant while his or her own system of antibody protection matures." This has been known for a long time, ever since infection has been known, which is over a hundred years, and it was culturally understood long before that.

Another feature of the breast-feeding controversy deals with satiety. This is a new situation for mothers and they are understandably tense about it. The question is: Has baby had enough? there was a time, earlier in this century, when a scales was handy to weigh the baby before and after the meal. Then came the bottle; baby had to finish four ounces, or whatever had been said by the pediatrician. These procedures were peculiar, and were certainly not based on the cultural experience of time. For it is well known that a suckling infant controls his or her intake, both in amount and frequency. This is a feature well understood by the mothers of the seventies. But we are about to ship crateloads of baby food formulas to the poor people of the third world. What they need is better food for the mothers, wherewith to feed their own infants in their own approved fashion. This was well illustrated in a television program in late October, 1980, when the poverty-stricken mothers of Eritrea and Somalia, surely the world's worst off, showed the cameraman their shrivelled breasts, pleading for the food that they had to have in order to suckle their infants properly.

We have to guard against our own arrogance
in these matters, and be prepared to meet the real
needs of the people. For the story told in this
book is hopefully one that will lead us to solutions to the problems on a cultural as well as a
practical basis. We have tended, it seems to the
author to become mesmerised by arithmetic. Have
you have your vitamins today?   if not, here is
a supplement, a tablet. This does not do for the
world's poor. We have to return to a closer relationship between the people and their food, both
in time and in place. Food has to be grown locally,
and eaten soon after.

Certainly the food package from abroad is
useful in an emergency, and for special purposes.
But in the long run, the receipt of such packages
destroys the pride and the self-sufficiency of the
recipients in ways that are not hard to understand.
The dependency loops must not be so large that there
is no control, and no hope of freedom from want.
We have to realise the anomoly; the rich are eating
poorly, and the poor are eating poorly; but for
entirely different reasons. It behooves us, it
seems to me, not to export poor eating habits to
the world's poor under the guise of magnanimity.

THE WRONG ROAD

We have to recognise the direction in which
progress lies. First we have to define progress.
As a matter of fact this is tied up with affluence.
According to Jean d'Ormisson, the decline of
the west dates from the time of our prosperity.
And yet we speak of progress. What is progress?
we have probably made our largest mistakes in
failing to identify our needs. We have satisfied
only a part of them, and that is the least important
part, namely the mechanisation of our lives.

A cogent example of the problem of progress
comes from Brazil in October 1980. It identifies
"progess" in Brazil as "the cultural survival of
the rich". Once-poor people there are now a

destitute class, living and dying in the streets.
And yet we hear little of this aspect of Brazilian
life, possibly because we are blinded by the physical
growth of a city like Sao Paolo. Evidently we in
America have few words of wisdom to offer these
people, although our own recent histories are re-
plete with example of poor decision-making in
the matter of the development of cities. This is
just the kind of circumstances which will exacerbate
the north-south conflicts of the future. For
America's post World War II bounty and munificence
in helping nations struggle to their feet is one of
the great chapters of our history. But that was
over 30 years ago. As has been pointed out
forcefully by Professor Roy Laird of the University of Kansas, America now feeds the wealthy, not
the poor. Of the 1978 food grain shipments, over
two thirds went to the wealthy countries.

We are preoccupied with our own problems and
have devoted less attention to those of other
people. According to Dr Jean Mayer, of Harvard
University School of Public Health, the progress in
the last fifty years has been unimpressive. He
pointed out that in 1974 there had been practically
no redistribution of wealth since 1925. The top
25% of our population still controlled 50% of the
income as they did then. The bottom 25% controlled
only 4%. Even with the enormous emphasis on, and
application of, welfare programs of every description, corrective programs and food stamps, which did
not exist in 1925, we have only been able to maintain the status quo.

Dr Arnold Schaefer, along with Dr Mayer
testified at the McGovern hearings in 1972 that
25 million Americans were obvious risks nutritionally; and that "they could in no way, shape or
manner conceivably obtain an adequate diet."

But there are hopeful signs. According to a
recent significant book by Paul Harrison, ("The
Third World Tommorrow"), there is great promise in
new programs financed by the World Bank and Education

Foundation to generate self-help measures. For by 1969, it became obvious to all but the most obtuse, that a "trickle-down" theory would entail the lapse of centuries to wipe out poverty, if ever it could. These programs center on reducing inequalities in areas as diverse as Java and Upper Volta. It is Harrison's belief and hope that the West's resistance to an international new deal will thereby be made less harsh.

For indeed we need a global perspective. Aurelio Peccaei, President of the Club of Rome, outlines the cost of compartmentalised thinking, and the inward looking that characterises much of our limited thinking. He pleads for recognition of the pitfalls and dangers in the present situation, and stresses how we are all in the same boat. Man's struggle for food goes on, and it shows no signs of letting us off easily. The rest is up to us.

REFERENCES

479 "..STARVED INTO CAPITULATION." Drummond, J.C. ibid, chap XXIV p 432. (1939).

479 GERMANY WAS THE FIRST TO SUFFER. Eltzbacher. P. Die deutsche Volksehrnahrung und die Englische Aushungerplan (1915).

480 "AT THAT TIME I WAS OF THE OPINION.." Preface to studies of Rickets in Vienna (1919-1922) Medical Research Council, Special Report No 77 (1923).

481 LEAGUE OF NATIONS' MINIMAL DIET. Diet in reation to small incomes; Bull. Health Organisation. Vol II No 1 (1933).

481 MILK CONSUMPTION. J. Proc. Agric. Economics Soc, Vol IV No 2 (1936).

482 DIETARY DEFICIENCIES. Orr, John Boyd, Food, Health and Income (1936).

482   WORLD WAR II: Drummond, Sir Jack: Scientific Approach to Food Problems during the War. Nutrition, Dieteticsm Catering (1947).

484   VALUE OF BREAST FEEDING: Wall Street Journal March 21, 1980.

486   FEEDING THE WEALTHY NOT THE POOR: Laird, Professor Roy, University of Kansas: Christian Science Monitor, July 9, 1980.

487   LITTLE PROGRESS BETWEEN 1925 AND 1974; Mayer, Dr. Jean. U.S. Nutrition Policies for the Seventies: Report of ACS Committee on Chemistry and Public Affairs p 2 (1974).

487   25 MILLION AMERICANS NUTRITIONAL RISKS: Schaefer, Arnold E and Mayer, Jean: McGovern Hearings 1972.

487   SELF-HELP MEASURES: Harrison, Paul; The Third World Tomorrow; World Press Review p 48 November 1980.

488   COST OF COMPARTMENTALISED THINKING: Peccari, Aurelio: President, Club of Rome. World Press and Report. March 1980 p 42.

ILLUSTRATIONS

STAMPEDING OVER A CLIFF: CAVE PAINTING   5
from the Huntingdon Library, San Marino,
California

TRAPPED MAMMOTH: CAVE PAINTING IN SOUTH-   7
ERN FRANCE

FIELDS AT HARVEST TIME: TOMB AT THEBES: 39
reproduced by courtesy of the Trustees
of the British Museum

DAILY MEAL WITHIN THE TOMB OF DJEHUTI,   42
THEBES: reproduced by courtesy of the
Trustees of the British Museum

BABYLONIAN PLOWING SCENE, 14th century, B.C.   47

MOSES GIVING HIS CONSTITUTION TO THE SONS OF   54
ISRAEL: Beginning of the Book of Exodus,
Alcuin's Bible; Ms Add. 10546; reproduced
by courtesy of the Trustees of the British
Museum

HARVESTING OLIVES: Ancient Greece at work.   65
C.K. Ogden (1926); Attic Vase in the
British Museum

ROMAN ROTARY MILL: from Vatican Museum   94

GLADIATORS: 109

NINTH CENTURY SOLDIER: from A short   119
history of the English People; John
Richard Green; I p 86 (1894); reproduced
by courtesy of the Hamlyn Group, Feltham,
England

NORTHERN WARRIOR: from John R. Green.   130
I, page 4

KUCHI YURT IN AFGHANISTAN, 1966; photograph   140
by the author

491

EARLY WATER WHEELS: fourteenth century   148
Paris; from Tannahill p 90

A WOOD FOR TWO PIGS: early 14th century;   153
from John R. Green; II, p 478, courtesy
of the Hamlyn group.

PLOUGHING, A.D. 1340. Loutrell Psalter;   159
from John R. Green. II. p 473; courtesy
of the Hamlyn Group

CHICHESTER MARKET CROSS: from J. R. Green;   165
II, p 614; courtesy of the Hamlyn group

A FORESTALLER IN THE PILLORY: Vetusta   171
Monumenta, from John R. Green. II. p 591;
courtesy of the Hamlyn group

CARDING AND SPINNING: Loutrell Psalter;   180
from John R. Green, II, p 499; courtesy
of the Hamlyn Group

WINDMILL, 14th CENTURY: MS Bodley 264   182
f 49; courtesy of the Bodleian Library,
Oxford

QUEEN ELIZABETH I; age 24: Statues of   189
the Order of St. Michael and St. George;
after John R. Green, II p 732; courtesy
of the Hamlyn group

EARLY SHIP: 200

SADDLE QUERN, EGYPT: from Ancient Egyptian   210
Paintings; Davies and Gardiner

INDUS VALLEY SEALS: reproduced by courtesy   223
of the Trustees of the British Museum

DISCOVERIE AND CONQUEST OF THE PROVINCES   250
OF PERU: Horizon Book of the Elizabethan
World

"MISTRESS OF THE SEAS":   Ms in Pepys   296
Library, Magdalene College, Oxford; from
John R. Green, II p 612; courtesy of the
Hamlyn Group

PURITAN FAMILY MEAL: Roxburgh Collection,   308
British Museum; reproduced by courtesy of
the Trustees

COLLIERY, (1806) from John R. Green Vol IV   362
p 1735 courtesy of the Hamlyn Group

BACK-TO-BACK HOUSING: Advances in Techno-   404
logy ed. Asa Briggs.   #51; courtesy of
Thames, Hudson Ltd, London

STAFFORDSHIRE COLLIERS: from Penny   416
Magazine, after Green, ibid Vol IV,
p 1835; courtesy of the Hamlyn group

SLITTING FISH IN EGYPT: from Food in   459
Antiquity, by D.R. Brothwell, after
Wilkinson

DANISH MILKING MACHINE: from Journal   464
of the Academy of Science and
Engineering (1892)